Praise for *JUSTINIAN*

"Effortlessly erudite, lucidly written, with a sharp eye for the telling detail, Peter Sarris has written the great biography of the greatest of the Byzantine emperors."
—Rory Stewart, *New York Times*–bestselling author of
The Places in Between

"Justinian's long life mirrored that of ancient Rome itself: both rose from lowly origins to supreme power, survived revolt and conquered rivals, crafted laws, and erected mighty monuments, only to be worn down by insurgents, invaders, and plagues. In a stunning tour de force, Sarris brings one of history's most momentous dramas back to life."
—Walter Scheidel, author of *The Great Leveler*

"Justinian looms so large in the landscape of the ancient Mediterranean that it is almost impossible to take his measure. Yet Sarris has done so convincingly, offering a lucid and persuasive account of a ruler as invested in the mechanics of government as in waging wars of conquest. A remarkable achievement."
—Kate Cooper, author of *Queens of a Fallen World*

"Sarris's *Justinian* is magnificent. A vivid and authoritative biography of one of Rome's most fascinating rulers, *Justinian* is also a vibrant portrait of an entire world—a resurgent Roman Empire suddenly devastated by tragedy."
—Kyle Harper, author of *The Fate of Rome*

"Spectacularly good: a wonderfully colorful biography of the man who remade the Roman Empire. Sarris plunges us deep into a world of imperial conflict, religious paranoia, pandemics, and climate change, while never losing sight of the extraordinary character at its heart. Based on decades of scholarship, this is the definitive history of the emperor and his times, and a thrilling testament to the glories of Byzantium."

—Dominic Sandbrook, cohost of *The Rest is History*

JUSTINIAN

ALSO BY PETER SARRIS

The Novels of Justinian: A Complete Annotated
English Translation (editor)

Byzantium: A Very Short Introduction

An Age of Saints? Power, Conflict and Dissent in
Early Medieval Christianity (co-editor)

Empires of Faith: The Fall of Rome to the Rise of Islam, 500–700

Aristocrats, Peasants and the Transformation of
Rural Society, 400–800 (co-editor)

Procopius: The Secret History (editor and co-translator)

Economy and Society in the Age of Justinian

JUSTINIAN

EMPEROR, SOLDIER, SAINT

PETER SARRIS

BASIC BOOKS
New York

Basic Books
Hachette Book Group
1290 Avenue of the Americas, New York, NY 10104
www.basicbooks.com

Printed in the United States of America

First US Edition: November 2023

Published by Basic Books, an imprint of Hachette Book Group, Inc. The Basic Books name and logo is a trademark of the Hachette Book Group.

The Hachette Speakers Bureau provides a wide range of authors for speaking events. To find out more, go to www.hachettespeakersbureau.com or email HachetteSpeakers@hbgusa.com.

Basic books may be purchased in bulk for business, educational, or promotional use. For information, please contact your local bookseller or Hachette Book Group Special Markets Department at special.markets@hbgusa.com.

The publisher is not responsible for websites (or their content) that are not owned by the publisher.

Print book interior design by Bart Dawson.

Library of Congress Cataloging-in-Publication Data
Names: Sarris, Peter, author.
Title: Justinian: emperor, soldier, saint / Peter Sarris.
Other titles: Justinian, emperor, soldier, saint
Description: First US edition. | New York: Basic Books, 2023. | Includes bibliographical references and index. |
Identifiers: LCCN 2023024728 | ISBN 9781541601338 (hardcover) | ISBN 9781541601345 (ebook)
Subjects: LCSH: Justinian I, Emperor of the East, 483?-565. | Emperors—Byzantine Empire—Biography. | Byzantine Empire—History—Justinian I, 527-565.
Classification: LCC DF572 .S274 2023 | DDC 949.5/013092 [B]—dc23/eng/20230525
LC record available at https://lccn.loc.gov/2023024728

ISBNs: 9781541601338 (hardcover), 9781541601345 (ebook)

LSC-C

Printing 1, 2023

To James Howard-Johnston and Turlough Stone

CONTENTS

CONTENTS

PART 4: THE GREAT UNRAVELLING

Каждую ночь
мертвец
приподнимает гробовую плиту
и проверяет на ощупь:

не стерлось ли
имя на камне?

—КУПРИЯНОВ ВЯЧЕСЛАВ, *Сумерки тщеславия*

Every night
The dead man
Slightly lifts the lid of his tombstone
And checks by touch

Whether his name
Has worn away.

—VYACHESLAV KUPRIANOV, *Twilight of Vanity* (tr. P. Sarris)

The Roman Empire in the Second Century

ATLANTIC
OCEAN

BRITAIN

River Rhine

GAUL

SPAIN

Corsica

Rome

Sardinia

Sicily

Carthage

Mediterranean Sea

AFRICA

N
W E
S

0   150   300   450   600 miles
0   150   300   450 600 km

Map 1

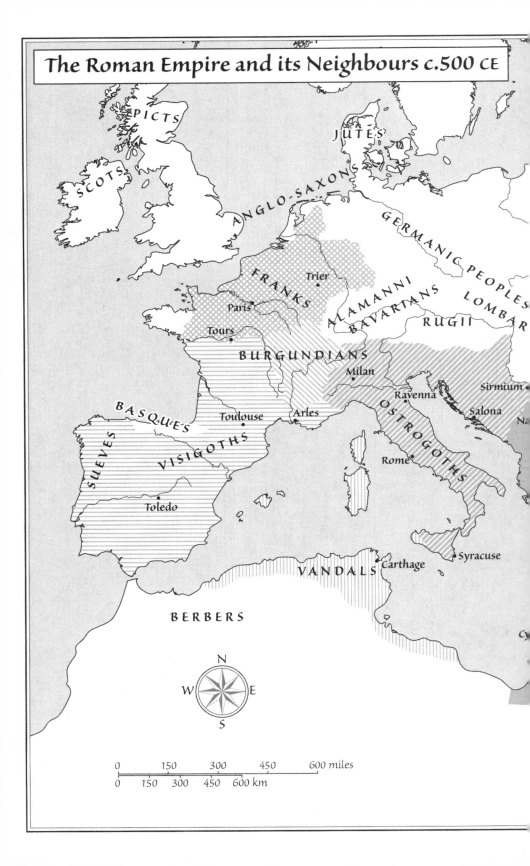

The Roman Empire and its Neighbours c.500 CE

PICTS

JUTES

SCOTS

ANGLO-SAXONS

GERMANIC PEOPLES

FRANKS

Trier

ALAMANNI

BAVARIANS

LOMBAR

RUGII

Paris

Tours

BURGUNDIANS

Milan

Ravenna

Sirmium

BASQUES

Toulouse

Arles

Salona

Na

SUEVES

VISIGOTHS

OSTROGOTHS

Rome

Toledo

Syracuse

VANDALS

Carthage

BERBERS

Cy

N
W   E
S

0   150   300   450   600 miles

0   150   300   450   600 km

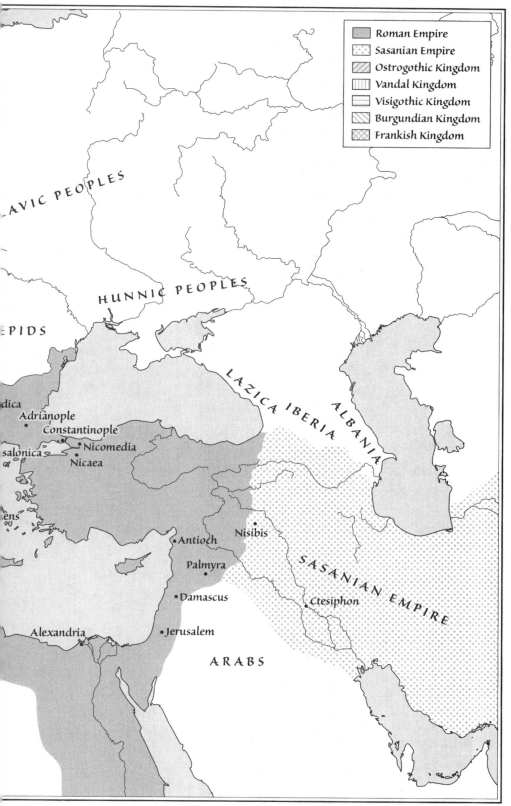

SLAVIC PEOPLES

HUNNIC PEOPLES

EPIDS

LAZICA IBERIA

ALBANIA

dica

Adrianople

Constantinople

salonica

Nicomedia

Nicaea

ens

Antioch

Nisibis

Palmyra

SASANIAN EMPIRE

Damascus

Ctesiphon

Alexandria

Jerusalem

ARABS

Map 2

The Mediterranean at the End of Justinian's Reign

FRANKS

LOMBARDS–

Milan

Ravenna

Busta
Gallorum

Rome

Arles

VISIGOTHS

Naples

Carthage

Tricamarum

Syr.

Ad Decimum

Septem

BERBERS

Tripoli

N
W   E
S

0   150   300   450   600 miles

0   150   300   450   600 km

Map 3

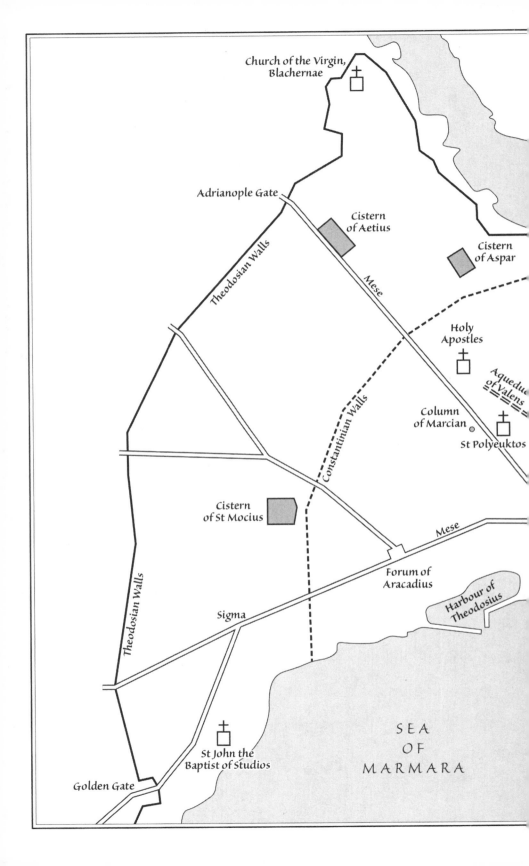

Church of the Virgin, Blachernae

Adrianople Gate

Cistern of Aetius

Cistern of Aspar

Theodosian Walls

Mese

Holy Apostles

Aqueduct of Valens

Constantinian Walls

Column of Marcian

St Polyeuktos

Cistern of St Mocius

Mese

Forum of Aracadius

Harbour of Theodosius

Theodosian Walls

Sigma

St John the Baptist of Studios

Golden Gate

SEA
OF
MARMARA

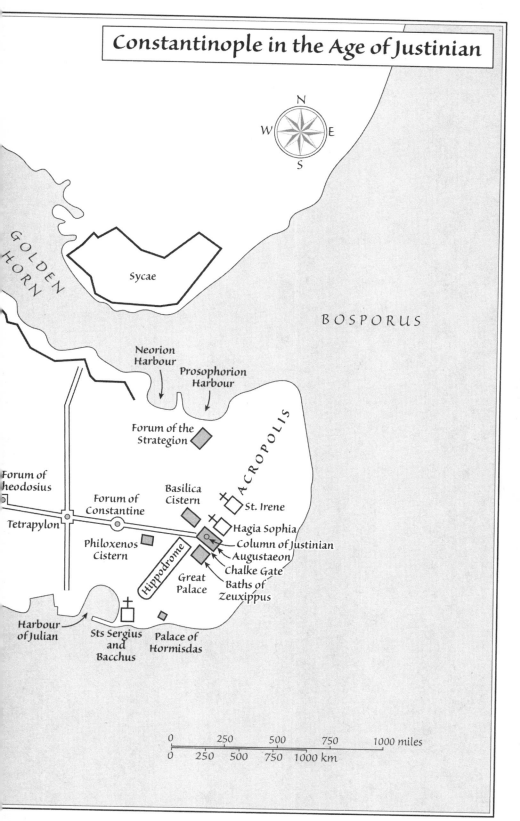

Constantinople in the Age of Justinian

N
W E
S

GOLDEN HORN

Sycae

BOSPORUS

Neorion Harbour

Prosophorion Harbour

Forum of the Strategion

ACROPOLIS

Forum of Theodosius

Basilica Cistern

Forum of Constantine

St. Irene

Tetrapylon

Hagia Sophia

Philoxenos Cistern

Column of Justinian

Hippodrome

Augustaeon

Great Palace

Chalke Gate

Baths of Zeuxippus

Harbour of Julian

Sts Sergius and Bacchus

Palace of Hormisdas

0   250   500   750   1000 miles
0   250   500   750   1000 km

Map 4

Justinian— The Light and the Shade

In March 2020, as the new coronavirus began spreading like wild-fire from its European epicentre in northern Italy, the authorities in the Turkish city of Istanbul were obliged to close the city's greatest ancient monument to visitors. The Cathedral Church of Hagia Sophia ('Holy Wisdom' in Greek) had been formally inaugurated by the Roman emperor Justinian (r. 527–565) in 537, and over the centuries it had served successively as a bastion of Christian spirituality, an Ottoman mosque, and, more recently, a museum—although the Turkish government would soon once again make it a Muslim place of preaching and prayer.[1] As the janitors and officials, wrapped from head to toe in masks, gowns, and gloves, began the painstaking task of disinfecting the vast structure, once the largest enclosed space in Christendom, to expunge it of the virus, the angels, archangels, emperors, and saints in the great mosaics adorning its walls, ceilings, and domes, dating from the time of Justinian and his successors to the throne of Constantinople, appeared to look on. Clearing the building seemed to have briefly restored its inner harmony: it was as if the images could now once more enter into dialogue with one another. Pictures transmitted across the globe depicted a scene eerily reminiscent of that evoked by the great Russian poet and dissident Osip Mandel'shtam in the verses he had composed in honour of the monument just over a hundred years earlier:

> *The church, bathed in peace, is beautiful, and the forty windows are a triumph of light; finest of all are the four archangels in the pendentives beneath the dome.*

> *And the wise, spherical building will outlive nations and centuries, and the resonant sobbing of the seraphim will not warp the dark gilded surfaces.*[2]

The combination of panic and misery which the coronavirus unleashed on the world in the early months of 2020 would have been all too familiar to Justinian. Just as governments and scientists in our own day found themselves suddenly confronting a new and unfamiliar disease, which destabilized even the most sophisticated of economies and regimes, so, too, had Justinian's reign been rocked by the sudden and seemingly unprecedented appearance of bubonic plague.[3] Arriving in the empire just four years after the completion of Hagia Sophia, the pestilence would lay low many hundreds of thousands of the emperor's subjects. It was even rumoured that Justinian himself, secluded in the imperial palace, had contracted the disease and somehow recovered.

Justinian has long fascinated me—ever since I wrote an undergraduate essay on him in Oxford in the early 1990s in response to the question 'Did Justinian ruin the empire he set out to restore?' In many ways, I have spent much of the subsequent thirty years trying to answer that question and attempting to come to terms with the emperor and his reign. Even without the intervention of the plague, Justinian's career would have stood out from the pages of ancient and medieval history for its energy, ambition, and drama.[4]

From the imperial capital of Constantinople, which had been founded by the emperor Constantine the Great some two hundred years earlier, Justinian ruled over a vast domain which, at the start of his reign, extended from Greece and the Balkans in the West to the deserts of Syria and Arabia in the East (Map 2). It encompassed not only Asia Minor and Anatolia (modern Turkey), but also the fantastically wealthy territory of Egypt, at the time the most economically productive and sophisticated region of the Mediterranean world. Yet, for all its apparent grandeur, the empire that Justinian inherited in 527 was haunted by a profound sense of anxiety, failure, and insecurity, which the new emperor was determined to address.

A chief, though not the only, cause of anxiety was the fact that although Justinian claimed to be Roman emperor, sole heir and successor to the emperors Augustus, Marcus Aurelius, and Constantine, the area he ruled no longer embraced the Roman Empire's former core territories of Italy, North Africa, Spain, and Gaul. Along with Britain, these lands had been lost to direct Roman rule as the result of a period of pronounced political and military crisis between roughly 410 and 480 CE. His empire did not even include the city of Rome itself—although the city of Constantinople had long before been accorded the title of 'New Rome'.[5] Glorious and extensive as it was, many already understood the empire of Justinian to be an imperial contradiction. 'Barbarian' rulers who had carved out autonomous kingdoms for themselves in the West now openly contested its claims to universal Roman authority.

In response, early in his reign Justinian would spearhead an imperial reconquest of Africa, Italy, and ultimately part of Spain (Map 3). His campaign began in 533, with the daring decision to

3

send an expeditionary force across the sea-lanes of the Mediterranean from Constantinople to what is now Tunis. The former
Roman provinces of Africa, embracing much of modern Tunisia,
Algeria, and Morocco, as well as part of Libya, had been invaded
in the middle decades of the fifth century by a group, primarily
of Germanic origin, known as the Vandals. From their capital at
Carthage, the Vandals had set about establishing a significant maritime presence in the Western Mediterranean, thereby undermining and threatening key Roman interests. Justinian's expeditionary
force, however, caught them off guard, rapidly defeating them in
battle and capturing the Vandal king, Gelimer. The entire kingdom passed back into Roman hands. The breathtaking success of
this African mission would soon encourage Justinian to direct his
armies into Italy in a determined effort to restore Roman rule over
the ancient heartland of empire. This attempt, too, would prove
largely successful, although in Italy, where Justinian's armies met
with more concerted resistance, the result would be to inflict much
greater damage on the fabric of the reconquered territories, including the city of Rome itself, than the 'barbarian invaders' of the fifth
century had ever done.[6]

At home, Justinian cracked down on tax evasion by members
of the senatorial elite, who repeatedly schemed and plotted against
him. He also dramatically overhauled the inherited body of Roman
law. Justinian's aim was to impose order and clarity on the sprawling mass of legal texts governing the administration and regulation
of the empire, thus facilitating speedier justice. The reformed law
would express one unified vision and will: that of the emperor himself. So effective was this act of autocratic fiat that it is now very difficult to work out in any real detail what Roman law was like before
Justinian; the emperor determined the form in which Roman (or
'civil') law would survive into the Middle Ages and beyond. Indeed,
to this day, principles derived from Justinianic law form the basis of
the legal systems operating across much of Europe.[7]

Whilst locked in political conflict with members of the elite, who often resented his legal and fiscal reforms, the emperor attempted to appeal to the broader populace of Constantinople. He did so by investing in lavish building projects, epitomized by Hagia Sophia, and engaging in prodigious acts of generosity and charity, primarily targeted at the urban poor. Above all, Justinian sought to recast the Roman Empire, turning it more fully into a Christian state, in which religious outsiders, dissidents, and those deemed morally or sexually deviant were subjected to ever more draconian punishments. As churchmen who were deemed 'heretical' saw their writings burned on the streets, and were themselves consigned to prison or exile, and as the emperor's many Jewish subjects found themselves openly discriminated against by state officials, with active imperial encouragement, it became increasingly clear that Justinian's accession had heralded the advent of a more intolerant age.[8] To some of his enemies he was a demon; to some of his admirers he was a saint. But whether they viewed him as a 'holy emperor' or a 'demon king', many of his contemporaries understood that Justinian was a ruler of remarkable vision and drive.

Justinian helped lay the foundations for Orthodox Byzantium as it took shape in the centuries ahead. In many ways, however, his achievement was more fundamental than that. In his recasting of the Roman state as an 'Orthodox Republic' (as he described it in one of his laws), he ultimately laid the ideological and psychological foundations for medieval Christendom as a whole. He also bequeathed a major legacy to the Islamic world that emerged in the Near East in the seventh and eighth centuries.[9] On a broader level, through his energetic reform programme, and his no less energetic self-glorification, Justinian recast what it meant to 'rule', providing a model of statecraft to which future Byzantine emperors, along with medieval kings, Muslim caliphs, and Ottoman sultans, would come to aspire.

At the same time, a series of factors beyond Justinian's control undermined his attempts at imperial renewal. Chief amongst these were the rival ambitions of a neighbouring superpower: Persia. Ruling over the lands of what are now Iran and Iraq, the emperors (or *shahs*) of the Sasanian Empire were by far the most politically, economically, and militarily sophisticated foe that the Romans faced. Just prior to Justinian's rise to power, warfare between the Romans and Persians had erupted on a massive scale. Containing Persian aggression in Syria and the Caucasus (modern Armenia, Georgia, and Azerbaijan), which the two empires divided between themselves, was thus a pressing concern throughout Justinian's reign. Further challenges emerged as a result of instability on the Eurasian steppe that brought hordes of Central Asian nomads sweeping westward towards imperial territory, and, crucially, a major period of climatic instability that probably facilitated the arrival of the bubonic plague. It was the first major eruption of that disease in the known history of the Mediterranean world. Justinian's reign therefore combined unprecedented optimism with unanticipated calamity, severely testing the resilience of both emperor and empire.

To date, many studies of Justinian, especially in English, have focussed on his military policies and adventures rather than on his internal reforms, with historians relying more heavily on sources concerning military history than on the legal and religious sources which reveal his broader policy agenda.[10] As a result, few have successfully synthesized the different aspects of his reign. Nor has any single work so far managed to draw out the emperor's personality, or how Justinian's personal vision of empire and his policy agenda across the military, legal, religious, and domestic spheres all related to one another and cohered. Yet, as we shall see, especially through his legal works and theological interventions, the emperor's personal voice comes across much more clearly and consistently than has often been supposed.

INTRODUCTION

These sources enable us to catch the urgent tone of Justinian's unremitting insistence on the need to elicit divine favour; his constant impatience; his tendency to infuse even the most mundane administrative tasks with spiritual and religious significance; his obsession with detail; and his close personal dependence on his consort, the infamous empress Theodora, so strong that, after her death in 548, his focus would initially begin to drift and his grip on power to loosen. The same sources reveal Justinian's determination to crush his opponents, and his blistering contempt for those who were seemingly oblivious to the virtues and superiority of imperial Christianity. The emperor's legislation reveals a man moved by genuine sympathy for the poor, for orphans, and—perhaps with his wife's encouragement—for widows and other vulnerable women, such as country girls trafficked to Constantinople for the purposes of prostitution. In terms of his own self-representation and interests, Justinian was an emperor deeply immersed in the minutiae of administration and law, a soldier committed to the expansion and defence of the Roman realm (despite his own relative lack of front-line military experience), and a pious Christian preoccupied with the definition and propagation of what he regarded as the 'true faith'.

In the Church of San Vitale, in the northern Italian city of Ravenna, there stands to this day a magnificent mosaic, dating from the sixth century, depicting the emperor Justinian in procession with his courtiers, across from an equally magnificent mosaic of Theodora and her attendants. The portrait of Justinian that this mosaic preserves is the most famous image that we have of the emperor. As Justinian stares out at us from the walls of the church, it is easy for the viewer to be mesmerized by the radiance of the imperial diadem, or the splendour of the emperor's bejewelled raiment. Yet the gold, silver, and other luminous tesserae of the emperor's crown, robes, and visage stand out and captivate primarily by virtue of the darker fragments of glass that frame them.

Likewise, Justinian—and his age—were composed of both light and shade, and in order to understand the emperor himself and come to terms with his reign, we have to appreciate both. For Justinian's reign was marked not only by an unprecedented degree of charity but also by an unprecedented degree of intolerance and cruelty, and the emperor's strong sense of personal mission and commitment to what he perceived to be the common good was matched by his strongly autocratic tendencies and his keen (and often prickly) sense of his own dignity and pride.

The key message of this book, however, is that despite the many centuries that separate us from Justinian, this very ancient figure remains our contemporary. For as our recent experience of pandemics reminds us, many of the challenges that Justinian faced, and even some of the solutions that he and others devised in response to them, continue to resonate. Above all, the emperor's legacy remains all around us: in the architecture inspired by his building programme—of which the most beautiful and influential manifestation is surely Hagia Sophia; in our legal systems; and in our culture and history, through Justinian's fundamental contribution to both the formation of Christendom and the making of the Islamic world. As such, for all his complexity and contradictions, Justinian and the history of his reign continue to speak to us today.

PART 1

The Rise to Power

Chapter 1

An Empire Divided

CRUCIBLE OF EMPIRE

Even those who knew Justinian up close found him a difficult man to read and understand. The sixth-century writer Procopius was a close colleague of one of the emperor's most trusted military advisers. Yet in his account of Justinian's reign, he admitted that he struggled to find words to describe him: Justinian's character was beyond his 'powers of accurate speech'.[1] The first task in coming to terms with this enigmatic and arresting figure is to make sense of the turbulent world from which Justinian emerged. As we shall see, his keen awareness of a series of military crises and religious controversies that convulsed the Roman Empire in the centuries and decades before his birth was central to his reign. These challenges determined the institutional and political context in which Justinian was obliged to operate, as well as the ideological and cultural milieu that shaped both the emperor and those around him. Justinian and his regime represented the culmination of several centuries of increasingly fraught and dramatic Roman history to which he was determined to respond. As emperor, Justinian would present himself not just as omnipotent ruler, but also at times as historian, theologian, and judge, and to understand why, we must begin with the troubled religious and military history of the Roman Empire in the years that preceded his accession to the throne.

The point of origin of the Roman Empire was, of course, the city of Rome itself, from which Julius Caesar and his heirs had led their armies to conquer and subdue much of Europe and the Mediterranean world. It was also in Rome, in 31 BCE, that Julius Caesar's adoptive son, Octavian, had declared himself to be first citizen and supreme ruler, claiming the title of *Augustus* (meaning both 'venerable' and 'superhuman').[2] By the second century CE, Roman rule extended from Britain and Spain in the West to Armenia, Syria, and Palestine in the East, and from the rivers Rhine and Danube in the North to the Atlas Mountains and the far reaches of the Upper Nile in the South (Map 1).

At its second-century height, the Roman Empire was characterised by a very high degree of ideological and cultural domination from the centre and a remarkable measure of practical provincial autonomy on the ground. Rome was undeniably the centre to which, proverbially, all roads led, and to which the spoils of war and conquest flowed. The city's striking architectural enrichment under Augustus and his heirs is still manifest to this day in the extraordinary standing remains of the Colosseum, the Forum of Trajan, and other imperial monuments. Rome was the seat of the emperor, from where he sent out instructions to his governors in the provinces and directed his generals, dispatching them to the frontiers to quell any signs of local disaffection or trouble. A careful balancing act was generally maintained between the emperors—who had dynastic ambitions, and a natural tendency to wish to see members of their own families succeed them to the imperial office after their deaths—and the city's leading citizens, the senators, many of whom sought to preserve aspects of Rome's earlier 'Republican' traditions.

At a provincial level, the empire was almost self-governing, with much of the day-to-day business of governance, including tax collection and the workings of justice, being entrusted to councils of local landowners, largely resident in the cities. The cities of the empire were the nodal points of communication, administration, and commercial life in the Roman world. In Rome's western provinces, in particular, there was a highly devolved system of government held together by strong cultural ties deliberately cultivated and propagated by Rome.[3] By entrusting local elites with so much of the business of government, as well as positions from which they could derive both profit and prestige, the Roman authorities had managed to co-opt them into the business of empire. Drawn into the cities the empire had founded, members of local elite families had been exposed to Roman cultural values, learning Latin and studying Roman history and literature, and had come to think of themselves as Roman. Indeed, in 212, Roman citizenship had been extended to all subjects of the emperor, save for those who bore the status of slaves. As a result, rights under and access to Roman law had been significantly extended, further helping to embed a sense of belonging to Rome well beyond the ranks of the elite. Ideological and political commitment to the empire was especially pronounced, for example, amongst the rank-and-file of the military, who were expected to fight and die for Rome.

To the East, in Greece, Asia Minor, and Anatolia (modern Turkey), as well as in Syria, Palestine, and Egypt, the situation was rather different. Here the Romans had projected their rule over societies and cultures that had been conquered in the fourth century BCE by Alexander the Great of Macedon, whose empire had then been divided up amongst his generals into a series of so-called

Hellenistic kingdoms after his untimely death. As a result, the elites of the Near Eastern territories beyond the Hellenic heartlands of European Greece and Asia Minor had acquired Greek language, literature, and cultural values. In these eastern provinces, dense networks of cities already existed, and thus did not have to be built up and invested in from scratch by the Roman authorities. In the East, therefore, the Romans encountered elites that already possessed a high culture and an infrastructure well suited to Roman forms of administration. The challenge here was to align the established Hellenistic cultural values of each region with the Romans' own strong sense of imperial mission.

As a result, while to the West, the cultural basis of empire rested upon the successful Romanization of local elites, to the East the Romans had to tailor their message to suit and appeal to local political and cultural expectations. To take one example, in order to marry his political ambitions with Roman tradition, Octavian, upon adopting the name and title of *Augustus*, had presented the imperial office as a sort of amalgam and assemblage of preexisting 'Republican' and civic ones. He accorded himself the rank of 'chief magistrate' of the Roman Republic, and the title of 'first amongst equals' (*primus inter pares*), rather than anything more overbearing. The Roman Republic, after all, had been founded in 509 BCE, when the last king of Rome, Lucius Tarquinius Superbus, had been expelled from the city. As a result, it was important for Octavian and his heirs to avoid presenting themselves to a Roman political audience after a manner that smacked too obviously of 'monarchy'. The imperial office was instead presented and understood in essentially 'Republican' terms, not only in the city of Rome but also in the western provinces.[4]

In the East, very different political conditions prevailed. Alexander and his followers had conquered territories in Syria, Egypt, and Persia with long-established traditions of 'divine monarchy';

here, kings were treated like gods and their subjects were described as little more than actual or proverbial slaves. Alexander and his heirs had adopted the political language, ideologies, and ceremonial aspects of divine monarchy in these regions to convey their authority to their new subjects in terms they understood. Roman emperors followed suit: when addressing their eastern subjects, they had quickly begun to use the same language of power and style of rule, assuming titles such as 'world ruler' (*kosmokrator*).[5]

A wish to appeal to the political and cultural sensibilities of the Greek-speaking elites of Rome's eastern provinces informed not only how emperors presented themselves stylistically and rhetorically, but also how they conducted their foreign policy. By virtue of their cultural Hellenization under Alexander and his heirs, the elites of many of the cities of Syria, Palestine, and Egypt thought of themselves in cultural terms as Greek, just as processes of acculturation and education to the West led Latin-speaking western elites to think of themselves as culturally Roman. The traditional enemy of the Greek-speaking world, going back to the fifth century BCE, had been Persia. The Persian Empire of the Achaemenid dynasty, which the united Greeks had defeated at the Battle of Salamis in 480 BCE, had represented the much demonised 'other' against whom the Greeks had defined themselves, and this cultural and political animosity towards Persia continued amongst the Greek-speaking elites of the Hellenistic East. Accordingly, Roman emperors soon learned that an effective means of appealing to the political instincts of their Greek-speaking subjects, and harnessing them for the purposes of empire, was to be seen as taking war to their ancestral enemy by leading campaigns against the Persians. Such campaigns enabled emperors to depict themselves as rightful heirs to Alexander and helped to cement Roman rule in the East as well as facilitating the emergence of an incipient ideological alignment between cultural Hellenism and Roman political identity.[6] As a result, to the East, what has been termed a 'Greek Roman Empire' gradually emerged.[7]

CRISIS OF EMPIRE

By the end of the second century, the northern frontiers of the Roman Empire in Europe had essentially come to rest along the rivers Rhine and Danube, as beyond these natural borders were a series of politically disunited tribal groupings that posed little direct threat to Roman power. The Roman army had engaged in policing activity along these frontier zones to deter incursions and periodically punish raids whilst also maintaining a series of trading posts within the 'barbarian' world to the north, where Roman goods were in high demand. Such flows of Roman wealth northwards were manipulated by the Roman authorities for political and strategic purposes. They were preferentially funnelled through or sometimes gifted to Roman client-rulers and chieftains, who were mobilised by Rome against their potentially troublesome neighbours. A zone of Roman political and economic influence thus extended beyond the Roman frontier proper, with some of the 'barbarians' (as the Romans regarded them) even appearing to have used Roman money to facilitate transactions between themselves.[8]

By the middle of the third century, these flows of Roman wealth beyond the frontier zone, and attempts on the part of the Roman authorities to build up the power of local chieftains, had begun to have consequences which, from a Roman perspective, would prove to be highly counterproductive. Cumulatively, they undermined the relatively egalitarian social structures of many of the barbarian peoples on the borders of the empire and catalysed the emergence of increasingly powerful warrior elites, who were capable of forging larger and militarily more effective tribal confederations that began to challenge Roman power. From the middle of the third century, a series of ever larger and more successful incursions into Roman territory had begun to take place, spearheaded by new barbarian groups emerging from the north, such as 'the Painted Men' (*Picti*) in Britain; the 'Brave' (*Franci*) and the 'All Men' (*Alamanni*) from beyond the Rhine; and the *Greutingi*, better known to posterity as the Goths, a confederacy from what is now Ukraine, who struck from beyond the Danube. These groups sought to seize directly from Rome what they had hitherto obtained through service, subsidy, and commerce.[9]

Most ominously of all, at around the same time the Roman Empire found itself subject to growing military pressure from the east. In the closing years of the second century CE the Romans had extended their eastern frontier at the expense of the ruling Persian dynasty, the Arsacids, expanding their zone of influence and control into the strategically crucial region of Armenia. This defeat at the hands of Rome had led to the downfall of the ruling dynasty and a bitter struggle for power between the different aristocratic families. This protracted civil war finally ended in 224, when the new Persian ruler, Ardashir, was crowned the first shah of the Sasanian dynasty. From his capital at the city of Ctesiphon (near modern Baghdad), Ardashir sought to unite the fractious military aristocracy of Persia behind him by launching a series of raids deep into Roman territory. This policy of aggression culminated in 260, when Ardashir's successor, Shapur I, launched a daring campaign into Roman Syria, sacking the city of Antioch and capturing and humiliating the Roman emperor Valerian (*r.* 253–260 CE).[10]

The Roman authorities found themselves in an increasingly dire position. The gravity of the situation was exacerbated by the fact that Roman military manpower had been largely concentrated along the empire's frontiers, so that once an enemy managed to break through the frontier zone, there was little military presence in the provincial hinterland to prevent the raiders from running amok.[11] Likewise, the governance of the empire was so highly delegated to city councils that it was almost impossible to marshal and reallocate resources from those regions least affected by enemy attack to those that were bearing the brunt of them. Most serious of all, a political establishment led by a single emperor ruling primarily from the city of Rome, surrounded by senators of predominantly civilian backgrounds unfamiliar with military affairs, was demonstrably incapable of facing down and coordinating resistance to simultaneous military challenges to the north, east, and west. The emergence of these new and more dangerous foes meant the Roman Empire of the third century found itself in the grip of a severe military crisis.[12]

Along with the deteriorating military situation, there was increasing political instability, as the leaders of the Roman army in the field and politicians in Rome began to respond to what they perceived to be the failings of their rulers by deposing reigning emperors and appointing or acclaiming new ones. The army's officer corps supported new emperors with military backgrounds, leading to a series of 'soldier emperors'. At the same time, a number of what are perhaps best thought of as 'local' Roman regimes emerged, whereby the leading members of provincial society in, for example, northern Gaul and Syria, exasperated at the inability of the central Roman authorities to defend them, gave their support to local warlords, who took battle to the enemy and claimed the imperial title. Between 258 and 274, the provincial elites in much of Britain, Gaul, and Spain aligned themselves behind a general named Postumus, who headed up a so-called Empire of the Gauls, whilst to the East, the client ruler of Palmyra—Odenathus—led resistance to the Persians.[13] Although the imperial authorities in Rome viewed such men as rebels leading separatist regimes, there is every sign that they regarded themselves as Roman rulers defending Roman civilization.[14]

Historians have traditionally regarded the coups and usurpations of the third century as signs of chaos and disorder. But over time, they would arguably prove to be the key to Roman survival. The empire of the Gauls and the Palmyrene statelet managed to repel foreign invaders with considerable success, as did the soldier emperors who came to power at this time. Most of these new soldier emperors came from the region of Illyricum and adjacent territories in the Balkans, which had emerged as the Roman Empire's main military recruiting ground. Since the second century CE, advancement through the ranks of the Roman army, and ultimately appointment to the rank of general, had also increasingly been on the basis of ability rather than birth. This meant that the men raised to the imperial office by their troops were often highly talented soldiers of humble social background, who were ideologically committed to the survival of Rome, impatient of failure, and willing to innovate. These were men who knew how to fight and were determined to win. As a result, across the still militarily disrupted years of the 260s to the 280s, the foreign insurgents were increasingly driven out of Roman territory, and the 'local' Roman regimes to the East and West successfully reincorporated into the overarching structure of the empire.[15]

It is conventional to regard the 'crisis' of the third century as drawing to a close in around 284 with the accession of the emperor Diocletian, who overcame his imperial rivals, cowed the empire's foes, and established personal mastery over the Roman world. From 284 until the end of his reign in 305, the empire would know a period of relative peace such as it had not experienced since the 220s. This enabled Diocletian and his entourage to consolidate a series of improvised measures and reforms whereby he and his late third-century predecessors sought—and managed—to contain the various aspects of Rome's military and political crisis.[16] These reforms would shape and determine many of the administrative structures of empire that Justinian would inherit upon his accession to the throne.

It had become increasingly apparent, for example, that one emperor, resident primarily in the city of Rome, could not possibly hope to contain multiple and simultaneous military threats along the vast expanse of the empire's frontiers.[17] What the empire needed was more devolved leadership located closer to the main sources of military threat. A system of 'power sharing' thus emerged, which Diocletian consolidated and entrenched, whereby there were now two emperors—or *Augusti*. One of these was located primarily in the East to face down the Persians, and the other based primarily in the West to safeguard the Rhine frontier. Given that the most sophisticated and concerted threat to Roman power came from the Sasanians, it made sense for the senior of these two emperors to base himself in the East. Crucially, these emperors now ruled not from Rome, which found itself increasingly politically marginalised, but rather from cities nearer the frontiers of the empire, such as Trier in Gaul or Antioch in Syria, which Diocletian, as the senior *Augustus*, made his base. Each *Augustus* was also appointed a deputy or *Caesar* to provide an additional level of military and political flexibility. This arrangement helped to counter a long-standing weakness of the Roman political system resulting from the inherited Roman antipathy to hereditary monarchy: uncertainty over succession to the imperial title. Each *Caesar* would now serve not only as deputy, but also as nominated heir to his respective *Augustus*. Historians often refer to this new articulation of imperial power as the 'Tetrarchy' or the 'Rule of Four'.

Major efforts were made at this time to provide the Roman Empire with much greater defensive and bureaucratic cohesion. The size of the army was significantly increased, and military units were dispersed more widely.[18] The provinces were split up into smaller units and kept under tighter supervision. These smaller provinces were then grouped together into larger transregional units known as *dioceses*, each under the command of an official known as the *vicarius* and his staff. who were directly answerable to the emperor and his court at the nearest 'Tetrarchic' capital. The dioceses would later be grouped into still larger units called 'prefectures', each under the authority of a 'praetorian prefect'. For the first time in Roman tradition, something approximating to a central imperial bureaucracy emerged with responsibilities over and above the level of the city and province.[19]

Such reforms—and especially the expansion of the army—needed to be paid for. In order to finance these new arrangements, Diocletian and his government achieved a remarkable feat. Surveyors were sent out to assess the taxable and productive resources of each and every province of the empire, and to report back on the extent and quality of agricultural land and the number of people available to cultivate it. Simultaneously, efforts were made to calculate the budgetary needs of the Roman state. Calibrated tax demands were then issued, balancing the needs of the state against the ability of local populations to pay. Instructions were given that such surveys were to be conducted on a regular basis, and in order to make the flow of taxes more dependable, taxpayers were increasingly legally bound to reside in the communities in which they were registered for purposes of taxation: councillors in their cities, villagers in their villages, agricultural labourers on the estates on which they toiled.[20] Only recruitment into the ranks of the burgeoning imperial bureaucracy or the expanding army offered a way out. Crisis had thus led to an institutional upgrading and enhancement of a now much more tightly administered empire, albeit one in which the city of Rome itself had been relegated from the centre of imperial power to a much revered but largely marginalised provincial backwater.[21]

The changes which took place in the Roman world across the late third and early fourth centuries had very marked implications for the evolution of Roman political culture. The decision of Diocletian, as the senior emperor, to establish himself primarily in the East to face down the Persian menace heralded a fundamental relocation of authority and power. Henceforth, only very rarely would any 'senior' emperor base himself for an extended period of time to the West of the Balkans. This, in turn, affected how imperial power was conveyed and understood, for it meant that the senior emperor was now operating in a political context in which, to project his power effectively, he had to do so within the traditions of divine monarchy. As a near contemporary, Aurelius Victor, declared of Diocletian, 'He was a great man, but with the following habits: he was the first to want a robe woven with gold, and sandals with plenty of silk, purple, and jewels; although this exceeded humility and revealed a swollen and arrogant mind, it was nothing compared to the rest, for he was the first of all the emperors after Caligula and Domitian to allow himself to be called "master" [Latin *dominus*] in public, to be worshipped and addressed as a god.'[22] The imperial office had become both highly militarized, by virtue of the rise of the soldier emperors, and highly ceremonialised, with the emperor increasingly depicted—in both eastern and western contexts—as the representation of divinity on earth. Diocletian himself claimed to hold power under authority from Jupiter, the father of the gods in the traditional Roman pantheon.[23] This emphasis on the emperor's supposedly divine personal associations no doubt helped to distract attention from his lowly Illyrian roots. The most important point was that the centre of gravity of the Roman Empire had shifted decisively eastwards.

NEW DYNASTIES AND NEW RELIGIONS

Perhaps because he did not have a son to whom to pass on power, and also, perhaps, as a nod to traditional Roman constitutional values, Diocletian never attempted to turn the Tetrarchy that he established into a dynastic system, although the families of the various tetrarchs did intermarry. The man he appointed as his co-ruler in the West (a fellow Illyrian soldier named Maximian), and their respective eastern and western deputies (Galerius and Constantius, also from the Balkans), had been chosen primarily on the basis of their trustworthiness, their talent, and the loyalty of their troops.

The system of power-sharing was effectively held in place by the overarching authority and personality of Diocletian himself.

In 305, the now elderly emperor made a remarkable and rare decision: he announced that he would retire from imperial politics, taking himself off to live in a palace he had constructed at Spoletum on the Dalmatian coast. From within this massive structure the modern Croatian city of Split would later emerge. He ordered his junior colleague, the western *Augustus* Maximian, to step down at the same time, and power was transferred to their respective *Caesars*, Galerius in the East and Constantius in the West, to whom new deputies were in turn appointed. An apparently peaceful transition of power seemed to have been achieved, but it was not to last long. The following year, as the new western *Augustus* was preparing to campaign against the Picts to the north of the empire's frontier in Britannia, he died. Encamped outside the city of York, the late emperor's army responded by acclaiming as his successor not the late emperor's duly appointed *Caesar*, but rather Constantius' son, Constantine. This act of effective usurpation encouraged others to follow suit, and the army around the city of Rome declared the former western emperor Maximian's son, Maxentius, as emperor in the West. A third claimant to the western throne emerged in Africa. Within barely a year of Diocletian's retirement, the Tetrarchy had been torn asunder by rival dynastic and political ambitions, fuelled by the support given to the imperial pretenders by their armies in the field, who clearly felt they had much to gain, in terms of pay, supplies, and prestige, by being led by an emperor and showing loyalty to his family.

Over the course of the ensuing civil war, the young prince Constantine managed to progressively eliminate each of his western rivals, culminating in his victory over Maxentius at the Battle of the Milvian Bridge outside the city of Rome in 312. A parallel civil war erupted in the East, which was settled in favour of the general Licinius. An East-West balance was restored. Relations between Constantine and Licinius, however, were never easy, and in 324 Constantine concocted a pretext to lead his armies eastwards, bearing down upon Licinius, who was based at Nicomedia (modern Izmit), on the Asian coastline opposite to the Bosphorus. Defeating Licinius first on land, and then at sea (at the Battle of Chrysopolis near the Golden Horn), Constantine captured and then executed his last imperial rival.[24] As the late fifth- or early sixth-century *Chronicle* of the pagan historian Zosimus would record, 'The whole empire now devolved on Constantine alone.'[25] In celebration of his victory at Chrysopolis, Constantine renamed the nearby Greek city of *Byzantion* after himself, redesignating it 'The City of Constantine the New Rome'—*Konstantinoupolis Nea Romê*—and adorning it with an array of splendid public monuments befitting an imperial foundation: a palace, a hippodrome, city walls, and a magnificent Christian cathedral. For, unlike Diocletian, Constantine was not a worshipper of the old gods of Rome and a devotee of Jupiter: rather, he was an exponent of a relatively recently established faith, which many at the time would have thought of as the 'Christ cult', but which we refer to as Christianity.[26]

In order to appreciate the significance of Constantine's adherence to Christianity, we have to return to the imperial crisis of the third century, which had witnessed many changes not only in Roman society but also in Roman religion. The traditional 'pagan' religious culture of Rome (as of Greece) was polytheistic, meaning that the Romans believed in a multiplicity of gods. As Roman rule had spread to the East and West, and the Romans had encountered the various cults of their new subject peoples, Rome had signalled a willingness to absorb the religious traditions of the provinces and identify local deities with the established Greek and Roman ones. As a result, the Romans were largely tolerant in matters of religion. The official propagation of the so-called imperial cult, to which all the emperor's subjects were expected to sacrifice and show due respect, gave the devotions of Roman subjects unity, cohesion, and focus. Temples to the imperial cult had been built throughout the empire, and upon death Roman emperors were accorded the title of *divus* (meaning 'deified').

The only significant body of the empire's subjects which had refused to participate in the imperial cult and sacrifice to it had been the Jewish community, which was heavily concentrated in Palestine (though with a presence throughout the urban centres of the empire, especially in the Near East and Mediterranean). The ancestral religion of the Jews was strictly monotheistic (meaning they believed there was only one true God), and this had made it impossible for them to sacrifice to the imperial cult or participate in its rituals. Judaism was widely regarded as a venerable religion, and in refusing to sacrifice the Jews were understood to be upholding the traditions of their ancestors. Such loyalty to the traditions of one's forefathers was regarded as morally virtuous within Roman culture, and as a result the Jews were largely excused their nonparticipation. The breakaway sect from Judaism known as Christianity had been spreading since the first century. Its followers claimed that an itinerant preacher known as Jesus of Nazareth, or Jesus Christ (from the Greek term *Christos*—'the anointed one'), had been the son of God, and that this Jesus, who had preached salvation for all mankind, had been crucified by the Roman authorities under the emperor Tiberius (*r.* 14–37 CE). The movement had experienced particularly rapid expansion in the urban centres of the empire across the third century, when the readiness of its members to provide charitable assistance to the poor and the sick at a time of widespread economic disruption and disease had won it many admirers and devotees.

Like the Jews, the Christians also refused to sacrifice, but unlike the Jews, their nonconformity could not be excused on the grounds of filial piety and tradition, as theirs was a new religion. Consequently, the Christians were viewed with considerable suspicion by the Roman authorities, with many regarding their refusal to sacrifice to the imperial cult to be not only antisocial, but also a potential cause of divine displeasure. In the reign of the emperor Diocletian, in particular, their refusal to sacrifice had unleashed a period of persecution. Many Christians were executed, becoming 'martyrs' (from the Greek *martyros*, 'witness') to their faith. Their memory was cultivated and celebrated by the Christian community, or Church (Greek *ekklesia*, 'assembly'), which declared them to be 'saints'. Their dedication to the faith was thought to have elevated them above the common mass of mankind and drawn them closer to God.

According to subsequent statements issued by or on behalf of Constantine, the emperor had adopted the 'Christ cult' just prior to the Battle of the Milvian Bridge in 312, having supposedly witnessed a cross miraculously appearing in the sky which Christians in his entourage enabled him to interpret and understand.[27] He ascribed his victory over Maxentius to the Christian God and began to lavish patronage and largesse upon the leaders of the Church, allowing them to draw upon state coffers to construct places of worship. The largest of these—the 'cathedral churches'—were established as the residences of the local heads of the Christian communities in each city, known as the bishops (Greek *episkopoi*, 'overseers'). Christian bishops and priests were excused from the obligation to serve on city councils and, like government officials, were able to travel across the empire for free using state-supplied mounts and pack animals (a system known as the *cursus velox*, approximating to 'high-speed super highway' or 'fast post'). The emperor thus signalled that Christianity was now his personally favoured cult.

As Constantine's centre of power shifted eastwards after his defeat of Licinius in 324, the emperor came under growing Christian influence, as it was in the cities of the eastern part of his empire that Christian communities were at their largest and most self-assured. At no point did Constantine initiate persecution of those who disagreed with him on religious grounds—he worked pragmatically and cooperatively with his generals, administrators, and potentates irrespective of religious affiliation. It was made clear, however, that sharing the faith of the emperor was something of an advantage when it came to promotion through the ranks of the imperial government, and conversion to Christianity on the part of ambitious members of the new bureaucratic and military elite snowballed across the course of the fourth century, both under Constantine and under his successors.

The leadership of the Church meanwhile increasingly sought to marry Christian faith and imperial ideology. The influential bishop and courtier Eusebius, for example, penned a speech praising the emperor in which he lauded him as the Christian God's one true deputy on earth, thereby providing a Christianised vision of the relationship between imperial and divine power that drew upon deep-rooted traditions of divine monarchy.[28] In return, under Constantine's patronage the Christian Church achieved unprecedented institutional and doctrinal development. In 325, Constantine presided over the first universal (or 'Ecumenical') Council of the Church, convened at the city of Nicaea, both to clarify issues of belief and to establish the organizational life of the Church, creating a system of Church government that shadowed that of the Roman state, with a bishop in every city and a 'metropolitan' bishop or archbishop in every province.[29] A significant process of religious realignment and transformation was underway, one which would reach an important milestone in 380 when the emperor Theodosius I (r. 379–395) felt sufficiently confident to declare Christianity to be not only the favoured religion of the emperor, but also the official religion of the Roman state.[30]

HERETICS, BISHOPS, AND SAINTS

From the very origins of Christianity, the movement had been characterised by a strong aspiration to unity alongside very wide disparities of actual belief.[31] Down to the fourth century, conflicting versions of Christ's life and teachings (known as gospels) remained in circulation.[32] Which of these were true? Jesus was called the 'Son of God'. But what did this mean in practice? Was he divine? Or had he simply been a very holy man?

These debates mattered to Christians, because they held that erroneous belief—heresy—closed the pathway to salvation.[33] Only those who accepted the true faith—orthodoxy—shared in the forgiveness of sins and the eternal life which the religion promised. Such concepts—orthodoxy and heresy—central to the new faith, were completely alien to traditional Roman ways of thinking about religion.[34] Prior to the age of Constantine, what the leaders of the Church had lacked was a means of defining orthodoxy and suppressing heresy. Constantine's adoption of Christianity made this possible for the first time. Traditionally, Roman emperors had felt an obligation to maintain the 'peace of the gods' (*pax deorum*). This essentially meant they were expected to intervene to prevent violent disputes from breaking out between different sects. The leaders of the Christian communities managed to convince Constantine that with his adoption of their faith he was now obliged to crack down on heresy and help settle disputes within the Church.

It was this expectation that had led the emperor to convene the Ecumenical Council at Nicaea (modern Iznik) in 325, over which he presided in person. For a dispute had arisen within the Church in Alexandria in Egypt which needed settling if it was not to destabilise the Church as a whole. Christians considered Jesus to be the 'Son of God', but in Alexandria, one priest, Arius, had been teaching a variation on this concept: that although Jesus was divine, God 'the Father' must have existed before God 'the Son', and thus the Father was superior to the Son.[35] Arius' opponents believed that the Christian God consisted of three coeternal and equal elements—God the Father, God the Son, and the Holy Spirit—which united and interceded between the heavenly and earthly realms. They taught, therefore, that Jesus had been both fully man and fully God, and that his divine aspect had existed before and throughout all time. At the Ecumenical Council of 325, Arius' position was condemned and deemed 'heretical'. Orders were given that his writings be burned and that Arius himself should be sent into exile. By the end of the fourth century, the 'Trinitarian' doctrine of Arius' opponents had been accepted as orthodoxy and the condemnation of the 'Arian' heretics had become a cornerstone of imperial religious policy. Beyond the empire, however, Christian missionaries loyal to the memory and theology of Arius were busy spreading the faith (and his interpretation of it) amongst the various barbarian peoples resident north of the Danube and beyond, such as the Goths and their neighbours. As a result, Arian Christianity would put down deep roots amongst the barbarians.

The Council of Nicaea was ultimately successful: by the end of the fourth century, the mainstream body of the Church within the Roman Empire had come to accept that Jesus Christ had been both 'fully God' and 'fully man'. This element of the faith was vital to the Church's doctrine of salvation. Most Christians believed that Jesus had died on the cross in order to atone for the sins of mankind, and that by ascending into heaven he had opened the pathway to salvation for his followers. In order to atone for the sins of mankind, he had to be fully human, just like us. Yet in order to ascend into heaven and wipe away mankind's sins, he also had to be fully divine. But how was this to be defined and understood? Was Jesus Christ a unique blend of the human and divine? Or did he have two separate natures, a human one and a divine one?

This issue—known as 'Christology'—caused a series of increasingly acrimonious disputes within the Church, and Constantine's successors to the imperial throne attempted to resolve them by drawing together rival bishops to debate and define the true faith. By the fifth century, the bishops of certain cities were considered to be the most prestigious of these: the bishop of Rome (who was believed to be the heir to Saint Peter, who had been martyred in the city not long after the crucifixion of Christ); the bishop of Alexandria in Egypt (believed to be the heir to Saint Mark, who had penned one of the earliest and most authoritative gospels); the bishop of Antioch in Syria (where the church had been founded by Saint Peter before he had made his way to Rome); the bishop of Jerusalem (where Jesus' followers had first gathered after his death); and the bishop of Constantinople (where the emperor Constantine—by that point widely regarded as a saint—had been buried upon his death in 337). These five bishops would come to be known as 'patriarchs' because of their seniority and authority within the Church.

In the mid-fifth century, a series of new Ecumenical Councils were convened in an effort to settle the burgeoning dispute over the relationship between the 'human' and 'divine' in the person of Christ.[36] The concern of those who believed in the two separate natures of Christ was that if the human and divine within him formed a single nature unique to him, then he could never have been either fully like God the Father in his divinity or fully like mankind in his humanity, and thus his death and resurrection could not have opened the pathway to salvation for mankind as a whole, as his resurrection and ascent into heaven could have been regarded as unique to him. Overemphasis upon the union, mixing, and blending of Christ's two natures, they claimed, thus threatened to produce a Jesus who was neither fully God nor fully man, just as water mixed with wine was neither water nor wine. This position had been most aggressively argued earlier in the fifth century by a patriarch of Constantinople, Nestorius.

Nestorius' emphasis, often referred to as *dyophysite*, from the Greek for 'two natures', elicited opposition from other elements in the Church that were equally determined to uphold what they believed to be the authentic teachings of the faith. For these thinkers, led by the brilliant theologian Cyril, patriarch of Alexandria, overemphasis on the distinction between the human and divine in the person of Christ threatened to undermine the entire concept of salvation, by making it impossible to explain or comprehend how the human and divine within Christ had been able to interact, relate, and cohere, just as oil and vinegar could be contained in the same vessel but never truly become one inseparable substance.[37] Cyril and his followers believed that without the full assumption of Christ's humanity by the divine, there could be no salvation through his death and resurrection. At the resurrection, none of Christ's humanity could be left behind. It had to be fully underpinned and embraced by his divinity. This position is often referred to as *miaphysite*, from the Greek for 'one nature'. At a council convened at Ephesus in Western Asia Minor in 431, Nestorius' teachings were condemned (or 'anathematized') and the patriarch deposed.

This issue caused continuing unrest within the Church, especially in Rome and Constantinople, where sympathy for the two-nature position was strong. Eventually, in 451, a follow-up council was held at Chalcedon, near Constantinople, in an attempt to establish a compromise formula. There, the majority of bishops present agreed to uphold the condemnation of Nestorius, but—in a gesture towards the two-nature party—asserted that Christ existed '*in* two natures, which undergo no confusion, no change, no division, no separation', with both natures being preserved and coming together 'into a single person'.[38] This was too much for Cyril and his followers amongst the leaders of the Church in Syria and Egypt, who would have preferred the formula that the person of Christ had been formed '*from* two natures', thus emphasising unity.

As a result, Cyril and his supporters refused to accept the decrees of the Council of Chalcedon. Subsequently, opposition to Chalcedonian doctrine became deeply rooted in Egypt, as well as in Syria and Palestine, where Cyril had many sympathisers. This refusal on the part of Cyril and his supporters to accept the definition of the faith established at Chalcedon constituted a direct challenge to imperial authority and unity. If, in the fourth century, Constantine's decision to convene the first Ecumenical Council had helped give greater definition and clarity to the Christian faith, the fifth-century councils had helped to bake in the divisions that had emerged. For Cyril was too popular a figure for the imperial government to move against, and his supporters were concentrated in some of the empire's wealthiest and most important provinces. The authorities could not afford to alienate the burgeoning Christian population in those regions.

It is sometimes difficult for the modern reader to appreciate the importance of the doctrinal disputes of the fourth and fifth centuries. The theology at the heart of the arguments was often complex and derived much of its terminology from Greek philosophy. But these disputes touched upon the core of Christian belief, and the hopes that many Christians cherished that if they believed correctly, acted correctly, and prayed correctly, they would be rewarded with forgiveness of sins and eternal life in the hereafter. These disputes, however, were also political. With the institutionalisation of the Christian Church in the age of Constantine, bishops had become powerful political figures.[39] Constantine had allowed them to preside over judicial hearings of his Christian subjects, and in the cities of the empire they had emerged as ever more influential power-brokers. Ecumenical Councils such as those held at Nicaea and Chalcedon were not polite tea parties at which kindly prelates debated theology. Rather, they were often brutal affairs, at which basic issues concerning the politics and administration of the imperial Church had to be thrashed out—sometimes literally so. At the Council of Nicaea in 325, for example, Bishop Nicholas from the city of Myra was later reputed to have slapped Arius round the face (a claim which might surprise those who are aware that Nicholas of Myra is the saint on whom the genial figure of Santa Claus was originally based).

In terms of Church politics, at the Council of Chalcedon it was agreed that the bishop of Rome (also known as the pope) should be accorded a 'primacy of honour' over the other leading bishops, by virtue of the fact that Jesus was believed to have accorded Saint Peter authority over his disciples. It was acknowledged at the same council that the bishop of Constantinople was of equal standing to the bishops of Alexandria, Antioch, and Jerusalem, despite his office having been of relatively recent creation, and the 'patriarchal' status of the bishop of Jerusalem was also confirmed. The bishops of Constantinople and Rome emerged from the Council of Chalcedon as winners in both political and theological terms, whereas the bishop of Alexandria was obliged to retreat from the council with his authority diminished in both respects. Perhaps unsurprisingly, subsequent popes in Rome and the patriarchs of Constantinople would be determined to uphold every aspect of the Chalcedonian settlement, while later patriarchs of Alexandria would be equally determined to see the council's work undone.[40]

NEW KINGDOMS

The establishment of Christianity as the official religion of the Roman Empire, and its increasingly central role in Roman imperial ideology, were pivotal to how the emperor Justinian would view the world around him and his place within it. Wrestling with the ramifications of the dispute over the Council of Chalcedon would be a major preoccupation of his reign. But a series of other events occurred at around the same time which would also prove highly significant and elicit a vigorous response from Justinian: the recently reorientated and newly stabilized Roman Empire found itself once again under threat.

The events of the third century had demonstrated that the military security of the Roman world was highly sensitive to developments amongst the barbarian peoples north of the Rhine and the

Danube. The late fourth and early fifth centuries would in turn demonstrate that these tribal groupings were highly vulnerable to any threat emerging from the Eurasian steppe—the plains and grasslands extending beyond the Danube via Ukraine to Central Asia and ultimately to the borders of China. In the mid- to late fourth century, a major reconfiguration of power in Central Asia led to the rapid movement westwards of groups of warriors known as Huns, who laid claim to the political legacy of an ancient nomadic empire known as the *Hsiung-nu*, who centuries earlier had humiliated and rendered tributary the emperors of China.[41] One confederation of Huns struck into the eastern territories of the Sasanian Empire of Persia, where they carved out a kingdom for themselves centred on the wealthy commercial entrepôts of Samarkand, Bukhara, and Khiva. This group (who would come to be known as the 'Hephtha-lite' or 'White' Huns) soon extended their control over the lucrative flow of Eurasian trade in silk and other goods which had developed in the preceding centuries, attempting to prevent such merchandise from travelling by sea to Persia, in order to force the trade through the land routes over which they now held sway. The loss of these Central Asian territories was a great blow to the Sasanians. As a result, the Persians would begin to identify the Huns rather than the Romans as their primary foe.

Other Hunnic groups rapidly reached the 'Pontic' or Ukrainian steppe north of the Black Sea. These invaders primarily consisted of hordes of mounted warriors, who were raised on horseback from infancy and possessed unrivalled cavalry skills, their military effectiveness being further enhanced by their remarkable skill with the light composite bow, which enabled them to rain arrows down on any advancing enemy and slaughter many of them before hand-to-hand combat could even commence. They were a foe the Chinese had long come to fear, but the likes of which the Romans had never encountered before on any substantial scale. In the 370s, bands of

34

these Huns began to bear down on the Goths, and in 376 large numbers of Gothic refugees arrived on the northern bank of the Danube. They begged to be admitted into Roman territory, the menfolk offering their military service to the empire if their families were granted lands within it. The reigning eastern emperor, a former general named Valens, agreed to this request, and the imperial authorities granted food and supplies to the Gothic settlers.[42]

As the desperate plight of the Goths became ever more apparent, however, the Roman commanders on the ground took advantage of the situation to mistreat and humiliate the empire's 'guests' (as the imperial government liked to think of them). In 378, the Gothic army rose up in revolt, and, at the Battle of Adrianople, inflicted a humiliating defeat on the Romans: two-thirds of the Eastern Roman field army was slaughtered, along with the emperor Valens himself. Although the new emperor, Theodosius I, managed to restore peace, allowing the settlers to form their own division in the Roman army under their own leadership and to settle in the Balkans, the standoff was an uneasy one.[43]

The continued presence of the Goths in Rome's Balkan territories negotiated by Theodosius I constituted an ongoing threat to the security of the Eastern Roman Empire (the division between 'East' and 'West' under separate *Augusti* having now become both culturally and politically entrenched). But the Goths posed a growing threat to the western authorities, too, and as a result the western court relocated itself from Gaul into northern Italy, in part to keep an eye on the Goths. In the West, the late fourth century had witnessed the gradual emasculation of the imperial office. Ever since the emergence of the Sasanian threat and the Diocletianic reconfiguration of Roman government, power and authority had increasingly come to be concentrated in the East. Now firmly established in their new imperial capital of Constantinople, the eastern emperors did not want to have to worry about potential rivals and challengers from the West. Consequently, the eastern authorities had increasingly sought to secure the appointment there of more biddable, effectively 'puppet' rulers, often bound to the eastern *Augustus* by dynastic ties. They were even willing to see 'boy emperors' appointed to the western throne, knowing that they would be easier to manipulate and control.[44]

This shift had two main consequences. The first was that the courts of these 'puppet', boy rulers were dominated by their courtiers, and particularly by 'overmighty subjects' (typically military commanders, themselves often men of barbarian origin who had been recruited into the Roman army). Second, the weakening of the imperial court led to growing political anxiety within provincial society in the West, where local elites were used to having access to an emperor who meant business, and where an appreciation of the empire's potential military insecurity had remained acute. This sense intensified dramatically in the early years of the fifth century, when the commander of the Gothic army, Alaric, led his troops into Italy in an effort to extract enhanced levels of pay and supplies from the imperial authorities there. As negotiations with the western government floundered, in the year 410 he and his men sacked the city of Rome.[45]

Even before that point, many of the leaders of Roman society in the West had come to feel neglected and abandoned by the empire, by virtue of the withdrawal of the imperial court into Italy. This sense of abandonment had been exacerbated around the year 406, when additional bands of Goths, as well as other barbarian groups, described as Vandals, Sueves, and Alans, crossed the Alps and the frozen Rhine and once more began to fan out over imperial territory.[46] Crucially, the imperial authorities in the West proved themselves largely incapable of driving these invaders back. A series of internal power struggles ensued as different generals and commanders attempted to take the situation in hand. By the end of the second decade of the fifth century, much of the Western Empire was in a state of chaos, with barbarian armies operating throughout Gaul and Spain, fighting for, with, and against different Roman commanders and claimants to imperial power. In this protracted Roman civil war, barbarian participants came to play an ever growing and ultimately decisive role.[47]

As the Roman Empire in the West fragmented into a series of local Roman or 'Romano-barbarian' regimes, it was inevitable that the Huns, too, would want to get in on the act. By 445, the growing number of Huns in Europe had united under the leadership of a single ruler—Attila—who soon forged a vast empire extending from the Rhine to the Caucasus, encompassing much of the barbarian world to Rome's north.[48] In 451, Attila led his armies into Gaul, where at the Battle of the Catalaunian Plain—the location of which remains a mystery to this day—his forces clashed with remaining detachments of the Roman army along with anti-Hunnic barbarian troops.[49] Although Attila was stopped, and the Hunnic Empire would begin to collapse upon his death in 453, it had become clear that insofar as the Western Roman Empire existed at all beyond Italy and the Alps, it now did so only as a shifting series of alliances between individual military commanders and warlords. The military retinues and armies of these commanders felt little loyalty to the increasingly distant and ineffectual figure of a western emperor, whose court was now based at Ravenna. In 476, Romulus, the last of the Roman emperors resident in Italy, was deposed by his commander-in-chief, Odoacer, who was of Gothic origin.[50] Odoacer then set himself up as king and informed the emperor in Constantinople that there was no longer any need for a separate emperor in Ravenna and the West. Titular authority in the region could instead finally pass to the eastern *Augustus*, a legal fiction that served to mask the emergence in the West of a patchwork quilt of increasingly independent and autonomous kingdoms ruled by

Frankish, Gothic, Vandal, and other primarily barbarian war-lords and kings. The Eastern Roman Empire, ruled from Constantinople, was thus effectively all that now remained of the Roman Empire of old.

NEW POLITICS

Within Constantinople itself the demise of the Western Roman Empire had coincided with significant processes of political change. Constantine's decision to found a new city on the Bosphorus in the 320s had been an act of self-glorification, but it had also been a carefully calculated act of *Realpolitik*. Beyond the ranks of the Christian Church and clergy, Constantine had come to the East with no natural base of support, and in Licinius he had deposed and murdered an emperor who had been popular amongst pagan and Christian alike. Constantine's foundation of Constantinople had enabled him to remove himself from an alien and potentially threatening political environment and to establish his position in the East in a setting of his own choosing and his own creation.[51] It also gave him the opportunity to build up a network of wellborn and influential clients, who could serve as the emperor's representatives, allies, and supporters, and he made a concerted effort to draw leading members of eastern provincial society to the city, as their support would strengthen his new regime. He made generous land grants to such men and their families, allowing them to build private residences, and in 332 he instituted the free distribution of bread rations, derived from the rich corn supply of the province of Egypt. This grain was shipped in vast quantities across the sea-lanes of the Mediterranean to help bolster and expand Constantinople's population. Crucially, Constantine's son and successor, Constantius II (r. 337–361), had also founded a Senate in the city, into which its leading citizens were enrolled. By the end of the fourth century, the Senate of Constantinople had been accorded equal status to the Senate of Rome, and all the greatest landowners of the Eastern Empire, along with the region's leading civil servants and military top brass, were granted membership of it.[52] The long-term effect of this policy was to draw together the social and political elite of the Eastern Mediterranean into a single political community, giving a sense of common interest and common identity to the ruling classes of the eastern provinces as a whole, focused on the city of Constantine.[53]

By the end of the fourth century Constantinople had become firmly established as a permanent imperial residence: no longer would emperors relocate to Antioch to face down the Persians, as Diocletian, and even Constantius II, had done. With emperors now ensconced in the great palace complex at the heart of the city—adjacent to the Hippodrome, where the population assembled to watch chariot races and circus performances; the Cathedral Church of Holy Wisdom (*Hagia Sophia*), where the patriarch prayed; as well as the Senate House, where members of the imperial aristocracy assembled to discuss the direction of imperial policy—a new power dynamic emerged. Whereas the Roman emperors of the first century had been strongly influenced by members of their own families and by the Senate, and the soldier emperors of the third century by their armies, by the end of the fifth century East Roman emperors were increasingly subject to the lobbying of a whole range of interest groups whose demands they needed to balance. These included the army (above all the palace guard); the upper echelons of the bureaucracy; members of the Senate of Constantinople (largely representing the 'landed interest'); representatives of the Church (headed by the patriarch); and even the urban population of the capital itself, where intermittent bouts of rioting sometimes broke out in protest against unpopular policies, and where crowds gathered in the Hippodrome and chanted their approval or disapproval of the emperor and his entourage seated in the imperial box (the *kathisma*).[54] Keeping these interest groups in check was no easy matter.

AN AGE OF ANXIETY

By the end of the fifth century, it would have become increasingly apparent to political circles in Constantinople that across the former Roman heartlands in the West a new generation of Frankish, Gothic, Vandal, and other barbarian rulers had carved out kingdoms of their own. The most sophisticated of these were the Vandal kingdom, which had been established in the former Roman provinces of North Africa, centred on the city of Carthage, and the kingdom of Italy, where the Gothic king Theoderic had deposed Odoacer, initially with the active encouragement of the East Roman authorities. To add insult to injury, many of the new rulers subscribed to the theology of the disgraced churchman Arius, whose followers had translated the Bible into Gothic. Core territories of the Roman world had thus not only been lost to the direct rule of the empire but had even come to be ruled over by 'heretics'.

By the start of the sixth century, Roman power only projected westwards from Constantinople as far as the nearer parts of the region of Illyricum, which, in the preceding decades, had been repeatedly subjected to both Gothic and Hunnic attack.[55] Beyond that, the Roman Empire was effectively no more. To the East, Syria, Palestine, and Egypt remained under imperial control, but within these provinces religious tensions were riding high. In particular, drawing upon deep-rooted but mounting 'eschatological' traditions in the Near East, which foretold the arrival of the 'Anti-Christ', and then God's final judgement, many Christians concluded that they were living in the 'Last Days' and that the end of the world (known in Greek as the *eschaton*) was nigh.[56] Syria, moreover, remained highly vulnerable to Persian attack. Indeed, a sudden resumption of warfare between the two powers in 502 would contribute to a dramatically heightened sense of insecurity across the Near East as a whole. Within the imperial capital itself, political conditions had become increasingly unstable, with the recent reign of the emperor Zeno (r. 474–491) having witnessed a series of conspiracies and revolts.[57] In Constantinople by around 500, a profound sense of crisis was in the air and political anxieties were rife. The one remaining 'Roman' emperor no longer governed Rome and faced renewed military challenges from the east. God's 'deputy on earth' found his authority openly challenged by leading elements within the supposedly 'imperial' Church, and the world seemed to many to be on the verge of falling apart. Such was the city to which the young Justinian had recently made his way and where he would soon begin his ascent to the acme of political power.

Chapter 2

From Rags to Riches

THE EMPEROR AND HIS HOMELAND

In September 2019, after a long and exhausting drive from Belgrade, a small car containing two distinguished Serbian professors of archaeology, along with me and my partner, pulled up at the bottom of a dusty dirt track in the remote countryside. The track led up to the remains of the city of 'Justiniana Prima', founded by the emperor Justinian southwest of the city of Naissus (Niš), the birthplace of the emperor Constantine. Over time, the ancient city has been reduced to a set of shallow, grass-covered structures and steep, overgrown earthen banks. To the untrained eye, it might appear as uninspiring as the bleakly desolate landscape over which the acropolis of Justiniana Prima once presided. But decades of painstaking excavation, led by my hosts that day, Vujadin Ivanišević and Ivan Bugarski, have revealed findings of incomparable fascination to anyone interested in both the person of the emperor and the drama of his reign.[1] For this was where, as Justinian would declare in one of his laws, 'God granted that We should make our original entry into this world'.[2] In other words, it was where (or very near to where) Justinian claimed to have been born.

The site may tell us much about the way Justinian saw himself and wanted others to see him. The most striking feature to emerge from decades of archaeological research at Justiniana Prima is the city's overwhelmingly religious character. Approaching it at its height in the middle years of the sixth century, one would initially have had to pass through the sprawling suburbs outside the city's formidable defensive walls.[3] The suburbs were home to many of the city's civilian inhabitants and housed monasteries, hospices, and hospitals, testament to the emperor's charitable instincts. The city proper covers about eight hectares. Entering through the great monumental gateway in Justinian's day, one would have been struck by the remarkable water features that his engineers had provided for the amenity and wonder of its population: a vast cistern, a water tower, pools, fountains, and wells. All were supplied by an aqueduct, some twenty kilometres in length, that snaked out across the landscape to the distant reaches of Mount Radan, where the rich springs are known to this day as the *Dobra Voda* (good water). At the same time, walking along the main processional avenue, or *embolos*, one would have had the chance to enter—and marvel at—a series of churches built in a row, each constructed in a different architectural style, perhaps to represent the building techniques and decorative schemes of churches from different regions of the empire. Moving on through the gateway that connected the Lower City to the Upper City, one would have passed an additional church, and the main buildings and monuments where much of the administrative and commercial life of the town was conducted. Chief amongst these monuments was a circular plaza in which there stood a bronze statue, probably of the emperor Justinian himself.

Finally, one would have made one's way up to the heart of Justiniana Prima: the acropolis. This was effectively a city within a city, entirely ecclesiastical in character, comprising a magnificent triple-apsed cathedral, a baptistery, and associated buildings where the archbishop of the city resided, leading prayers on behalf of the emperor and his empire. As the location of this remarkable 'Church quarter' makes clear, this was a city placed under divine protection and entirely subject to priestly jurisdiction and control. In essence, Justiniana Prima appears to have been conceived of not just as a monumental celebration of the emperor and his achievements, or an act of self-glorification akin to Constantine's foundation of Constantinople, but as a pilgrimage site to which pious Christians were expected to flock for prayer, healing, and contemplation, as they would have done to the shrines of saints and martyrs across the empire. In addition to its religious character, the city also had a strongly military aspect, its walls and ramparts reinforced by a series of some forty towers, each manned by a host of soldiers and officers, whose helmets and belt buckles (signifying their military rank) have been found amongst the debris excavated on the site. This was a city dedicated to a man, in short, who seemed to regard himself as a unique mixture of emperor, soldier, and saint.

Justinian was evidently determined to convey a breathtakingly elevated sense of his own dignity. Many contemporary critics, however, would have interpreted such lofty pretensions as a deliberate attempt on the part of the emperor to distract from his distinctly lowly origins. Certainly, as the location of Justiniana Prima reveals, the young Justinian—originally named Petrus—was born and raised far from Constantinople, in the empire's northern Balkan territories. In the fifth and sixth centuries, many members of the elite would have regarded it as the empire's largely lawless 'wild west', perched on the very edge of civilization. For the province in which Justiniana Prima was situated was one of the least urbanized in the entire Roman world. It was a land of farmers, herdsmen, and miners, renowned for their hardiness and brute strength, and the menfolk of the region were valued as good soldiers. The area had traditionally constituted the empire's main military recruiting ground, and many of the soldier emperors of the third and fourth centuries had originated from there. Despite this, many members of the civilian and bureaucratic elite in Constantinople and the other great cities of the empire deemed such 'Thracians' and 'Illyrians', as they were known, as little better than the 'barbarians' against whom the Roman army was meant to fight. As a result, they would always view Justinian with considerable suspicion. Indeed, Procopius went so far as to claim that the future emperor's birth had been the result of an unholy sexual encounter between a peasant girl and an evil spirit. It was almost certainly with deliberate irony that in one of his public works the historian would describe Justiniana Prima as the place 'whence sprung Justinian . . . founder of the civilized world'.[4] How could such a man possibly have ascended the imperial throne? What had drawn him to Constantinople in the first place?

JUSTIN AND THE ROAD TO CONSTANTINOPLE

Justinian's journey from provincial obscurity to the imperial crown began with his uncle Justin, who, in around the year 470, set out from the fortified settlement of Vederiana in their mutual home-land to seek employment in the army in Constantinople. Probably travelling for much of the way along the Via Militaris ('military highway'), connecting the Balkan territories via Naissus, Serdica (modern Sofia), Philippopolis (modern Plovdiv), and the city of Adrianople (modern Edirne) to the capital, a distance of well over seven hundred kilometres, Justin made the trek (which would have taken him just under a month) accompanied by two friends, Zemarchus and Dityvistus, who also hoped, in the words of Pro-copius, to escape the 'conditions of poverty and all its attendant ills' in which they had been raised and 'to better their lot'.[5] Today, the landscape around Justiniana Prima (located near Vederiana) is desolate and scarcely populated, never having really recovered from the damage inflicted by the two world wars of the twentieth century, and the region is a net exporter of young people in search of better opportunities elsewhere. It was much the same when the young Justin and his companions headed towards Constantinople on foot, 'carrying', Procopius tells us, 'cloaks slung over their shoulders' in which they carried the husks of dried bread that were meant to sustain them on their way. Justin appears to have been born around the year 450, and in the years leading up to his birth the lands where he and his family lived had been subjected to devastating raids and attacks orchestrated by Attila, who unleashed his Hunnic armies on the region in order to extract tribute from the Roman authorities. Visiting the site of the city of Naissus in 448, the Roman diplomat Olympiodorus had reported back to Constantinople, 'We found the city had been deserted since it had been laid waste by the enemy. Only a few sick people lay in the churches. We halted a short distance from the river, in a clean space, for all the ground adjacent to the bank was full of the bones from men slain in war.'[6]

The chronic military insecurity caused in the region by the Huns would have persisted throughout Justin's childhood and adolescence. For in the aftermath of the breakup of Attila's empire, the lands around Justiniana Prima had remained vulnerable to barbarian attack, with much of the Roman population obliged to seek refuge in fortified redoubts and a dense network of hilltop citadels and fortresses, such as at Vederiana, where they were able to preserve their cultural memory and political identity.[7] It is striking, for example, that Justin was able to speak Latin (which Justinian would later describe as his own native tongue), despite having begun life, according to a later Byzantine source, as a swineherd.[8] It is possible that when Justin began his journey to Constantinople, their homeland was effectively under barbarian rather than Roman rule. At best, it was probably a war-torn no-man's-land over which no one power exercised control.[9] Whilst Justin and his friends had decided to head east in pursuit of military service to the emperor, near contemporaries of theirs were just as likely to have ended up in the Gothic king Theoderic's army, which also numbered poor Romans in search of employment amongst its ranks.[10]

Justin and his companions made their way to Constantinople at a time of profound crisis in the Roman Empire, which was progressively contracting with every passing year. Although a western emperor still sat on the throne in Italy, his days were numbered. Beyond the Italian Peninsula imperial control in the West had largely faded away, just as it may have done in Justin's native land. The city of Constantinople, however, the 'New Rome' and capital of the Eastern Empire, would have been a magnificent sight. It is uncertain whether the trio of Justin, Zemarchus, and Dityvistus would have been able to enter the city freely: perhaps they were intercepted prior to or upon their arrival at the gates of the capital by military recruitment officers or other agents of the state, eager to vet or interrogate new arrivals. If permitted to enter and wander at will, the young men would probably have come through the so-called Charisius or Adrianople Gate, located roughly five kilometres from the milestone known as the *milion* in the heart of the city, which marked the end point of the Via Militaris, and from which all distances in the empire were measured.[11] From there the final stretch of the military road would have led them past the magnificent Church of the Holy Apostles, in which the body of the emperor Constantine lay, until they reached the 'capitol', or *philadelphion*—the monument of 'brotherly love'. This was so-named after the two sets of red porphyry statues of the first Tetrarchic emperors and their deputies (Diocletian, Maximian, Galerius, and Constantius) that stood there embracing one another—and which now famously survive outside Saint Mark's Basilica in Venice, having been looted by the Venetians during the Fourth Crusade in 1204. From the capitol they would have turned left onto the main monumental highway of Constantinople, the *mese*, or 'middle road', and then proceeded on to the Forum of Theodosius I, centred on an imposing column with a statue of the emperor on top of it dressed in military costume, flanked by statues of his sons on horseback.[12]

Finally they would have passed through the circular Forum of Constantine, at the centre of which there stood a forty-metre-high column of red porphyry topped with a golden effigy of Constantine himself. Depicted with golden rays of sunlight shining forth from his head, he brandished a sceptre and globe, symbolising his universal authority. According to one near contemporary account, by a certain Hesychius, from atop this column Constantine 'shone like the sun upon the citizens'.[13] We might imagine the overwhelming impression these accumulated marvels would have made on the minds of three young lads from the war-torn and impoverished reaches of Illyricum. Beyond the forum lay the main offices of government (the *praetorium*) and the Hippodrome, where the population of Constantinople gathered to watch horse races and to stare and shout at the emperor and the highest officials of the state. And finally, there stood the imperial palace itself, adjacent to yet another magnificent cathedral church, dedicated to the Holy Wisdom (*Hagia Sophia*) of God.[14]

Whether at a recruitment station outside or within the city, the three young men would have been subjected to physical examinations and conceivably some assessment of their actual or potential fighting skill. In any case, Procopius relates that 'as they were all men of very fine figure', they were not only enrolled in the army, but specifically enlisted in the ranks of the 3,500-strong palace guard, known as the *scholae palatinae*, receiving official letters to that effect signed by the reigning emperor, Leo I (*r.* 457–474), who at that time was engaged in reform of both the palace and its guarding arrangements.[15] This was a remarkable piece of good fortune, as it suddenly propelled the young Justin into close proximity to the seat of power in the greatest city of the known world. It was a lucky break that he evidently owed in no small part to his good looks: the contemporary historian John Malalas, for example, noted how even in old age, Justin was strikingly handsome, possessing a good nose and a ruddy complexion.[16] At the same time, both Malalas and Procopius tell us, he was blessed with a generous disposition and an easygoing nature.[17] What he lacked, observers agreed, was education.[18] Indeed, Procopius went so far as to claim that Justin was largely taciturn (presumably on the grounds of not being able to speak 'properly') and 'a right peasant' (*agroikizomenos malista*).[19] Nevertheless, he clearly had talent and potential which were recognised.

The duties of the palace guards into whose ranks Justin enrolled in approximately 470 combined ceremonial and guarding duties in the imperial palace in Constantinople with tours of active military service, fighting alongside units of the regular army and barbarian mercenaries who had signed up to serve the emperor (known as *foederati*, or 'federate' troops).[20] In the decades that followed, these tours allowed Justin to witness firsthand many of the challenges the Eastern Empire was facing at this time on the military front line. In 491, for example, when he would have been in his early forties, the imperial title passed to an official named Anastasius. The previous emperor, Zeno (r. 474–491), had been a military man whose origins were with the hardy mountain folk of the territory of Isauria in the hinterland of Asia Minor. Many such men were enrolled in the palace guard alongside the young Justin. Zeno's reign had been a tumultuous one, and in 475 he had been briefly deposed in an ultimately unsuccessful coup. The accession of Anastasius sparked off an Isaurian uprising in their homeland, and Justin, by this time a commander, was amongst those sent to help crush it. A bitter and bloody campaign ensued that lasted from 492 to 497, fought under the leadership of a draconian general, John 'the Hunchback'.[21] During the course of this campaign, Procopius would later claim, John had Justin arrested and imprisoned for an unspecified offence.

He intended to have him executed, but was dissuaded by a series of dreams in which a 'creature of enormous size and in other respects too mighty to resemble a man' came to him, threatening him with a terrible fate if he did not release the detainee.[22]

We next hear of Justin around the years 502–505, when he held the position of 'count of military affairs' (*comes rei militaris*) in the East Roman army that was sent against the Persians, who had occupied the important frontier city of Amida in Syria. By 515—now once more in Constantinople, and by this point in his sixties—Justin was one of the officers charged with containing and defeating an uprising led by General Vitalian, who disapproved of Anastasius' religious policies, and probably his economic policies too.[23] In a long and distinguished military career, Justin likely experienced more than one close brush with death.

At some point between his initial enrolment in the palace guards and the revolt of Vitalian, Justin had been transferred from the *scholae palatinae* to the three-hundred-strong elite guards' regiment of the *excubitores* (so-named because they were housed in the *exkoubita*, or side entrances to the palace, in close proximity to the main entrance). This regiment guarded the innermost sections of the palace complex and the person of the emperor himself. The excubitors were meant to be distinguished in both appearance and military record. They stood out from the other palatine detachments of the army by virtue of their high-laced boots and military uniforms, which, as the sixth-century bureaucrat, scholar, and antiquarian John Lydus noted, deliberately preserved and replicated the appearance of the armies of ancient Rome.[24] By 515, Justin had been appointed the commander-in-chief of these men, bearing the title of *comes excubitorum* ('count of the excubitors'), which also automatically accorded him senatorial rank. He had come a remarkably long way from the pig styes of Vederiana.

Members of the better-educated bureaucratic and 'mandarin' class of the Eastern Roman Empire, as well as members of the aristocracy, were used to assuming that military men of humble social background such as Justin were senseless brutes, good with a sword, but unaccustomed to the pen, and devoid of inner thoughts and feelings of any quality or substance. But Justin probably received from the army a rather better education than the likes of Procopius might have been willing to admit. It is almost inconceivable that he would have been able to fulfil his official responsibilities as an officer if truly illiterate. The Roman army, after all, was a world awash with paperwork—indeed, in a law issued in 534 it would be stated that both literacy and knowledge of imperial legislation were common amongst the military.[25] Likewise, Justin clearly had views and thoughts of his own on issues of considerable complexity.

Since the mid-fifth century the imperial Church had been increasingly wracked by disputes as to the nature of the relationship between the human and divine in the person of Christ. The definition of that relationship proposed and accepted by a majority at the Council of Chalcedon in 451 still held sway, but had been the subject of concerted opposition by the leaders of the institutional Church in Egypt as well as in significant parts of Syria and elsewhere. Support for the Chalcedonian formula was most entrenched amongst the leaders of the Church in the West, led by the bishop of Rome— the pope—and in those regions that were traditionally under papal authority, such as Justin's home region of Illyricum, as well as within Constantinople itself. In the interests of holding an increasingly divided empire together, both the emperor Zeno and his successor, Anastasius, had attempted to find a way of reworking the Chalcedonian definition of the faith so as to address anti-Chalcedonian concerns. In 482, Zeno had issued a statement of unity (known as the *Henotikon*) devised on his behalf by Acacius, patriarch of Constantinople, meant to supplement the Chalcedonian formula. This document had failed to win over the major anti-Chalcedonian factions whilst simultaneously offending the pro-Chalcedonian leadership. In 484, Pope Felix III had cut off contact with and 'excommunicated'

Acacius, leading to a breakdown in ecclesiastical relations between Rome and Constantinople that persisted even after Acacius' death in 489. This dispute would be known as the 'Acacian schism'.

Under Anastasius, who was highly interested in matters of theology, the *Henotikon* remained the cornerstone of imperial ecclesiastical policy, and the emperor made repeated efforts to engage with the anti-Chalcedonians. In 512, he appointed as patriarch of Antioch a high-profile opponent of Chalcedon, the brilliant theologian Severus. This appointment led to widespread protest and informed General Vitalian's decision to rise up in revolt: pro-Chalcedonian orthodoxy was strongly supported not only by significant elements within the population of Constantinople, but also by many of the units of the imperial army stationed in and around the capital.[26] Despite Justin's readiness to loyally obey orders and help quell Vitalian's mutiny, he, too, was a determined supporter of the pro-Chalcedonian party, and would be recognised as such by contemporary sources concerned with the dispute.

It would be easy to assume that Justin, Vitalian, and the protesters on the streets of Constantinople and elsewhere had little understanding of the abstract, complex theology informing the differing perspectives of the theological factions locked in debate at this time.[27] Yet clearly, members of both lay and military society were sufficiently engaged to put their own lives at risk. They accepted that it was worthwhile to do so, out of fear that erroneous belief could close the pathway to salvation, both for themselves and for all mankind. For Justin, in particular, a commitment to orthodoxy as defined and supported by the pope in Rome was also probably bound up with his overlapping social identities. 'Barbarian' groups such as the Goths were, from a sixth-century East Roman perspective, associated with 'heresy' and the condemned teachings of the fourth-century churchman Arius. It was by virtue of their heretical standing that the imperial authorities had come to ban such outsiders from serving in the palace guard, or even serving in the

East Roman army, save in their own separate units. Commitment to orthodoxy is thus likely to have been tied to regimental and professional identity and may have been felt especially keenly by a man such as Justin, who had grown up witnessing the consequences, and perhaps living in the shadow, of barbarian domination. As a result, there are signs that Justin may have been considerably more engaged with matters of faith than one might imagine of a man whose career was overwhelmingly concerned with the affairs of the world.[28]

As well as being capable of thought, faith, and belief, Justin was also capable of genuine affection, a fact demonstrated in his choice of a wife. Through his career in the imperial army and the connections he would have forged in the worlds of palace and court, Justin could easily have acquired for himself a partner of rather better birth than his own. Yet he found and married a woman whose social standing was even lower than his had been when he began his journey to Constantinople as a young man. His wife, the historian Procopius tells us—and we have no reason to doubt him—was a former slave girl of barbarian origins by the name of Lupicina (the best English translation would be 'Foxy'). Had he simply wished to enjoy a sexual relationship with her, Justin could have kept her as his concubine (as many Roman elite men chose to do with respect to women of low social standing, despite the increasingly shrill protests of the Christian clergy). Instead, he chose to make an 'honest woman' of her, later giving her the new and more decorous name of 'Euphemia' ('Of Good Repute'). The only logical explanation for Justin's actions was that he genuinely loved her. Even Procopius, who was no fan of the family, had to admit that Justin's wife was 'very far removed from wickedness', although she had in common with Justin the manners of a peasant (she was, he wrote, *very* rustic').[29] There are also indications that she, too, was deeply religious, and perhaps rather fastidious when it came to what company she was minded to keep.

There is every reason to believe that Justin and his wife were blessed with a happy marriage. They were not, however, blessed with children. Justin therefore contacted his sister (whose name is not, alas, recorded), who still lived very close to the settlement of Vederiana with her husband—Sabbatius—and their children, Vigilantia and Petrus, in a village called Taurisium. Justin invited the boy, Petrus, to come and join him in Constantinople, where he would later adopt him as his son, giving him the name Petrus Sabbatius Justinianus, or Justinian. Clearly keen to gather his family around him in the capital where they could share in his good fortune, Justin was also joined by his brother, whose sons Germanus and Boraïdes were signed up for the army.[30]

We do not know at what age the young Petrus left his parents and sister behind and made his way to the imperial city. If part of the purpose of Justin's invitation was for the boy to acquire an education, then he was probably about eight years old (Justinian would later invite a young relative, another Germanus, to join him at that age).[31] Petrus seems to have been born in about 482, so he may have made the journey around the year 490, just before the emperor Anastasius ascended the throne, by which point Justin would have been around forty and his career already well established.[32] If so, the uncle is likely to have had a profound influence on the young boy—Justin might have regaled him, for example, with accounts of his exploits during the Isaurian War (though perhaps not of his short-lived imprisonment).

The precise extent and nature of the education the young Petrus received are also, unfortunately, not entirely clear. Later in life, Justinian would provide his kinsman Germanus with a top-notch education. According to the contemporary historian Agathias, Germanus even went on to attend lectures at the university in Constantinople.[33] But the course of study Germanus followed probably represented the education that Justinian would have wished for himself, rather than the one he actually received. He clearly studied Greek in addition to his native language of Latin, receiving instruction in grammar and perhaps the basics of rhetoric (his later writings, even in Latin, reveal an aspiration to a rhetorical style rather than an actual mastery of it). He may also have studied Roman history and the rudiments of Roman law, each of which clearly caught his imagination.[34] Justinian's later writings reveal a knowledge of Christian doctrine, although whether he had studied it formally with a religious instructor, as opposed to at his own instigation, is uncertain.[35] Unlike that of his relative Germanus, Petrus' education probably stopped just at the point at which higher rhetorical and literary education would have been expected to begin.[36] He was clearly educated with a view to a career in the palace, but more on its military than on its administrative side.

Subsequently, Justin managed to secure for Justinian not only recruitment to the palatine guard, but ultimately enrolment into the ranks of the elite guards' unit of the *candidati*, a corps of just forty men who served as the emperor's personal bodyguard. Like his uncle, Justinian was evidently regarded as being of good physical stock—even when at his most critical, Procopius had to admit that 'he was not bad looking', whilst John Malalas describes him as 'handsome' like his uncle.[37] The *candidati* were meant to be of impressive appearance and bearing.[38] They wore special white dress uniforms and received privileged rations, presumably to help bulk them up. Service in their ranks thus provided the perfect perspective from which to observe the innermost workings of the court. Unlike Justin, Justinian does not appear to have seen active military service beyond the capital on the imperial front line—although it is conceivable he may have visited the Armenian front in about 526.[39] Given the propagandistic use Justinian might have been able to make of any such experience later in life, it is probably safe to assume that he did not, and the years between about 507, when, according to Roman law, he would have reached the age of full majority, twenty-five, and 518, by which point he clearly had become a *candidatus*, were, in any case, militarily relatively quiet ones from the perspective of the East Roman authorities. Instead, he was able to spend his time cultivating connections in the palace.

The period of Justinian's service in the palace under Anastasius was characterised by three important developments. The first was a general strengthening of the empire's position in the Balkans as the imperial authorities reasserted control over its Danubian frontier. The second was the initiation of a major programme of investment in the defensive infrastructure of its eastern frontier in response to the recent Persian war. Third was a heightening of religious tensions, especially within Constantinople, in response to Anastasius' ongoing efforts to reach out to anti-Chalcedonian dissidents which had led to General Vitalian's mutiny against Anastasius. Although pro-Chalcedonian officers, such as Justin, had dutifully helped to contain the revolt, it was probably with a view to not testing their loyalty to the breaking point that Anastasius had chosen not to track down and execute the rebel commander, who may have been regarded as something of a hero on the streets of Constantinople. Certainly, there was a series of major riots in the city directed at opponents of Chalcedon, who were deemed to be exercising too much influence at court: during the course of one such riot, a crowd in the Hippodrome had taken up the cry 'A new emperor for the Roman state.' A renowned eastern monk who was well known for his opposition to the Chalcedonian formula was killed by the mob, and his head paraded through the streets of the city as his killers chanted, 'Here is the enemy of the Trinity!'[40]

Such riots are unlikely to have been entirely spontaneous. The Hippodrome was the great meeting point between the classes of Constantinople, and the chariot races were popular amongst Romans of all backgrounds. In the capital and across the cities of the empire many young men joined so-called Circus Factions, which were originally supporters' clubs for the four chariot-racing teams. The divisions were the same in every city: the Whites, the Reds, the Blues, and the Greens. Over time, these Circus Factions had emerged as an important point of contact between upper-class and lower-class males, and they provided their members with networks that extended throughout the empire. A Green supporter from Constantinople finding himself in Antioch, for example, would be guaranteed a warm welcome amongst the Green supporters there.[41] Procopius complains of the outlandish fashions and haircuts that faction members adopted in Constantinople (huge billowing shirts and 'Hunnic' hairstyles—short at the sides but long at the back, akin to the 'mullet' once favoured amongst British football players in the 1980s). But the factions could also be associated with considerable lawlessness. Procopius reports how faction members would assault and rob people on the street, rape women, morally and sexually corrupt the sons of wellborn citizens, and force people to change their wills, but escaped punishment because of the fear they inspired and the influence their more aristocratic and senatorial supporters could wield.[42]

Because of this special license they enjoyed, the Circus Factions played an increasingly important role in the political life of the empire, and especially of the capital. As the imperial party sat in the royal box at the Hippodrome, chants would go up amongst the crowd, led by the Circus Factions, criticising or praising aspects of current imperial policy. The emperor Anastasius was publicly and crudely berated in the Hippodrome for what were perceived to be his parsimonious fiscal and monetary policies.[43] At the same time, figures at court and in the Senate were keen to cultivate connections amongst the 'factionalists', encouraging (and probably paying) the lower-class ones to riot in protest against individual policies, or to target individual ministers, bishops, and other figures whose removal they desired. As a result, the Circus Factions were drawn into the ever more politicised doctrinal disputes of the day, with the Blues generally supporting Chalcedon, and the Greens opposed. In Constantinople, in particular, these were the two most powerful of the four clubs, and they were each funded by wealthy patrons who were keen to see their political and religious agenda supported on the streets.

The Circus Factions had also become increasingly institutionalized. Their members could be summoned, for example, to help defend the walls of a city when under enemy attack, and they had even acquired a role in imperial coronations.[44] According to political convention, each new Roman emperor was meant to be appointed and acclaimed by the Senate, the army, and the people. In Constantinople, the 'people' were represented ceremonially by the factionalists, who would chant their support as the new emperor was presented to them.[45] So long as the palatine officials and highest officers of the Senate could negotiate and agree on a smooth transition of power to a commonly recognised heir within the walls of the palace, and present their choice as a fait accompli to the representatives of the army and the factions, all was well. Any prevarication, confusion, or delay, however, could suddenly allow the military and the mob to intervene and attempt to impose a candidate of their own. Just such a situation would soon arise.

'OUR MORTAL LORD HAS PASSED AWAY'

By 518, the emperor Anastasius' health was failing, and he had not made any clear arrangements for his succession. Although childless, he had three adult nephews, each of them a plausible contender for the throne. The most able of these, the general Hypatius, was commander-in-chief of the eastern field army (*magister militum per orientem*), while his brother, Pompey, was commander of the main Balkan field army (*magister militum per Thraciam*). The third nephew, their cousin Probus, had held high civilian office in Constantinople. Faced with choosing among them, Anastasius had prevaricated, and had failed to line up any one of them.[46] Another widely favoured candidate in the capital was a young aristocrat,

Olybrius, who was married to a niece of Anastasius and was the son of the well-connected and fantastically wealthy Anicia Iuliana. A surviving member of the Theodosian dynasty and descendant of one of the last western Roman emperors, she was eager to see a member of her household take up what she evidently regarded as their rightful place on the throne.[47] Indeed, the rioting mob that had recently called for 'a new emperor for the Roman state' had marched to the residence of her husband, the general Areobindus—who was of known pro-Chalcedonian sympathies—and attempted to persuade him to seize the throne. The Circus Factions had an uncanny habit of turning to members of Iuliana's family at times of crisis, although in this case, they were unsuccessful.[48] Another candidate was within the court, where the chamberlain Amantius apparently had high hopes that the throne could be secured for his protégé Theocritus, a committed supporter of Anastasius' favoured religious policy of anti-Chalcedonian engagement.[49]

On the night of 9 July 518, Anastasius passed away without resolving the issue of his succession. Of his nephews, Hypatius was with the army in Antioch, whilst Pompey was some 450 kilometres away overseeing the army in Marcianople (in modern Bulgaria). Probus was probably in the capital, but may not have been in the palace, where a decision had to be made, quickly.[50] Fortunately, a sixth-century courtier, Peter 'the Patrician', preserved crucial details of the struggle for power that now ensued.[51] Those in attendance upon the emperor (known as the *silentarii*) sent news of Anastasius' death to the two highest officers of the imperial guard, who met at the palace and conferred. One of these men was the head of the emperor's private retinue of *scholarii* (known as the *magister officiorum*), Celer; the other was the commander of the *excubitores*, Justin.[52] They knew each other well, having served together both at court and in the field against the Persians. According to another contemporary source, Celer had also been Anastasius' closest friend.[53] Having consulted with Justin, Celer explained the situation to the troops on duty and under his charge in the palace, including Justinian and the other *candidati*, whilst Justin informed the *excubitores* and other military officials. The heads of the palace guard thus seem to have attempted to choreograph and control the succession to Anastasius. According to Peter the Patrician, Justin and Celer addressed their men with what was clearly a mutually agreed statement: 'Our mortal Lord has passed away. We must all confer together and choose a new emperor pleasing to God and beneficial to the empire.'

By this point the chamberlain and head of the emperor's bedchamber (the *praepositus sacri cubiculi*), Amantius, had arrived on the scene and begun to take charge of the situation. At dawn the next day, members of the Senate resident in Constantinople began to arrive at the palace dressed in appropriate mourning garb. Crucially, news of the emperor's death had also been leaked to the Circus Factions, particularly—it would appear—the Blues (with whom, Procopius tells us, the *candidatus* Justinian was affiliated). Certainly, they would play a much more active role in the events that ensued than their rivals. Chants began to rise up from the Hippodrome directed at the senators as they made their way into the palace: 'Many years for the Senate! Senate of the Romans may you be victorious! A God-given emperor for the army! A God-given emperor for the world!' along with, Peter tells us, 'many other cries'.[54]

The senators now convened in the chamber of the palace known as the Hall of the Nineteen Couches, which was reserved for gatherings of the greatest ceremonial and political importance. There they were joined by the patriarch of Constantinople, John, whom Anastasius had only recently appointed on the condition that he affirm his opposition to Chalcedon. A series of inconclusive debates and discussions ensued as a number of potential candidates for the throne were discussed, none of them garnering widespread support. Accordingly, the *magister officiorum* intervened, warning that unless a decision was reached speedily, those assembled within the chamber risked losing control of the situation, especially given the growing presence outside of the faction members and, increasingly, it would seem, the army.[55]

As the arguments inside the palace continued, Justin's troops in the Hippodrome, as if on cue, intervened. According to Peter the Patrician's account, 'The *excubitores* up in the Hippodrome proclaimed as emperor a tribune [army officer], and friend of Justin, John . . . and they raised him on a shield. But the Blues were dissatisfied and pelted him with stones, and some were even shot down by the *excubitores* with arrows.' The Blues having rejected an ally of Justin's, the troops of the *scholarii* now attempted to acclaim as emperor a friend of their boss Celer, a general named Patricius, who just happened to be present, and whom they raised up on a couch with a view to symbolically crowning him. This time it was the *excubitores* who were dissatisfied, and they pulled Patricius to the ground. According to Peter, Patricius only survived with his life because Justinian, who had now arrived amongst the other *candidati*, intervened. The *excubitores* pleaded with Justinian to take the throne himself, but he demurred. Perhaps his candidacy had not been sanctioned by Justin, and he felt he needed to stay on his uncle's good side. As the different sections of the palace guard proposed different candidates, some of them began to bang on the ivory doors of the palace, demanding to be given the robes of state with which to invest a new emperor. Psychological pressure on those inside the palace intensified. With the soldiers literally hammering at the gates, the senators were compelled to reach a compromise: they settled on Justin, whom, Peter said, they 'somehow persuaded' to don the imperial robes. Given his advanced age, many of those who acquiesced to Justin's candidacy at this point may have done so on the assumption that he was unlikely to be emperor for long, and their initially favoured candidates might have a better chance the next time round.[56]

Justin had been nominated as emperor by the senators but it would be fair to say that they did so under considerable duress. Even amongst the troops under the command of Celer, his nomination did not win universal approval. Peter reported that 'some *scholarii* who were dissatisfied went up to him, with the result that one even gave him a blow with his fist and split his lip'—hardly decorous behaviour, given that Justin would have been an old man of some sixty-eight years of age. 'Otherwise,' we are told, 'the opinion of all of the senators and soldiers and faction-members prevailed and he was carried up to the Hippodrome.'[57] There his coronation was agreed to by both the Blues and the Greens, who were now also on the scene, but who, unlike their rivals, had not had any discernible impact on the proceedings.

In the imperial box, or *kathisma*, of the Hippodrome, Justin was joined by the patriarch of Constantinople, and the imperial chamberlains brought the vestments which the soldiers had hitherto demanded in vain. With the crown on his head, and brandishing a spear and shield, the new emperor received the acclamation of the crowd: 'Justin *Augustus*, may you be victorious!' He then addressed his subjects, promising that every soldier would receive a donative of five gold coins and a pound of silver to mark his accession. His formal declaration was read out by the court clerks, as the chief legal officer, known as the *quaestor*, could not be found, and his colleague Celer, it was claimed, had suddenly fallen ill. The new emperor's statement announced, 'Since we accede to the imperial power by the judgement of almighty God, and by your common choice, we invoke heavenly foresight. Through his love of mankind, may he encourage us to achieve everything that is of benefit both to you and to the public good. It is our intention . . . to set you on the path to every success, and to guard each and every one of you, with every form of good cheer, and support, and freedom from care.' The crowd responded with cries of 'Many years for the New Constantine! . . .

Worthy of the imperial power! Worthy of the Trinity! Worthy of the City!'[58]

The banalities with which Justin regaled his audience on the morning of 10 July 518 would hardly suggest that he was a man who had been preparing for power, with a governing agenda ready to hand. Peter the Patrician believed that the circumstances that had led to his accession had been 'almost unplanned', and that Justin had been reluctant to accept the crown. The ecclesiastical historian Evagrius would write later in the century that his accession had been totally unexpected.[59] Justin himself would shortly write to Pope Hormisdas in Rome to announce his elevation, informing him that he had ascended the throne unwillingly.[60] Procopius ascribed his sudden emergence as emperor to the power of his office as *comes excubitorum* rather than the power or foresight of the man himself.[61] It would later be claimed that the court chamberlain Amantius had given Justin funds to distribute amongst the guards to buy up support for his chosen candidate Theocritus, but that Justin had then used that money to buy support for himself.[62] If so, the bribes are likely to have been distributed amongst the troops by Justinian rather than by Justin, who had remained enclosed in the *Hall of the Nineteen Couches* with Celer and the other senators.[63]

Despite these accusations, there is no clear evidence that Justin deliberately engineered his own coronation, although he and Celer may have sought to ensure that the new emperor was a military man, and probably a pro-Chalcedonian. This would explain the manner in which their respective troops had sought to acclaim the army officers John, who would subsequently become a bishop, and Patricius, who had nurtured pro-Chalcedonian connections whilst also playing nicely with the Anastasian party.[64] Although Celer, as a loyal friend to Anastasius, had gone along with the latter's ecclesiastical policy, Justin would soon permit him a role in negotiating an end to the Acacian schism with the papal authorities in Rome, a decision that would have been inconceivable had he considered him to be genuinely anti-Chalcedonian himself.[65]

The story of Justin's rise to power reads almost like something from a fairy tale. Indeed, according to a fascinating anecdote preserved by a sixth-century Church historian, a court official, one Marinus, who had been a protégé of Anastasius, had the entire rags-to-riches story of Justin and his family, and their journey from provincial backwater to the pinnacle of political power, turned into a painted mural used to adorn the public baths in the capital. This visual representation of the emperor's origins may have been a little too graphic for Justin's tastes: we are told that Marinus was summoned before the emperor and asked to account for himself. Marinus replied, 'I have employed [these] pictures for the information of the observant, and for the edification of those with discernment, so that the great men, the rich, and the children of important families, should not trust in their power, their wealth, and the importance of their noble families, but in God, who [quoting Scripture] "raises the unfortunate man from the dung pile and places him at the head of the people".'[66] It is testament to how easygoing the new emperor could be that Marinus escaped with his life. In any case, the 'great men' and 'noble families' of Constantinople probably did not need a tableau to tell them what was plain for all to see: that with the sudden ascendancy of Justin and his family, any ongoing imperial ambitions they nurtured had been thwarted—in the short term at least—in a most extraordinary way.

Chapter 3

Succession

RESTORING UNITY: JUSTIN, THE POPE, AND THE WEST

A lthough Justin was originally an outsider to the world of the imperial court in social terms, through his many years of service there he had clearly learned to understand its workings in intimate detail. A contemporary Latin source records how the late emperor Anastasius would wake up in the morning to find Justin guarding his bedside and relates that Justin had attended to the emperor so closely that he even trod on his robe.[1] Now emperor himself, the dutiful Illyrian set about getting to grips with what he perceived to be the top priority—the restoration of full ecclesiastical unity with Rome. Pro-Chalcedonian agitation, both at court and on the streets of Constantinople, provided the impetus for this rapid reorientation of imperial policy. On 15 July 518, just five days after he participated in Justin's coronation in the Hippodrome, John, patriarch of Constantinople—whom Anastasius had only appointed a couple of months earlier—was barracked by clearly preorchestrated pro-Chalcedonian chanting by members of the public as he entered the Cathedral Church of Hagia Sophia. They demanded that he not only publicly affirm his support for the Council of Chalcedon (which Anastasius had obliged him to renounce), but also condemn anti-Chalcedonian theologians and churchmen whom Anastasius had indulged, such as the intellectually formidable patriarch of Antioch, Severus.

The imperial troops guarding and patrolling the vicinity of the cathedral, which was adjacent to the palace, made no effort to intervene or to maintain order. John attempted to calm the mob, first by publicly endorsing the Chalcedonian definition of the faith, and then by agreeing to celebrate a Mass in its honour the next day and to condemn ('anathematize') Severus. But the protests continued, with the militants demanding that three names that Anastasius had ordered to be removed from the official records of the Church be restored: that of the late pope Leo, and those of two pro-Chalcedonian patriarchs. These records, known as 'diptychs', were writing tablets on which were inscribed the names of officeholders both dead and alive whom the ecclesiastical authorities wished to commemorate or celebrate.[2] Patriarch John acceded to these demands on condition that Justin grant his assent and a council of bishops in and around Constantinople be convened to approve them.[3]

With respect to the emperor, the mob was, of course, pushing at an open door, and it is very likely that those associated with Justin were behind the demonstrations in the first place. Imperial and conciliar consent was rapidly forthcoming, and instructions were sent to the patriarch of Jerusalem and other eastern bishops to convene synods to condemn the increasingly isolated and now dangerously exposed Severus, who, along with many of his followers in Syria (comprising both bishops and abbots), was soon deposed and driven from office. Severus fled to Egypt, where the depth and extent of anti-Chalcedonian feeling made it much harder for the imperial authorities to arrest him.[4] By 519, the newly appointed patriarch of Antioch, Paul, was actively cracking down on those who were loyal to the theology of Severus in and around the city.[5]

Justin also took the opportunity to summon back from exile or politically rehabilitate a number of high-ranking figures whom Anastasius had dismissed on account of their Chalcedonian affiliations. Chief amongst these was General Vitalian, whom he immediately placed in charge of the army around Constantinople (as *magister militum praesentalis*), and whom he nominated to the high-profile rank of consul for the year 520, succeeding Justin himself.[6] This would have involved Vitalian organising and presiding over a series of public celebrations and games in the Hippodrome, and so would have been a very clear signal to the population of the capital that a significant page had been turned in terms of the imperial government's religious stance. Others whom Justin summoned back included the wealthy Egyptian landowner Flavius Apion, who had overseen the provisioning of the East Roman field army during Anastasius' Persian War. Justin appointed him to the position of 'praetorian prefect of the East', effectively chief finance minister for the empire.[7]

The path was now clear for Justin to reach out to the papacy, and on 1 August 518 he sent a letter to Pope Hormisdas announcing his election. The missive is strangely straightforward: the new emperor simply informs the pope of his appointment and asks him to pray for his success in strengthening the empire. The emperor's pro-Chalcedonian sympathies must have already been well known in Rome and did not need trumpeting: the pope's reply made it clear that he recognised Justin as an ally, whom divine providence had brought to the throne to rid the empire of its religious lawlessness. In a follow-up letter sent in September, Justin opened negotiations, informing Hormisdas that the patriarch of Constantinople and the bishops gathered around him had drafted a set of proposals for the pope's perusal aimed at restoring ecclesiastical unity, orthodoxy, and concord. He was sending these to Rome along with an interlocutor.[8]

In the discussions that ensued, the papal authorities played hardball, evidently seeking to press home the advantage which they perceived the accession of Justin now gave them. By doing so, they could maximise the embarrassment of those moderate pro-Chalcedonian churchmen who had sought to triangulate between the *diktats* of faith and the expectation of loyalty to a reigning emperor by engaging in a positive way with Anastasius and the *Henotikon*. The pope demanded, for example, that the name of Acacius, patriarch of Constantinople, who had drafted the *Henotikon*, as well as the names of four of his successors and all the bishops who had subscribed to it, be erased from the diptychs. Even the names of Emperors Zeno and Anastasius were to be expunged from the public commemorations of the Church. Rome, moreover, was to be recognised as the sole repository of orthodoxy. These demands were presented by a papal delegation which was formally received by the emperor on 27 March 519.[9] The following day, the patriarch of Constantinople agreed (probably under considerable pressure from the emperor) to accede to the pope's demands. On 31 March (Easter Day), Justin announced that the schism was over.[10] His prime objective—restoration of religious unity with Rome—had been achieved in less than a year. As a papal source known as the *Book of the Pontiffs* would declare, 'And a council was held before Justin Augustus . . . and they all, even Justin Augustus, cried out together, saying "Damnation to Acacius, here and in eternity!" . . . And thus it came to pass that there was harmony from the East unto the West and the peace of the Church prevailed.'[11]

As news of what many churchmen in the East effectively regarded as an imperial capitulation to the papacy spread, there were, predictably, signs of growing discontent. The members of the papal delegation had been instructed to prolong their stay in the empire to ensure that the imperial authorities delivered on their commitments, but even in Thessalonica, where the Church had long-standing institutional connections and affiliations to Rome, one of the legates was physically assaulted: his lodgings were burnt to the ground, and his host and two of his servants were killed by a rampaging mob, furious at the demand that the bishop of Thessalonica sign the accord. Repeated efforts were made to persuade the pope to relent on his demand that the bishops who had subscribed to the *Henotikon* be condemned and expunged from the diptychs. This requirement was causing considerable unhappiness, especially in the provinces, where previous bishops were often revered by the faithful. Rome refused to engage; as a result, even many moderate pro-Chalcedonians chose to simply ignore the concordat's provisions. Others provided those who had signed up to the *Henotikon* an opportunity to publicly affirm their pro-Chalcedonian credentials whilst making it clear that they had not interpreted the text in a miaphysite way.[12]

When engaging directly with his provincial subjects to the East, Justin was willing to respond positively to the anxieties of moderates on both sides of the Chalcedonian dispute.[13] But it was crucial for the emperor and his new regime to be seen to send a clear message, to the leaders of the Christian communities in both the Old and the New Rome, that he was committed to unity and concord on the basis of Chalcedonian orthodoxy. This approach cemented loyalty to him in the army and on the streets of Constantinople. It also won him allies in the West. Having grown up in Latin-speaking Roman territory periodically subject to barbarian rule, Justin was predisposed to engage closely with pro-Chalcedonian churchmen and Christians in the West in general, and Italy in particular. Yet doing so also allowed him to put out feelers to ascertain the prospects for an imperial revival there. The Gothic king in Italy, Theoderic, was by this point an old man and had failed to produce a son to succeed him to the throne, raising the inevitable questions as to what would happen to the territory after his death.[14] Justin's initial emphasis on ecclesiastical unity with Rome at any price was not without its risks, but makes more sense in this context.

Certainly, it is striking that the years following Justin's rapprochement with the papacy would witness signs of growing tension between the Gothic regime and the papal authorities in Italy, which the emperor and those around him deliberately sought to exacerbate. In 526, Theoderic even had Pope Hormisdas' successor—John I—arrested, accusing him of conspiring with Constantinople.[15] Similar accusations were made against a number of high-ranking senators in Rome, including the philosopher and statesman Boethius, who was executed.[16] Such emergent divisions within the Italian kingdom were potentially to the empire's great advantage. But Justin's policy of reaching out to the pope was not simply a political move. Justin was also strongly motivated by a keen sense of personal faith, which, as we shall see, he had passed on to his nephew Justinian, who, by this point, had become his adopted son.

EMPEROR, SON, AND POPE

At the same time that he was corresponding with the new emperor, Pope Hormisdas was also corresponding with other major figures. Some, such as Justin's wife, the empress Euphemia, he probably wrote to out of politeness. She was clearly thrilled to be able to exchange letters with the pontiff: 'We have received the letters of your Beatitude with a grateful and giddy mind,' she informed the pope, celebrating and commending his 'integrity of life and consistent commitment to the true faith'.[17] There are, however, no signs she was actively involved in policy formation, although one anti-Chalcedonian author informs us that she refused to take Holy Communion from prelates who did not publicly subscribe to the

Council of Chalcedon.[18] Others the pope clearly corresponded with because he regarded them either as important power-brokers in Constantinople or as well-placed allies from whom he could derive useful intelligence. These included Justin's erstwhile colleague Celer and his protégé Patricius, Anastasius' nephew Pompey, and the powerful and well-connected princess Anicia Iuliana. The pope's correspondence with Justinian probably fell somewhere in between. In any case, Justinian made sure that the messenger conveying letters from the emperor back to Rome—whom he regarded as a good friend—also carried a personal message from himself.[19]

Through this letter, we hear Justinian's voice for the first time, and encounter the future emperor's distinctive personality and style.[20] The text was evidently written (or dictated) by Justinian in person, as no clerk trained in the elegant discourse of the imperial Chancery would have written to the pope in such terms.[21] It is urgent and insistent, adopting a startlingly providential and theological tone, coming as it does from someone who at this point may still simply have been one of the imperial bodyguards, or *candidati*.[22] 'The longed-for time', Justinian informed the pope, 'which we have wished for with the greatest of prayers, has been granted through divine clemency, with a view to the sufferings of the human race, that all the catholic and those who are perfectly faithful to God may be able to entreat themselves to his majesty.' Emphasising his intimate connection to the new ruler in Constantinople, Justinian assured the pontiff that 'Our Lord, the most invincible Emperor, has always clung to the orthodox religion with a most ardent faith, and desired that the holy churches should be called back to unanimity . . . since the greater part of the details of the faith have been established under the authority of God [*deo auctore*]'. In order to resolve remaining issues, Justinian urged the pope to hasten in person to Constantinople: even a moment of further delay would be intolerable, given the urgent need to restore unity to 'the whole world' in regions under imperial control. 'Hurry up, most holy

Lord!,' he beseeched the pope, that 'by the favour of Our Lord Jesus Christ' the matter be settled with the emperor once and for all.[23]

In subsequent correspondence, Justinian's tone would become still more expressly theological as he tried to engage Pope Hormisdas in detailed discussion of doctrinal issues. In one letter, Justinian warned him of 'Scythian monks' (from the modern Dobrudja) who were on their way to Rome to propose a compromise position that had no official standing in the East. In a follow-up letter dispatched soon thereafter, Justinian presented a discourse upon the theological solution the monks had proposed. He was warming to their position, citing in justification the writings of Saint Augustine, the fifth-century Latin bishop and theologian whose teachings were revered in the West. He ended the letter with a medical analogy to justify carefully targeted theological remedies to the problems within the Church with which he was clearly rather pleased: 'For by custom', he reminded the pope, 'we praise the doctor, who manages simultaneously to cure long-standing illnesses, without causing new wounds.'[24] Such medical metaphors would reappear in Justinian's subsequent legislation.[25] In a more forthright epistle, he again urged greater haste, as God was watching them all, the pope included: 'Your Apostolicity has been fully aware of what ardent faith your son the most serene emperor, and we ourselves (nosque) have borne from the start: and how we have never ceased to strive with respect to those matters that pertain to the upholding of the divine religion. . . . Therefore we respectfully beseech your reverence, that there be no opportunity for any prevarication, but rather we need to hurry up, operating as we are—in every respect— under the eyes of divine judgement.'[26]

Hormisdas' responses to Justinian were not, in the first instance, qualitatively different from those which he sent to his other well-connected correspondents in and around Constantinople, including Justinian's cousin Germanus, who was now emerging as an important military figure. But Justinian's letters to the pope were qualitatively different to anything he received from them. Anicia Iuliana, for example, criticised the enemies of true religion in a general way, dismissing them as 'rabid dogs', without engaging in anything approximating to theological discussion. She would clearly never have dreamed of writing to the pope, as Justinian did at one point, assuring him that the position enunciated by the Holy Father was, in theological terms, fully acceptable ('for we believe the position intimated to us in your religious response', he informed the pope, 'to be catholic').[27] It is hard to believe that such a tone would not have raised an eyebrow or two in the papal curia.

Especially in their early correspondence, Hormisdas was careful not to get drawn in by Justinian. He did not respond directly to his invitation to hasten to Constantinople, and he politely sidestepped efforts by the guards officer to engage him in doctrinal debate. He was, however, grateful for the intelligence Justinian passed on with respect to groups such as the Scythian monks, and kept Justinian informed as to how he had responded to them. The pope also praised Justinian for his manifest zeal and commitment to the cause of unity and his determination to crush heretics (whereas the pontiff's letters to Anicia Iuliana tended to dwell on her impeccably blue blood and noble character).[28] Justinian's letters had clearly made a mark, and may have succeeded in conveying the message he was determined to get across: that he was a powerful figure at court, and an active participant in his adopted father's rule. Both he and the emperor, Justinian had emphasised to the pope, had striven on behalf of the true faith *jointly*.

This point is an important one. As we shall see, the historian Procopius would later claim that from Justin's accession in 518 onwards, Justinian was the real power behind the throne, dictating and determining the course of imperial policy. Justin, Procopius would claim, was no more than 'an old man tottering to his grave', an illiterate who 'had never learned to tell one letter from another': 'extraordinarily like a stupid donkey, inclined to follow the man who pulled the rein, his ears waving steadily all the while'.[29] Justinian, he would have us believe, was the man holding the reins. The truth was rather more complicated.[30] But at its core, the picture presented by Procopius—that Justinian was the person *really* running the empire, on behalf of his elderly adoptive father—probably reflected what Justinian *wanted* people to believe. It is striking—and perhaps ironic—that throughout his negative critique of Justinian, Procopius was inclined to feed off and subvert Justinian's own propaganda, and it would appear that was true even with respect to his account of Justin's reign.

So what was the reality of the situation? Justin's accession had necessarily raised both the profile and importance of his adopted son, Justinian, who, for example, was charged with receiving the papal delegation upon their arrival in Constantinople on 25 March 519. He did not do so alone, but rather alongside the influential figures of General Vitalian and Anastasius' nephew, Pompey.[31] Justin had granted Justinian a sumptuous palace just south of the Hippodrome, adjacent to the Sea of Marmara (it became known as the Palace of Hormisdas—both the palace and the pope were named after a fifth-century Persian convert to Christianity). Justinian was keen to inform the papal legates that he was building a church within it dedicated to Saints Peter and Paul (who were strongly associated with the city of Rome); he requested that they intercede with the pope to obtain some holy relics for him to keep there. Rather than being a sign that he possessed unusual influence or power, this is more likely to have been an attempt on Justinian's part to ingratiate himself with the papal authorities by conveying a strong sense of personal piety.[32]

In fact there is no evidence that upon ascending to the throne the new emperor favoured Justinian or propelled him into high office. While Justin did set about clearing the palace of those who had been too closely associated with the figure of Anastasius, none of the posts that were vacated are known to have gone to his adopted son.

Indeed, both Vitalian and Justinian's cousin, Germanus, would initially appear to have been promoted in preference to him.[33] In a letter to the pope in April 519, Justinian bore the title of *comes* (count), but this may have been a purely honorific rank, albeit one that would have had the effect of bestowing senatorial status.[34] It is also possible that Justin had appointed Justinian to his old job of *comes excubitorum*, as we do not otherwise know who filled that post—but a near-contemporary source from outside the empire claims that Justinian remained a *candidatus* until 520.[35] As the emperor's son, Justinian would have been worth courting politically, but, if anything, Justin appears to have gone out of his way not to alienate opinion by being seen to lavish too many favours upon him straightaway. Locking Vitalian into the regime was a much more pressing priority, and he and Justin travelled to the city of Chalcedon together to jointly affirm their commitment to the decrees and definition of the council that had been held there.[36]

By the summer of 520, Justinian had been promoted to the high-ranking military post of general of the army stationed around Constantinople (*magister militum praesentalis*) alongside Vitalian, whom Justin had already appointed to this rank.[37] Vitalian now also held the office of consul, further bolstering his profile in the city and establishing him as the most powerful figure at court after the emperor himself. Soon after the papal delegation had finally left Constantinople, however, Vitalian was suddenly and unexpectedly cut down and killed in a parade ground near the palace, probably by members of the palace guard. According to a later anti-Chalcedonian source, Justinian was present when the murder occurred, and Procopius would later insist he had orchestrated it.[38] A near-contemporary source from outside the empire concurred, saying that a coterie (*factio*) loyal to Justinian was behind the assassination. Whether or not this is true, there can be no doubt that the death of Vitalian worked to Justinian's great advantage, and Justinian succeeded him as consul in 521.[39] It does seem likely that he was involved in the 'hit' on Vitalian. The assassination was justified by claims that Vitalian had been plotting against the emperor, an accusation that Justin seems to have accepted and ultimately believed.[40]

Between Justin's accession to the throne in July 518 and the death of Vitalian in July 520, Justinian appears to have been busy building up his public profile and political reputation. He reached out to the papacy, may have coordinated the elimination of his chief rival, and attempted to convey the sense that he was a key power-broker at court and potentially the real power behind the throne, however detached from reality such claims might have been. According to Procopius, he also entered into private correspondence with powerful figures within the Vandal kingdom of Africa, such as the Vandals' Prince Hilderic, with whom he exchanged lavish gifts (although the date of this supposed episode is uncertain).[41] Significantly, Justinian seems to have built up a following in the army and on the streets of the capital: some of the imperial guard had already attempted to acclaim him emperor in 518, and we are told by Procopius and other contemporary sources that Justinian nurtured connections with the 'Blue Faction' of the Hippodrome to acquire influence beyond the world of the court.[42]

Justinian's determination to build up a political following not only at court, but also on the streets of Constantinople, became evident upon his accession to the consulship in 521. The consul was expected to preside over a series of games, celebrations, public theatrical performances, animal hunts, and parades over the course of his year in office. The processions took place not only in the Hippodrome, but also on the streets of the imperial capital. In a later law, Justinian would detail seven of these: the initial parade in January at which the consul was granted his badge of office; the chariot races, where he would kick off events by throwing down his napkin (*mappa*); the 'theatre hunt', in which exotic animals were chased, fought, and killed; prize-fighting and wrestling, in which men contended against both animals and each other; a bawdy procession through the streets of the capital known as the parade of the whores (*pornai*), which would conclude at the theatre with shows by comedians, tragic actors, staged choruses, and song and dance; a further set of chariot races; and lastly a spectacle to mark the consul's resignation.[43] Events such as the 'parade of the whores' evidently possessed a strongly burlesque character. Later in the century, legislation would be issued to prevent actors, actresses, and prostitutes from dressing up as monks and nuns for the titillation of their audiences or clients.[44] Within contemporary attitudes, the distinction between 'actresses' and 'prostitutes' was so blurred as to be practically nonexistent: not all prostitutes were actresses, but all actresses were assumed to be prostitutes. In terms of consular celebrations, Justinian himself is likely to have hosted rather more events than those listed in the law (the legislation in question was aimed at cutting down on the expenses associated with the post).

As well as funding these events, the consul traditionally distributed 'largesses' to the people, scattering gold and silver coins and objects, such as apples and cups crafted in precious metals— although the imperial government had increasingly come to disapprove of this practice, in part because some consuls treated the associated expenditure as a 'claimable expense', which they could claw back from the government.[45] According to Procopius, it was customary for the consul to spend and distribute 2,000 pounds weight of gold in this fashion over the course of the year, equivalent to some 144,000 gold coins (*solidi*), at a time when even a skilled worker such as a stonemason might have received no more than 12 gold coins for an entire year's work.[46] No wonder the consulship was regarded as the perfect way to launch or buttress a political career: it effectively gave the man who held the post the opportunity to legitimately buy the support of the citizens of the capital. During his year in office, Justinian is reported to have given away some 4,000 pounds weight of gold—double the customary amount.[47] It is inconceivable that he would have been able to do so without the support and subvention of the emperor, perhaps as a reward to Justinian for his loyalty, and to help him amplify his political reputation and renown. The contemporary chronicler Count Marcellinus, who served as Justinian's private secretary, or *cancellarius*, prior to his accession to the throne, would record in his account how Justinian 'made this consulship the most famous of the eastern ones by being considerably more generous in his largesses. For two hundred and eighty-eight thousand *solidi* were distributed to the people or spent on spectacles.' And that was not all: Justinian also 'exhibited simultaneously in the amphitheatre twenty lions and thirty panthers, not counting other wild beasts'.[48] The crowds clearly loved it.

THE PROSTITUTE AND THE PRINCE

Like all consuls, Justinian marked his period of office with pairs of carved ivory plates, typically attached at the hinge, bearing his name and other elements. These objects, which, like the official records mentioned earlier, were also called 'diptychs', often included the portrait of the consul concerned, as well as a résumé of his career prior to the consulship, and were intended for distribution to members of the Senate. Three copies of Justinian's diptych have survived: perhaps significantly, they count amongst the largest examples of this type of artefact in Roman history (each leaf of the largest of the extant examples was originally about 38 centimeters long, 14.5 centimeters wide, and 12.5 millimeters thick). Curiously, whilst carrying his name ('PETRUS SABBATIUS IUSTINIANUS'), Justinian's diptychs do not bear his image. Sparingly decorated with representations of acanthus flowers and lions' heads, they are striking for their relative lack of ornamentation. Why this should have been the case is uncertain, although it has been plausibly suggested that these three may be lower-quality examples of his diptychs, presented to senators and officials of humbler standing, whilst more ornate and portrait-bearing examples may have been reserved for more exalted recipients.[49]

Fortunately, we do have a near-contemporary description of what Justinian looked like by the 520s. According to the mid-sixth-century chronicle written by an author known as John Malalas, who was broadly sympathetic to the regime, he had 'a good chest, a good nose, was fair-skinned, curly-haired, round-faced, handsome, with receding hair, a florid complexion, with his hair and beard greying'. He was also, he added, 'magnanimous' and 'Christian'.[50] By the end of his period as consul in 522, Justinian would have been around forty years of age, and would have had every reason to feel good about the world and his place within it. He was now the son of an emperor, a high-ranking general, and a political figure of demonstrable influence and growing popularity. His chief political rival for the throne—on which he clearly had his eye—had been done away with. Those of whom he disapproved theologically—and he clearly took matters of religion very seriously—were in a state of disarray, even if the pope in Rome had not listened to him and engaged to quite the extent that he might have liked. And he had met the woman he loved.

For it would seem that, along with his good looks, another feature that Petrus Sabbatius Justinianus shared with Justin was a romantic streak, and, like Justin, he would marry for love rather than out of political calculation. It was not, however, when in his full pomp as a young army officer that Justinian first encountered and forged a bond with the great love of his life, but rather when he was already approaching middle age. By around 521 Justinian was sharing the Palace of Hormisdas with a woman possibly some ten to fifteen years younger than himself by the name of Theodora.[51] By the early 520s, this woman had become well known amongst anti-Chalcedonian Syrian churchmen in the imperial capital for being sympathetic to their cause, despite Justinian's own commitment to the Chalcedonian definition of the faith. After Justin had moved so decisively against anti-Chalcedonians in Syria who were under the leadership of Severus of Antioch, a Syrian priest by the name of Stephen, assistant to the bishop of Amida (whom Justin exiled to Petra in 521 or 522), had made his way to Constantinople on the bishop's behalf. Directed to Theodora, he asked that she might try to persuade Justinian to intervene with the emperor to take pity on the bishop, who was finding life in his place of exile difficult to bear. This she did, making the 'entreaty' to Justinian 'even with tears', and Justin eventually permitted the bishop to relocate to Egypt (but not to return home).[52] The account, written by an important churchman, John of Ephesus, was highly sympathetic to Theodora, praising her for her piety and spirituality. At the time of her encounter with Stephen, John says, she held the elevated courtly title of *patricia*.[53] Rather more startlingly, she had originally come, he reports, 'from the brothel' (*porneion*).[54]

This extraordinary detail—coming, as it does, from an author who was deeply committed and grateful to Theodora—suggests that we should give credence to his claim. The term he used is a very strong one and cannot be convincingly interpreted metaphorically.[55] The point is corroborated by two completely unrelated sources. One of these is a somewhat later western chronicle, which relates openly that Justinian met his future partner in a whorehouse (*lupanar*).[56] The other is from the historian Procopius, who states that Theodora and her elder sister had worked as prostitutes from when they were children. Procopius further implies that Theodora had mixed with the lowest stratum of the city's sex workers, who operated either on the streets or from the relative comfort of a home: 'those', he tells us, 'whom men of ancient times used to call the "foot-troops"'.[57] To John of Ephesus, there was no shame in Theodora's past. Like Mary Magdalene in the New Testament, and a whole host of fallen women whose transition to sanctity the early Church had celebrated, it arguably made her spiritual journey and her manifest devotion to

Christ and those who served him all the more praiseworthy. After all, as Jesus himself was said to have declared, 'There will be more joy in heaven over one sinner who repents than over ninety-nine righteous persons who need no repentance.'[58] Procopius, by contrast, regarded the whole relationship as shocking, and was firmly of the opinion that Theodora had not changed her ways.

Procopius' account of Theodora proved to be one of the most effective and disturbing pieces of character assassination directed against a powerful and influential woman in the long history of male misogyny. However, Procopius rarely simply made things up: even when he was at his most outrageous, there was typically at least a grain of truth in what he asserted. With respect to Theodora, that grain of truth seems to have primarily consisted of the nature of her past—and the extent of Justinian's remarkable devotion to her.

Despite the increasingly 'Christian' nature of both the imperial government and the imperial capital, Constantinople in the early sixth century was home to a flourishing 'flesh-trade'. A law issued in the 530s, which aimed to crack down on prostitution, described how pimps and procurers would tour the countryside inducing young girls to sign spurious contracts of employment in return for shoes and fancy clothes. Once in the capital, these people traffickers would force the girls into prostitution to pay off these debts, effectively imprisoning them against their will as sex slaves, hiring them out to their clients, and pocketing the profits. As the law stated, the 'cruel and odious' practice had grown to such an extent that there were brothels 'almost throughout this sovereign city and its suburbs across the water, and, worst of all, even near its holy places and most venerable houses', with girls as young as nine years old being abused and sold. The pimps, the law relates, would continue to pursue and drag back the women even when 'certain persons, out of pity . . . have made frequent efforts to get them away from this work, and settle them in a lawful relationship'.[59] This law, issued by Justinian himself, may well have drawn on Theodora's own personal knowledge and experience. Indeed, the implication of one contemporary account is that Theodora had actively lobbied for it.[60]

Theodora appears to have been born around the year 490 (although some have argued for a later date).[61] According to Procopius, her father, Acacius, was the chief bear-keeper (or 'master of bears') for the Green Faction in Constantinople, where the bears would have been made to fight and trained to dance.[62] We have no reason to believe that she was born anywhere other than the capital city (although later sources would try to associate her with both Cyprus and Syria).[63] Her father is said to have died when Theodora and her two sisters, Comito and Anastasia, were still children, the eldest of them not more than seven years old.[64] Their distraught mother speedily remarried, in the hope of saving the family from penury, and tried to acquire her late husband's job for her new husband. Although the position was given to another man, a rival faction—the Blues—took pity on the family, and Theodora's new stepfather found employment supervising their menagerie of captive bears. As the girls were pretty, their mother had them enlisted in the troupe of dancers who performed at and around the Hippodrome. Procopius claims that it was from around this time (and before she had reached sexual maturity) that Theodora was traded in the brothel. As she grew up, Theodora progressed to dancing on the main stage and, so Procopius said, offering her services as a 'prostitute in her own right'. She began to participate in the staged comedies and to be noticed by the well-placed young men of the Blue Faction, who frequented the theatre with a view to inviting actresses to perform (and entertain) at their private dinner parties and functions. It was claimed that Theodora was notorious for the lascivious dances she would perform at these bibulous events. Procopius would accuse her of being famously adept at far more than just dancing and acting.[65]

It was probably through the connections forged at events such as these that Theodora became the concubine of an imperial official

named Hecebolus, whom she accompanied to Libya on the western border of Egypt when he was appointed governor there. Con-
cubinage, an arrangement which allowed upper-class men to form
relationships with lower-class women without marrying them,
was legally recognised but increasingly regarded by the Church as
morally unacceptable. When Hecebolus tired of her and set her
aside, she had to work her own way home, travelling via Alexandria
and, according to Procopius, 'making a tour of the whole East . . .
plying her trade in each city'.[66] By this point Theodora seems to have
been accompanied by a daughter, probably fathered by her erstwhile
lover. Indeed, it may have been the pregnancy resulting in the birth
of this child that spurred Hecebolus to abandon her. Subsequent
claims that Theodora also gave birth to a son whom she later murdered can probably be dismissed as vicious palace gossip.[67] Contrary
to Procopius' claims, there are hints in an Egyptian source that it
was whilst she was travelling through Alexandria that Theodora's
spiritual awakening began (if such a 'Damascene conversion' took
place at all).[68] Once back in Constantinople, she made the acquaintance of and rapidly formed a relationship with Justinian, the most
likely point of contact between them being the links to the Blue Faction they had in common.[69] Procopius relates, for example, that just
prior to meeting Theodora, Justinian had been corresponding with
a famous dancer associated with the Blue Faction based in Antioch
in Syria, who had encountered Theodora as she was attempting to
make her way home. By this point, Theodora may have been around
thirty years of age, and we are informed that 'Justinian conceived
for her an overpowering love', and lavished her with gifts, 'for she
seemed to him the sweetest thing in the world, as is wont to happen
with lovers who love extravagantly'.[70]

The writings of Procopius preserve two rather conflicting
accounts of Theodora's appearance. In one of these, meant for public consumption, the author declared that 'to express her loveliness
in words, or to portray it in a statue, would be, for a mere human

being, altogether impossible'.[71] In his more private account, meant for circulation after Justinian and Theodora were both dead, the words suddenly tripped off his pen: 'Now Theodora', he wrote, 'was fair of face and generally attractive in appearance, but short of stature and lacking in colour, being, however, not altogether pale, but rather sallow, and her glances were always intense, and made with contracted brows.'[72] The sources agree that she possessed a sharp intelligence and a ready wit, combined with a great capacity for loyalty to both people and causes, enormous reserves of determination, and a strong vindictive streak.[73] Even Procopius comments on the sharpness of Theodora's repartee, although he also complained that she was so lacking in decorum that she would burst out laughing in public, which no respectable Roman lady would ever have done.[74] Although capable of great generosity and kindness, she was not a person to cross. And the empress Euphemia did not like her at all.

Although Justinian had formed a relationship with Theodora by around the year 521, he did not marry her at this point. Procopius blames this entirely on the opposition of Justinian's elderly adoptive mother, who clearly felt that a woman such as Theodora simply would not do for her handsome and now distinguished (albeit increasingly middle-aged and still unmarried) son. As Procopius wrote, 'So long as the empress was still living, Justinian was quite unable to make Theodora his wedded wife. For on this matter alone the empress went against him, though opposing him in no other matter.'[75] Justinian's inability to marry the woman he loved, at this moment in time, is the clearest evidence we have of the inaccuracy of Procopius' claim that Justinian was running the whole show on behalf of his moribund uncle from the start. Justin was still in control, and, on family matters, he listened to his wife. The empress conceivably disapproved of what she had heard of Theodora's early 'career' both on and off the stage; she might have been wary of the woman's rumoured anti-Chalcedonian sympathies; and she might have just thought she was too *old*. In any case, she was having none of it, and her will prevailed.[76]

At some point between the summers of 521 and 522, Euphemia died, clearing the way for Justinian to make an honest woman of his beloved.[77] The next problem he faced was that it was actually illegal for a man of senatorial rank such as himself to marry an ex-actress such as Theodora, by virtue of the fact that she had once belonged to what was deemed to be a 'disreputable profession'.[78] In order for their marriage to be legal, Justinian needed to persuade his uncle to change the law—something which Euphemia would never have allowed. This, Procopius tells us, Justin agreed to do. As Procopius put it, 'Since it was impossible for a man who had attained the senatorial rank to contract marriage with a harlot . . . he compelled the emperor to amend the laws with a new law, and from then on he lived with Theodora as his married wife, and he thereby opened the way to betrothal with harlots for all other men.'[79]

Between June 521 and July 522, Justin issued a remarkable law which was clearly promulgated with a view to Theodora's circumstances, and in which we can effectively hear the elderly emperor attempting to reason with his deceased wife.[80] The late empress had been an ex-slave. In order to make their marriage socially acceptable, her former master would have had to apply to the reigning emperor for her to be granted 'restitution of free-birth status'.[81] This process enabled the authorities to expunge all legal trace that a person had ever been a slave: the beneficiary was, effectively, born again with full freedom. The emancipated Lupicina had become an ex-slave, but with the restitution of free-birth status, Euphemia had become as fully 'free' as anybody else.[82] Thereafter, no social stigma or stain could attach to her because of her past.

In the new legislation, issued by Justin but manifestly at Justinian's behest, the emperor asks why it should be possible to free ex-slaves of their past, but not lower-class free women who had been drawn into disreputable professions (such as 'those who have got involved in theatrical productions'), but who had now repented of their past sins, and wished to marry men of high status who in turn wished to marry them. How could it be Christian to deny redemption and forgiveness to such women, and deprive them of 'the hope of a better marriage prospect'? Rather, Justin declared, he would grant such women 'an imperial benefit, which would bring them back to that condition, in which, if they had done no wrong, they could have remained'. So long as they would abandon 'their bad and dishonourable way of life, embrace a more advantageous lifestyle, and devote themselves to honourable pursuits', they could petition the emperor to have their proverbial slate wiped clean and 'proceed to a valid marriage'. These marriages were even to be permitted with men 'who enjoy high rank or who are for any other reason forbidden to marry actresses'. In order to ensure that a proper marriage was intended, a dowry would have to be provided, and 'written documents' furnished (presumably including a confession and renunciation of her past ways on the part of the woman).[83]

The law for which Justinian (and, presumably, Theodora) had lobbied was one which now promised to wipe away her past. Crucially, it also potentially did the same for her sisters, as well as her daughter, thus paving the way for her child to be introduced to high society and eventually find a good husband of her own. For even a young lady born whilst her mother was still working as an actress could apply, and was, 'without hindrance', to receive an official letter from the emperor, 'through which it shall be allowed for them to marry in such manner as if they were not daughters of an actress mother'.[84] And for a girl born after her mother's renunciation of her past and subsequent social rebirth, no such application was necessary. Moreover, all children born of a penitent ex-actress and an upper-class man united in wedlock, Justin closed his law by emphasising, were now to be regarded as fully legitimate.

Clearly, Justin hoped that Theodora's childbearing days were not over. However much Euphemia had disapproved, the old man may well have recognised that Justinian was utterly devoted to Theodora, and that the two of them had forged a deep emotional (and—it would transpire—political) bond. That bond would be attested to in a range of contemporary sources, including Justinian's own legislation, where he would make explicit mention of how he consulted his wife when drafting his laws, and evidently drew upon her experiences in doing so. Early in his reign, Justinian would make the legal pathway to social rehabilitation for ex-actresses even more straightforward in a law aimed at 'allowing no one to drag a woman . . . onto the stage or into a chorus against her will, or to prevent one desiring to leave from doing it'. Those who repented of their past lives, this law would decree, could marry anyone they wished 'at their own discretion'.[85] Theodora had never consented to the circumstances she had been forced into in her early life: evidently, as soon as she was able, she pressed the men around her to help not just her, but also other women like her. She would thus emerge as an unusually influential (and consequently much reviled) woman in this age of ambitious and powerful men.

Justin's remarkable legal intervention on behalf of Justinian and Theodora reveals that Justinian's power was now truly on the ascendant. Perhaps in the absence of his wife, the elderly Justin was drawing closer to his adopted son. His health, too, may have been failing: in another law issued in 521, the emperor expressly sympathized with the blind and those suffering from deteriorating sight and memory, or otherwise 'troubled by thoughts of death'.[86] When Roman emperors speak in their laws in such intimate terms, it is likely because they shared such concerns or ailments themselves, or had seen them afflict their loved ones. Such publicly stated anxieties may also have informed Procopius' later accusation that, towards the end of his reign, Justin would become 'foolish as well as very old', perhaps hinting at a measure of what we would today call dementia.[87]

Justinian's efforts to consolidate and strengthen his position in the Senate and on the streets of the capital proceeded apace. With respect to the latter, he almost got himself into serious trouble in 523. In that year, major riots occurred in Constantinople and other cities in the East orchestrated by the Blue Faction, which Justinian continued to court. In response, the emperor ordered the urban prefect of Constantinople, Theodotus (nicknamed 'the Pumpkin'), who was responsible for maintaining law and order in the city, to move against those he believed to be behind the violence.[88] Accordingly, Theodotus arrested and executed a high-ranking official, Theodosius, and was even rumoured to be preparing to arrest Justinian himself, who was ill and hence vulnerable at the time.[89] Justin appears to have intervened to protect his nephew, who then arranged for Theodotus to be dismissed. Further attempts on Justinian's part to have the ex–city prefect accused of trumped-up charges—of poison, murder, and sorcery—failed, however, as the empire's chief legal officer, a brilliant intellectual by the name of Proculus, spoke up in his defence. Instead, Theodotus decided the safest option available to him was to flee the capital. He escaped to Jerusalem, where he hid himself in a monastery.[90]

Justinian's efforts with the Senate proceeded along a smoother course. It was in response to petitions from the Senate, for example, that Justin agreed to accord him the honorary rank of *nobilissimus* ('most noble'), which was traditionally reserved for the sons of emperors.[91] It is claimed that they had earlier petitioned Justin to declare Justinian co-emperor, a request that he had denied, ostensibly on the grounds that he regarded him as too young to rule (though it is unclear when this request was supposedly made).[92] Justinian was also careful to continue to curry favour and forge alliances with members of the ecclesiastical establishment, funding the construction and restoration of a number of important places of worship across the capital.[93] Nurturing his contacts within the army, Circus Factions, Senate, and Church was all part of a carefully targeted strategy to secure his accession to the throne.

By 525, it was quite clear that Justinian was the heir apparent: the chief legal officer, Proculus, is even recorded to have openly alluded at court to Justinian's ambition to succeed to the throne. The Persian ruler Kavad, we are told, had suggested that he and Justin replicate a diplomatic arrangement between the two empires which had first been instituted around a hundred years earlier, whereby each emperor would ceremonially 'adopt' the other's son and intended heir. Proculus is reported to have quipped to Justinian that were this to happen, Kavad's son, Khusro, rather than he, might end up on the Roman throne.[94] At around this time, Justin also formally appointed Justinian his deputy, or *Caesar*.[95] Once again, the decision appears to have been taken in response to a request from members of the Senate, but conceivably instigated by Justinian himself, and Justin is reported to have bestowed the title reluctantly.[96] Those senators aligned with Justinian would have been eager to ensure a smooth succession of power upon the death of Justin, thereby avoiding the chaos that had ensued upon Anastasius' demise. Justinian, for his part, was clearly itching to finally get his hands on the reins of power.

FROM CAESAR TO EMPEROR

In April 527, the now obviously ailing emperor ordered that a new gold coin be minted and distributed throughout the empire. Such coinage was the basis of the empire's monetary system, in which taxes were paid, wages and prices reckoned, and commodities bought and sold. At the same time, the imperial government used the images placed on such coins to convey clear political messages to the emperor's subjects. The portraits and names of new emperors were emblazoned on the coins to advertise their accession to power; images of barbarians being speared, or the ancient Roman personification of Victory, were sometimes also included to help raise morale and strengthen resolve.

The message that Justin now wished to convey through the new coinage would have been immediately apparent to the bankers and money-changers who were obliged to release it to the public. A copy of the coin survives to this day in the collection of the Dumbarton Oaks Museum in Washington, DC: on one side, the emperor Justin sits enthroned, facing forward, with a golden 'nimbus', or halo, around his head, holding in his left hand a globe, symbolizing his universal authority. Alongside him, unlike on his previous coinage, there now sits his nephew, Justinian, similarly enthroned, haloed, and globe-bearing. Around the imperial portrait, we read the abbreviated Latin inscription 'DN IVSTIN ET IVSTINIAN PP AVG' ('Our Lords Justin and Justinian: Pious Rulers and Emperors'). On the other side of the coin is depicted a winged angel, carrying a long cross and another cross mounted on a globe, surrounded by the words 'VICTORIA AVGGG' ('To the Victory of the Emperors!'). The newly issued coins were designed to announce the fact that Justinian had finally been made co-emperor to rule alongside, and succeed, his uncle. Whatever doubts the old man may previously have harboured with respect to his adopted son, he had evidently either set them aside or forgotten them. Revealingly, the coins were produced and distributed with unusual haste.[97]

This is important for two reasons. The first was that the emperor was evidently fading fast (an old war wound of his, we are told, had come to life and was causing him much pain).[98] Justinian and his allies urgently needed to choreograph his final succession to the throne if the whole process was not to be hijacked at the last minute. Theodotus' planned arrest of Justinian in 523, after all, had demonstrated that he still had many well-placed enemies as well as allies.[99] The second reason was that Constantinople was still home to a number of wealthy and well-connected families whose members were keenly aware that their recent ancestors had themselves held the imperial title, and they were desperate to reassert their control over the office of emperor once Justin was out of the way. Anicia Iuliana, for example (whose imperial lineage Pope Hormisdas had gone out of his way to praise in 519), had recently built the magnificent Church of Saint Polyeuktos in the heart of the capital to advertise her family's significance and prestige.[100] A poem carved on the arches of her great church described her as 'inheriting royal blood' and as 'the mother of a noble race'.[101] While Anicia Iuliana's husband had previously declined the invitation of the rioting mob to try to usurp the throne in the 510s, a relative by marriage of hers, the emperor Anastasius' nephew Hypatius, was now a significant figure in the imperial Senate.[102] Iuliana and others likely viewed Hypatius as a suitably blue-blooded potential candidate for the throne, one well placed to attract support from both pro- and anti-Chalcedonian factions. Justin (and now Justinian) had effectively wrong-footed such dynastic cliques by presenting Justinian's succession as a fait accompli.

Having previously been made *Caesar* by Justin, Justinian, according to court protocol, did not have to be acclaimed by the army and people in the Hippodrome. On 1 April, after Justinian's allies in the Senate had once more petitioned Justin to elevate Justinian to the rank of *Augustus*, Justin publicly appointed him co-ruler in the Great Hall (*consistorium*) of the palace.[103] Three days later, Justinian was formally acclaimed emperor by the palatine officials and guards in the *Delphax* parade ground, where Vitalian had been cut down some seven years before.[104] At the same time, Theodora was acclaimed as empress.[105] Justin was now too ill to attend the proceedings. Justinian was then formally crowned by the patriarch of Constantinople, who led prayers on his behalf.[106]

The emperor Justin died on 1 August 527. A modest man and a

reluctant emperor, he chose not to be buried in the company of Constantine and his other distinguished predecessors in the Church of the Holy Apostles, a location he had probably marched past as an awe-struck military recruit back in the 470s. Rather, he was laid to rest in a monastery alongside his beloved wife, Euphemia, who may have founded the institution concerned (known as the 'Monastery of the Augusta') as an act of piety.[107] Justin would have been about seventy-seven years of age at the time of his death, whilst Justinian was in his mid-forties. By virtue of the careful efforts that had been made to ensure that Justinian succeeded his uncle, the new ruler was able to consolidate his hold on power as sole emperor in the face of only muted opposition. Justinian would go out of his way to convey to his subjects a clear sense that, with his accession, a new age had dawned.

PART 2

A Turbulent Beginning

Chapter 4

Confronting the Enemy

AN EMPIRE AWAKENS IN THE EAST

The early years of Justinian's reign would witness a remarkable outburst of creativity and energy informing both internal policy and external relations. At home, the emperor would direct a sudden and harsh crackdown on pagans, heretics, and others he regarded with particular disapproval (such as those he considered sexual 'deviants'), as well as those deemed guilty of 'lawlessness' in general. There was a widespread belief amongst Christians in the early sixth century that mankind was living in the 'Last Days' and that divine judgement was imminent. A text known as the *Oracle of Baalbek*, for example, predicted how after the death of the emperor Anastasius, an era of chaos would ensue, and said that at this time men would become 'rapacious, greedy, rebellious and barbarian', 'hating their mothers' and 'raiding their own ancestral lands', until

'He who was crucified on the wood of the cross will come from the heavens, like a great and flashing star'.[1] Justinian's determination to purge his empire of those whom he saw as sources of moral corruption or religious error may have been partly informed by an awareness of such sentiments and his desire to ease the path to salvation for the rest of his subjects when 'Judgement Day' finally came.[2] Disorder and lawlessness at the grass roots of East Roman society were major concerns, and apocalyptic anxieties conceivably intensified them. But the first and primary duty of any Roman emperor was to defend the empire and protect it from attack. Justinian was no exception: what was distinctive about the new emperor's foreign policy in the first five years of his reign was the unprecedented extent to which it would be informed and advanced by means of religious diplomacy.

Ever since the revival of warfare between the Romans and Persians in 502, the imperial authorities in Constantinople had made concerted efforts to invest in the defensive infrastructure of the empire's eastern frontier to render it less vulnerable to enemy attack. The city of Dara, perched on the edge of the Roman-Persian border in Syria, became the focus of a great deal of military investment.[3] The resumption of hostilities between the two great powers had also led each empire to seek diplomatic advantage over the other amongst the peoples of the Caucasus to the north and Arabia to the south. During Justin's reign, the Romans had significantly advanced their position in both of these areas. In the year 521–522, the king of the strategically crucial West Caucasian kingdom of Lazica, which controlled the eastern coast of the Black Sea, defected from a pro-Persian stance and adopted Christianity, taking the emperor Justin as his godfather.[4] This was followed by further defections to Constantinople on the part of the already Christian rulers of the central Caucasian kingdom of Iberia in return for promised military assistance.[5] In 525, the Romans provided logistical support for the invasion of the southern Arabian kingdom of Himyar (Yemen) by the empire's close allies, the East African Christian kingdom of Axum.[6] The pretext for this invasion was the supposed persecution of the region's Christian community by the ruler of Himyar, who was regarded as an agent of Persian influence. Himyar, however, was also the most politically important kingdom in Arabia and played a vital role in international trade—its merchants and sailors venturing far across the Indian Ocean—so the extension of Roman influence here was a long-standing imperial objective. Both of these interventions show how the Roman authorities were learning to 'weaponise' Christianity and deploy it to the empire's diplomatic and military advantage. The Roman interventions in both Iberia and Himyar occurred at around the same time that Justinian had been appointed *Caesar*, and it is reasonable to assume that he would not only have been consulted on these moves but may even have actively encouraged them.[7]

Tensions between the East Roman Empire and Persia had heightened over the course of Justin's reign, with the Persians protesting in the most strenuous terms at the extension of Roman authority in the Caucasus, which they regarded as a traditionally Persian 'sphere of influence'. They objected as well to the empire's ongoing programme of investment along the direct Roman-Persian frontier in Syria. Although the Romans regarded the new fortifications at Dara to be entirely defensive in character, from a Persian perspective it looked dangerously like the town was being transformed into a forward base for a potential assault on the city of Nisibis, which was just sixteen miles away, and which the Romans had been obliged to surrender to the Persians in the fourth century. Many of the most economically productive cities of the Sasanian Empire were near the Roman frontier zone, meaning that any intensification of the Roman military presence there was bound to put Persian nerves on edge. The Persians had repeatedly mobilised their clients amongst the Arab tribes on the desert fringe south of Roman Syria to make forays and raids into Roman territory and disrupt the building work.[8] Such raids had intensified in 527, as news reached Persia of the emperor Justin's failing health and then death, with the Persian shah, Kavad, attempting to exact payment of tribute from the Romans. This, in turn, had led to a series of Roman retaliatory raids towards Nisibis. Amongst Justinian's first acts as emperor was to issue orders speeding up the defensive building programme in the East in anticipation of an imminent large-scale war.[9] He also appointed a new commander-in-chief of Roman forces in Armenia to oversee military operations in the Caucasus, which was always a decisive theatre of war in any Roman-Persian conflict, as each empire was highly vulnerable to attack from the river valleys and mountain passes crisscrossing its lands.[10]

Justinian's emphasis on Armenia and the Caucasus would prove crucial to the future strategy of the empire. Hitherto, the Romans had been primarily reliant for the defence of their Armenian territories on the private armies raised by members of the local Armenian nobility who recognised Roman overlordship. Justinian did away with that, establishing Roman garrisons and more fully integrating the Armenian provinces into the empire at large.[11] He also imposed direct rule on the mountainous territory south of Lazica, known as Tzanica, so as to tighten Constantinople's grip on this key Caucasian territory, building roads, forts, and—significantly—churches. For here, as elsewhere, Justinian's military strategy had a strong religious element, as he sought to impose Christianity on Tzanica's recalcitrant population. In 528, a Persian offensive against the empire's Laz allies was successfully contained. The empire's position in the Caucasus was further strengthened in 528–529 by the negotiation of a military alliance with the powerful Queen Boa, of a group known as the Sabir Huns (who dwelled north of the Caucasus and could pose a threat to both Roman and Persian interests there). According to the *Chronicle* of John Malalas, after the death of her husband, Boa was 'won over by the emperor Justinian with many gifts of imperial raiment, and a variety of silver vessels, and not a little money'.[12]

Justinian had taken immediate steps to bolster the empire's position along the northern (Caucasian) sector of its eastern frontier and speeded up the pace of fortification in its central sector in Syria and adjacent territories, where the empire faced Persia directly. At the same time, he instituted a major reconfiguration of the empire's clientage arrangements amongst the desert tribes to the south, so as to make it harder for the Persians or their allies to strike or raid along the empire's extensive and largely undefended desert frontier. The various pro-Roman Arab tribes were brought under the overarching authority of the head of the Christian Jafnid clan, to whose ruler, al-Harith, Justinian granted 'the dignity of king'.[13]

What is perhaps most striking is that Justinian was able to press ahead with this attempt to consolidate and strengthen the empire's position to the East despite a series of unexpected shocks and challenges that might have knocked a less determined ruler off kilter. In 528–529 a harsh winter brought hunger to much of the region, and Antioch and a number of other cities in Syria were struck by earthquakes.[14] Justinian responded by attempting to rally the spirits of his Christian subjects in Antioch (as well as to secure divine favour) by renaming it *Theoupolis* (the 'City of God'). At the same time, he sought to reach out to members of the local landowning elite by appointing them all to the highest senatorial grade (that of *illustris*, which conveyed significant social advantages), whilst also granting them a three-year tax exemption.[15]

Then, in 529, a major uprising by the Samaritan peasantry of Palestine, led by a charismatic messianic figure known as Julianus ben Sahir, attempted to cast off Roman rule. The Samaritans—descendants of ancient Israelite communities that remained religiously and ethnically distinct from the Jews of the region—had been growing increasingly restless for many years, but not for centuries had a core territory of the Roman Empire witnessed anything like this. Justinian crushed the revolt with much bloodshed, aided by his Jafnid allies. According to the contemporary chronicler John Malalas (who worked at the offices of the imperial government in Antioch—the chief city of the East—and so may have had access to official records), twenty thousand Samaritans were killed, many others fled, and a further twenty thousand Samaritan children were sold as slaves to Arab tribesmen.[16] As further punishment, Justinian issued a law ordering all Samaritan places of worship ('synagogues') to be pulled down, and forbidding their replacement.[17]

All this time, the upgrading of defences and preparations for war continued, but Kavad, the Persian shah, struck first. In June 530, a large Persian army—estimated at fifty thousand men—headed out from Nisibis and marched on Dara, where the recently appointed commander-in-chief of the Roman field army in the East (*magister militum per orientem*), Belisarius, was overseeing the ongoing building work.[18] He had previously served as a member of Justinian's private military retinue, when the future emperor had held the position of general under Justin, and he, too, hailed from the empire's Balkan territories. The two men had clearly got on well, and Belisarius' ability had caught Justinian's eye.[19] Fortunately for posterity, Belisarius was accompanied in Dara by his military legal adviser and secretary (*assessor*) Procopius, whose firsthand experience of the battle would inspire him to write a multivolume history of his own times. In that work, he detailed the wars 'which Justinian, Emperor of the Romans, waged against the barbarians of the East and the West'.[20]

According to Procopius, the Persians outnumbered Belisarius' forces by two to one—but the fact that he was present at Dara at all, with twenty-five thousand men, would suggest that he was probably planning an assault on Persian territory after his work on the defences was complete. Presumably because the work was not finished, Belisarius was obliged to meet the Persians on the open field. The battle began with each side unleashing wave upon wave of arrows. The infantry troops then met in hand-to-hand fighting. The Persians initially seemed to have the advantage in this melee, and the Roman army's left flank began to give way. Prior to the battle, Belisarius had devised a plan with the commander of barbarian allied troops from the Balkans (known as Heruls). With their commander, Pharas, these men, numbering just some three hundred, had positioned themselves out of sight behind a hill on the edge of the battlefield. When the signal was given, they suddenly emerged, catching the Persians by surprise. As Procopius would relate, 'The three hundred Heruls under Pharas from the high ground got into the rear of the enemy and made a wonderful display of valorous deeds . . . and the Persians, seeing the forces [of the Roman commander] Sunicas too coming against them from the flank, turned to flight. And the rout became complete, for the Romans here joined forces with each other, and there was a great slaughter of the barbarians.'[21]

A series of simultaneous Persian assaults on Roman positions in Armenia were contained with similar success by the new commander-in-chief there, proving the wisdom of Justinian's strategy.[22] Although the Persians were able to defeat Belisarius and his army in the spring campaigning season of 531, at the Battle of Callinicum, Kavad's decision to test and take on Justinian achieved little other than to prove the strength of the new emperor's steel.[23] Later that year, the elderly shah was succeeded to the throne by his son Khusro, who was eager to sue for peace. Initially Justinian was reluctant to engage, perhaps waiting to see whether Khusro could overcome internal opposition to his succession on the part of his brothers. Once it was clear that Khusro was secure, and hence worth negotiating with, Justinian relented. An agreement was speedily reached to exchange prisoners and declare a truce. More detailed negotiations took place in the spring of 532. These would culminate in the so-called Endless Peace between the two empires announced later that year, whereby the Persians were effectively obliged to acknowledge Constantinople's strengthened position in the East, and in return Justinian would not station a military commander (*dux*) at Dara and would pay the Persians a significant sum of money (11,000 pounds weight in gold, or some 792,000 *solidi*). This was supposedly meant as a contribution to the cost of maintaining Persian defences at a set of mountain passes known as the 'Caspian Gates', which were crucial to preventing steppe nomads from raiding across the Caucasus. In the face of the challenge posed by the Huns in the late fourth and fifth centuries, it had previously been agreed that the Persian and Roman Empires had a common interest in fending off such attacks.[24]

Justinian's readiness to pay such large sums to the Persians, and to certain of the empire's other neighbours, would soon occasion rumblings of discontent on the part of members of the Senate in Constantinople, as well as others who did not approve of Roman taxes being given away to 'barbarians'.[25] Nevertheless, from Justinian's perspective, this peace made sense. He had consolidated and secured the Roman gains of the 520s in the western Caucasus; he had successfully accelerated the fortification programme on the eastern frontier; and he had proven the worth of his reconfiguration of the empire's military command structure and clientage arrangements. Justinian had no further significant territorial ambitions to the East, so peace through strength with Persia was a good outcome. The emperor was fully aware that the Persian shah could only sell such a peace to the great noble families of Iran, who dominated his court, if he could show them that he had returned from the negotiations bearing Roman gold, which carried enormous symbolic significance within Sasanian ideology.[26] Justinian also especially wanted peace in the East at this time, as new opportunities were emerging elsewhere.

While facing down the Persians, for example, Justinian had also been attempting to extend the empire's influence along the northern shores of the Black Sea. The Crimea, and the peninsula of Cherson, in particular, were of great strategic significance to the Roman authorities. A Roman presence there could potentially serve as a 'listening post' on the western end of the Eurasian steppe, allowing Constantinople advance notice of any movement westward towards its Balkan territories—and the imperial capital itself—by a new nomadic confederacy or foe. The Romans had learned in the late fourth and fifth centuries the scale of the threat such steppe powers could pose. A major Roman diplomatic offensive amongst various Hunnic groups who remained in the region had taken place in 528 and 529. This drive to win over new allies had secured the support of Queen Boa, but at the same time as the alliance with her was being forged, we are told, 'the king of the Huns near Bosporos [the Crimea], named Grod, also came over to the Emperor'. In what sounds very much like a conscious redeployment of the religious diplomacy which had been used to secure the defection of the Laz king some seven years earlier, a contemporary chronicle records that 'he came to Constantinople and was baptized. The emperor stood sponsor for him at baptism and after bestowing many gifts upon him sent him away to his own country, to guard the Roman territory.'[27]

On returning to his own people, King Grod was soon murdered on the orders of pagan priests, furious at his conversion, and in particular at his policy of melting down silver idols, which he had then exchanged with the Romans for coin. The Huns also swept down and wiped out the Roman garrison guarding the city of Bosporos, which had been established as the empire's point of contact with the Crimean Huns. Justinian retaliated by dispatching a large army by sea to the Strait of Kerch. These troops, under the charge of a general holding the newly established title of 'Count of the Pontic Straits', had sent the Huns scattering.[28] Although the conversion of King Grod had perhaps not gone entirely to plan, the overall strategic aims of Justinian's Crimean intervention had been achieved.

DEFENDING THE BALKANS

By 528 a distinctive strategy had been established in both the Caucasus and the Crimea. First, concerted efforts were made to draw the rulers of neighbouring peoples into Constantinople's diplomatic embrace, preferably through their adoption of imperial or 'Orthodox' Christianity. This diplomatic drive was then consolidated by putting military boots on the ground in the newly acquired spheres of imperial influence. The use of imperial Christianity to advance imperial interests was not entirely new. The emperor Anastasius, for example, had secured the conversion of the Frankish king Clovis to imperial Christianity in about 508 so as to lock him into a pro-Constantinopolitan and anti-Gothic axis.[29] But no emperor had tried to deploy the policy on so many fronts, and with such success, simultaneously. For in the western Balkans at the same time, the leader of the powerful Germanic barbarian confederacy known as the Heruls had likewise made his way to Constantinople for baptism, forging a military alliance while he was there. As the chronicler John Malalas again would record, 'In that year [528] the king of the Heruls, named Grepes, came over to the Romans and arrived in Byzantium with his own force. He made obeisance to the emperor Justinian and asked to become a Christian. He was baptized at Holy Epiphany with the emperor Justinian acting as his sponsor in holy baptism. His leading men and twelve of his relations were baptised with him. When Justinian had bestowed many gifts upon him he dismissed him, and he travelled with his forces to his homeland, with the emperor of the Romans informing him, "Whenever I want you, I will inform you."[30]

At this point Grepes and his followers appear to have been settled in northern Illyricum, an area which Justinian and his family, of course, knew well. As a result of their alliance with the emperor, they were now granted permission to establish themselves around the city of Singidunum (modern Belgrade), thereby helping to further consolidate the imperial military presence on the ground there.[31] Other Heruls joined the empire's field armies to fight on other fronts: they were the troops, for example, who would swing the Battle of Dara in Belisarius' favour in 530.

As well as seeking to strengthen the empire's position on the ground in the Balkans by successfully drawing the Heruls and other groups into alliance with him, Justinian also sought to entrench and consolidate the empire's position by following in the footsteps of his immediate predecessors and investing heavily in the region's military and defensive infrastructure there. This wave of investment would probably reach its peak in the period from about 534 to 540, but is discernible from the earliest years of Justinian's reign. The newly founded city of Justiniana Prima, for example, appears to have been occupied by its new citizens as early as 530. As part of this programmatic upgrading of Balkan defences, Justinian had provincial cities, frontier fortresses, and principal military routes fortified or reinforced. He also fortified towns and cities well beyond the frontiers, as far south as the Peloponnese in Greece, whilst simultaneously providing the rural population with fortified citadels, in which to take refuge during periods of enemy attack.[32] The emperor aimed to provide the Balkan provinces in general with much greater 'defence-in-depth', limiting the damage any marauding foe could inflict.[33] This strategy may have been partly informed by Justinian's own personal appreciation of the nature of warfare in the region and the acute vulnerability of its rural population. After all, the sorts of militarised farmsteads and rural redoubts that the emperor's policy caused to proliferate throughout the Balkans were akin to the fortified village his uncle had originally called home, Vederiana. In their native land, such networks of fortified redoubts had helped to preserve a sense of Roman identity amongst the local population despite years of intermittent barbarian domination.[34] They might yet prove useful elsewhere.

In his homeland, Justinian's foundation of Justiniana Prima, with its strongly military and religious character, bolstered the region's defences and enhanced the new emperor's reputation in the eyes of the provincial population. Elsewhere in the Balkans, inscriptions were placed on the newly enhanced defences emphasising Justinian's personal role in their construction. The words 'Justinian Who Loved to Build', or simply 'Justinian', have been found on a number of such inscriptions and on brick stamps throughout the region of the Lower Danube and Black Sea (in modern Bulgaria). In the vicinity of the Greek city of Corinth, inscriptions reveal, the local bishop, Victorinus, was also keen to get in on the act. One building, for example, was adorned with a text declaring, 'Light from Light, true God from true God, protect the emperor Justinian and his pious servant Victorinus, as well as the inhabitants of Greece, who live according to God.' The brick stamps bearing the emperor's name and lauding his building projects were very likely mass-produced in Constantinople and then dispatched to the provinces. Justinian was clearly determined to convey to his subjects a strong sense of his personal commitment to their security, as well as to the broader strengthening of the empire which God had entrusted to him, in the hope that in doing so he would elicit both their support and their prayers. In the case of Bishop Victorinus in Corinth, this policy evidently met with considerable success. Another of the inscriptions associated with this bishop reads, 'Holy Mary, Mother of God, protect the empire of the Christ-loving Justinian . . . along with the inhabitants of Corinth.'[35]

WEAKNESS TO THE WEST

Justinian had an eye for talent. This would be most apparent in the legal and administrative spheres, but it also had very important implications for his military strategy. He had evidently been the one to notice General Belisarius' potential, for example (although the latter would be subjected to a 'Commission of Enquiry' in the aftermath of the defeat at Callinicum in 531). Likewise, in 529, Roman military capability in the Balkans had been significantly enhanced by Justinian's recruitment of a Gepid prince, named Mundo, who was a figure of real political authority in the region, with a fearsome reputation and a large army of his own. Justinian rapidly appointed Mundo commander-in-chief of the imperial army in the western Balkans. The Gepids were one of the Germanic barbarian groups that had been subject to Hunnic overlordship in the fifth century; they had come to settle in the western Balkans in the aftermath of the breakup of Attila's empire, seizing the city of Sirmium (modern Sremska Mitrovica in Serbia) from the Romans. In 488, as he led his armies out of the Balkans into Italy, the Gothic king Theoderic had seized Sirmium and killed the Gepid king, Mundo's uncle. Notwithstanding his uncle's demise, Mundo had gone on to serve Theoderic and his regime in Italy, becoming an important military commander. His decision to make his services available to Justinian was a major coup, and in 529–530 he played a vital role in containing attacks on imperial territory, not only by Huns and by the former Hunnic subjects known as Bulgars, but also by his own Gepid kin. Mundo was probably key to the subsequent negotiation of a new Roman-Gepid pact, which, in 530, would result in a sudden and unprovoked assault upon Sirmium, aimed at driving out the Gothic garrison there.[36] Mundo's utility to Justinian would not end with the forging of that alliance, however, and Justinian's determination to recruit him indicated that he had further ambitions, not just in the Balkans, but beyond.

The decision to mobilise Justinian's recently acquired Gepid allies against Sirmium was perhaps the first and clearest sign that Justinian's military focus and interests were beginning to shift westwards. The primary importance of Sirmium was that it stood at a key point along the Roman road network that extended from Naissus and Singidunum towards Italy. No army advancing by land from East Roman territory into the Italian Peninsula could do so unless it either controlled or was allowed to pass through the city of Sirmium, or, alternatively, that of Salona (which the Goths also held).[37] Hence, the Roman-backed Gepid assault inevitably caused considerable anxiety amongst the Gothic high command, which continued to be based at the old imperial capital of Ravenna. There, political conditions had become increasingly unstable. In 526, the Gothic king, Theoderic, had died after a long and glorious reign. Owing to his failure to father an adult male heir to succeed him, the crown in Italy had passed to Theoderic's grandson, the boy-king Athalaric, who was only eight at the time of his grandfather's death. As a result, effective power in the kingdom had passed to an unsteady and faction-ridden council of regency, headed by Athalaric's mother and Theoderic's daughter, Queen Amalasuntha.

The regent was clearly a woman of some talent. The Italian courtier Cassiodorus would note in particular her linguistic skills, including her ability to speak fluently in Greek as well as Latin and Gothic.[38] But she was regarded with considerable suspicion by elements within the Gothic nobility, who knew that, as a woman, she was incapable of providing the Gothic army with the active military leadership its members expected. They were also suspicious of what they regarded as the over-Romanising education she was providing to her son.[39]

Perhaps because of the lack of effective military leadership, the new regime had also failed to inspire in the kingdom's barbarian neighbours the fear and trepidation with which Theoderic had been able to keep them in check. Consequently, territory in southern Gaul over which Theoderic had previously extended his rule had to be surrendered to the Franks.[40] Within the Italian kingdom itself, there were signs of growing lawlessness at a local level. Gothic lords and military commanders on the ground took advantage of the absence of a strong figure of royal authority in Ravenna to illegally encroach upon or even seize estates belonging to local landowners, thereby heightening tensions between the regime and members of the Roman landed elite.[41] There was, in short, every reason for Justinian to sense vulnerability on the part of the Gothic regime in Italy, and to begin to consider a political or possibly even military intervention there. The attempted expulsion of the Gothic garrison from Sirmium would make sense in terms of Justinian beginning to lay the groundwork for just such a move.

There are clear indications that a number of those who were or had been around Justinian, forming his core body of assistants and advisers prior to and after his ascent to the throne, were ideologically predisposed towards making such an intervention should the opportunity arise. It had suited those in power in Constantinople in the late fifth century to convince themselves of what many members of the western senatorial elite in Italy may also have felt at the time: that the forced retirement in 476 of the last western emperor resident in Italy, Romulus, had been of no particular significance.[42] Viewed from the ground up, much of the substance of the empire in the West persisted, including the political, administrative, and cultural infrastructure of the Roman Empire. The Roman Senate, city councils, Roman law, and Roman education all remained intact, and all that Italy lacked was an emperor. Others took a more hardline perspective. Count Marcellinus, in his *Chronicle*, for example, was of the opinion that the deposition of Romulus in 476 had signalled that the 'Western Empire of the Roman people' had 'perished'. Marcellinus was an Illyrian, and amongst Illyrians anti-barbarian sentiment may have been especially strong.[43] He had also served as private secretary (*cancellarius*) to Justinian prior to his accession, so it is possible that his view of events in Italy and the West may have accurately reflected that of Justinian and his circle. To Marcellinus and those who thought like him, Roman power in the West was no more, and it was the duty of the emperor to restore it.

If the situation in Italy was such that a direct intervention from Constantinople was looking increasingly possible, in Africa such an intervention was looking increasingly necessary. In 523, when Justinian's associate Hilderic had ascended the Vandal throne, he had set in motion an important diplomatic reorientation away from Theoderic's regime in Ravenna (with which the kingdom had formerly been allied), and in favour of Constantinople. As a result, the position of the imperial or 'Catholic' Church in Africa had also improved considerably: the persecution that had hitherto been orchestrated by the Arian authorities had been lifted (although there is good reason to believe that our contemporary and largely Catholic sources had always exaggerated its extent). Hilderic was not, however, a militarily effective king, and his armies suffered a number of defeats at the hands of Berber tribesman from along the fringes of his realm. In a world in which martial prowess was deemed central to the nature and function of kingship, this was serious. Hilderic was already unpopular amongst elements of the Vandal nobility for his broader reconfiguration of royal policy, and in 530 he was deposed and incarcerated by a distant cousin of his, Gelimer.[44] The loss of so well placed an ally as Hilderic was unfortunate, but were the new regime to reinitiate the persecution of the region's Catholic clergy, then Justinian, as a religiously highly committed ruler, would feel obliged to respond.

Any tilt towards a more aggressive policy in either Italy or Africa would have been greatly assisted by Justinian's ongoing and extravagant courting of the papacy. Although this predated his rise to power, he pursued it with considerable fervour upon his accession to the throne. In the first few months of his reign, Justinian issued an official confession of faith, underscoring his determination to uphold and strengthen the renewed ecclesiastical unity between Rome and Constantinople that Justin had achieved, and signalling his absolute commitment to follow in 'the tradition and confession of the Holy Catholic and Apostolic Church of God'. In 533, Justinian would write to a new pope, John II, directly, informing him in a lengthy and detailed theological exposition of how, as the emperor put it, 'we have hastened to make all priests of the whole orient subject to the See of Your Holiness and to unite them with it'. The text we have of this letter reveals that the emperor had even signed it off in person: 'May the Deity', he wrote, 'preserve you for many years, holy and most pious father.'[45] But before the emperor could take advantage of or respond to the reconfiguration of power that was underway within the barbarian kingdoms of Africa and Italy, he first of all had to address more pressing matters at home.

Chapter 5

The Body of the Law

CRACKING THE WHIP

In the early years of his reign Justinian had undertaken a series of bold, assertive moves to strengthen and consolidate the empire's military and diplomatic position. By these means, as Procopius wrote, the emperor could claim to have 'bolstered the Roman domain, which everywhere lay exposed to the barbarians'.[1] These efforts built upon those of his predecessor and uncle, Justin, to whose policy agenda Justinian is likely to have contributed, first as general, then as *Caesar*, and ultimately as co-ruler. But under Justinian there was more than simply a continuity of policy: the pace and determination with which policies were pursued escalated and intensified considerably, and nowhere was this more evident than in matters of internal administration and the law.

Contrary to how it might have suited others to present him, Justin had never been lax when it came to matters of legislation: the number of extant laws issued per year during his reign is comparable to the legal output under the emperor he succeeded, Anastasius.[2] Justin was also capable of making major, carefully targeted governmental interventions if necessary. When in 525, for example, much of the city of Antioch was destroyed by a devastating earthquake, the emperor ordered that the sum of more than one-third of a million *solidi* be assigned to the rebuilding of the city. This would have been equivalent to almost one-half of all the money the imperial government collected each year through taxation from Egypt, the wealthiest and fiscally most productive region of the Roman world.[3] Left to his own devices, however, Justin was clearly not inclined to make significant innovations: as Procopius put it, the emperor 'did not succeed in doing his subjects any harm nor any good either'.[4] In legal terms, he had been a great believer in letting sleeping dogs lie.

The rate of output and tone of Justin's legislation changed dramatically once Justinian was appointed co-emperor, such that approximately one-third of all the laws we have for Justin's reign were issued in those five months alone.[5] Having spent almost nine years of his life watching his adopted father running the Roman state at a relatively leisurely pace, Justinian was clearly desperate to speed things up. Here was a middle-aged man in a hurry, determined to finally make his mark. Indeed, turning from reading the legislation of Justin to that issued under the joint names of Justin and Justinian is akin to being woken up from a light doze by somebody grabbing you by the shoulders and shouting at you. And once Justinian started shouting, he did not easily stop. In just one month after he became sole emperor (June 528), Justinian issued more extant laws than his uncle had done in the entirety of his eight and a half years of sole rule; whilst Justin had issued some thirty laws from 518 to 527, during the first nine years of his reign Justinian would issue well over four hundred.[6] Throughout, we hear the same hectoring and insistent tone already familiar to us from Justinian's letters to Hormisdas, which became an instantly recognisable feature of many of his subsequent laws.

The first wave of Justinian's legislation addressed the full range of issues that had long concerned Roman emperors: the technicalities of the Roman law of marriage, inheritance, commercial exchange and loans, property ownership, and the regulation of legal proceedings at court, to name but a few. There are also hints that Justinian and Theodora were actively engaged in what might be considered feathering their own nests and rewarding their favourites. The tone adopted in this legislation is likely to have aggravated critics of the new regime. In April 529, for example, it was decreed that all gifts and property transfers between the emperor and the empress were to be regarded as automatically valid, irrespective of earlier restrictions. In December 531 further measures were issued along these lines, loosening the rules on gifts granted by the imperial couple to their chosen beneficiaries. This law refers explicitly to Theodora as 'our most serene Augusta, our consort,' and criticises those who 'do not acknowledge Imperial Majesty' or who fail to recognise the 'contrast between private fortune and imperial greatness'. 'For why', Justinian asked somewhat haughtily, 'should they who by their counsel and work labour day and night for the people of the whole earth not have a prerogative worthy of their fortune?'[7] The law suggests that Theodora was already playing an active part in imperial affairs.

Justinian's initial focus, however, was overwhelmingly religious in nature. One of the first clearly dated laws that survives from his reign forbade bishops from having children or grandchildren, and regulated the running of hospices, infirmaries, poorhouses, and orphanages under ecclesiastical care. It also cracked down on bribery to secure Church appointments and complained of priests paying others to perform their duties for them—including conducting Church services. Justinian believed in the imperial Church, but he was under no illusions as to the moral failings of many of its personnel. Six years later, in 534, he would complain of bishops playing dice, betting on horses, and attending stage shows, musical performances, and boxing matches, when, in fact, 'it behoved them', the emperor declared, 'to devote themselves to fasts, vigils, the study of the divine scriptures and prayers on behalf of us all'.[8]

Even so, Justinian's religious ire was overwhelmingly directed at pagans, heretics, Jews, and the Samaritans of Palestine, all of whom were banned from holding public office in the Roman state.[9] The emperor's hostility towards the Samaritans would soon intensify in response to the uprising of 529, but each of these groups witnessed an ominous escalation in the tone of the imperial rhetoric directed against them and the severity of the penalties the government sought to impose. Earlier legislation was essentially set aside and replaced with a set of far more draconian measures so as to push these heterodox communities to the fringes of Roman society. In 527, in a law issued jointly with his uncle, Justinian had prohibited heretics from holding 'assemblies, sectarian gatherings, or synods; celebrating ordinations or baptisms . . . or managing or administering lands'. This prohibition had to be repeated in 530 in the face of widespread evasion of the law—including in Constantinople. As a result, Justinian ordered that all 'so-called patriarchs, companions, bishops, presbyters, deacons, or other clergymen' associated with heretical groups be driven from the city, 'lest some of the simple folk hear their absurd stories, and, following their impious teachings, lose their own souls'.[10] The implication is that earlier emperors had legislated against such groups in principle, but had in fact allowed their priests and ministers to operate relatively unmolested even in the capital city. Justinian was now determined to put the legislation into practice.

This was particularly true with respect to pagans (a term used to describe devotees of the pre-Christian religions of Greece and Rome). Emperors since the late fourth century had passed increasingly draconian legislation seeking to prohibit public acts of pagan worship and other practices associated with paganism, such as astrology. Large concentrations of pagans survived within the empire, however, in places such as Baalbek in Lebanon, where a magnificent pagan temple continued to be thronged with worshippers, and parts of Asia Minor, including the highlands of Lycia, where Christianity would appear to have made relatively little impact on the rural population. A striking lack of archaeological evidence for church building in Greece suggests that here, too, the spread of Christianity may have been considerably slower than the imperial authorities would have liked.[11] An adherence to pre-Christian religious traditions and beliefs also appears to have persisted amongst elements of the civic elites of the empire, and even within well-connected families in Constantinople itself. Such families had probably adopted a strategy of tactful silence on religious affairs, conforming religiously in public as and when necessary, whilst keeping their inner thoughts largely to themselves.[12] Well-connected networks of pagan intellectuals survived, especially in the main centres of philosophy in the empire, such as Alexandria and Athens.

In an important law probably issued in 529, Justinian made it illegal not only to perform pagan rituals or rites, but even to be a pagan.[13] Those who were found to have made only false or nominal conversions from what he termed 'the insanity of the unholy pagans' to Christianity (primarily 'for the sake of keeping their position in the imperial service, their rank, or property') were to be 'subjected to the ultimate punishments'—which in Justinian's legislation generally meant the death penalty. 'Those who have not yet been deemed worthy of worshipful baptism', the emperor declared, 'must make themselves known . . . and go with their wives and children and their whole household to the most holy churches to be taught the true Christian faith.' Those who failed to convert would be exiled. Those caught performing pagan rites could be killed.[14] Pagans were also expressly banned from teaching, reflecting anxiety that educational institutions were being used to surreptitiously preserve and disseminate pre-Christian religious traditions and modes of thought.[15] This was the most extreme anti-pagan legislation that any Christian emperor had ever passed.

Justinian's primary concern at this point was with upper-class or 'establishment' pagans, whose presence in the 'body politic' was regarded as morally polluting. The implementation of such legislation, however, required the cooperation of local civic officials, such as provincial governors, city-level legal officers known as *defensores civitatum* ('defenders of the cities'), and agents of the Church, all of whom were encouraged to act upon accusations made by informers.[16] The Church possessed an army of legal officers, the *defensores ecclesiae* ('defenders of the Church'), who were already being used to investigate accusations of heresy, and who were now directed against those suspected of crypto-paganism. There was always a danger, to which Justinian was alert, that wealthy pagans could simply bribe governors and other officials (even bishops) to look the other way and let them be, and in those parts of the empire where anti-Chalcedonian feeling was strong, many churchmen are likely to have been loath to act on Justinian's instructions to initiate widespread religious persecution.[17] The difficulties the imperial authorities had in enforcing religious policy in largely anti-Chalcedonian Egypt, for example, probably afforded the pagan philosophers of Alexandria an unusually high degree of protection. In the late fifth century, the strongly anti-Chalcedonian patriarch of Alexandria, Peter Mongus, is recorded to have come to an understanding with the head of the philosophical school there which his successors may have felt obliged to respect.[18]

But Justinian's new legislation did mean that in those areas where the instincts of governors and bishops were more fully aligned with his own, such officials now not only had carte blanche but clear encouragement to go after those well-connected or wealthy pagans whom they may hitherto have regarded as potentially too influential or powerful to touch. The enforcement of this legislation in Athens was sufficiently draconian for the leading pagan philosopher there to abandon the city in the company of his chief colleagues and students ('dissatisfied', we are told by a near-contemporary source, 'with the prevailing belief about the supreme being among the Romans'). They headed for Persia, where, they had been informed, the authorities were more appreciative of the merits of the Greek philosophical tradition.[19] The philosophers would later decide to return to Roman territory, but only after the new Persian shah, Khusro, in negotiations with Justinian, had persuaded him to allow them to do so unharmed.[20]

Justinian also extended the scope of his purge to include anyone whose lifestyle he felt to be injurious to public morality. Around the same time, he decided to move against a group which had largely been ignored by the moralising legislation of earlier Christian emperors: men who had sex with other men. In that year, according to the chronicler John Malalas, 'some of the bishops of various provinces were accused of living immorally in matters of the flesh and of homosexual practices'. Malalas cited specific individuals as being targets: 'Isaiah, Bishop of Rhodes, an ex-prefect of the watch at Constantinople, and likewise the bishop from Diospolis in Thrace named Alexander'. 'In accordance with the sacred ordinance', he continued, 'they were brought to Constantinople and were examined and condemned by Victor the city prefect, who punished them.' Malalas went on to record how the prefect 'tortured Isaiah severely and exiled him and amputated Alexander's genitals and paraded him around on a litter. The emperor immediately decreed that those detected in pederasty should have their genitals amputated. At that time many homosexuals were arrested and died after having their genitals removed. From then on there was fear amongst those afflicted with homosexual lust.'[21] Procopius, whose account confirms Malalas' testimony, regarded Justinian's persecution of homosexual men as an act of unnecessary cruelty.[22] Justinian's 'Christianizing' legislation thus differed from that of his predecessors in many ways: not just in the number of laws and the issues they addressed, but also in the ferocity with which they were implemented.

'THE BOOK OF CONSTITUTIONS'

The outpouring of legislation during the first few years of Justinian's reign is rendered still more extraordinary by the fact that it also coincided with a major programme of legal codification and reform such as no previous Roman emperor had ever attempted. The volumes of codified and reformed law that resulted from these efforts would form the basis of the legal systems that would operate across much of Europe until the Age of Napoleon, and would also be a formative influence on Islamic law. The three great legal texts that Justinian would bequeath to posterity—the *Codex*, the *Digest*, and the *Institutes*—stand to this day as amongst the greatest intellectual achievements to survive from the ancient world. They are testimony to the remarkable erudition and talent of many of those whom Justinian drew to his court, despite the hostile attitude the emperor had adopted towards many educated pagans, and the evident discomfort many felt living under his rule. Taken together, along with the emperor's subsequent legislation, these works would come to be known as the *Corpus Iuris Civilis* (the 'Body of Civil Law').[23] These volumes reveal Justinian's absolute determination to assert personal ownership, authority, and control over the entire legal system standing at the heart of the empire's constitution, ideology, political culture, and system of government, and to dedicate them to the service of God.

At the start of Justinian's reign, empire and emperor were faced with two overriding legal challenges. The first—and most serious of these—was, in a sense, hardwired into Roman legal culture and the course of its historical development. The origins of Roman law went back to a text known as the Twelve Tables (dating from about 450 BCE). Like all legal texts, the Twelve Tables inevitably contained ambiguities which led to queries, and the law evolved over the centuries to face new challenges and accommodate novel situations. This had resulted in a huge outpouring of legal opinions, clarifications, amendments, and supplements, some issued by governmental or legal officers (such as *praetors* and members of the Senate), and others by legal experts (known as 'jurists' or 'jurisconsults'), who possessed an almost priest-like status in traditional Roman culture.[24] These, in turn, had been further augmented by pronouncements issued by emperors which carried legal authority, typically in response to petitions directed towards them by their subjects. There had been such a proliferation of legal opinions and statements that it had become increasingly difficult for lawyers, judges, and litigants to ascertain what the law on any particular subject actually was. The fear was that the situation would lead to a lack of respect for the law, which, Justinian believed, could threaten the effective cohesion of the empire and the proper workings of the state.

The second challenge was that from the third century onwards, the amendment, development, or updating of Roman law had come to be regarded as an imperial prerogative. Across the fifth and early sixth centuries, however, the new barbarian rulers in southern Gaul and Spain had begun to respond to legal queries addressed to them by their Roman subjects by issuing their own laws, updating the inherited Roman legal framework and issuing compilations or 'codifications' of these replies and updates.[25] They had done this in part to make themselves look more imperial, and thus more authoritative in the eyes of their subjects, but it was seen as a direct affront to the authority of the emperor in Constantinople, who alone possessed the right to legislate for Romans. The situation required a firm imperial response.[26]

There had been a number of attempts to impose order on the

constantly expanding mass of legal texts. Under the reign of the emperor Diocletian (r. 284–305), two private compilations of imperial legal pronouncements had been collated for the use of legal practitioners: these were known as the *Codex Gregorianus* and the *Codex Hermogianus*. In the early fifth century, the emperor Theodosius II had issued an official *codex*, or compilation, of such 'constitutions' (as imperial legal pronouncements were known) organised chronologically by subject, allowing lawyers to ascertain both the state and development of the law.[27] This text had been validated in the East on 15 February 438.[28] In the ninety years between then and Justinian's accession to the throne, many more such constitutions had been issued. Theodosius had shied away from the idea of attempting to impose order on and clarify the opinions of the classical jurists, whose writings ran to nearly two thousand separate volumes (although he did issue guidance as to which of the jurists were to be given precedence).[29]

On 13 February 528, only six months after becoming sole emperor, Justinian addressed the Senate in Constantinople to inform them of his intention to compile and officially promulgate a new 'Book of Constitutions' which he would name after himself: the *Codex Iustinianus*. This work was to be far more than a mere updating of the *Codex Theodosianus* of 438: rather, the constitutions of past emperors stretching back to Hadrian (117–138 CE) were to be pared down, edited, and abridged, with a view to removing all superfluous material and purging them of any contradiction.[30] They were to be recast to express a single unified opinion and will, presented as being that of the emperor Justinian himself.

Typically, the emperor was determined to present his project in fundamentally Christian terms. 'This material,' he declared, 'which many past emperors have considered to be in urgent need of correction, though none of them, in the meantime, ventured to bring such a project to completion, We, with the aid of Almighty God, have now determined to provide for the common good: namely, to make lawsuits less long-winded by abridging the host of constitutions . . . and by compiling, under Our auspicious name, a singe codex.' As in his earlier correspondence with Pope Hormisdas, Justinian was eager to convey to the Senate his sense of urgency: 'We have hastened, therefore,' he informed its assembled members, 'to bring these matters to your attention, so that you may know the extent of Our daily solicitude for the common welfare, desiring that constitutions shall hereafter be certain, authoritative, and collected in one codex [such that] the citation of constitutions may expedite the resolution of litigation in all trials.'[31]

The task of editing, compiling, and recasting was entrusted to a law commission comprising several high-ranking governmental and legal officials, including the current chief legal officer (or *quaestor*), a former chief legal officer, the head of the bureau of petitions, a former praetorian prefect of the East (effectively chief finance minister of the empire), and Tribonian, a barrister who had been appointed to an ad hoc position in the palace, conceivably to assist with the project. The committee was joined by Theophilus, professor of law in Constantinople, and two other high-ranking practising barristers.[32]

The commission took little more than a year to complete its work. On 7 April 529 the emperor formally confirmed the 'Code of Justinian', declaring that 'Almighty God has granted his support to Our zealous undertaking on behalf of the State', and ordering that henceforth only 'this codex, which will endure forever,' was to be cited in court.[33] There are signs, however, that—urged on by the emperor—the commissioners had signed off their work in excessive haste. As the codex began to be introduced into legal proceedings, practical difficulties with it began to emerge. Justinian was obliged to report to the Senate, for example, that 'some of the laws, by reason of facts arising later and after fuller deliberation, required some changes or correction', and it was decided that others still needed to be deleted, discarded, or supplemented.[34] Accordingly, a second version had to be prepared—this time under the supervision of Tribonian—which would not be formally released and distributed to the empire at large until 534. It is a sign of the remarkable effectiveness and cohesion of the empire's legal chancery under Justinian that today barely a trace of the first edition of the code survives, save for some fragments discovered in the deserts of Egypt.[35] The Code of Justinian as it would be transmitted to posterity would be the second, improved version. This time, in announcing the promulgation of the work, the emperor was careful to make no reference to eternity.

One of the complicating factors which may have led to the deficiencies within the first version of the codex was the ongoing legal uncertainty arising from both the huge number of juristic writings still in circulation and a lack of clarity as to how they were meant to relate to Justinian's new 'Book of Constitutions'. Consequently, shortly after the promulgation of the first code, Justinian had issued a pronouncement known as the 'Fifty Decisions' (*Quinquaginta decisiones*), which no longer survives, and which sought to address outstanding juristic controversies arising from the ancient texts.[36] Even this was evidently deemed insufficient to resolve the broader legal difficulties. Perhaps encouraged by Tribonian—whose learning, industry, and talent had clearly made a profound impression on Justinian—it was decided that what was now needed was a paring down, editing, and recasting of the vast writings of the classical jurisconsults.

'THE TEMPLE OF JUSTICE'

By 530 Justinian had appointed Tribonian to the position of chief legal officer, or *quaestor*. Even Justinian's fiercest critics were obliged to acknowledge the brilliance of his new appointee. According to the historian Procopius, himself a lawyer by training, 'Tribonian

possessed natural ability and in educational attainments was infe-
rior to none of his contemporaries.' He was also, Procopius claimed,
'extraordinarily fond of money', and knew how to ingratiate himself with the emperor.[37] Later generations of scholars in Byzantium
would suspect Tribonian of paganism, but if their suspicions were
correct, his extraordinary knowledge and understanding of the law
evidently afforded him a measure of protection.[38]

On 15 December 530, Justinian announced his decision to set
up a new law commission under Tribonian's charge to condense,
clarify, and codify the writings of the ancient jurists. The declaration, which was addressed directly to Tribonian, opened with
the words 'Through the agency of God' (deo auctore), which twelve
years earlier Justinian had deployed with rhetorical relish in his
correspondence with Pope Hormisdas. Indeed, the emperor made
it clear from the start that he regarded the imposition of order on
the empire's legal system as forming part of his providential mission.[39] As he informed his quaestor, 'We have hastened to achieve
the most ambitious, most extensive emendation of the law; both to
collect and amend all Roman lawmaking and to present in one volume the scattered works of so many authors, a project for which no
other has dared either to hope or to wish, and which has appeared
to us most difficult, indeed even impossible.' Then, emphasising
the divine purposes of the project, he added, 'But lifting up Our
hands to Heaven and imploring the aid of the Eternal, We have
preserved . . . this ambition . . . trusting in God, who in the greatness of His power can both grant and bring to fruition utterly desperate undertakings.'[40]

Informing Tribonian that his work on the code had convinced
him of his genius, Justinian ordered the quaestor to handpick the
best law professors and state advocates and gather them to work
jointly on the project within the Great Palace itself. These men would
include not only the two leading professors of law in Constantinople, but also two professors from the renowned school of Roman law

in Beirut. The commissioners were to 'read and refine the books on Roman law by the ancient jurists to whom the most sacred emperors granted the authority to draft and interpret laws, so that the whole substance may be gleaned from them and all repetition and contradiction omitted'. 'Once this material has by the supreme generosity of the Godhead been collected,' Justinian continued, 'you shall set it forth in a work of the greatest beauty and thus dedicate it, as it were, as a proper and most holy temple to justice, and you shall arrange the law in fifty books.' No juristic writings outside of these fifty books were henceforth to be cited in court: the 'ancient law, in a state of confusion for some 1,400 years and now distilled by us,' would thus be 'as if fortified by a wall, with nothing outside it'. The condensed compilation of ancient law, Justinian instructed Tribonian, was 'to bear the name of *Digest* or *Pandects*' (meaning something akin to the modern usage of the word 'encyclopaedia'), and any discrepancies between the authors would be resolved by the emperor himself. Despite the scale of the task, Justinian still regarded speed to be of the essence. Tribonian was told 'to accomplish all these things and bring them to a concise and rapid conclusion . . . so that the work . . . may be presented by Us . . . as proof of the providence of Almighty God and to the glory of Our rule and your service'.[41]

Tribonian got to work on the *Digest* with remarkable dynamism and vigour whilst also sorting out the issues that had arisen with the code. He appears to have set his commissioners a very tight timeline of just three years in which they were to gather together, read, excerpt, and harmonize, under imperial scrutiny, the classical juristic writings, which, as we have seen, ran to nearly two thousand volumes, or some three million lines of Latin text.[42] This task was delegated to six senior commissioners, organized into three committees, to whom Tribonian allocated the work (known to scholars as the Sabinian, Edictal, and Painian committees), with the writings of different authors being assigned to different groups. It is testimony to the *quaestor*'s seemingly boundless reserves of energy and commitment that he chose to chair the first of these committees himself. The lawyers then pored over and debated the texts, identifying which passages were best and most useful. Just 5 percent of the literature they read ultimately made it through this initial sifting. The excerpts then had to be edited and pieced together to make sure they made sense in their excerpted forms both grammatically and legally (this was probably the work of separate subcommittees, with the excerpts they made that were meant for inclusion being stored in 'pigeon-holes' in the palace, where Justinian ordered the commissioners to work).[43] As the newly recombined texts were assembled, they were read out and discussed to see how they would sound in court, with the advocates on each committee presumably performing the recitations.[44] They were also vetted by the emperor.[45] The task of excerpting the texts appears to have taken some eighteen months. Assembling the new text and gaining official approval for its constituent parts probably took about the same amount of time. The job of the commissioners was further complicated by the fact that copies of some of the legal works they required only arrived relatively late in the day, and so had to be abstracted and inserted by a separate committee.

During the first phase of the process, each committee probably scrutinised, discussed, and excerpted around 1,500 lines a day (or 25 pages).[46] Debating the relative merits of the opinions of some of the towering intellectual figures of Roman law, and deciding which of their writings to keep or jettison, however, is likely to have been an intense and exhausting affair. Justinian had been clear that no automatic preference was to be given to any one author: passages were only to be selected on their merits.[47] It says a great deal for the intellectual autonomy and rigour of those charged with compiling the *Digest* that at the end of the day, about 40 percent of the text they produced would be derived from the writings of a third-century jurist by the name of Ulpian (duly reworked and revised), despite the fact that his original writings had listed constitutions hostile to Christians, making it easier for governors to persecute them.[48] Ulpian's writings had been primarily entrusted to the committee chaired by Tribonian—hence, perhaps, the *quaestor*'s later reputation in Byzantium as a pagan.[49] The overall result was to recast the inherited mass of juristic opinions into a coherent and updated compilation to be read alongside the corresponding titles of the *Codex Iustinianus* (consisting of legal enactments issued by emperors).[50] So effective was the achievement of this editorial feat, and so ruthless the process of discarding those passages and writings of the classical jurists deemed by the committee to lie 'beyond the wall' of the fortified 'Temple of Justice', that it is now extraordinarily difficult for legal scholars to reconstruct what Roman law looked like *before* Justinian and his commissioners got to work.[51] Although the emperor professed to have been motivated by a 'reverence for antiquity', Justinian had in fact recast the entire inherited legal tradition to meet contemporary needs.[52]

'THE CRADLE OF THE LAW'

Nor did the emperor's plans for the law (and Tribonian's responsibilities towards them) end there. In instructing Tribonian to get to work on the *Digest*, Justinian had also signalled his intention to produce a condensed and introductory textbook of the reformed law: a set of *Institutes* (Latin *Institutiones*) or *Elements* (Latin *Elementa*) meant to serve the needs of students, and which effectively provided an overview or map of how the law worked and how the different parts of it related to one another.[53] The students who formed the core of the work's intended readership would have included many who dreamed of a future governing the empire, as legal training was expected not only for a career in the law courts, but also for entry into the civil service.[54] If the *Codex Iustinianus* drew inspiration and much of its material from the *Codex Theodosianus*, and if the *Digest* relied to a significant extent on a carefully revised and distilled version of the writings of Ulpian, the *Institutes*, on which Tribonian set to work immediately after the conclusion of the *Digest* project, with the aid of two of the law professors on his team, were largely modelled on the writings of a second-century jurist named Gaius along with earlier 'institutional' (educational) literature.[55] Once Tribonian and the professors had completed a first draft of the *Institutes*, Tribonian edited, polished, and modernized the whole.[56] The official promulgation of the *Digest* was held back until this task too had been completed.

The first of the works to be released (on 21 November 533) was the *Institutes*, which the emperor dedicated to those whom he described as 'the young enthusiasts for law', for whom he had now provided 'a cradle of the law, not based on obscure old stories but illuminated by the light of Our imperial splendour'. 'Study our law,' the students were urged. 'Do your best and apply yourselves keenly to it. Show that you have mastered it. You can then cherish a noble ambition, [and] when your course in law is finished you will be able to perform whatever duty is entrusted to you in the government of our state.'[57] A few weeks later it was announced that the *Digest* would go into effect on 30 December. Copies of it were dispatched throughout the empire (no small feat, given that even the heavily condensed work that the commissioners produced was still roughly one and a half times the size of the Bible).[58] 'Thus', Justinian informed the Senate of Constantinople on 16 December, 'the entire assemblage of Roman law has been compiled, completed in three volumes, that is, the *Institutes*, *Digest* or *Pandects*, and *Constitutions* [the first version of the code] and finished in three years, a work which when the materials first began to be divided [for the committees], we expected not to be finished in ten years. We have piously offered this work to Almighty God for the preservation of mankind, and We have given ample thanks to the Supreme Deity, who has enabled us to wage wars successfully, to win an honourable peace, and to lay down the best laws not only for Our own but for every age, both present and future.'[59]

In associated legislation, Justinian would overhaul the entire basis of legal education in the empire, placing his newly codified law at the heart of the professional training of those planning to forge careers in imperial service or in the courts. Law students at the end of their first year of study, which would focus mostly on the *Institutes*, were henceforth to be known as *Iustiniani*—'the Justinians'.[60] They were to be the crack troops at the forefront of the emperor's drive to restore imperial authority both at home and abroad. As Justinian had declared when issuing his new textbook, 'Imperial Majesty should not only be graced with arms, but also armed with laws, so that good government may prevail in time of war and peace alike. The head of the Roman state can then stand victorious, not only over enemies in war but also troublemakers, driving out their wickedness through the paths of law.'[61]

But who were these 'troublemakers'? Why were they so much on Justinian's mind in the year 533? Contemporaries would have known exactly who he meant. For however extraordinary the rapidity with which Tribonian had completed the programme of legal codification entrusted to him by the emperor, it is likely that he would have been able to accomplish the task even more speedily had a major uprising led by the Circus Factions not occurred in Constantinople in January 532. These rioters had demanded that both Tribonian and the praetorian prefect at the time—John the Cappadocian, a ruthless bureaucrat—be removed from office. Actively encouraged by members of the Senate, they had then attempted to depose Justinian himself. It is to that attempted coup and its aftermath that we must now turn.

Chapter 6

The Voice of
the People

'OUR SCEPTRED SOVEREIGN AND
GOD-CROWNED THEODORA'

On the morning of Tuesday, 20 January 532, the centre of Constantinople presented a scene of utter devastation. Many of the buildings around the Hippodrome and adjacent to the palace had been burnt to the ground. 'No one', a later source tells us, 'dared to go out, but only the shops which provided food and drink for needy people were open.' Across the city, an atmosphere of 'great imperial terror' prevailed.[1] This was the result of seven days of unprecedented politically motivated violence and destruction which had almost driven Justinian from the throne.

There had been rumblings of discontent against Justinian's rule from the very start, perhaps exacerbated by the way in which the new emperor had sought to promote not just his own political profile, but also that of his wife. Such grumblings seem to have first emerged from within circles associated with the household of the former emperor Anastasius. In 528, the *Chronicle* of John Malalas records, 'Probus the patrician, a relative of the emperor Anastasius, incurred anger for having slandered Justinian.' Probus was arrested and put on trial before a full meeting of the Senate. The emperor, however, 'took the proceedings and tore them up, saying to Probus, "I forgive you for the offence you committed against me. Pray then that God too may forgive you."' This act of magnanimity, John relates, earned Justinian the applause of his senatorial audience. Less generosity would be shown the following year, when an ally of the emperor, named Priscus, reputedly fell foul of the empress Theodora: as a result, his property was seized and he was forced into internal exile.[2]

The imperial couple were particularly sensitive and alert to the ongoing political pretensions of members of the Anastasian household and the family of the haughty and exceptionally wealthy dowager Anicia Iuliana. The construction of the Church of Saint Polyeuktos that she had funded, standing adjacent to the imperial mausoleum of the Church of the Holy Apostles, was a very public statement of their continued political ambitions. Anicia Iuliana had even declared in its dedicatory inscription—portions of which survive—that she alone had 'conquered time and surpassed the wisdom of celebrated Solomon, raising a temple to receive God'.[3]

In response, Justinian and Theodora ordered the construction of a new church next to the Palace of Hormisdas, adjacent to where Justinian had previously dedicated one to Saints Peter and Paul.[4] The new foundation was initially dedicated to the Syrian soldier Saint Sergius, although it would later come to be known as the Church of Saints Sergius and Bacchus, to include the memory of another Syrian soldier saint with whom Sergius was commonly associated.[5] Unusually for Constantinople, this church was constructed around a central dome—which may also have been true of the Church of Saint Polyeuktos. Perhaps more tellingly, the format of its dedicatory inscription very closely resembled that of Anicia Iuliana's church. Its message, however, was a direct refutation of the vanity and misdirected munificence of Justinian's predecessors and the great families of old. 'Other sovereigns', the carefully crafted epigram declared, 'have honoured dead men whose labour was unprofitable, but our sceptred Justinian, fostering piety, honours with a splendid abode the Servant of Christ, Begetter of all things, Sergius. . . . May he in all things guard the rule of the sleepless sovereign and increase the power of the God-crowned Theodora, whose mind is adorned with piety [and] whose constant toil lies in unsurpassed efforts to nourish the destitute.'[6]

By 532 unhappiness with the regime had begun to spread well beyond the ranks of the rival factions and dynasties who felt that the throne was rightfully theirs, coming to affect a much broader cross section of political society.[7] Whilst many hardline elements within the leadership of the Church and their supporters amongst the laity clearly welcomed Justinian's suppression of pagans, heretics, and others, to observers of a more conservative mindset such efforts to move against the 'enemy within' were cruel and unnecessary. They broke the fundamental rules of how the emperor was meant to govern and the sort of obedience he could reasonably expect.[8] Emperors were traditionally expected not to pry too deeply into the inner thoughts and beliefs of their subjects, who, in turn, were expected to make an outward show of conformity to such laws and regulations as the government issued. By cracking down on those who made public professions of Christian faith, for example, whilst perhaps maintaining older religious traditions in private, Justinian was considered to be overstepping the mark. Procopius was bitterly critical of Justinian's treatment of the Samaritans around his hometown of Caesarea, lambasting the emperor for persecuting people for their beliefs, whilst also praising those Samaritans who had made a purely nominal conversion to Christianity, so as to escape legal penalties. Likewise, what was the point of persecuting people for their sexual proclivities or youthful indiscretions? Procopius felt that it was akin to punishing people for being ill.[9] Religious fanaticism had its supporters, but it also had its critics, especially among some of the better educated members of the imperial bureaucracy and civil administration, where a more traditional Roman attitude of tolerance in matters of religion was still discernible.

Where imperial policy risked alienating the emperor's subjects more generally was when it came to touch not only on matters of religion and culture, but also on the material conditions in which people lived their lives. For at the heart of relations between emperor and subject stood the issue of taxation, which, in the East Roman Empire of the sixth century, was primarily levied on the land and those who owned and worked it—from the greatest senator, with his far-flung estates, to the lowliest peasant cultivating a tiny family plot.

Taxation in the Roman Empire had always been a bruising and brutal affair. One ancient Christian hymn, the 'Dies irae' ('Day of Wrath'), conceived of God, when on the Last Day he sits in judgement over mankind, in terms of the arrival of the imperial tax inspector.[10] Ever since the reign of the emperor Diocletian in the fourth century, officials had been sent out to the provinces on a regular basis to assess the taxable resources of the emperor's subjects. Extracting the information on which the fiscal system depended, and then forcing often recalcitrant communities or landowners to pay what was demanded of them, frequently depended upon threats of force or even acts of violence. City councillors who failed to collect taxes from their surrounding region could be held personally liable for such debts, and agricultural land that was unowned or uncultivated could be forcibly assigned to local landowners or villages, whose inhabitants thereby became liable for the taxes attached to it. In the reign of Anastasius, a system of tax-farming had been introduced to parts of the empire whereby individuals would bid for the right to collect local taxes and then take a cut of the proceeds. Predictably, such officials (*vindices*) came to be widely hated.[11]

From the fourth to the early sixth centuries, roughly half of all the tax revenues collected by the Roman state were probably used to fund the army.[12] The period of peace that characterised much of the second half of the fifth century in the East had allowed the imperial authorities to build up significant cash reserves. So while Anastasius' introduction of the office of *vindex* had proven unpopular, he had been able to abolish certain taxes, such as the so-called *chrysargyron*, effectively a tax on mercantile profits.[13] When the sudden revival of warfare with Persia demanded it, Anastasius had to use his accumulated reserves to engage in rapid and large-scale expenditure on the empire's eastern frontier, as well as to begin the refortification of Roman positions towards and along the Danube. The need for these fortifications continued during Justin's reign and beyond. Procopius suggests that the empire's coffers were significantly depleted by the time Justinian became sole ruler.[14]

One of the key priorities for Justinian, therefore, when he became emperor, was to ensure the steady and reliable flow of tax revenues. This meant enforcing laws against the acts of peculation and tax evasion that threatened to undermine the fiscal foundations of the state. Justinian considered fiscal inefficiency, like military inactivity, or the toleration of heretical and pagan sects, as an avoidable weakness resulting from the indolence of his predecessors. Many of the lands of the Roman Near East were enjoying unprecedented prosperity in the 510s and 520s, and the emperor judged that there was no reason to assume that his subjects (especially the wealthiest amongst them) could not afford to pay.[15]

His critics had a different view, regarding him as uniquely covetous of other people's money, and scandalously spendthrift once he had possession of it. Whilst Procopius had regarded Anastasius as the 'most stewardly' of emperors, to him Justinian was 'like an ever-flowing river: while each day he plundered and pillaged his subjects, yet the inflow all streamed straight on to the barbarians, to whom he would make a present of it'. In his damning critique of the emperor, Procopius even claimed that early in the reign of Justin, an acquaintance of his (whom he calls 'one of the notables') had received a prophetic dream: in it he had seen Justinian standing on the shore of Byzantium, from where 'he drank up all the waters of the sea', until, he reported, the future emperor had drained the very Bosphorus dry, and sucked out and consumed even the contents of the city's sewers.[16] This negative depiction of an all-consuming emperor would subsequently become a standard feature of Byzantine *Kaiserkritik* (any literature critical of the emperors): but with respect to Justinian specifically, the allegation of unprecedented fiscal cupidity which underlay it was evidently keenly felt.[17] His attitude towards taxation raised hackles across the social spectrum.

'THE FOUL CAPPADOCIAN'

As we saw with Tribonian, Justinian had an eye for talent and a knack for appointing those whose instincts and priorities chimed with his own. When it came to the collection of tax revenues and the careful scrutiny of state expenditure, his right-hand man would be a ruthlessly efficient bureaucrat who was openly reviled in the contemporary literary sources, John the Cappadocian. Justinian appointed John as praetorian prefect of the East (or chief finance minister) around the year 531, but John's influence on policy may well have predated his elevation to that post.[18] To Procopius, John was 'oppressive and severe alike with all men, inflicting blows upon those whom he met and plundering without respect almost all of their money'. He was, moreover, 'without the advantages of a liberal education; for he learned nothing while attending the elementary school except his letters, and these, too, poorly enough'. His constant priority, Procopius claimed, was 'to destroy the lives of many men for the sake of gain and to wreck whole cities'. Nevertheless, even Procopius was obliged to admit that John was possessed of great natural ability, and a rare talent for spotting problems and discerning solutions. John, he said, became 'the most powerful man of whom we know'.[19]

The contemporary scholar and bureaucrat John Lydus (who himself served as a legal official within the praetorian prefecture under John the Cappadocian) helps us to put more flesh on the bones of this evidently controversial figure. According to his account, 'the foul Cappadocian', as he calls him, originated from the city of Caesarea in Anatolia (not to be confused with the Palestinian city of the same name, from which Procopius hailed). From there he had entered imperial service as a financial officer (*scrinarius*) within the military administration, possibly serving on the staff of the *magister militum praesentalis* (the commander-in-chief of the army stationed in and around Constantinople) while Justinian held that post in the 520s.[20] It may have been at this point that he first came to Justinian's attention, for John Lydus tells us that the Cappadocian 'gained access to the emperor and won his friendship, and because he had promised to do things beyond belief on behalf of the government, he was promoted to the ranks of the intendants of finance'. Soon thereafter, Justinian appointed him to senatorial rank and suddenly 'hoisted him' into the 'prefectural dignity' (that is, appointed him as praetorian prefect). This despite the fact that, as John Lydus put it (in an expression of casual but heart-felt prejudice), 'Cappadocians are always foul; fouler, however, when appointed to office, and at their foulest when in pursuit of profit'.[21]

Lydus then goes on to provide a detailed critique of the Cappadocian's policies (some of which are also the subject of explicit criticism by Procopius, to such an extent that it has been frequently postulated that the two authors may have known each other, or at least must have been aware of one another's work).[22] He singles out in particular John's brutality towards those suspected of tax evasion, including an acquaintance of his, Antiochus, whom John the Cappadocian supposedly had tortured to death in an attempt to make him reveal where he was hiding his money. He complains of how John 'used to send out to every place and region . . . men who were similar to himself in his attempt to extract in the manner of a suction-pump any money which hitherto lay hidden'. He provides a vivid account of the activities of such tax collectors in his native city of Philadelphia, in the famously wealthy province of Lydia in Asia Minor, which, he claims, John's chief agent 'chewed up . . . so finely that after him, because it had become bereft not only of money, but also of human beings, it could no longer admit any opportunity of change for the better'.[23]

In particular, Lydus details how John brought ruin to many of the farmers and landowners of western Asia Minor (within what was known as the 'diocese' of Asia) by cutting back on the so-called *cursus velox*, or 'fast post'.[24] This was the system of state-supported posting stations, stables, offices, and hostels (akin to the later Islamic *caravanserais*) at which state officials, soldiers, and even representatives of the Church could obtain new horses, pack animals, carriages and wagons, and food and other supplies as they made their way across the empire. Located every twelve to twenty-five miles or so along all the major road networks, they facilitated the rapid circulation of news as well as orders and commands between Constantinople and the far-flung frontiers of the empire.[25] As John Lydus emphasises, such posting stations were also to the great benefit of the local rural population, members of which would gather at the fairs that grew up around these centres to sell goods to the government officials and other passing travellers stationed or sojourning there. The peasants and villagers would use the money they derived from these sales, he tells us, to pay their taxes. The Cappadocian, however, decided that in this part of western Asia Minor as well as elsewhere in the less militarily vulnerable parts of the East (as described by Procopius), the *cursus velox* was an unnecessary expense and should be curtailed.[26] It was only to be maintained on the route that connected Constantinople to the eastern frontier, which was known as the 'Pilgrim's Road', as it also provided the main route to the Holy Land.[27] The result, Lydus claims, was that many were unable to sell their goods at market, crops rotted in the fields, and peasants were forced into extreme hardship in order to pay their taxes.

Lydus' complaints against the Cappadocian were not entirely related to taxation. He also blamed him for a series of internal reforms within the praetorian prefecture itself which, he asserted, did great institutional harm, and which had a particularly deleterious impact on John Lydus' own career. This claim helps to explain the extraordinarily vitriolic nature of his account and his determination to pin all the difficulties Justinian would soon face on John.[28] He also blames him for a significant change within the legal culture of the prefecture, whereby Greek would replace Latin as the default and initial language in which new legislation was drafted and issued (save in respect to Latin-speaking regions or the highest offices of state, such as the Senate).[29] This change in practice cannot be entirely ascribed to John the Cappadocian, but is certainly reflected in the contemporary laws which survive. The measure was an entirely logical one in terms of governmental efficiency, given that, across the Eastern Empire, as even the Latin-speaking emperor Justinian was obliged to admit, Greek, not Latin, was the common tongue of the elite as well as of much of the broader population.[30] To John Lydus—who was deeply conservative by instinct, an antiquarian by nature, and ended up appointed by Justinian as professor of Latin in Constantinople—this was an act of pure cultural vandalism.

Whatever his motivation, John Lydus clearly states in his account that, as a result of the policies advocated by John the Cappadocian, both prior to and during his first year in office as praetorian prefect, 'immense wealth was amassed', such that 'he saw oceans of money flowing around him'. This is, of course, precisely what Justinian would have wanted (although John Lydus predictably accuses his nemesis of having kept much of the money for himself). The praetorian prefect also attempted to cement his position politically by courting the Green Faction. He was less successful, however, in his courting of the empress Theodora. According to John Lydus, 'endowed with understanding and sympathy towards those who had been wronged', the empress 'went to the emperor and informed him' of the mounting grievances of his subjects. In particular, Lydus claims, the streets of Constantinople were increasingly thronged by migrants from the countryside, fleeing ever more adverse conditions, and complaining of maltreatment at the hands of the authorities.[31] Such 'useless mobs', as Lydus calls them, were inevitably drawn towards the Hippodrome and the Circus Factions, whose leaders were in a position to offer both entertainment and support. Through their acclamations, the factions could give collective voice to the burgeoning unhappiness of the emperor's subjects.[32]

'WOULD THAT SABBATIUS HAD NOT BEEN BORN!'

There can be little doubt that a growing number of unemployed migrants and others were drawn to Constantinople at this time. Justinian would later issue legislation to curtail such inward migration. But even in the early 530s, Lydus relates, the authorities' treatment of those he describes as having 'abandoned the land of their birth', with a view to 'idling rather than working soberly' on the streets of Constantinople, was becoming increasingly harsh.[33] 'The officials', he tells us, 'lashed out rather vehemently against the crimes of the people.'[34] Some of the migrants whose activities the authorities sought to police may have initially arrived as petitioners, hoping to bring their complaints concerning the activities of tax collectors before the emperor. Tellingly, in 539 Justinian would issue legislation to curtail the flow of agricultural workers (*coloni adscripticii*) to Constantinople, where they hoped to bring lawsuits against their landowning employers. But the late fifth and early sixth centuries also appear to have witnessed considerable population growth across the lands of the Eastern Roman Empire as a whole, and it is conceivable that these broader demographic pressures were the main driver drawing unemployed migrants to the capital at this time.[35]

The emperor does not seem to have been terribly concerned at first by the complaints voiced by the Circus Factions, or those petitioning Theodora and others about the activities of John the Cappadocian. John's approach to taxation apparently reflected that of Justinian himself, as well as those immediately around him, who, John Lydus claims, 'used to speak in defence of the wicked Cappadocian'.[36] Moreover, the emperor's own attitude towards the Circus Factions may itself have been a cause of growing uncertainty and instability on the streets. During the reign of Anastasius, the political activities of the Circus Factions had been most conspicuous with respect to the controversial doctrinal politics of the day, although they had also complained about aspects of Anastasius' economic policies.[37] From the accession of Justin onwards, however, Justinian and his network of supporters had progressively drawn the Circus Factions in general, and the Blue Faction in particular, much more closely into the broader machinations of the political system, using them as a means of building up Justinian's support both at court and on the streets and taking advantage of their endorsement when he claimed the throne.[38]

Even so, once on the throne, Justinian had attempted to distance himself from his erstwhile supporters, adopting a harsh tone with respect to faction-related violence both within Constantinople and across the empire. According to John Malalas, he ordered that 'rioters or murderers, no matter to what faction they belonged', be punished.[39] When revealing himself before his subjects in the Hippodrome—as imperial ceremonial tradition and protocols demanded he do—Justinian could not prevent the Circus Factions from raising their voices and bringing their collective complaints to his attention. However, no doubt contrary to the expectations of the faction members, given his previous dealings with them, the emperor was no longer minded to act upon their requests. Indeed, the emperor's recently promulgated law code, the *Codex Iustinianus*, contained a statement which is perhaps indicative of how Justinian was now inclined to regard his recent allies: 'The worthless voice of the people', the code declared, 'should not be listened to. Nor is it right to give credence to their voices when they demand either that the guilty should be acquitted or that the innocent should be condemned.'[40] This sudden change in Justinian's attitude is likely to have occasioned both bewilderment and anger.

A later Byzantine source, in what seems to be a genuine and remarkable account, records increasingly bitter exchanges in the Hippodrome of Constantinople between the Green Faction and the emperor from around this time. As the faction members chanted their complaints against the recent deeds of an imperial official, named Calopodius, on the one side, and the emperor (speaking through his herald) summarily and contemptuously dismissed their petition on the other, what was meant to be an orderly and regulated exchange of information between the emperor and his subjects rapidly degenerated into a 'slanging match'.[41] The acclamations, the source reveals, had begun in a straightforward and respectable manner, with the Greens chanting, 'Long may you live, Justinian Augustus, *Tu vincas!* [You conquer]. I am wronged, O paragon of virtue, and cannot endure it!' But the Greens refused to accept the emperor's curt reply—of 'No one does you wrong!'—and drop the subject. Justinian's herald remonstrated with them: 'You have not come here to watch [the races] but only to insult your rulers! . . . Silence, you Jews, Manichaeans and Samaritans! . . . How long are you going to

curse yourselves? . . . I am telling you, get baptized in one [God]!'
The Greens soon gave back as good as they got: 'Would that Sabbatius [Justinian's father] had not been born, so that he would not have
a murderer for a son! . . . Farewell, Justice, you exist no more!'[42]

THE IDES OF JANUARY

On Saturday, 10 January 532, perhaps in accordance with Justinian's recent command that those charged with serious offences be
prosecuted, irrespective of their Circus Faction, the urban prefect of
Constantinople, Eudaemon, arrested a number of men, members of
both the Blue and Green Factions, and sentenced seven of them to
death for murder.[43] The miscreants were transported by boat across
the Golden Horn to the suburb of Sycae (Galata), where they were
to be hanged. However, as the sentence was being carried out, the
scaffold broke, and two of the condemned (one Green and one Blue)
miraculously survived. According to one account, a second attempt
to hang them was also botched, and the surrounding bystanders
demanded that the faction members be given sanctuary in a nearby
church. Accordingly, the two lucky felons were spirited away by a
band of monks, who gave them safe haven in the adjacent Church of
Saint Laurence.[44] The urban prefect responded by sending troops to
guard the church and await further instructions.

By tradition, the following Tuesday (13 January) marked the
start of a new series of races in the Hippodrome, and Justinian was
meant to preside over them. They were known as the *Ides*. Afterwards, the emperor was expected to host a banquet in honour of
those who had received promotion to high office in imperial service
during the preceding year. Surrounded by these newly elevated dig-
nitaries, Justinian could not afford to lose face at this event. Accordingly, when the Green and Blue Factions united in the Hippodrome
to call upon him to show mercy to the condemned murderers holed

up in the Church of Saint Laurence, he simply ignored the pleas of the crowd. According to John Malalas, the chants then continued all the way through to the twenty-second race of the day (out of a total of twenty-four). Thereafter, 'the devil prompted evil counsels in them, and they chanted to one another: "Long live the merciful Blues and Greens!" After the races the crowd went off united, having given themselves a pass-phrase with the word "Conquer" [*Nika!*] so as not to be infiltrated by soldiers. . . . And so they charged off.'[45]

Infuriated by the emperor's refusal to concede to their requests, the faction members now marched on the offices of the urban prefect in the praetorium. Failing to obtain a reply to their demand that the 'fugitives at Saint Laurence's' be freed, they engaged in a wave of rioting and arson. According to John Malalas, they set fire to the praetorium itself.[46]

The next morning, Wednesday, 14 January, Justinian decided to face down the mob and preside over the scheduled second day of races. But as the customary flag was raised to mark the opening of the games, the faction members burnt down the upper tiers of the Hippodrome and destroyed much of the neighbouring colonnade. The fire blazed as far as the nearby Baths of Zeuxippus, which contained a famous assemblage of statues on historical and mythological themes, and this monument, too, was destroyed.[47] By this time, both of the condemned murderers, whose failed execution had given rise to the riots—and many other faction members whom the authorities had been holding—had now been freed by the intervention of the mob, and it was not at all clear why the Circus Factions were still rioting.[48] Justinian sent three high-ranking officials out from the palace, including the battle-hardened Gepid general Mundo, to enquire what it was that the rioters now wanted.[49] Apparently, within the palace a lively debate had been underway as to how the emperor should proceed. According to a highly fragmentary passage in an otherwise reliable source, those around him (quite possibly meaning the empress Theodora) had been telling Justinian,

'When you are in trouble, you need to listen.' Word came back that the Circus Factions were now demanding that Justinian dismiss not only the urban prefect, Eudaemon, whose arrest of the Circus Faction members had sparked off the crisis, but also John the Cappadocian and Tribonian. Clearly under pressure from within and without the palace, Justinian immediately sacked all three.[50]

The demand that he dismiss these three officials was perhaps the first indication that the disturbances were being used by those with connections to the Circus Factions to achieve political change. The anger of the mob was being carefully harnessed to target and isolate the emperor's chief ministers: the ones he most relied upon, but whom anti-regime elements in the Senate and political society more generally had come to despise. John the Cappadocian was a highly controversial figure whose policy agenda was already impacting an increasingly broad cross section of society. Eudaemon was involved in the earlier incident that led to the protests. But it is hard to see how Justinian's chief legal officer, Tribonian, could have elicited so much animosity unless the conservative elements within the Senate and the bureaucratic elite had played a role. These forces may have regarded legal reform—as represented by the first recension of Justinian's code and the ongoing compilation of the *Digest*—as an act of dangerous and potentially tyrannical innovation.[51] To John Lydus, even issuing laws in Greek was a step too far.

Justinian had given ground, but he was not willing to lose control. Perhaps sensitive to the fact that he had been cornered by his opponents and forced to sacrifice those whom he most trusted (with the sole exception of his wife), the emperor now attempted to restore order on the streets, or at least to safeguard the palace complex itself, by making a show of force. Significantly, the general Belisarius also happened to be around the palace at this time. In the aftermath of the Roman defeat at Callinicum in 531, Belisarius had been subjected to a court-martial, removed from his post, and recalled to the capital.[52] His presence in time for the banquet for new officeholders associated with the Ides of January might suggest that Justinian either had already reappointed him or was about to do so.[53] Either way, the emperor now ordered Belisarius to move against the rioters.

Heading out of the palace with his private military entourage, we are told, Belisarius and his men ruthlessly cut down many of the insurgents gathered there.[54] The slaughter continued through to the evening.[55] Rather than restoring order, however, the general's intervention simply made matters worse. According to John Malalas, 'The mob was incensed and started fires in other places and began killing indiscriminately.'[56] By the end of the following day, the *Chalke* (Bronze) Gate, which guarded the entrance to the palace, the Senate House, and the Cathedral Church of Holy Wisdom (*Hagia Sophia*) adjacent to the palace, had all been destroyed.[57] The mob had even marched on the nearby palace of a nephew of the emperor Anastasius, Probus, gathering weapons and chanting, 'Another emperor for the city!'[58] and 'Probus! Emperor for *Romania*!' Not finding him at home, they burned it down.[59] But it was now clear that those directing the disturbances were determined not just to unseat Justinian's chief ministers—an objective they had now achieved—but to depose the emperor himself.

'YOU ARE STUFFED, ASS!'

On the following morning, Friday, 16 January, the rioters destroyed more governmental buildings, deliberately targeting the state archives, where taxation and other official records were kept. Amidst much indiscriminate incendiarism, they reduced a series of hospices, hospitals, and charitable institutions to ashes, including the so-called Hospice of Samson, where, we are told, 'all those who lay sick in it perished'. The faction members, a later but well-informed Constantinopolitan source would relate, were now 'murdering men at random, and dragging them away and throwing them into the sea like dung; and similarly too, they were murdering women'. This could have been a sign that the rioters were now completely out of control. Alternatively, the carnage may have been purposeful, encouraged by those who were eager to flush Justinian out of the palace and convince him to abandon the city. The emperor nevertheless remained ensconced behind the palace walls, and on Saturday, 17 January, military reinforcements arrived in the capital from Thrace, and extensive fighting between the soldiers and the rioters ensued.[60] Again, the troops were unable to restore order amid bitter hand-to-hand fighting throughout the streets of the city. Within the palace, Justinian and his advisers were yet again obliged to reconsider their approach.

On Sunday morning, in a final attempt to persuade the rioters to desist, Justinian exited through a heavily fortified palace door that opened directly onto the imperial box, or *kathisma*, of the Hippodrome, carrying his Bible. A detailed Constantinopolitan source tells us that 'when this was known, all the people went up, and the entire Hippodrome was filled with the crowds. And the emperor swore an oath to them, saying "By this Power, I forgive you this error, and I order that none of you be arrested—but be peaceful; for there is nothing on your head, but rather on mine. For my sins have made me deny to you what you asked of me in the Hippodrome." And many of the people chanted, "Augustus Justinian, may you be victorious!" But others chanted, "You are stuffed, ass!" And he desisted, and the emperor went down from the Hippodrome.'[61]

The following twenty-four hours would prove to be pivotal in Justinian's reign. Thankfully, they are unusually richly recorded in the contemporary sources, which include, amongst others, a detailed account of discussions within the palace written by Procopius.[62] Procopius, a close adviser to Belisarius, may have been present for the conversations he describes, or he may have relied on Belisarius' recollections for his account. In any case, Belisarius would play a crucial role in the events that followed. For although Justinian's display of public penance had won the approbation of certain of the faction members (probably overwhelmingly Blues), it had failed to move enough of them to his side to quell what was now a full-blown uprising against his rule. Key members of the Senate had been holed up within the palace, and the emperor gave them permission to head out and look to the defence of their own residences in the city. The ruins of Probus' home were perhaps still smouldering at this point. Justinian's invitation to the senators might have seemed to be an act of resigned generosity: there are indications, however, that a measure of calculation may also have been involved, for, on the Saturday, the emperor had specifically instructed the late emperor Anastasius' other nephews, Pompey and Hypatius, to leave the palace and 'go home as quickly as possible'.[63]

The mob on the streets was actively in pursuit of a new emperor, and Hypatius would have been regarded as an especially eligible choice, possessing as he did both blue blood and fine military credentials. That being the case, Justinian might have had every reason to wish to keep him as close to himself as possible. But, as the elevation of Justin as emperor in 518 had demonstrated, whoever controlled the palace essentially controlled the throne. By no means were all of the senators present within its walls that weekend in 532 necessarily committed to Justinian's survival; crucially, Procopius relates, even members of the palace guard were distinctly ambivalent as to the emperor's prospects.[64] Justinian may well have feared an imminent coup from within the palace itself, placing Hypatius or his brother on the throne.[65] Better to get them out of the palace, he seems to have thought, and let those senators less committed to the survival of his regime go with them. Hence, according to Procopius, Justinian had ordered the two princelings to go, despite the fact that they themselves feared that the mob would try to proclaim one or the other of them emperor, and warned Justinian of this possibility.[66]

What now transpired would demonstrate both the wisdom and

the danger of Justinian's strategy. As Hypatius and Pompey had predicted, after insulting the emperor in the Hippodrome, the rioters arrived at their door. According to Procopius, 'The body of the people hastened to them, and they declared Hypatius emperor, and prepared to lead him to the forum to assume power.' Despite the public protestations of both Hypatius and his wife, he was immediately taken to the Forum of Constantine, 'where they called him to the throne; then since they had neither diadem nor anything else with which it is customary for an emperor to be clothed, they placed a gold necklace on his head and proclaimed him Emperor of the Romans'. Those senators who had left (or had never joined) Justinian in the palace now met with Hypatius to discuss how to proceed. 'Many of them', according to Procopius, 'were of the opinion that they should go to the palace to fight.' Procopius clearly believed that they wanted to head there to fight *against* Justinian. The senator Origen proposed a counterargument: that a direct and bloody encounter could inevitably go either way, and that within the palace the emperor was likely to have the upper hand. It was better, he argued, to offer Justinian a way out: to make it clear to him that the game was up, but at least give him the chance of fleeing Constantinople with his life, and the prospect of perhaps trying to regroup with his supporters elsewhere.[67] Procopius records no senator at this gathering outside the palace speaking out in support of the emperor. This is telling, as his account of the insurrection would appear in his widely circulated and highly popular public history of Justinian's reign.

Hypatius, Procopius recorded, was of the majority opinion: that they should throw caution to the wind and head straight to the Hippodrome.[68] The rioters headed where this senatorial party led them—a further sign that what had begun as factional disorder had been successfully harnessed by Justinian's opponents to political ends. Once in the Hippodrome, Hypatius was placed in the imperial box, the *kathisma*. From there he received 'the people's acclamation in favour of him and the insulting utterances they spoke against the emperor Justinian and against the *Augusta* Theodora'. Only the heavy bronze doors of the palace separated Hypatius in the imperial box from Justinian within the palace. Outside the palace, too, members of the Green Faction were now beginning to arrive carrying arms and wearing breastplates, determined to 'open up the palace and lead Hypatius into it'.[69] In response, Justinian ordered that the corridor connecting the palace to the *kathisma* be barricaded.[70]

How are we to account for Hypatius' apparent willingness to play along with the plotters, and even to join them in discussing the best course of action? There are indications that he had attempted to keep a foot in both camps until he was finally persuaded that the throne was effectively his. But his decision to throw his lot in with the mob seems to have been the result of confusion and misinformation. According to a detailed account of the events of the day, Hypatius had sent a trusted intermediary to the palace to pass on a secret message to Justinian: 'See, I have assembled all your enemies in the Hippodrome. Do what you wish with them.' When this messenger attempted to gain access to the emperor, Justinian's personal physician informed him that the emperor had in fact already slipped away and abandoned the throne. The messenger reported back to Hypatius, 'Master, God prefers that you be emperor: for Justinian has fled, and there is no one in the palace.'[71]

According to a later Byzantine source, which preserves much genuine sixth-century material, Justinian had indeed considered taking flight (thus perhaps unleashing the series of rumours which ultimately reached Hypatius' ears). 'The emperor', we are told, 'in terror wanted to load his money on to a galley (*dromon*) and get away as far as Herakleia in Thrace, leaving General Mundo to guard the palace, along with Mundo's son and three thousand men.'[72] Procopius reports, however, that Justinian's nerves were steeled by his devoted consort, the 'God-crowned' Theodora, who had clearly had enough of the prevarication of those surrounding the emperor, and was determined to make her position clear despite the fact that for a woman to be seen 'to be daring in front of men, or to assert herself boldly,' as Procopius put it, broke all the rules of protocol. She was more man than most of the emperor's advisers were, and she publicly accused them of 'holding back [their views] out of cowardice'. Theodora was of the straightforward opinion that Justinian had no choice but to stand and fight: 'It would be unendurable', she declared, 'for a man who has been an emperor to end up as a fugitive.'[73]

There are good reasons not to accept the finer details of Procopius' account of Theodora's speech. But we have no reason to doubt that the emperor would have consulted her, or that he would have accepted her advice. Justinian had, after all, made it clear from the start that he regarded Theodora not just as an empress, but as his active and closest partner in the business of government. What is less clear is whether Justinian's proposed exit from the palace was meant to signify a total abandonment of the throne or, perhaps more likely, a tactical retreat such as Origen had proposed suggesting to the emperor.[74] Either way, their boldness stiffened by Theodora's exhortations, Justinian and his circle now set about planning how best to defend themselves and take on the emperor's foes in what was potentially a last stand. 'All hopes', Procopius tells us, 'centred on Belisarius and Mundo' and the battle-hardened troops who followed them as their private military entourages. The imperial guards and regular troops present in and around the palace could not be trusted, because, as Procopius claimed, 'They were neither well-disposed to the emperor, nor willing openly to take an active part in the fighting, but were simply waiting to see what the future would hold.'[75] Belisarius' and Mundo's men, by contrast, were bound by personal oaths of loyalty and service to follow their masters into battle. The evident devotion to Justinian of these two men was thus the single thread on which the emperor's hopes for survival now depended.[76]

Preparations were made for a triple-pronged assault on the

rioters and insurgents. First, an Armenian military commander and courtier, Narses (who had recently defected to the Romans from the Persians), slipped out of the palace, and, with the aid of his men, began to distribute money amongst members of the Blue Faction (with which Justinian had long been associated) in order to buy up their support. Soon, these erstwhile rioters 'broke away and began to chant, "Augustus, Justinian, may you be victorious! Lord preserve Justinian and Theodora!"' This turn of events provoked a furious backlash from members of the Green Faction, who 'rushed on them and stoned them'. Second, seeking to take advantage of the ensuing confusion—and distributing further bribes, in order to buy up support amongst the palace guard—Narses and his troops were joined by Mundo and his men, who emerged out of the palace complex and took up positions at the gate south of the Hippodrome.[77] Third, Belisarius and members of his entourage then attempted to break through to the *kathisma*, but their path was blocked by guardsmen unwilling to be seen to assist either side. Instead, he was obliged to lead his men out through the remnants of the Chalke Gate of the palace, through the 'ruins and half-burned-out buildings', and across to a colonnade to the right of the imperial box. There he found that soldiers loyal to Hypatius were guarding the narrow doorway that led up to it.[78]

Rather than trying to fight his way through this tight space and risk being trapped, Belisarius ordered his men to take up the war cry and join him in charging with swords drawn directly into the crowd, where the faction members were now busy fighting each other. Advancing from their respective positions, Mundo, Narses, and their men likewise joined the fray, initiating what would prove to be a prodigious slaughter of the rioters. As Procopius relates, 'Then indeed from both sides the insurgents who supported Hypatius were assailed and destroyed. When the rout had become complete and there had already been great slaughter of the populace, Boraïdes and Justin, cousins of the emperor Justinian, without anyone daring to lift a hand against them, dragged Hypatius down from the throne, and leading him in, handed him together with Pompey over to the emperor.' Procopius reckoned that over the course of the day, more than thirty thousand rioters were killed (the Hippodrome of Constantinople, it has been estimated, could hold roughly one hundred thousand spectators at any one time).[79] Although this figure (which may have amounted to somewhere in the region of 5 percent of the total population of Constantinople) is to be treated with some caution, the number conveys the author's sense of a massacre on a massive scale.[80] The next day, Monday, 19 January, Hypatius and Pompey were executed and their bodies thrown into the sea. 'The emperor', Procopius relates, 'confiscated all their property for the public treasury, and also that of all the other members of the Senate which had sided with them.' 'This', he wrote, 'was the end of the insurrection in Byzantium.'[81]

The 'Nika riots', as they would come to be known to posterity (*Nika* meaning 'Conquer'), were not the first outbreak of mass violence on the streets of Constantinople, nor would they be the last. In terms of scale, duration, and sheer destructiveness, however, they were unprecedented.[82] The uprising was initially fuelled by Justinian's shifting attitude towards the Circus Factions. As an aspirant to imperial power, he had manipulated the faction members to his own advantage. As emperor, he now wanted them to desist from their lawlessness, and accordingly, he had ordered his officers to crack down on their activities. From Justinian's viewpoint, this shift in policy was entirely rational. From the perspective of the factions themselves, it was at best confusing, and at worst a betrayal. The emperor's antagonistic attitude towards them in the Hippodrome itself had then set the scene for the crisis that would unfold. As the riots escalated, and the forces of law and order in Constantinople were shown to be incapable of restoring control, the crisis also provided an opportunity for Justinian's opponents in the city to move against first his chief ministers, and then ultimately the emperor himself. The anger of the mob had been fanned, manipulated, and harnessed by those well-connected elements within Constantinopolitan political society which had probably always regarded Justinian and Theodora as distasteful *parvenus*, as well as by others who were increasingly becoming alarmed by the direction of imperial policy. Procopius was of the opinion that the riots had broken out 'unexpectedly', before escalating into 'a very serious affair' which 'did a great deal of harm to both the people and the Senate'.[83] As the corpses of Hypatius, Pompey, and the other thousands of victims of the uprising bobbed and rotted in the sea off the Golden Horn, and as the core of the capital lay smouldering in ruins, many of Procopius' contemporaries are likely to have agreed.

Chapter 7

Building Heaven on Earth

'BETTER AND MORE BEAUTIFUL, STRONGER AND MORE SAFE'

In the aftermath of the crushing of the Nika riots, we are told, Justinian 'immediately announced his victory to all the cities under his sovereignty and the destruction of the usurpers who had risen against him'.[1] The uprising had rocked the regime to its very foundation and almost driven Justinian and Theodora to abandon the imperial capital, and with it their hold on power. Despite the fact that they did—just—retain control, the destruction of the monumental heart of Constantinople, and many of the buildings in which the highest offices of state had been based, had a tangible impact on the effective workings of government. It is striking that we have almost no evidence for any new legislation being issued between the uprising in mid-January 532 and the late autumn. The usual rhythm of imperial administration only began to resume in October: Justinian issued almost twenty new laws in that month alone, as opposed to barely any in the preceding nine. The one substantial measure he issued soon after the riots was an order to rescind an attempted reduction in the distribution of bread rations to the population of Constantinople—a clear sign that the emperor was now once more determined to buy up support on the streets of the imperial capital, as he had first done when he was consul.[2]

Justinian's initial political response to the insurrection was a revealing mix of opportunism and conciliation. As the Senate House lay in ruins, he took advantage of the situation to move against a number of his long-standing enemies and rivals who had previously made the Senate their base of operations, and seized their estates. He also restored John the Cappadocian and Tribonian to their respective offices, allowing the latter to resume work on the compilation and editing of the *Digest*. Belisarius was also reinstated as commander-in-chief of the field army of the East (*magister militum per orientem*). When the emperor did once more begin to issue new laws, he adopted a notably humbler tone than he had done prior to the uprising, and wrapped himself ever more tightly in the rhetorical embrace of his Christian faith. He would declare in a law issued in the early months of 533, for example, 'Serving the Saviour and Lord of All, Jesus Christ, our True God in all things, We also wish to imitate His humility, insofar as the human mind can comprehend it.'[3] At the same time, he attempted to rebuild political bridges with elements of the Constantinopolitan political establishment, including the household of the late emperor Anastasius and erstwhile allies of Anicia Iuliana (who may have been dead by this point). Anastasius' nephews, Hypatius and Pompey, were granted posthumous pardons. Justinian even ordered a cenotaph to be built to honour Hypatius' memory, bearing a carefully worded dedicatory epigram: 'I am the tomb of Hypatius; but small as I am, I make no claim to cover the body of so great a champion of the Romans.

The earth blushed to bury the mighty man beneath a paltry tomb-stone, and preferred to entrust him to the keeping of the deep.[4]

Justinian also reached out to alienated elements within the imperial Church. In the spring of 532—just a few months after the uprising—he personally convened a three-day conference within the Palace of Hormisdas: here, five pro-Chalcedonian and five anti-Chalcedonian bishops associated with the deposed patriarch of Antioch, Severus, met to discuss the prospects for a restoration of unity. The participants kept minutes of the conversations, and copies of these survive to this day.[5] According to the record of proceedings preserved in Syriac by the dissident party, after two days of tit-for-tat theological debate and point-scoring, Justinian addressed the anti-Chalcedonian representatives pragmatically and in a positive manner, making it clear that, for all their differences, he still regarded them as an essential part of the imperial Church. 'I am not of the opinion', he reportedly told them, 'that you do not think in an orthodox fashion.' Instead, their refusal to share communion with defenders of the Chalcedonian theological formula was due to what he regarded as 'excessive scruples over detail' on their part, over which he hoped to be able to reassure them.[6]

Justinian then asked the bishops if they would be willing to join an imperial delegation which the emperor hoped to send to Rome, Alexandria, Antioch, and Jerusalem to discuss the controversy. This they declined on the grounds of old age. Justinian then requested that they commit in writing not to ordain a separate and parallel clergy, or to try to win over defectors amongst the laity from pro-Chalcedonian congregations. Again, they refused, on the grounds that Justinian had already forbidden them from doing this, and that it would be insulting to the emperor for them to have to promise in writing to obey his commands. Nor were they willing to swear an oath orally to comply with these instructions, as Church law forbade priests from taking oaths.[7] Eventually, Justinian, no doubt increasingly exasperated, asked the bishops to at least try to make some concrete proposals for the restoration of unity. They refused to budge an inch. Finally, in a remarkable concession, the emperor proposed a compromise: Would they, he asked, be willing to accept the Council of Chalcedon insofar as it had denounced a series of hardline thinkers at *both* ends of the theological spectrum, whom most could agree were basically heretical, whilst agreeing to differ on the main issues in contention, and thus preserve their doctrinal integrity? Essentially, Justinian was asking the dissident bishops to accept the validity of the Council of Chalcedon with respect to its *disciplinary* provisions, whilst being allowed to continue to differ from its *theological* provisions, and thereby to be reintegrated into the main body of the imperial Church.[8] Aware that he would have to sell any such deal to the papacy in Rome, Justinian asked for the following concessions in return: that the dissidents drop their condemnation of a publicly circulated letter (known as the 'Tome') that the fifth-century Roman Pope Leo had composed setting out his two-nature Christology, which had acquired totemic status in the eyes of the Council of Chalcedon's western defenders; and that they drop their demand that a statement of faith (known as a *libellus*) issued by the late Pope Hormisdas be rescinded.[9] The *libellus* had ordered that the names of the bishops and patriarchs who had led resistance to the Chalcedonian definition of the faith be removed from the public records (the diptychs) of the Church that were read out during the liturgy.[10]

In the wake of the Nika riots, Justinian showed himself to be willing to make enormous theological concessions to opponents of the Council of Chalcedon in order to restore unity to the imperial Church. He even moved against hardline monastic supporters of Chalcedon (the *Akoimetai*, 'Sleepless Ones') in Constantinople, whose antics were in danger of scuppering his efforts. However, his request that the dissident bishops accept the '*libellus* of the Romans', as the Syriac account of the negotiations describes it, proved to be too much for most of them to bear, as it effectively required them to accept the legitimacy of Rome's condemnation of those theologians of the previous generation whom they and their followers regarded as heroes, and the talks broke down.[11] It was not for want of trying on Justinian's part, and the emperor's efforts would not end there. In March 533, he issued a lengthy and detailed public profession of faith composed with a view to drawing together moderate supporters and opponents of Chalcedon. It placed particular emphasis on his devotion to the Virgin Mary (known in Greek as the *Theotokos*, or 'she who bore God'), who had come to be regarded as the city of Constantinople's divine patron, and where she was revered by the overwhelming majority of Christians of both pro- and anti-Chalcedonian inclinations.[12]

Justinian's religious initiatives in the immediate aftermath of the Nika riots reveal both how he himself was coming to understand the events of that dreadful week and how he wished others to understand them. For at the same time that he was presiding over negotiations with the dissident clergyman, he and his supporters were making a concerted effort to shape and inflect public understanding of what had occurred in the capital. The emperor concentrated on blazoning his determination to put right the damage that had been done. His initial instinct, as reflected in imperial propaganda issued on behalf of the regime, had been to represent the uprising as an attempted coup, orchestrated by the emperor's political enemies with the assistance of lawless elements within the Circus Factions. Judging by the evidence, this was indeed what it had been. A well-informed Constantinopolitan chronicle, which drew in part upon official sources, recorded how, after crushing the rioters, 'the emperor Justinian . . . undertook to build the Great Church [*Hagia Sophia*] . . . and the palace, and all the public places of the city which had been burnt . . . after ordering the city prefect to punish those from the Blue Faction who had sided with the Greens and the remaining factions against him.' There are hints in the same account that Justinian was determined to future-proof the palace complex in which he had taken refuge against any further revolt. It records that he forthwith 'built *inside the palace* bakeries and granaries for the storage of grain, and likewise too a cistern for water in case of popular crises'.[13] Evidently, there had been moments during those dark days in January when he and those around him had been running short of supplies. The emperor wanted to make sure that would never happen again.

Progressively, however, a new interpretation of the events began to be expounded, which may help to contextualise Justinian's sudden change in ecclesiastical policy and his focus on reconciliation. This new narrative argued that the uprising and its associated wave of destruction and death were the result of collective sinfulness, as demonstrated by the spiritual pride of the opposing religious parties. It was this sin which had incited the wrath of God, who had intervened to punish mankind and call the emperor and his subjects back to the path of righteousness. As such, it was akin to an outbreak of severe famine, drought, earthquakes, or plague (occurrences which the emperor also understood as signs of divine displeasure). Some five years after the revolt, a public prayer was commissioned by the emperor from the brilliant contemporary hymnographer Romanos, to be celebrated in the imperial capital in remembrance of the uprising and its aftermath. The revolt, Romanos noted, had come in the wake of repeated earthquakes and famines: as mankind had failed to learn its lesson from these, God had been obliged to send the riots as a third and still more terrifying call to repentance: 'The Creator delivered a first blow, and a second, but he did not find that men were becoming better—rather, progressively worse. So, he placed despair on the very altar of grace and allowed to burn the hallowed precincts of the churches. . . . The wails of the mob poured out into the city's streets and churches, for fire would have destroyed everything, if God had not come out and given to us all eternal life.'[14]

The shift in divine attitude from one of punishment to compassion, Romanos argued, had been the direct result of imperial intercession. Justinian and Theodora had petitioned God on behalf of their subjects, with the emperor addressing the Lord directly: 'The city was buried beneath these horrors and cried in great sorrow. Those who feared God stretched out their hands to him, begging for compassion and an end to the terror. Reasonably, the emperor—and his empress—were in these ranks, their eyes uplifted in hope towards the Creator: "Grant me victory", he said, "just as you made David victorious over Goliath. You are my hope. Rescue, in your mercy, your loyal people and grant them eternal life."'[15]

The tone and language of the emperor's reported intercession deliberately depicted him to be as much priest as emperor. At the same time, the act of restoring and rebuilding the city would be presented in terms of the emperor emulating God himself, his re-creation of Constantinople echoing the Lord's primordial act of cosmic creation. As John Lydus would put it, 'The emperor's Fortune overcame, in all respects, the heap of ruins . . . just as if the Creator . . . were again calling forth the universe into light out of formless matter by the mere power of His volition.'[16] Justinian's top priority was the reconstruction of the 'Great Church' of Hagia Sophia, which he undertook, we are told, to build 'zealously . . . and better'.[17] He is reported to have begun work on it just a few weeks after the crushing of the Nika riots.[18] In a remarkable mobilisation of resources, he would achieve this feat in just five years and ten months, as part of a broader project to, in the words of Lydus, make the city 'better and more beautiful, stronger and more safe'.[19]

'THIS MIRACULOUS TEMPLE'

Viewed from the Bosphorus, the historical old town of Istanbul, located on the promontory overlooking the 'Golden Horn', remains to this day dominated by the stately domes of Justinian's rebuilt Cathedral of Holy Wisdom, or Hagia Sophia. After the Ottoman conquest of the city in 1453, a series of Turkish minarets, appointed like sentries guarding a much prized but slightly ramshackle possession, came to accompany it. The somewhat drab outer appearance of Hagia Sophia today preserves the outward form of the Justinianic church, but none of its lustre. The sixth-century original, recent archaeological excavations have confirmed, was clad with sheets of white marble that would have reflected the beams of the sun like a beacon of holiness, drawing in the faithful and illuminating the heart of the greatest city in the Roman world.[20] This was as nothing, however, compared to its spectacular interior, today muffled and occluded by blocked-out windows, scaffolding, carpets, and screens. For many centuries prior to the Ottoman conquest, the effect of entering this church—beholding the sunlight streaming in through its glass windows, hearing the divine liturgy being chanted in Greek by throngs of priests and the assembled ranks of the faithful, the scents of the incense wafting on the air, its smoke rising majestically to the upper reaches of its vaults and galleries—was deemed one of the most spiritually overpowering experiences a Christian could encounter. Especially when combined with the sacrament of Holy Communion—tasting the bread consecrated by the priests, and believed to be transformed into the 'Body of Christ'—it would indeed have constituted a total sensory experience.

In recent years, architectural historians, sound engineers, medieval musicologists (including my former colleague Alexander Lingas), and experts in computer-generated images, led by the US-based art historian Bissera Pentcheva, have learned how to re-create much of the unique visual, acoustic, and emotional impact of Hagia Sophia as a place of Christian worship in its prime.[21] In particular, through the recordings made by Lingas and his musical ensemble Capella Romana, we are able to appreciate why in the tenth century, for example, Scandinavian visitors from the recently founded principality of Kyiv chose to adopt imperial (or 'Orthodox') Christianity on the grounds that, in Hagia Sophia, they believed they had witnessed the place where God Himself dwelled.[22] The psychological and emotional impact of the church was not limited to Christians, or even to those considering adopting the religion. Since their restoration in the mid-2010s, visitors have once again been able to marvel at a series of mosaic images of angelic powers, or seraphim, in each of the four pendentives that seem to hover beneath the central dome. These depictions, which date from a later period of Byzantine history, are so overwhelmingly ethereal in appearance and impression that one medieval Muslim visitor to the city even reported back home that a great angel lived there.[23]

Justinian gave the commission to rebuild the Great Church to two architects, Anthemius of Tralles (a famous mathematician), and Isidore of Miletus. As was noted by the late Cyril Mango, professor of Byzantine and Modern Greek at Oxford, whose knowledge of the history of this building was unrivalled, 'We may imagine that they were chosen because they combined practical experience with a high degree of theoretical knowledge, but, in fact, we do not know of any other building that either of them had created.'[24] Rather as with his praetorian prefect, John the Cappadocian, and his chief legal officer, Tribonian, Justinian appears to have appointed these men on the basis of trust rather than track record. The emperor is also reported to have taken a personal interest in the design of his new church and its execution.

In terms of design, Justinian's new Hagia Sophia would signal a dramatic break with the past. The previous structure had probably been a five-aisled 'basilica' church, quadrilateral in form with a pitched roof, the standard model for cathedral churches in Rome since the fourth century.[25] The new church, by contrast, was to be built around a vast central dome. The concept of a domed church was not new: Justinian's Church of Saints Sergius and Bacchus had been built as an octagon around a dome, and Anicia Iuliana's Saint

Polyeuktos may also have been domed. A tradition of domed architecture also existed with respect to pre-Christian buildings in Rome (such as the Pantheon) and churches in Syria. In Rome, Thessalonica, and elsewhere, small domed baptisteries had been built. Nobody, however, had attempted to build a domed church on the scale which Justinian and his architects now appeared to be contemplating.[26]

When it was finally completed, Hagia Sophia, some ninety-seven metres long and seventy metres wide, was probably the largest building in the world. The 'scale and height of its great dome', it has been noted, 'remained unsurpassed until the Renaissance version of Saint Peter's in Rome was completed in the sixteenth century.'[27] It has been estimated that it was large enough to accommodate some sixteen thousand worshippers at any one time.[28] The current central dome, a slightly lower replacement of the original, soars almost fifty-six metres above the ground, with a diameter of thirty-one metres (or one hundred Byzantine feet). Its internal height is equivalent to that of a fifteen-story building. This dome rested on four massive piers (each over twenty-three metres tall) propped aloft a series of pendentives, with arch resting upon arch.[29] As Procopius wrote, rising above the central circle of the church was 'an enormous spherical dome, which makes the building exceptionally beautiful'. He continued: 'It seems not to be founded on solid masonry, but to be suspended from heaven by a golden chain . . . and so to cover the space. All of these elements, marvellously fitted together in mid-air, suspended on one another and reposing only on the parts adjacent to them, produce a unified and most remarkable harmony in the work.'[30] Viewed externally from street level, or as one sailed towards Constantinople, the new Hagia Sophia dwarfed even the tallest of the city's earlier structures and monuments (such as the column of Constantine).[31] As Procopius again described, 'It soars to a height to match the sky, and as if surging up from amongst the other buildings it stands on high and looks down upon the remainder of the city, adorning it, because it is a part of it, but glorying in its own beauty, because though a part of the city and dominating it, it at the same time towers above it to such a height that the whole city is viewed from there as from a watch tower.'[32] Whilst the inner space of Justinian's Hagia Sophia thus emphasised transcendence, its outer appearance arguably conveyed a sense of domination.[33] Neither impression would have displeased its great imperial sponsor.

So novel a construction inevitably posed great structural and technological challenges. As Cyril Mango put it, 'Justinian's architects strained to the utmost the technical possibilities at their disposal, and even overstretched them.' The brick and heavily mortared masonry that typified the built environment of Byzantine Constantinople had an inherent tendency towards unevenness in the course of construction: by the time one wall had been constructed, earlier walls would have settled, leading to internal tensions between them. The larger the construction, the more likely this was to lead to overall irregularity of execution, irrespective of how careful the initial plan.[34] The 'ingeniousness of the design' of Saints Sergius and Bacchus, it has been noted, had thus stood in contrast to the 'sloppiness of the execution' resulting from the need of the builders to engage in 'on the spot compensation' to resolve structural difficulties as they inevitably emerged. With Hagia Sophia, such problems were inevitably even greater. According to Procopius, at one point during its construction, the eastern arch supporting the central dome began to give way, and it was only salvaged by the personal intervention of the emperor himself, who proposed a solution to the despairing architects.[35] We have reason to be slightly suspicious of this account, but it probably conveys an accurate sense of the difficulties the builders faced.

Traditional studies of Hagia Sophia emphasise its remarkable architectural features, but what brought the building to life was the way in which the construction facilitated an extraordinary synergy between light, sound, and, ultimately, taste and smell. The sixth-century church as built by Justinian contained almost three hundred windows, which were carefully configured to capture the morning and evening light when the services of *matins* and *vespers* were performed. Indeed, the emperor would be credited with personally composing two hymns that were to be celebrated at or after these services: the *Monogenes* ('The Only Begotten Son') and the *Phos Hilaron* ('O Gladsome Light'). Further illumination was provided by a vast array of oil lamps and candles, which were harnessed to create what has been termed a 'hierarchy of light' within the church: a luminous *naos*, the central space where the liturgy was performed, surrounded by softer light in the church galleries, aisles, and narthexes.[36]

The subtly changing configuration of natural light within Hagia Sophia served to create a series of what were, to all intents and purposes, 'special effects' within the expanse of the church, making the white-grey marble on the floor and lower walls (transported to the site from the nearby island of Proconnesos) seem to shimmer and gently undulate like the sea.[37] The effects of both the sunlight and the artificial light on the stupendous array of golden glass tesserae on the vault surfaces and upper walls of the church resulted in a vast glowing effect and an overpowering sense of internal luminescence, which, in the words of Procopius, made it seem that 'the space was not illuminated by the sun from the outside, but . . . the radiance was generated from within', the light first mirroring the morning sun but then gradually building up and emanating outwards. The largely geometric scheme of internal decoration of the church would have intensified the worshipper's engagement with the light and its reflection off the gold, silver, and marble panelling of various shades and hues, leading the eye to respond to the overall effect of glitter and shine rather than attempting to focus on any particular image. As Procopius, again, described it, 'Thus the vision constantly shifts round, and the beholders are quite unable to select any particular element which they might admire more than all the others. No matter how much they concentrate their attention on this side and that, and examine everything with contracted eyebrows, they are unable to understand the craftsmanship, and always depart from there amazed.'[38]

These visual effects combined with the remarkable acoustic properties of the structure. The enormous inner space of the central dome, in particular (the nave has been estimated as containing a volume of some 255,800 cubic metres), amplified the voices of the four hundred or so priests, choristers, and other attendants who were employed to chant the liturgy in conjunction with the laity. A carefully engineered reverberation more than ten seconds in length transformed the human voice and human language into a euphonic whole which itself would have filled the space and absorbed the worshipper in contemplation of and participation in the divine mysteries. On top of this we should imagine the swirling clouds of incense and the ethereal jangling of censers and thuribles. The combined effect would have been one of total sensory immersion—'an aesthetic totality—optical and acoustic'.[39] To the late antique worshipper, it would have engaged the mind and elevated it to a state of divine contemplation. As Procopius put it, 'And so the visitor's mind is lifted up to God and floats aloft, thinking that He cannot be far away, but loves to dwell in this place, which He himself has chosen.'[40]

Procopius' emphasis on the intellectual and sensory responses elicited by Hagia Sophia is important, for in the sixth century, transcendence was believed to harness and sharpen the rational mind's ability to engage with and understand the cosmos, not as an escape from it (as it tends to be in some modern Western 'counter-cultures'). The design of Justinian's Hagia Sophia, and the careful engineering of the sensory experience within it, were intimately connected to the intellectual culture of the era and the way in which the educated viewer and worshipper would have understood the holy space. Light, for example, was understood as both a representation and embodiment of holiness. It was 'the symbol of God, and specifically Christ'. Gold, too, was associated with the divine.[41] The acoustic effects of the church not only conveyed a sensation of 'divine nearness', but also may have been understood as serving to transform the language of man into the otherworldly language of angels (especially through the chanting of the 'Alleluia' and during the celebration of the Feast of Pentecost, commemorating the day when the Holy Spirit had descended on Christ's disciples following the Resurrection and they had 'spoken in tongues').[42]

Above all, the great spherical dome, which presided over not just the church itself but over the entire city of Constantinople, would have been understood by the educated viewer in the context of a long tradition within ancient philosophy—namely, Neoplatonism—which would leave a deep imprint on Christianity. According to this view, the 'demiurge' (the supreme being, or the maker or creator of the cosmos) was believed to be capable of interacting with the created world through the 'luminous sphere', where heaven and earth met. The dome of Hagia Sophia was meant to evoke this sphere—it was the 'middle place' (Greek *to metaxu*), where mankind could experience the presence of God and achieve 'Holy Wisdom'. As the great sixth-century hymnographer Romanos described the church in celebration of its reinauguration under Justinian, 'This miraculous temple shall become known above all others as the most sacred dwelling space of God, the one which manifestly exhibits a quality worthy of God, since it surpasses the whole of mankind's knowledge of building. Both in its material form and through its liturgy it is seen to be—yes— and proclaims—a kind of heaven on earth which God has chosen for his own habitation.' Unlike the churches of the Holy Land or

Rome, which celebrated the places where Christ had lived or where the disciples had been martyred, Hagia Sophia was in and of itself a uniquely 'holy space'.[43]

'THE PROJECT GLEAMS IN GLORY'

The newly reconstructed and transformed Great Church of Hagia Sophia was formally consecrated on 27 December 537 by the emperor Justinian and Menas, patriarch of Constantinople. The hymn Romanos wrote to celebrate the event declared Justinian and Theodora to have surpassed even the biblical King Solomon in their architectural achievement (a claim which Anicia Iuliana had previously made). The name of Theodora is often passed over in accounts of the Justinianic reconstruction of Hagia Sophia, but at the time it was made clear that the project of reconstruction had been a joint enterprise between the emperor and his consort. Throughout Hagia Sophia (as also in the Church of Saints Sergius and Bacchus), marble columns were topped with capitals decorated with monograms bearing the names or titles of both rulers. Eighty-nine of these columns ascribe the work to Justinian, and thirty to Theodora.[44] Procopius saw the church as a sort of watchtower overlooking the city. Justinian and Theodora probably thought of it rather more as a divine guard-tower, defending it. In the centre of its great dome stood a cross to emphasise this role. As the sixth-century poet and courtier Paul the Silentiary would write in his account of the church, 'Above all rises into the immeasurable air the great helmet [the dome], which bending over like the radiant heavens, embraces the church. And at the highest part, at the crown, was depicted the cross, the protector of the city.' The same symbol was to be found in mosaic decorations throughout the church, along with the so-called Christogram (the Chi-Rho symbol, depicting the first two letters of the name of Christ, which the emperor Constantine had supposedly ordered his troops to place on their shields after his adoption of Christianity).[45] 'In this sign you conquer [*Nika!*],' Constantine had been told. Were these symbols perhaps also an allusion to and refutation of the chants of the Nika rioters?

Within the Great Church, various elements of design emphasised Justinian and Theodora's personal care for the well-being of their subjects and their efforts at divine intercession on their behalf. According to the same Paul, the richly embroidered silk cloth that adorned the high altar, for example, depicted scenes of the rulers acting 'as guardians of the city': 'Here you may see hospitals for the sick, there shrines. . . . And upon other veils you will see the monarchs joined together, here by the hand of Mary, the Mother of God, there by that of Christ, and all is adorned with the sheen of golden thread.'[46]

The reconstruction of Hagia Sophia was on so large a scale and completed in so short a time that it would long be regarded as little less than miraculous. Indeed, a later and popular Byzantine account claimed it had been designed by an angel, who revealed the plans to the emperor. The same source relates that Justinian spent the equivalent of one year's tax revenue from Egypt—the wealthiest province in the entire Roman world—on the project, and that the labour of ten thousand craftsmen was required to bring it to completion.[47] Large quantities of glass, gold, and silver were needed to make the mosaic tesserae that covered the almost ten thousand square metres of decorated space contained within the cathedral. These were probably mass-produced just outside the city walls.[48] 'The amount of co-ordination and pre-planning necessary for the enterprise', as a great authority on Byzantine architecture has noted, 'is staggering.'[49]

The speed with which the church was constructed necessarily came at a price. Justinian's constant refrain of 'Hurry!' (*Celerrite!*) was not always a wise one. Nearby provinces were ransacked for marble columns to reuse in the construction of the Great

Church—especially columns made in red porphyry, which came only from Egypt, and which had ceased to be quarried in the fifth century. The columns that were found were of uneven size, but were deployed anyway. 'Within the broad guidelines of the overall design', Cyril Mango noted, 'there is endless variation and improvisation—at times even sloppiness. This confers on the building a feeling of life, of the unexpected; it is, on the other hand, quite disconcerting to an observer steeped in the classical tradition, and we can readily understand the disappointment of travellers in the eighteenth and early nineteenth centuries, who found St. Sophia "Gothick".' Moreover, constructing a dome on so vast a scale and with contemporary building techniques and materials posed almost insurmountable difficulties: 'No architect at the time', Mango commented, 'could have calculated, even approximately, the thrusts that would be generated by a masonry dome of that size.' Indeed, the great dome would collapse and have to be rebuilt with a slightly lower curvature in 558. But it was remarkable that the original had survived as long as it did, and what did it in finally was not any inherent fault, but a series of earthquakes that struck the city in 553 and 557. No Roman or Byzantine emperor after Justinian would build a church even half the size of Hagia Sophia.[50] Never to be surpassed, the Great Church would thus come to stand as the epitome of both imperial and Christian architecture for centuries to come.

Justinian's construction of Hagia Sophia revealed and reflected much of the emperor's personality and mindset. The speed with which he ordered it to be constructed was testimony to his constant impatience. The audaciousness of the church's design mirrored his characteristic impetuousness, and its scale embodied the emperor's urge to dominate and surpass. Moreover, his determination to imprint on the monument not only his own name, but also that of his wife, provided further tangible proof of his utter devotion to Theodora. At the same time, Justinian seized the more general opportunity presented by the destruction wrought by the Nika riots to rebuild not just the monumental heart of his capital, but also much of the city beyond, in such a way that it would serve to celebrate his regime, consolidate his grip on power, and advance his ideological agenda. For one major effect of this wave of imperially sponsored construction was to imprint much more firmly in architectural form the Christian character of the city. Another was to impose the person of the emperor upon the capital as its presiding genius.

Over the course of the period from 532 to about 543, when the empire would undergo a sudden change in circumstances, Justinian directed an extraordinary programme of urban renewal.[51] In addition to the great water cistern built adjacent to the palace (known as the 'Basilica Cistern', or, in Turkish, the *Yerebatan sarayi*), this included thirty-two more churches, six hospices, palaces, public buildings and amenities (such as new government buildings and additional cisterns), and new harbours for the city. Although not on the scale of Hagia Sophia, some of these churches, such as the domed basilica church of Saint Irene, adjacent to the imperial palace, or the rebuilt Church of the Holy Apostles, in which the emperors since Constantine had been buried, were both large and exquisite.[52] The former remains to this day one of the finest standing monuments of Byzantine Constantinople, whilst the latter, although destroyed by the Ottoman Turks, constituted one of the two earliest examples of a cruciform church with multiple domes, a style with a long afterlife in Byzantine and Eastern Orthodox church building. It would also be the inspiration behind the construction of the magnificent basilica of Saint Mark's in Venice.[53]

The nature of the destruction wrought by the Nika rioters was such that Justinian could not completely neglect secular construction and monuments. Monumental squares, such as that of the *Augustaeon* (just south of Hagia Sophia), had to be rebuilt, as did the

Senate House and the Baths of Zeuxippus. However, the religious buildings were Justinian's main focus, not only in the city but also in its suburbs and on surrounding islands. This emphasis represented 'a radical reversal of previous imperial campaigns, where the greatest efforts had been directed toward the development of civic spaces and the institutions they housed', one historian has observed. As a result, Constantinople became the Christian city par excellence, less 'New Rome' and more 'New Jerusalem' (Map 4).[54]

Non-Christian antiquities that had hitherto adorned the capital but which had been damaged in the revolt were treated with relative indifference unless they had specifically imperial associations. So, for example, whilst the Baths of Zeuxippus were rebuilt, they were restored without any of the ancient sculptures that had formerly stood there, their statue bases reused as paving slabs for the new construction. A large number of pagan statues were also removed from the *Augustaeon* during its repair. Likewise, within the gloomy depths of the Basilica Cistern, it is still possible to discern the sculptures of gorgons and other mythological characters that were reused to support the columns that propped up the roof of Justinian's vast new subterranean reservoir. Many of these sculptures appear to have been deliberately placed upside down or on their sides by the sixth-century stonemasons and builders, perhaps to trap or to contain the demonic powers and magical properties with which Christians increasingly associated such statues and images.[55]

The projection of the personal authority and might of the emperor was another major objective of Justinian's project of urban renewal in the capital. Those passing through the rebuilt main entrance to the imperial palace, at the Chalke Gate which the rioters had destroyed in 532, for example, would have witnessed a series of magnificent mosaics which glorified the emperor. In the dome of the gatehouse were placed images of Justinian, Theodora, and the court, whilst the lower vaults contained scenes of military victories over which he had presided.[56] Of still greater visual effect, in the rebuilt square of the *Augustaeon*, Justinian erected an enormous column on which he placed a bronze statue of himself on horseback. This monument replaced a silver statue of the emperor Theodosius, which was melted down to pay for the new commission.[57] The new statue depicted Justinian facing east: in one hand he held a globe with a cross upon it (known as the *globus cruciger*)—a symbol of universal authority and Christian triumph. His other hand was raised aloft, outstretched and palm facing forward, as if, according to Procopius, he were ordering the 'barbarians' of the East—the great rival power of Sasanian Persia—to halt and advance no further.[58] Such crosses and globes also feature prominently in the decoration of Justiniana Prima.[59]

As with Hagia Sophia, the scale of this column and its associated 'equestrian statue' was vast. Looming over the city of Constantinople—the column alone is estimated to have stood at some seventy metres—it was, in the words of the author of a fascinating recent study, Elena Boeck, 'the tallest free-standing column in the pre-modern world . . . crowned by arguably the largest metal, equestrian statue created anywhere in the world before 1699'. The horse itself appears to have been reused from a monument which had previously stood in the Forum of Theodosius, but the column was both new and novel. Unlike previous such monuments, it consisted of a masonry column clad in luminous bronze so as to catch and reflect sunlight. As Boeck has noted, 'We have to imagine the towering column of the *Augustaeon* engaging in a close visual dialogue with the Great Church: both were shimmering, literally dazzling monuments (marble on the exterior of Hagia Sophia and glowing bronze on the monument, the shaft, and capital), both were breathtakingly tall, both celebrated Justinian, and both redefined the skyline of Constantinople.' Probably erected in 543, it would mark the culmination of Justinian's transformation of the imperial capital. Until its destruction by the Ottoman Turks after their conquest of Constantinople, the statue would long be famed as one of the great marvels of the medieval world.[60]

NEW OPPORTUNITIES

At the same time that he was rebuilding his capital, Justinian was also engaged in major building projects along the empire's eastern and northern frontiers. These were primarily, although not only, of a defensive nature. But many of the structures he ordered to be built in these regions were also of remarkably high quality. 'The Age of Justinian', as Cyril Mango put it, 'certainly represents the high point of Early Byzantine architecture. In many ways it is comparable to the age of Louis XIV.'[61] Within Constantinople itself, the net result of the emperor's building programme, a recent commentator has concluded, was effectively to turn the 'City of Constantine' into the 'City of Justinian'.[62] Political conditions both within the city and across the empire more generally were also transformed. In the years that followed the Nika riots, Justinian would increasingly turn to members of his own family to fill high-ranking posts, especially military ones.[63] As well as rebuilding the Senate House, the emperor effectively reinvented the Senate of Constantinople itself, progressively limiting active membership in that body to actual officeholders and diluting its hereditary character.[64] Projections of imperial authority and power also became increasingly Christian in character and form. The emperor came to be depicted on his coinage gazing directly out at his subjects—such as was common in contemporary images, or 'icons', of Christ and the saints—and holding aloft the same globe and cross which he also brandished atop his column in Constantinople.[65] His opportunism in the face of the attempted coup against him had been breathtaking both in its audacity and its success. The events of January 532 had perhaps demonstrated to Justinian the wisdom of the ancient Latin proverb that 'Fortune favours the brave'.[66] This was important, for in the aftermath of the Nika riots, new opportunities arose both at home and abroad. They, too, required daring and self-belief, but having faced down his foes in Constantinople, Justinian was now lacking in neither.

PART 3

Imperial Expansion and Power

Chapter 8

The African
Campaign

SAINTS AND SINNERS

The remains of the ancient harbours of Carthage now lie
enroute towards the drab port facilities of a district outside
the modern city of Tunis, known as 'La Goulette'. Only the vagu-
est of outlines of the Roman and Vandal inner harbour are still
visible to the naked eye, a faint reminder of the vast commercial
wealth underpinning the fortunes of this once magnificent Mediterranean entrepôt. When I visited La Goulette in the late 1990s,
my host looked at me somewhat askance when I suggested that we
head there so that I could peer at the watery remnants of the site.
While Tunis by then had lost much of the salacious reputation that
had made it such a popular destination for bohemian travellers

and writers earlier in the twentieth century, ports inevitably tend to possess a somewhat seedy character. And even in the context of ancient Mediterranean seaports, Carthage in the fifth and sixth centuries was regarded as especially louche. Writing around the middle years of the fifth century, the Christian clergyman Salvian of Marseilles had denounced its brothels and fleshpots, which, he claimed, were notorious for the availability within them of male transvestite prostitutes: 'men pretending to be women without even a hint of modesty or a cloak of shame'.[1]

From Justinian's perspective, the moral character of the city had further deteriorated under the Vandals, who had conquered Carthage and the territories of Roman North Africa in the fifth century before forcing the imperial authorities to sign a treaty acknowledging the legitimacy of their rule there. For while the Vandal leadership was nominally Christian, the Vandal priests advocated the theology of the fourth-century churchman Arius, whom the imperial authorities in Constantinople regarded as a heretic. The Vandals, in turn, regarded the leaders of the imperial (or 'Catholic') Church in the territories over which they ruled as hostile agents of imperial influence.

Faced with resistance from anti-Arian Catholic priests within their new domain, the Vandal authorities had initiated a persecution of the most recalcitrant amongst them. This process reached a peak under King Huneric in the late fifth century, who had presided over a council of the pro-Arian church, which began to develop a richer and more complex theology. As a result of his hardline policies and the stiffening of 'Arian' doctrine under his rule, many had fled to Constantinople, imploring the imperial authorities to intervene on their behalf. Around the year 500, an African clergyman, Bishop Victor of Vita, had penned a deliberately lurid account of the sufferings of the Catholic Church under the Vandals which was clearly intended to elicit an imperial response.[2] Likewise, many of the wealthiest African landowners, who had found themselves at the wrong end of repeated land grabs by the Vandal leadership, petitioned emperors in Constantinople to intervene.

Lobbying of this sort was still underway in Constantinople in the early 530s, intensified by the recent fall of Justinian's ally, the erstwhile Vandal king Hilderic. The sixth-century Syrian chronicler Zacharias the Rhetor records how certain refugees from Hilderic's court encouraged Justinian to strike at the Vandal kingdom by emphasising both the injustices they had suffered and the potential strategic and material benefits of war: 'There was then', he related, 'in Constantinople certain African nobles, who because of a quarrel that they had with a prince of that land [Gelimer], had quit their country and sought refuge with the emperor [Justinian], and they had given him information about this land and urged him to act, saying that this country . . . dreamt of a war with the Romans, but was locked in a war with the Berbers, a people established in the desert and living like the Arabs on brigandage and raids.' They also emphasised to the emperor that the capital of the kingdom, Carthage, was packed with treasures which the first Vandal king Geiseric had seized when he had sacked the city of Rome in 455.[3] These would be ripe for the picking if Justinian were to make a move.

Such stories had wide circulation. Procopius reported in similar terms how all the booty and wealth which the Vandals had ransacked from the Roman Empire had ended up being amassed in their kingdom.[4] Likewise, both he and Count Marcellinus related an extensively reported claim (the earliest version of which is to be found in the writings of Victor of Vita) that some Catholic priests who had their tongues ripped out by the Vandals were then exiled to Constantinople, where they had miraculously recovered the power of speech so they could bear witness to their sufferings. As Victor recorded, King Huneric had ordered a royal official 'to cut off their tongues at the root and their right hands': 'When that had been done, through the presence of the Holy Spirit, they spoke and continue speaking, as they had done previously.'[5] Not everybody, of course, believed such tales. Procopius, for example, went on to describe how certain of these 'holy men' had equally miraculously lost their power of speech again when caught consorting with prostitutes in the imperial capital. There is every indication, however, that Justinian did believe such stories, or at least he regarded them as sufficiently credible to refer to them in one of his laws.[6]

CONTEXTS AND PRETEXTS

Upon learning of the deposition of Hilderic in 530, Justinian had sent a diplomatic delegation to Carthage to fulminate against the new king Gelimer's act of usurpation. Gelimer's seizure of the throne, it was claimed, had breached the terms previously agreed between the imperial authorities and the Vandals as to how power was to be transmitted (or, from a Roman perspective, delegated) within the kingdom. Predictably, Gelimer rejected the emperor's demand that he step down from the throne and restore Hilderic to what Justinian regarded to be his rightful place. In response, Justinian sent a second delegation, threatening war if Gelimer would not at least agree to release Hilderic and his brothers from prison and let them live as exiles under imperial protection in Constantinople. Gelimer responded by telling Justinian to mind his own business, making the reasonable assumption that Justinian's threat to go to war in support of Hilderic was mere bluster.[7] The most recent attempt by Constantinople to intervene militarily in the region had ended in disaster in 468, when Geiseric's fire ships had destroyed an imperial armada. Would the Romans really make the same mistake twice?

For all his sabre-rattling, Justinian did not in fact immediately unleash his military in retaliation for the deposition of his ally. In 530 and 531, the emperor was preoccupied with containing the Persians on the empire's eastern front, as well as strengthening its position along its northern frontier. Facing down Persia was always bound to be his primary foreign policy concern, no matter how tempting the opportunities elsewhere. Moreover, institutional memory of the empire's humiliation in 468 remained strong amongst members of the 'mandarin' class on whom the imperial administration in Constantinople depended. If Gelimer suspected that those in power in Constantinople were inclined to oppose any substantial military move against him, events would prove him to be right, at least with respect to members of the civil service.

What would appear to have finally tipped the balance at court in favour of intervention in Africa was a combination of circumstances in Persia and a shift in political perspective in Constantinople. First, although the new Persian shah, Khusro, had initially continued his father's aggressive policy in relation to Roman activities in the Caucasus and the empire's investment in defensive infrastructure in Syria, political conditions within Persia were highly unstable. Khusro needed to focus his energies on confronting his own 'enemy within', in the form of his brothers and other malcontent elements within the Persian nobility, rather than escalating tensions with Justinian. As a result, a period of détente in Roman-Persian relations, which would enable Justinian to justify military intervention elsewhere, was in the interest of both rulers. Second, the Nika riots had almost toppled Justinian's regime, and the emperor needed to reach out to conservative and alienated elements within the political classes and the Church in order to restore his battered credibility. An intervention against the Vandals presented an opportunity to achieve just this. Third, the Vandal kingdom was famously wealthy and was locked into broader networks of Mediterranean commerce focused on Constantinople. A quick victory there could potentially deliver major financial benefits at a time when the empire was increasingly in need of greater revenues.

Justinian's domestic response to the Nika riots had already

revealed his tendency to present (and perhaps even understand) opportunistic and circumstantially driven power grabs in terms of moral duty, as well as his remarkable ability to turn events to his own advantage. That same approach would now be extended to the international stage as Justinian summoned his courtiers together to make the case for war, his decision to do so reinforced by one additional but ultimately overpowering personal characteristic: vanity. Gelimer's curt missive to Justinian advising him to mind his own business and focus instead on trying to sort out affairs within his own realm had not gone down well. As Procopius records, 'The emperor . . . upon receiving this letter, having been angry with Gelimer even before then, was now still more eager to punish him. And it seemed to him best to put an end to the Persian war as soon as possible and then to make an expedition to Libya [Procopius' favoured term for the Vandal kingdom]; and since he was quick at forming a plan and prompt in carrying out his decisions, Belisarius, the General of the East, was summoned and came to him immediately.'[8]

Justinian's characteristically precipitous decision to go to war did not elicit a positive reaction from his chief courtiers and advisers. Because he had summoned Belisarius to lead the campaign, Procopius—the general's legal secretary—recorded the debate that ensued in detail, including it in his eyewitness account of Justinian's wars. Memories of the disastrous campaign of 468 loomed large: 'When Justinian disclosed to the magistrates that he was gathering an army against the Vandals and Gelimer,' Procopius wrote, 'most of them began immediately to show hostility to the plan and they lamented it as a misfortune, recalling the expedition of the emperor Leo and the disaster of Basiliscus, and reciting how many soldiers had perished and how much money the state had lost.' The praetorian prefect, John the Cappadocian, and his fellow chief financial officer (known as the 'Count of the Sacred Largesses') were especially hostile to the proposal, 'for they reasoned that while it would be necessary for them to produce countless sums for the needs of the war, they would be granted neither pardon in the case of failure nor an extension of time in which to raise the sums'. Nor was there any enthusiasm for the war amongst the military top brass, who were seemingly unaware that the emperor had fingered Belisarius to lead the campaign: 'And every one of the generals, supposing that he himself would command the army, was in terror and dread at the greatness of the danger, if it should be necessary for him, if he survived the perils of the sea, to encamp in enemy territory, and using his ships as a base, to engage in a struggle against a kingdom both large and formidable.'[9]

John the Cappadocian, the only critic who was willing to publicly speak out in the emperor's presence, presented in quite stark terms what today would be regarded as the 'cost-benefits analysis' of his proposal. Procopius recorded the prefect's words: 'If you have confidence', John told Justinian, 'that you will conquer the enemy, it is not at all unreasonable for you to sacrifice the lives of men and expend a vast amount of money and undergo all difficulties of the struggle; for victory, coming at the end, makes up for all the calamities of war. But if in reality these things lie on the knees of God, and if it behoves us, taking example from what has happened in the past, to fear the outcome of war, on what grounds is it not better to love a state of quiet rather than the dangers of mortal strife?' The logistics of the campaign, he pointed out, would be a nightmare, and even if it was successful, securing and consolidating control of Africa would also require Justinian to conquer Sicily, thereby rendering a war with the Goths in Italy inevitable.[10] It would be wiser for Justinian to pull back now, John concluded, before it was too late.

No state or military official rose to argue against the points that John had made—nor do we hear of the empress Theodora playing any part in the debate over the wisdom of Justinian's military plans. Procopius suggests that the emperor seemed minded at this point to heed his anxious prefect's advice. A decisive intervention in favour of war was then made to Justinian by an eastern bishop, however, who, Procopius claimed, had asked the emperor for a private audience. The bishop supposedly informed Justinian 'that God had visited him in a dream and instructed him to go to the emperor and rebuke him, for, after undertaking the task of protecting the Christians in Libya from tyrants, he had, for no good reason, become afraid. "And yet", God had said, "I will Myself join with him in waging war and make him lord of Libya."' According to Procopius, 'When the emperor heard this, he was no longer able to restrain his purpose, and he began to collect the army and ships, and to make ready supplies of weapons and food, and he announced to Belisarius that he should get ready, because he was very soon to serve as commander-in-chief in Libya.'[11]

Whether this bishop really existed or related a dream we will never know. Clearly, to Procopius' mind, in deciding to go to war with Gelimer, Justinian was prioritizing religious factors and his own sense of providential mission over financial concerns. But the story he relates with respect to the bishop's intervention may have had some basis in fact. The sixth-century biography (or 'Life') of a Christian holy man, Saint Saba, claims that during an audience with Justinian he had told the emperor that if he should follow his advice, God would grant him victory over the Vandals in Africa so that he could extirpate the heresy of Arianism.[12] Saba—an abbot, rather than a bishop—died in 532, and the audience had supposedly taken place in 531, but the author of the 'Life' and Procopius preserve what were probably related memories concerning ecclesiastical lobbying in favour of war. Rumours would even circulate in the West that the emperor himself had received a vision in which an African saint who had been martyred under the Vandal king Huneric had urged him to go on the offensive.[13]

Whatever changed his mind, Justinian's attitude towards the campaign appears to have been far more flexible in terms of overall military objectives than Procopius and such religious propaganda would perhaps have us believe, and different justifications would be deployed to sell the campaign to different interest groups. To Vandal opponents of Gelimer and those Romans in the region who were essentially content with Vandal rule, the intervention could be represented as a punitive exercise, undertaken to restore Hilderic and uphold the original constitutional settlement that Geiseric had agreed with the empire in the fifth century. To the leadership of the imperial Church and those to whom Christian orthodoxy mattered most, it was depicted as a bold move undertaken in defence of the faithful, and a war against heresy. And to Roman traditionalists in Constantinople, Africa, and elsewhere, it was an effort to restore Roman liberty to those of the emperor's subjects who found themselves subjected to the ignominy of barbarian rule, and to reestablish Roman authority over what was by rights Roman territory. Different messages were thus crafted for different audiences as the emperor sought to carry political opinion with him. Keeping so many groups 'on board' with the campaign was no mean task, but the broader the coalition invested in the campaign, the easier it would be for the emperor either to reap the political benefits of success or to insulate himself against the perils of failure.

News soon reached Justinian that political conditions in Africa were even more propitious than he had hoped. For the downfall of Hilderic and the ensuing struggle for power at the apex of Vandal society had provided an opportunity not only for the Berber warlords who lived along the frontiers of the kingdom to make significant inroads into it, but also for others to attempt to carve out their own breakaway regimes or to reach out to Constantinople. A Roman subject of Gelimer's by the name of Pudentius, for example, 'one of the natives of Tripoli in Libya', said Procopius, 'caused the district to revolt against the Vandals, and sending to the emperor he begged that he should despatch an army to him: for, he said, he would with no trouble win the land'. Likewise, in Sardinia (over which, along with Corsica and the Balearic Islands, the Vandals exercised authority), Gelimer's appointed governor, Godas—'a Goth by birth, a passionate and warlike man possessed of great bodily strength'—established independent rule over the island in his own name. An imperial envoy was quickly despatched to the island to propose an anti-Vandal alliance. There, the ambassador found Godas 'assuming the title and wearing the dress of an emperor'. Whilst Justinian was welcome to send troops to the island to help him fight the Vandals, the ambassador was informed, Godas was not minded to accept the emperor's kind offer to also appoint an imperial governor there.[14] Godas' imperial pretensions apart, such signs of political fragmentation within and on the borders of the Vandal kingdom boded well for Justinian's imminent military venture.

JUSTINIAN'S ARMADA

With his new military commission now officially in place (Justinian awarded him the title of 'supreme commander', or *strategos autokrator*), Belisarius and his commanders set about gathering together the expeditionary force as speedily as they could. Again, as Belisarius' right-hand man, Procopius provides crucial testimony as to the scale and nature of the enterprise. Once fully mustered, the troops placed at Belisarius' disposal would appear to have numbered 10,000 infantry; 5,000 cavalry, probably made up of some 1,500 Roman recruits and 3,500 'barbarian' allies and mercenaries; a specialised unit of 1,000 Herul and Hunnic horse-archers (including 400 Heruls led by Pharas, who had distinguished himself at Dara); and an unknown number of *buccellarii*, troops who swore oaths of personal loyalty to their commanders, supplementing the general oath of loyalty that all troops made to the emperor, serving as a private military entourage.[15] Procopius later tells us that Belisarius maintained 7,000 such troops attached to his own household, but that was after he had enjoyed considerable further personal enrichment.[16] At this point a figure somewhere in the region of 1,000 to 3,000 or so such private troops would probably be reasonable.[17] The total expeditionary force thus probably consisted of some 20,000 men.

But what did these numbers mean? How significant were they? In broad terms, the Roman army of the early sixth century was divided into three distinct groups. The *limitanei* guarded the frontiers of the empire, where they were settled with their families. *Comitatenses* were mobile troops both conscripted and recruited from amongst the empire's native or subject populations. *Foederati* were troops of non-Roman origin, recruited into Roman service, and typically organised in their own 'ethnic' units and under their own leadership (Pharas' Heruls being a prime example). The distinction between these last two units would become increasingly blurred over the course of Justinian's reign, but at this point it still held. The mobile field armies, made up of *comitatenses* and *foederati*, were supplemented by units of elite guard troops (such as the future emperor Justin had served in) stationed in and around Constantinople, and, as we have seen, individual generals also maintained significant numbers of armed retainers (the *buccellarii*).[18] Belisarius had served as *buccellarius* to Justinian during his time as a general. The more militarily specialised the troop units concerned, the more predominant the barbarian element tended to be—hence Belisarius' decision to mobilise the Herul and Hunnic mounted archers for the African campaign. The 'total size' of what one might term the 'mobile' military establishment later in Justinian's reign—excluding *limitanei*—was possibly somewhere in the region of 150,000 men (a number we derive from the sixth-century military historian Agathias, who would take over from Procopius as the main narrator of Justinian's wars).[19]

Some 25,000 men had fought under Belisarius at Dara in 530, and the field army operating in the hinterland of the Balkans beyond Constantinople itself likely stood somewhere in the region of 10,000 to 15,000 troops. When placed in that context, the army Justinian directed towards Africa was significant, but not exceptional. Only Belisarius' *buccellarii* were removed from the eastern frontier (to which the general had briefly returned) for the purposes of the African campaign. Despite later claims to the contrary, Justinian evidently made the careful and rational decision *not* to strip the eastern frontier of military manpower for the purposes of an opportunistic foray to the West.

Mobilising and mustering the troops needed to attack Africa was one thing: getting them there was another matter entirely. Perhaps surprisingly, the East Roman Empire appears to have had a relatively small standing navy. Whilst the state did maintain a certain number of attack vessels (known as *dromons*) armed with a frontal battering ram for purposes of ship-to-ship fighting, the movement of large numbers of troops and bag-carriers along with their supplies (including food, clean water, arms, and horses) necessitated the requisitioning of merchant vessels.[20] Some 500 such ships of various sizes and carrying capacity were mobilised. They were to make their way towards Africa flanked and guarded by 92 warships. The sailing and rowing of the merchant vessels themselves required the services of some 30,000 sailors, mostly made up of Egyptians, Greeks from the Ionian islands, and Cilicians (from the southern coastline of Asia Minor). The warships were rowed by 2,000 specialist marines recruited from the citizen body of Constantinople.[21]

By late June 533 the fleet was ready to sail. Procopius relates how, prior to his departure, he was 'exceedingly terrified' at the dangers that lay ahead. Belisarius' ship (which, in addition to Procopius, also carried his wife, Antonina, who insisted on accompanying him on campaign) was anchored off the dockside adjacent to the imperial palace, from where Justinian had considered taking flight barely eighteen months earlier. As a sign of the perceived religious significance of the looming war, the patriarch of Constantinople,

Epiphanius, blessed the ship and presented Belisarius with a newly converted and baptized soldier to accompany him on campaign. With Belisarius' vessel at the head of the armada, the fleet began what was initially a slow and painstaking departure from the capital. It paused for five days at Heracleia, on the Sea of Marmara (modern Ereğli in Turkey), in order to board horses for the cavalry units, which had been collected from imperial stables and stud farms across the plains of Thrace. It then proceeded to the port of Abydus, which controlled access to and from the Hellespont. There Belisarius' progress was delayed by four days due to lack of wind, and the general was obliged to have two Hunnic soldiers (known as 'Massagetae') publicly impaled for having murdered a comrade of theirs during a drunken altercation.[22]

Once more favourable weather conditions returned, the fleet's progress resumed. Procopius relates that in order to stop it from being scattered by strong winds, Belisarius had the three leading ships, containing him and his entourage, painted with red markings and festooned with lamps, so that they could be identified in the event of poor visibility. Trumpets sounded from these ships each time they set out. As the ships proceeded via the Aegean to Cape Malea at the southern tip of the Peloponnese, they sometimes had to be pushed apart with poles to prevent them from crashing into and wrecking one another.[23] Finally rounding the potentially treacherous Cape Matapan in the Mani (the southernmost point of mainland Greece), the fleet put in at Methone on the southwest coast.

John the Cappadocian had from the very start been anxious about the likely expense of the African campaign and the logistical effort required to pull it together in such short order. According to Procopius, the prefect had ordered that the military 'hard biscuit' or soldiers' 'tack' that was issued to troops on campaign (*bucellatum*— hence the designation of private military retainers as *bucellarii*, or 'biscuit boys') only be cooked once, rather than twice, so as to save money on firewood.[24] The result was that by the time Roman forces had reached the Peloponnese, the biscuits had broken up and started to rot, leading to the death of some five hundred men. Belisarius ordered that new rations be purchased from the locals, and he sent a report to the emperor complaining about the Cappadocian's potentially disastrous penny-pinching. From Methone the fleet made its way to Zakynthos to restock on water prior to crossing the Adriatic. Languid winds meant that the next phase of the journey took longer than expected, and by the time Belisarius and his accompanying vessels reached Sicily some sixteen days later, the fleet's drinking water had spoiled. Finding a relatively uninhabited spot in the near vicinity of Mount Aetna, Belisarius disembarked, to consider his next move whilst on dry land. Importantly, the imperial authorities had received permission from the Gothic ruler, Theoderic's daughter Queen Amalasuntha, for the Roman fleet to stop off there to buy supplies from local markets, and then move on.[25] She probably wanted the fleet to be as far away from her territory as quickly as possible.

According to Procopius, Belisarius was at this point preoccupied by two concerns. First, he had little idea as to the actual military strength or state of preparedness of the Vandals, or even where in Africa he was to land. It is likely that Justinian had provided him with a relatively flexible mandate, to enable him to cut his cloth according to circumstance. If the Vandals were found to be relatively weak, then a full-blown reconquest of the region could be attempted; but should resistance be rather stiffer, so long as actual defeat at the hands of the Vandals could be avoided the whole exercise could be rebranded as a punitive expedition to put Gelimer in his place and induce him to adopt a more cooperative attitude. Second, he was aware of rumblings of discontent amongst his troops, who were anxious about being attacked by the Vandals while at sea. In order to try to allay each of these concerns, Belisarius ordered Procopius to head to Syracuse on a reconnoitring exercise. There, under cover of purchasing supplies for the fleet, he was to find out 'whether the enemy had any ships in ambush keeping watch over the passage over the sea, either on the island [Sicily] or on the continent, and where it would be best for them to anchor in Libya, and from what point as base it would be advantageous for them to initiate the war against the Vandals'. Procopius was then to rendezvous with Belisarius and rejoin the rest of the expeditionary force at the port of Caucana to the west.[26]

Once in Syracuse, Procopius had a remarkable stroke of luck. Having just arrived in the city, he records, he 'unexpectedly met a man who had been a fellow-citizen [of Caesarea] and friend of his from childhood, who had been living in Syracuse for a long time engaged in the shipping business'. The merchant, it transpired, had an employee (the word used would suggest that he was probably a slave) who had returned from Carthage just three days earlier, and this man reported that there was no need to worry about any ambush, for the Vandals clearly had no inkling whatsoever that an army had been sent against them from Constantinople. Gelimer's best troops had recently been sent to Sardinia on expedition against Godas, under the leadership of the king's brother, Tzazo. Gelimer himself was staying inland, four days' march from Carthage and the cities of the African coastal zone. With respect to landing the Roman expeditionary force, the coast was, literally, clear. Hearing this, Procopius whisked the slave off to report all of this in person to Belisarius at Caucana, leaving his bemused friend on the dockside at Syracuse. Our author goes on to relate that 'Belisarius, when the servant had come before him and conveyed his story, became exceedingly glad, and after bestowing many praises upon Procopius, he issued orders to give the signal for departure with the trumpets'. They quickly departed and stopped off at the islands of Gaulus (Gozo) and Melita (Malta): 'There a strong east wind arose for them and on the following day it carried the ships to the promontory of Libya, at the place which the Romans call . . . "Shoal's Head", for its name is "Caputvada". And the place is just five days' journey from

Carthage for an unencumbered traveller.' In September 533, three months after setting out from Constantinople, Belisarius led Roman troops onto African soil.[27]

What, one wonders, was Justinian doing during this nerve-wracking time? Unusually, for him, the answer would appear to have been 'fretting'. The period from June to September of that year saw no laws issued by the emperor, although around the time the fleet was setting off we do see him reaching out to the papal authorities in Rome and engaging in a detailed correspondence with the new pope, John II. These letters were perhaps partly motivated by a wish to secure western ecclesiastical—and divine—support for his military foray.[28] Tribonian's reports concerning the final editorial phase of the *Institutes* and *Digest* may also have provided some much-needed distraction.

Once the Roman expeditionary force had successfully anchored off the tiny settlement of Caputvada (which Justinian would later redesignate as a city by virtue of its felicitous military associations),[29] Belisarius convened his officers to discuss how to proceed. One of his commanders proposed immediately launching a naval assault on Carthage, as he felt the Roman forces were too exposed where they were. But given his men's anxiety about potentially having to fight at sea, Belisarius advised against this. Instead, it was agreed to establish a bridgehead and dig in where they were. Troops were then sent out to acquire supplies. When, the following day, Belisarius discovered that certain of his men had forcibly requisitioned produce from local peasants, he had them punished, insisting that wherever possible his soldiers buy supplies off local markets and traders so as not to alienate the population.[30]

In preparation for the march on Carthage, Belisarius also sent a detachment of *buccellarii* to the city of Syllectum (modern Salakta in Tunisia), one day's travel away, along the coastal road which led to the Vandal capital. The cities of Africa had been left largely undefended since the fifth century, when Geiseric had torn down their defensive walls to limit the ability of the natives to resist the Vandal takeover. Interestingly, Procopius reveals that Berber raids in the region had become so extensive by this point that the citizens of Syllectum had erected makeshift ramparts to fend off incursions from the tribal zone. Rather than launching a frontal assault on the town, Belisarius' men slipped into it during the early hours of the morning, when farmers and traders were bringing goods into market. Once inside, their commanding officer summoned the local bishop and other notables and, on Belisarius' instruction, informed them that they had come 'for the sake of the people's freedom', and that 'a thousand good things' would soon come their way. Belisarius' military prospects were much aided by the defection of the director of the public post (*cursus velox*), who handed over to him all the kingdom's horses that were stabled nearby. An official messenger was also captured, who agreed to carry a statement to Carthage and distribute it amongst his fellow officials. This statement had been prepared by Justinian to win over those civil servants who were most deeply implicated in the Vandal regime. Revealingly, the flyer made no mention of heresy, of divine visions, or of freeing Romans from barbarian rule. Instead, Justinian claimed, the goal was simply 'to dethrone your tyrant . . . who has imprisoned your king': 'Join forces with us, therefore, and help us free you from this wicked tyranny, so that you will be able to enjoy both peace and freedom. For we give you pledges in the name of God that these things will come to you by our hand.' Procopius informs us that the message was circulated, but only in private, and that it largely failed to convince its recipients.[31]

THE BATTLE FOR CARTHAGE

Belisarius now began to head towards the capital, unsure where and when the Vandals would strike. He sent a crack unit of three hundred *buccellarii* out some four kilometres ahead of the main body of the expeditionary force, whilst Hunnic cavalry flanked the army four kilometres to its south in order to report back on and impede any suddenly advancing foe. Additional cover was provided by the fleet along the coast, as the army followed the coastal road. Belisarius and his best soldiers brought up the rear, indicating that this was where the general most expected Gelimer to strike.[32] The army's rate of progress would have been roughly seventeen kilometres a day, and it would have made camp each night either in a city or in an otherwise defensible position—Syllectum, Leptis Minus (Lamta), Hadrumetum (Sousse)—before finally reaching Grassa, seventy-four kilometres south of Carthage near Gelimer's private estate. From there they crossed the Cap Bon peninsula, passing between the Lake of Tunis and the salt lake at modern Sabhket Sijoumi, approaching Carthage from the west.[33]

By now the Vandal king was fully aware that Belisarius was advancing on Carthage and that he and his regime were in serious trouble. The cream of the Vandal army had indeed been sent, as Belisarius had been informed, to Sardinia to face down the rebel ruler there. As Gelimer awaited their return, he had little choice but to make the most of such manpower as was at his disposal. He sent orders to another of his brothers, Ammatas, who had been sent to Carthage to execute Hilderic, to gather together Vandal forces to confront the expeditionary force at the suburb of Ad Decimum, some fifteen kilometres south of the city, where the road narrowed and the Roman forces could potentially be trapped. A further detachment of some two thousand Vandal troops, under the leadership of his nephew Gibamund, was to strike the Romans from the west, whilst Gelimer's own army would complete the triple-pronged ambush by attacking from the southwest.[34]

The strategy was a sound one: the problem for Gelimer was that his timings were out. Ammatas and the advance guard of the Vandal host of Carthage arrived at Ad Decimum earlier than they were supposed to, with much of the army making its way behind them in a barely coordinated series of dribs and drabs. As a result, Belisarius' advance guard encountered and eliminated Ammatas and much of his personal retinue and was then able to initiate a dash towards Carthage, slaughtering or putting to flight the bands of Vandal warriors they encountered in their path, and managing to reach the gates of the city. Likewise, Belisarius' Huns encountered Gibamund's forces eight kilometres west of Ad Decimum, at Sabhket Sijoumi, and easily put them to flight. Prongs one and two of Gelimer's three-pronged assault had thus been dealt with.

Belisarius himself at this point (still accompanied by his wife) was busy fortifying a camp some seven kilometres from Ad Decimum, so that his infantry troops and baggage carriers could rest whilst the cavalry prepared to advance against the enemy. According to Procopius, he was oblivious to what was going on elsewhere. The first of his troops to reach Ad Decimum were the *foederati*. There the locals informed his officers of the fate that had befallen Ammatas and the other Vandals. At the same time, they could tell from the clouds of dust billowing up from the landscape before them that Gelimer was now rapidly approaching with his army.[35] Gelimer, too, was apparently totally unaware of what had happened to his brother's and nephew's troops. Unsure how to proceed, when confronted by Gelimer's army the *foederati* fell back towards Belisarius' camp in considerable disorder, spreading further confusion amongst the units of Roman troops they met in the course of their flight.[36]

Had Gelimer pursued these men and marched directly against Belisarius, or had he headed to Carthage and caught the Roman fleet, which was now within striking distance of the city, he would probably have put an end to Justinian's dreams of reconquest once and for all. This result would have justified each and every one of the warnings that John the Cappadocian had issued to the emperor just a few months earlier. Instead, and to the evident bafflement of Procopius, he did neither. Encountering the corpse of his brother at Ad Decimum, Gelimer insisted that his army pause, so that the prince could be accorded his due and proper burial rites. This decision inevitably caused consternation and confusion amongst the rank-and-file of the Vandal army: it meant that Gelimer's troops were in no position to offer coordinated resistance when Belisarius and his men suddenly appeared. Gelimer and his retinue had to retreat to the plain of Boulla and the road leading to Numidia.[37] Carthage now lay ready to receive Belisarius.

The general was wary of entering the city too quickly, fearing ambushes on the part of remaining Vandal troops, and anxious that discipline amongst his men should not break down, and the 'liberation' of the city descend into a looting spree. As Procopius records, 'On the following day the infantry with the wife of Belisarius came up and we proceeded together on the road towards Carthage, which we reached in the late evening; and we passed the night in the open, although no one hindered us from marching into the city at once. For the Carthaginians opened the gates and burned lights everywhere and the city was brilliant with the illumination that whole night, and those of the Vandals who had been left behind were sitting as suppliants in the sanctuaries.' Within the city, the iron chain which protected the harbour at time of war was reeled in so as to permit the Roman fleet to dock, and those political prisoners who had not yet been executed on the instructions of Gelimer were released. Revealingly, these included those whom Procopius describes as 'eastern merchants' whom the Vandal king had suspected of having 'urged the emperor to go to war'.[38]

On the following morning, 15 September 533, Belisarius and his troops made their formal entry into the capital of the Vandal kingdom, one of the wealthiest and most cosmopolitan cities of the entire Mediterranean world. Those troops who had accompanied the fleet towards Carthage were ordered to disembark, and the general led the massed ranks of the Roman army into the city in battle formation, lest a surprise attack should emerge. Strict instructions were issued to the Roman troops to conduct themselves as liberators rather than conquerors.[39]

Once in the city, Belisarius found that the resistance he had feared from the Vandals had melted away. Accordingly, he made his way directly to the royal palace, where he sat on Gelimer's throne and received complaints from local merchants and shipowners: contrary to his instructions, the previous night Roman sailors had ransacked their cargoes. After receiving assurances (which Procopius believed to be false) from his captain-in-chief that this was not the case, Belisarius and his entourage retired to enjoy a lavish lunch which had been prepared by the palace staff for the Vandal king. As Procopius reminisced, 'And we feasted on that very food and the servants of Gelimer served it and poured the wine and waited upon us in every way. . . . And it fell to the lot of Belisarius on that day to win such fame as no other man of his time ever won nor indeed any of the men of old.'[40]

TRIUMPH AND HUMILIATION

The occupation of Carthage by Roman forces and the billeting of Belisarius' troops are recorded to have gone smoothly. The general offered generous terms to those Vandal soldiers and families who had sought asylum in the city's churches. He also ordered that the city be provided with proper defences to prepare it in the event of a retaliatory attack. Justinian, as we have seen, had attempted to present his intervention to the Roman functionaries of the Vandal government as merely an attempt to restore Hilderic and punish Gelimer. With Hilderic now dead, that claim was no longer credible. Belisarius, in addressing his men and the local civilian population, emphasised the theme of liberation: he was freeing Romans from the barbarian yoke (despite the fact that many of his best troops were themselves barbarians). With the capital of Vandal Africa now in Roman hands, the religious dimensions of the campaign now came to the fore. Arian priests were driven out from the great cathedral church dedicated to a famous third-century African saint, Cyprian, and the building—full, we are told, of 'beautiful votive offerings . . . lamps . . . and treasures, with everything laid out according to its appropriate use'—was handed back to those whom Procopius called 'the Christians who conform to the orthodox faith'.[41]

Controlling Carthage did not mean that Belisarius controlled the kingdom. Beyond it, Gelimer was busy rallying his remaining troops. He was also attempting to literally buy up support from amongst the African peasantry, by putting a price on the head of each Roman soldier they were able to kill. This remaining activity rendered the Romans highly vulnerable to attack when venturing out of the capital or moving between the coastal towns they had occupied, and Procopius records how local farmers in the countryside ambushed reconnoitring parties.[42]

Gelimer's decision to retreat towards Numidia in the aftermath of his defeat at Ad Decimum might at first seem a curious one, but it made sense in terms of his urgent need to mobilise additional sources of support. From the plain of Boulla he was able to reach out to the leaders of the Berber confederations of the tribal zone. His approaches, however, were rebuffed. The idea of the Roman Empire and the image of the emperor clearly still continued to carry great authority and prestige amongst the mixed Roman and Berber population, and Belisarius was able to harness this fact to his military advantage. As Procopius related, 'All those who ruled over the Moors [i.e., the Berbers] in Mauretania and Numidia and Byzacium sent envoys to Belisarius saying that they were slaves of the emperor and promised to fight with him. There were some also who even furnished their children as hostages and requested that the insignia of office be sent to them according to the ancient custom.'

He was referring here to the 'tokens of office'—a gold-tipped silver staff, a silver crown, and a white cloak fixed with a gold brooch—that Berber tradition required a potential ruler to obtain from the Romans in order to assume authority. 'Though they had already received these from the Vandals,' Procopius said, 'they did not consider that the Vandals held the office fully.' Gelimer's spirits were raised, meanwhile, by news that his brother Tzazo and his men had been victorious in Sardinia, and aware of the king's plight, were on their way to join forces with him. When the two brothers finally met at Boulla, we are told, they embraced each other and silently wept.[43] They then led the Vandal host towards Carthage to face down Belisarius, preparing to blockade the city by destroying a section of the aqueduct supplying it with water.[44]

The decisive engagement took place on 15 December 533 at Tricamarum, about thirty-two kilometres outside the city. It was a disaster for the Vandals, who appear to have been expecting to engage in hand-to-hand combat with the Roman infantry only to find their ranks broken and harried by the Roman cavalry.[45] Prior to the Vandal rout, the Romans had lost only fifty men, whereas Gelimer's troops lost some eight hundred, including Tzazo, who died on the battlefield sword in hand. The Romans then hunted down and killed all the Vandal combatants they could and enslaved their women and children. The Roman victory signalled the final demise of the Vandal kingdom. Gelimer fled to an inaccessible redoubt on Mount Papua in the Atlas Mountains, and the Herul commander Pharas was sent there in pursuit of the king. Unable to overcome the Berbers who had agreed to protect him (and whose sense of the obligations of hospitality was clearly strong), Pharas entered into negotiation with Gelimer, whose long-pampered family members were finding the harsh conditions on Mount Papua almost unbearable. Indeed, several of them are reported to have starved to death.[46]

In his correspondence with Pharas, the king denounced Justinian for having launched an unprovoked war on the basis of spurious pretexts. The Herul (who was himself of princely blood) advised Gelimer that it would be 'better to be a slave among the Romans and beggared there than to be a monarch on Mount Papua with Moors as your subjects'. In any case, Pharas continued, he had been informed that Justinian was minded to let the king retire to Roman territory with a considerable pension in money and land, and was even considering making him a senator and granting him patrician rank. Belisarius, he said, would vouch for the offer. Why hang on? Why not be a fellow servant of the emperor, like Belisarius? He could be like Pharas himself, and learn to derive pride from service to Constantinople.[47]

Eventually, in the spring of 534, Gelimer gave in: once Belisarius' representatives had confirmed these terms under oath, they accompanied the king to Carthage. There, when he was presented to Belisarius, Gelimer is reported to have broken down into hysterical and uncontrollable laughter. Many supposed that he had lost his mind, though his friends and allies attempted to put a more philosophical spin on his conduct, claiming that he had been reduced to such hilarity through contemplation of the extraordinary vicissitudes of fate.[48]

Justinian did not fully renege on the terms which had been sworn to Gelimer (although he was never made a senator or *patricius*, because, we are told, he refused to abandon his Arian faith). It would be fair to say, however, that the emperor breached the essential spirit of the deal. For after his encounter with Belisarius, when the ex-king was shipped to Constantinople along with the contents of the Vandal royal treasury, he was publicly and ritually humiliated in the context of a carefully orchestrated ceremony, or 'triumph' (the first such event, Procopius claimed, for almost six hundred years).[49] Belisarius, as the victorious general, presented to the emperor not only the amassed wealth of the Vandals, but also Gelimer and his family, displaying them, as the contemporary bureaucrat and scholar John Lydus put it, 'just as though they were worthless skivvies'.[50] The former king was led as a slave through the streets of the imperial capital in chains, along with his family and 'as many of the Vandals as were very tall and fair of body'. Upon reaching the Hippodrome, Gelimer 'saw the emperor sitting upon a lofty seat, and the people on either side, and realized as he looked about what a terrible plight he was in'. At that point, Procopius writes, 'he neither wept nor cried out, but kept on repeating to himself the words of scripture "Vanity of Vanities, all is Vanity." And when he came before the emperor's throne, they stripped off his purple garments and forced him to fall flat on the ground and prostrate himself before the emperor Justinian.' Just to make it clear who was in charge, the general Belisarius was also made to perform the same formal act of obeisance.[51]

As a reward for the African victory, Belisarius was appointed consul. Upon the start of his one year in office on 1 January 535, he effectively turned his consular celebrations into a second military 'triumph'. During his procession through the streets of the capital, Procopius reports, the general was 'borne aloft by the [Vandal] captives and, as he was thus carried in his consular chair, he threw to the populace the very spoils of the Vandal war. For the people carried off the silver plate and golden girdles and a vast amount of the Vandals' wealth of other sorts as a result of Belisarius' consulship.' Such generosity is likely to have helped the citizen body of Constantinople forgive, if not entirely forget, the crucial role the general had played in the massacring of the faction members and their supporters in the Hippodrome almost exactly three years earlier. It is also likely to have established him as a figure of some political significance and a potential claimant to the imperial throne in his own right. Indeed, Procopius later wrote that the general let it be known that 'never, *while the emperor Justinian lived*, would Belisarius seize the imperial title'.[52] The inference was that Belisarius was unwilling to make the same commitment to anybody else.

CONQUEST AND CONSOLIDATION

Justinian had been characteristically impatient for victory and had not waited for Gelimer to be captured to declare that his enemy had been defeated. For him, the seizure of Carthage sufficed: hence, in the constitution which he issued promulgating the *Institutes* on 21 November 533, he had adopted the triumphal titles of *Alanicus, Vandalicus,* and *Africanus* ('victor over Alans, Vandals, and Africans'), declaring, 'The barbarian nations which we have subjugated know our valour, Africa and other provinces without number being once more, after so long an interval, reduced beneath the sway of Rome by victories granted by heaven.'[53] When confirming the *Digest* in December, he drew the public's attention to the fact that 'a third part of the world has been annexed by us, for after Europe and Asia the whole of Libya has been added to our empire'.[54] Any post-Nika modesty on the part of the emperor was now a thing of the past.

Justinian gave careful consideration as to how the African territories were to be administered and incorporated into his realm. As early as April 534, just one month after the surrender of the Vandal king, he issued two lengthy and detailed laws concerning the civil and military arrangements that were to be made for the province.[55] Two features of this legislation stand out. First, it has been argued, on stylistic grounds, that Justinian wrote or dictated these laws *in person*.[56] Second, they set out details for the administration of parts of the Vandal kingdom which Justinian's troops had not yet occupied, and which it is conceivable they never actually would.[57] In terms of propaganda, Justinian used these laws to hone his justifications for the invasion. This was clearest in the first law, concerned with the civil administration of Africa, which contained a lengthy and highly rhetorical preface. The conquest was, the emperor declared, the will of God; and as a result of it, through Justinian's efforts, God had liberated his people from the yoke of servitude. The emperor then reminded his subjects of the indignities and outrages which, it was claimed, had been perpetrated against those Christians in Africa who had upheld the true faith: the imposition of Arianism by force; the conversion of Catholic churches into stables; the torture and exile of holy men. In explicit reference to the stories circulating concerning African Catholic exiles in Constantinople encountered earlier, Justinian also described how 'we ourselves saw venerable men who, with their tongues cut out at the root, miraculously spoke of their punishment'.[58]

In terms of administration, Justinian ordained that the former Vandal kingdom was to constitute a single prefecture of Africa under its own praetorian prefect. It would be divided into seven provinces, including Sardinia, Corsica, and the Balearic Islands, which had also been subject to Vandal rule. These arrangements owed next to nothing to the pre-Vandal Roman administration of the region and constituted a contemporary response to contemporary realities. The parallel legislation on military governance and occupation decreed that military commanders (duces) were to be established in five of these seven provinces, with Roman troops notably absent from two of the three provinces embracing the frontier zone of Mauretania. These provisions indicated that here the empire expected to work with Berber clients to secure the defence of the region (paralleling the situation with Arab clients along the empire's desert frontier to the East).[59] These duces were to serve under a new general: the magister militum per Africam.[60] An effort was also to be made to establish new limitanei supported by land grants to secure the frontier zones.[61]

Justinian's African legislation of 534 has something of a 'wish list' quality about it. As intimated earlier, it is far from clear how many of the territories and cities in which his new *duces* were to be based were actually under Roman control at the time these laws were issued.[62] It should perhaps be thought of as a blueprint for the future administration of the new prefecture, not all of which would or could necessarily be put into effect. The military narrative provided by Procopius would suggest that Justinian's priority (and perhaps the initial military objective of the campaign) was control of Carthage, the coastal towns, and as much of the inland zone as was required to defend them, as well as securing the key Mediterranean islands that had been subject to Vandal rule. Hence Procopius emphasises the occupation of Caesarea in Mauretania (modern Cherchell in Algeria) and Septem (Ceuta), which carried with it mastery of the Strait of Gibraltar, as well as Sardinia, Ibiza, Majorca, and Minorca.

These were all locations of great strategic value, but they hardly constituted a springboard for the invasion of the hinterland of the kingdom. Just as the empire had established positions in the Crimea which could be used as a 'listening post' on the world of the West Eurasian steppe, so too was the emperor explicit in his legislation on the broader strategic significance of Septem, where a fleet of warships was to be posted. The commander of this fleet was not only to police the crossing between Spain and Africa, but also to monitor and report back on events in the Gothic kingdom in Spain (often referred to as that of the 'Visigoths') and the Frankish kingdoms beyond. Belisarius' troops also attempted to seize the fortress at Lilybaeum (Marsala) in Sicily. The Gothic garrison there successfully repulsed Roman forces, but the episode reveals that securing control of the Strait of Sicily was an additional Roman war aim.[63]

It is conceivable that with respect to Africa, anything beyond control of the coastal zone and the islands was regarded as a bonus. This sense is also conveyed by much of the defensive and building work completed by Belisarius and his immediate successors in Africa. These investments concentrated on the improvement of the civic defences of Carthage and the other towns under Roman rule and the creation of a denser 'religious' infrastructure to help bolster a state-sponsored revival of the imperial Church in the region. In his *History of the Wars*, Procopius describes how in Carthage, Belisarius rebuilt the city walls, whilst in another of his works (*Buildings*), he adds that the imperial government also invested in a broader programme of imperial renewal in the city, which was renamed *Carthago Iustiniana* ('The Carthage of Justinian'), building new public colonnades and baths as well as a monastery and shrines dedicated to the Mother of God (the *Theotokos*). Archaeological work, which has largely confirmed Procopius' claims, reveals that the city's commercial ports were also extensively redeveloped.[64]

Beyond Carthage, Procopius describes the construction of new fortifications under Belisarius and his successors in and around an additional thirty-five African cities to help protect the inhabitants against 'the inroads of the Moors' as well as new religious institutions.[65] In Leptis Magna, for example, the centre of the city was fortified and five new churches were built (including another church devoted to the *Theotokos*).[66] To the East, the coastal city of Tripoli was fortified, as were two isolated monasteries south of Bernike (modern Benghazi), 'as bulwarks against the barbarians'. Quite often, Procopius describes the building of citadels within the circuit walls of the towns. In Carthage, even the new monastery was simultaneously 'an impregnable fortress'. Given the largely unfortified nature of the cities of Africa under the Vandals, it may not have been entirely apparent to the locals whether they were being liberated (and protected) or occupied. The reality on the ground was probably a mixture of the two. The only region where Procopius describes attempts to create a significant number of inland fortifications is

Numidia, where he claims fortresses would be constructed in the context of subsequent conflict with the Berbers.[67]

The emphasis on new religious foundations dedicated to the Virgin Mary is telling. The *Theotokos* was the patron saint of Constantinople, the New Rome. She, in a sense, travelled with its armies. It is interesting in this context that as well as commercial vessels of a more standard sort, maritime archaeologists have identified wrecks of ships carrying cargoes of what can only be described as 'flat-packed' churches that traversed the Mediterranean at this time, their loads comprising marble church decorations of eastern origin and conforming to a common architectural plan.[68] As the population of Tzanica on the eastern frontier had discovered, in the empire of Justinian, arms and religion travelled hand-in-hand.

Predictably, the establishment of rule from Constantinople in the former Vandal territories had immediate religious ramifications which went well beyond just church-building. Arianism and all other heresies were banned, and Arian churches and all their property handed over to the imperial Church. Concerted efforts were now made to police and reinforce the confessional boundaries between pro- and anti-Nicene (or Catholic and Arian) Christians, which had become increasingly blurred as Vandals and Romans had come to mingle and intermarry. Significantly, Justinian also ordered that all Jewish synagogues in the new prefecture be destroyed, indicating that he regarded the region's Jewish community to have been actively implicated in Vandal rule or opposition to the Roman reconquest. The normal deadlines for landowners who wished to apply for the restitution of stolen or lost property were relaxed with respect to the claims of the Church, so as to enable it to reclaim its extensive African estates. African émigrés who had made a home in Constantinople and had been lobbying for the region's invasion could now reclaim their lands. They had to make such claims, however, within five years, or the emperor would be able to seize the lot.[69]

This and related economic dimensions of the conquest were important. For mastery of the coastal towns of formerly Vandal Africa and the agriculturally highly developed hinterlands that supported them, as well as the ports and islands of Carthage and the Western and Central Mediterranean, such as Corsica and Sardinia, had opened up significant economic opportunities which Justinian was evidently eager to grasp. The redevelopment of the port facilities at Carthage signalled a desire to take advantage of the agricultural productivity of the region.[70] The Vandals had levied significant tariffs on trading vessels operating out of Carthage, and these, too, could now be used to bolster imperial coffers.[71] Likewise, at the port city of Leptiminus, archaeological excavations have revealed a major wave of investment in the industrial production of *amphorae* (clay vessels, in which African produce, such as olive oil, was exported), as well as ironworking, which may to some extent have been state sponsored.[72]

The symbolic value of confiscating the vast Vandal royal treasury and sending it to Constantinople was clear. It was claimed that it even included precious objects from the Temple of Solomon, which the Romans had removed from Jerusalem but which Geiseric had then spirited away from Rome when he had attacked the city in 455 CE. Of more political and economic significance was the transfer of ownership of most of the rich landed estates that had belonged to the Vandal kings to the imperial household. These, and their revenues, were placed directly under the emperor's control. With Roman armies, there always came Roman tax collectors. At around the same time that Belisarius was heading back to Constantinople, with Gelimer in tow, Procopius records, the emperor sent two high-ranking officials 'to assess taxes for the Libyans each according to his proportion [of land]. But these men seemed to the Libyans neither moderate nor endurable.' Landowners in Africa were not used to paying Roman levels of taxation.[73] Geiseric, Procopius tells us, had destroyed the tax records of earlier Roman administrators in the region. With the return of the Roman government, they were in for something of a shock.

RESISTANCE AND UNREST

Justinian's African legislation of 534 reveals an emperor with a plan. How realistic that plan was is another matter. It had been conceived, after all, in the immediate aftermath of an unexpectedly rapid and—from a Roman perspective—relatively bloodless victory. Belisarius' decision to head back to Constantinople along with Gelimer had been partly informed by political considerations, after officers around the general had begun to accuse him of planning to seize the kingdom for himself. According to Procopius, Belisarius had felt it necessary to have a word with the emperor in person so as to clear his name. The emperor was also probably quite keen to have a word with Belisarius. The absence of the general who had humiliated the Vandals, however, immediately led to a resurgence of Berber raiding activity in the area. The newly appointed praetorian prefect of Africa, Solomon, would have to deal with this problem. At a site that was probably west of Kairouan, he thus attacked a large Berber encampment, reportedly killing upwards of ten thousand men and capturing and enslaving many women and children.[74]

In a pattern that would also be repeated elsewhere on the empire's frontiers, however, more assertive Roman military action only elicited a more determined and coordinated response from the empire's rivals and foes, leading to further, increasingly serious Berber raids on Byzacena. Again, Solomon targeted enemy camps, pinning down a major settlement on the slopes of Mount Bourgaon. The resultant Berber casualties were said to number some fifty thousand, and the number of slaves taken was such, Procopius tells us, that a Berber boy could be bought for the cost of a sheep.[75] Whoever was having their liberty 'restored' in post-conquest Africa, it clearly was not the Berbers.

Not all of the Berber groupings, of course, had turned against the Romans in the wake of Belisarius' departure for Constantinople, but their responses were mixed. The dominant warlord in the vicinity of Byzacena, the formidable Antalas, remained largely cooperative. The leading figure in Numidia, a warrior by the name of Iudas, was decidedly hostile, leading repeated raids on sedentary communities. Both men offered safe haven to survivors of the recent Roman-led massacres. In 536, Solomon decided to lead his forces towards Iudas' base in the Aurès Mountains, but he was hampered by mounting unrest amongst his own troops. Turning an army of conquest into an army of occupation was never going to be an easy matter, especially when so many of the men were effectively foreign mercenaries who had been recruited or employed to fulfil a specific mission. Around the time of Easter in 536, a major mutiny broke out, led by the Herul general Stotzas, who received enthusiastic support from barbarian troops of Arian faith. These troops were not happy that they were not allowed to celebrate the Christian rites as they chose, and they believed they were entitled to the military landholdings which the rank-and-file of the Vandal army had formerly possessed, but which Solomon and his officials were busy transferring to the imperial household.[76]

There is every indication that Stotzas may have been on the verge of declaring himself king of a reconstituted African realm.[77] Certainly, Solomon was obliged to flee Carthage, and the city seemed on the verge of surrendering to the mutineers who were encamped outside its walls, when Belisarius unexpectedly arrived by sea and rapidly began reinforcing and buying up support amongst the Roman troops. In a successful engagement, he managed to drive the rebels from the city, and the remaining mutineers fled with their leader to Numidia. For reasons that will become apparent shortly, Belisarius was soon obliged to head back to Sicily, and Justinian sent his cousin (another nephew of Justin's), Germanus, to Africa to help restore order. When he finally arrived to quell the revolt, Germanus found that an estimated two-thirds of the remaining army had gone over to the rebels. Unhappiness over arrears in military pay was mounting.[78] Getting this situation back under control would require a major injection of both goodwill and hard cash, neither of which necessarily flowed that readily from Justinian's court. The Vandals may have been conquered, but the struggle for Africa was far from over. But why was Belisarius rushing off to Sicily when his services were manifestly still needed in Carthage? The reason was that Justinian's armies were now engaged in a new and still more ambitious war of reconquest.

Chapter 9

The Battle for Italy

THE STRUGGLE FOR POWER IN RAVENNA

Justinian and those around him had probably always favoured military intervention in Italy at some point. Relations between King Theoderic and the imperial authorities had never been easy. At his court in Ravenna, the monarch had been feted by Roman senators and foreign princes after a manner that was bound to grate.[1] The king had also adopted a highly imperial style of rule which would have further offended political sensibilities in Constantinople. Procopius went so far as to comment that, in his conduct, 'Theoderic was as true an emperor as any who had ever distinguished themselves in this office from the beginning'.[2] His regime even issued a celebratory gold coin bearing Theoderic's portrait and according him the imperial title of 'pious ruler, forever invincible'. The imperial authorities believed that only Roman emperors had the right to issue such coins and would have been deeply affronted. Roman forces had previously raided the Italian coastline under Anastasius; East Roman and Gothic interests had clashed over Sirmium; and when Theoderic was succeeded by the boy-king Athalaric and a faction-ridden council of regency under his mother, Queen Amalasuntha, Justinian smelled weakness. As John the Cappadocian had rightly pointed out, consolidating the empire's military control over the new African territories effectively presupposed that the government in Constantinople would try to prise Sicily from Gothic hands. Belisarius' attempt to seize the fortress at Lilybaeum (Marsala) perhaps signalled that the establishment of an imperially controlled enclave in Sicily had been a war aim from the start. There was every reason for the Roman conquest of Carthage to cause alarm and consternation at the Gothic court.

On 2 October 534, circumstances tilted further in favour of an intervention. In Ravenna, King Athalaric died, at the age of only about sixteen, after struggling for some time against a wasting disease, and this left Queen Amalasuntha dangerously politically exposed. In a desperate attempt to shore up her authority, she had reached out to her nearest male kinsman, a cousin and nephew of Theoderic's named Theodahad, who had clearly been machinating against her with the aid of some senatorial support. Theodahad now acceded to the throne, alongside Amalasuntha as co-ruler, and wrote to the Senate of Rome declaring, 'Your whispers in my favour might have been a source of danger, but now your openly expressed acclamations are my proudest boast.'[3] Noted for his cupidity, he was unsuited to kingship both in temperament and in lifestyle. Procopius described him as 'a man who abhorred to have a neighbour', as he had repeatedly seized the property of others until he had become the dominant landowner in Tuscany. Such greed might have been forgivable if it were balanced by a reputation as a warrior, but Theodahad was a Goth gone native. A devotee of the philosophy of Plato and a lover of Latin literature, deeply versed in biblical and theological scholarship, he was entirely unaccustomed to war.[4] We can see why he might have appealed to some members of the Senate, but it is hard to see what he had to offer the members of the Gothic nobility and the military rank-and-file, who had been hoping for a proper Gothic warlord to lead them. Platonic philosophy was about to be put to the test: Did anybody *really* have a use for a 'philosopher king'?

When writing to the emperor to announce her cousin's accession, Amalasuntha curiously failed to mention him by name, almost as if she could not quite bring herself to do so. He was simply 'a man bound to us by fraternal relation'.[5] United only by their weakness, Amalasuntha and Theodahad were soon manoeuvring and plotting against one another, and Justinian was more than happy to get drawn into the fray, as their anxious subjects began to ask where true authority lay.

According to Procopius, each of them tried to mobilise Justinian against the other whilst also putting out feelers to see, if the worst came to the worst and they were obliged to flee, whether Constantinople would offer them a home.[6] Even prior to the accession of Theodahad, when members of the nobility were plotting against her, Procopius claims, Amalasuntha's agents had approached Justinian asking if he would place the queen under his protection. He even reports that she had sent ships carrying much of her private wealth out of Italy to the imperial port of Dyrrachium on the Adriatic, in advance of her anticipated flight, which never in the end quite transpired. Likewise, Theodahad, Procopius reports, had recently offered to hand Tuscany over to the empire in return for a large cash payout, membership of the Senate in Constantinople, and a home there.[7]

When, in 534, Belisarius sent his troops against the fortress at Lilybaeum, Amalasuntha had sent the emperor a stinging public rebuke for attacking Gothic territory. Simultaneously, however, according to Procopius, she had written to the emperor in private, secretly agreeing 'to put the whole of Italy into his hands'. At the same time, Justinian's agents returned from Italy vouching for

Theodahad's offer, adding that he 'enjoyed great power in Tuscany, where he had become owner of most of the land and consequently would be able with no trouble at all to put the agreement into effect'. The emperor, 'overjoyed at this situation', had sent a trusted diplomatic agent to Italy, the courtier Peter the Patrician, to tease out further potential sources of support within the Italian kingdom.[8] With Theodahad and Amalasuntha battling for control of a throne which neither seemed determined to keep, so long as the other could not have it, the prospects for Justinian were looking better and better.

In April 535, the struggle for power at the Gothic court came to a head. Theodahad's allies seized and imprisoned Amalasuntha on an island on Lake Bolsena, and she was forced to write a letter of abdication. Theodahad forwarded it to Constantinople, accompanied by a high-ranking diplomatic delegation. According to a Gothic convert to Catholic Christianity named Jordanes, who wrote a history of his people later in Justinian's reign, the queen 'spent a very few days of sadness before she was strangled in the bath house by his [the king's] servants'.[9] Theodahad denied any responsibility for the queen's murder whilst simultaneously rewarding her killers. In Constantinople, the leading senatorial member of the delegation sent to dissuade Justinian from intervening, an éminence grise of the Roman Senate named Liberius, defected and sought political asylum.[10] The murder of Amalasuntha, whom Justinian had recognised on the throne, and whose father's position in Italy had been ratified under imperial treaty, now provided Justinian with a pretext to invade.

To some, the chain of events looked a little too convenient. Procopius would later suggest that the empress Theodora, who maintained separate lines of communication to Theodahad and his wife, Gundelinda, had encouraged the execution of the unfortunate queen.[11] This accusation is not entirely implausible, as we possess a suspiciously opaquely worded letter from Theodahad to the empress telling her that he had arranged to sort out a 'particular person' in such a manner as 'we believe agrees with your particular designs'.[12] Theodora may have kept out of the African campaign, but contemporary evidence suggests she was fully implicated in the Italian one. The imperial couple clearly regarded the meltdown of the Gothic monarchy as too good an opportunity to miss, and Justinian again entrusted the war of reconquest to Belisarius. As Jordanes put it, Justinian 'lost no time in marching his army, with their weapons still dripping with Vandal blood, against the Goths, under the same commander'.[13]

THE ROAD TO ROME

Over the course of the fifth century, the former provinces of the Western Roman Empire had come to be dominated by warlords of primarily barbarian descent presiding over what were now king-focused societies ruled by an elite which was essentially martial in outlook and culture. Of course, the Roman Empire had been led by men of war too, but when the Goths had killed the ruling Roman emperor, Valens, at the Battle of Adrianople in 378, they had not captured or destroyed the empire, which had a bureaucratic and ideological resilience and depth independent of any one ruler or dynasty. By contrast, the capture of the Vandal king, Gelimer (like the death of King Harold at the Battle of Hastings in 1066), had sealed the fate of his entire realm. Such kingdoms were uniquely vulnerable to attack at times of disputed succession, or when the military credentials of those at the top were perceived to be in doubt. The fact that Justinian directed armies first to Africa and then Italy precisely at such moments of weakness would suggest that his decisions were informed by a carefully considered analysis of power in the West. Allies such as his royal Gepid general, Mundo, may have contributed to this way of thinking. The crisis in Ravenna arising from the murder of Amalasuntha presented a golden opportunity to strike, and Justinian's envoy to Italy, Peter the Patrician, informed Theodahad and the Gothic leadership that 'because of the base deed that had been committed by them, there would now be a war without truce between the emperor and themselves'.[14] Peter is also likely to have issued a stark warning to members of the Roman senatorial elite in Italy, saying that they would be well advised to cooperate with the armies of the emperor that were now on their way to liberate them from the 'tyranny' of Theodahad, as well as from what Procopius' continuator, Agathias, would later describe as the 'foreign domination' of the Goths, and to restore 'Sicily, Rome and Italy to their ancient way of life'.[15]

Justinian's armies initiated a two-pronged attack on Gothic-ruled territory in 535, whilst simultaneously trying to persuade the Franks to attack from the northwest. The emperor's envoys reminded the Frankish king, Theodebert, that the Franks and Romans were united by their rejection 'of the opinion of the Arians, and also by the enmity we both feel towards the Goths'.[16] Belisarius was despatched to Sicily, accompanied by his *buccellarii* and four thousand *foederati* and regular troops, three thousand Isaurians (highly skilled warriors from the highlands of Asia Minor), two hundred Huns, and three hundred Berbers who had been signed up to serve the emperor. Combined with the retinues that attended his subordinate commanders, the total expeditionary force might have reached a maximum of ten thousand troops—a relatively small army for the purposes of the conquest of Italy as a whole, but more than enough to secure Sicily and the south, which may have been Belisarius' initial aim.[17] He was instructed that if he met with effective resistance in Sicily, he was to withdraw, claiming he was only en route to Carthage, and that his intentions had been misconstrued. A second Roman army struck from the Balkans to the north, advancing through Dalmatia and achieving the long-standing imperial objective of seizing Salona, a crucial point along the network of Roman roads that connected Italy to the East. This force was led by the Gepid prince, Mundo, who was widely respected in the region.[18] Salona and Sicily were probably the initial core territorial goals: if Gothic resistance turned out to be weak and ineffectual, ambitions could be escalated. Alternatively, Theodahad might simply decide to throw in the towel in return for an easier life in Constantinople.

Because Belisarius was also accompanied on his Italian campaign by his legal secretary, Procopius, we possess a vivid eyewitness account of the rapid capitulation of Sicily before the Roman forces. Many of the cities on the island simply surrendered and opened their gates.[19] This was, of course, the part of the Gothic kingdom most closely locked into the broader networks of trade with Constantinople and the East (hence the presence in Syracuse of Procopius' old schoolfriend from Caesarea). Representatives of the Eastern Empire would thus have seemed far from alien. Only at Palermo did Belisarius meet with sustained resistance on the part of the Gothic garrison, which he overcame by sending ships heavily manned with archers into the harbour and raining arrows down onto the defenders. On 31 December 535, Belisarius celebrated both the end of his consulship and the successful conquest of Sicily by making a triumphal entry into Syracuse, 'loudly applauded by the army and by the Sicilians and by throwing golden coins to all'.[20]

This news was greeted rapturously in Constantinople. In a law issued less than three months later, Justinian expressed the hope that, God willing, the empire's recent successes in Sicily and Africa, alongside peace with Persia, might mark the start of 'our reconquest of all the rest of the lands that ancient Rome had conquered from the bounds of one ocean to the other, but then lost through inertia'. 'Emboldened by having God on our side,' he continued, 'we shun no extreme of discomfort, constantly enduring sleeplessness, fasting, and every other form of hardship for the benefit of our subjects.'[21]

In Ravenna, by contrast, Theodahad was in something of a panic. He attempted to offer terms to Justinian's trusted envoy to Italy, the same Peter whom the emperor had previously sent, as

Procopius put it, 'to throw the Goths and Theodahad into confusion'.[22] The king was willing to make many concessions: renounce all Gothic claims to Sicily; send a gold crown (weighing almost one hundred kilograms) each year to Constantinople, as a sign of his tributary status; provide three thousand Gothic soldiers to serve the emperor as and when required; disclaim any legal authority over senators, priests, and their property; ensure that the emperor's name was acclaimed before his own in the Hippodrome of Rome and all other official contexts; and make sure that statues of the king would only be erected in conjunction with statues of the emperor, with the latter placed in the position of seniority. Peter agreed to forward these proposals to Constantinople.

Theodahad then asked what would happen if Justinian rebuffed his offer. According to Procopius' account, when Peter replied that the war would continue, the king decided to write a letter to the emperor agreeing to surrender Italy in return for extensive estates and an annual income of just under ninety thousand *solidi*. Peter agreed that the second offer would only be put to Justinian if he rejected the first. Predictably, when Theodahad's interlocutor, Rusticius, a priest, made his way to Constantinople, it was the second offer that the emperor accepted. Arrangements began to be put in place to secure a peaceful transfer of power.[23]

Military events on the ground, however, soon intervened to put an end to the apparent concordat between Justinian and Theodahad. The main bulk of the Gothic settlement in Italy, and much of the Gothic military presence, had traditionally been concentrated north of the river Po. This was largely to prevent any invasion from precisely the direction from which Mundo and his army were now advancing. In Sicily and the south, by contrast, Belisarius was faced with a series of much more isolated (and isolatable) Gothic garrisons. In late 535, a large Gothic army entered Dalmatia to confront Mundo and his men. In an initial engagement between the Goths and a Roman reconnoitring party, led by Mundo's son, Maurice, the

Romans had the worst of it, and Maurice was killed. In such circumstances, any father would wish to avenge his son, and Mundo is likely to have been raised in a culture in which the 'blood feud' was one of the most strictly observed of social institutions. Accordingly, he led the main body of the Roman army in a frenzied charge against the Goths, whose forces were routed, with many of their leading nobles killed. As Procopius put it, 'Mundo went on killing and pursuing the enemy wherever he chanced to find them and was totally incapable of restraining himself due to the misfortune that had befallen his son.' The problem, from the Roman perspective, was that Mundo also fell amid the melee, thereby depriving the northern Roman expeditionary force of its leader, and Justinian of one of his most trusted and able generals. Leaderless, the Roman army pulled back from Dalmatia, whilst continuing to occupy Salona. A key component in Justinian's envisaged 'pincer movement' had been blunted. Sensing perhaps a moment of opportunity of his own, Theodahad now withdrew his offer and placed Justinian's envoys under house arrest.[24]

The war resumed in earnest in early 536, when another close military associate of Justinian, a commander named Constantianus, was despatched to Illyricum to raise new forces and advance into Dalmatia, where he forced the Goths (who had managed to briefly reoccupy Salona) to fall back to Ravenna. Simultaneously, to the south, Belisarius initiated the conquest of the Italian mainland, leading his men (as well as his wife) across the Strait of Messina to Rhegium whilst leaving garrisons in Syracuse and Palermo. As he marched through Bruttium and Lucania, with his fleet flanking him along the coast, the general received the surrender of all the major cities through which he passed, whose populations, Procopius tells us, were largely hostile to Gothic rule. He was also joined by a son-in-law of Theoderic, who defected along with his troops.[25] Belisarius then led his men into Campania, reaching Naples. Unlike the cities that had recently capitulated, however, Naples was well fortified and guarded by a substantial number of Gothic troops. Here the Roman advance paused as Belisarius and the Neapolitans pondered what to do.

A notable of the city, one Stephanus, was soon sent to negotiate. He pleaded with the general to bypass the city and proceed directly to Rome. The presence of the Gothic garrison, he explained, precluded the Neapolitans from simply surrendering, and the garrison would not do so, as Theodahad was holding their families hostage to ensure their loyalty. Any attack on the city would lead to the death of many innocent Romans. Procopius records that Belisarius told Stephanus they must 'receive into your city the emperor's army, which has come to secure your freedom and that of the other Italians'. The Gothic garrison, Belisarius continued, had a simple choice: agree to serve the emperor, withdraw from the city, and go home—or die. He added, in private, that if Stephanus was able to secure his compatriots' acquiescence, he would be well rewarded. Accordingly, Stephanus returned to the city and advised his fellow citizens (probably meaning the members of the city council and other notables) to surrender. He was supported in this by a man of influence: 'Antiochus, a man of Syria, but long resident in Naples for the purpose of carrying on a shipping business, who had a reputation there for wisdom and justice'. Stephanus was nevertheless asked to go back to Belisarius to receive further assurances, which he was willing to give. The general pointed out that their near neighbours in Sicily had recently 'exchanged their barbarian tyrants for the sovereignty of Justinian' to no harm.[26] Despite the evident displeasure of the Goths, the Neapolitans seemed on the verge of surrender.

They were eventually dissuaded from this course of action by two pro-Gothic *rhetors* in the city (the term in this context probably means 'practising lawyers'), who pointed out, in essence, that nobody likes a turncoat. Were they to throw the gates of the city open to Belisarius, and the Goths then prove to be victorious, they would be punished for their treachery. If the East Roman authorities ultimately triumphed, they would never respect or trust a population that had turned against its former masters. The leaders of the city's substantial Jewish population, who supported this position, 'promised that the city should be in want of none of the necessities'; the Goths, for their part, 'promised that they would guard the circuit wall safely'.[27] Naples said no to Belisarius and Justinian.

The hostility toward Justinian's armies evident on the part of the Jewish community of Naples is telling. Through commercial and religious networks, the Jews of Naples and southern Italy are likely to have been in relatively regular contact with the Jewish communities of the Roman Near East, who were already finding life difficult under Justinian and his aggressively Christianising regime. Theoderic, by contrast, had been largely protective of his Jewish subjects. As himself a member of what was, in Italian terms, a religious minority, the king had been highly sensitive to the precarious positions of other minorities in his realm. He had assured the Jews of Genoa that 'nobody can be made to believe against his will'.[28] Accordingly, despite Catholic protests, he had allowed the repair of synagogues. In Africa, meanwhile, Justinian had recently ordered all synagogues to be destroyed. The Jews of Naples thus had no real choice but to resist the Romans and remain loyal to the Goths. Indeed, Justinian would not have expected them to do anything else.

Accordingly, Belisarius initiated the siege of Naples. First he attempted to force the inhabitants into submission by cutting the aqueduct into the city to disrupt its water supply, but this tactic achieved little, because there were numerous wells within its walls. Gothic resistance was effective, despite the fact that casualties were high, and Theodahad failed to send the reinforcements for which the Neapolitans pleaded. Eventually, Belisarius' Isaurian troops found a route into the city via the point at which the aqueduct entered its walls. After the Neapolitans rejected one final offer from the general, he sent a detachment of men in under cover of nightfall.

These troops were able to overpower the Gothic defenders manning two towers on the northern side of the city, where Belisarius had massed the bulk of his army, and the Roman troops scaled the walls. The seaward defences of the city, manned by members of the Jewish community, were also eventually overcome, and the city was sacked and plundered after a twenty-day siege. Belisarius' Hunnic troops, in particular, were accused of slaughtering civilians who had taken refuge in churches until the general intervened, ordering that the killing stop and all those who had been seized as slaves be released. 'And thus it came to pass', Procopius noted ironically, 'that on that day the Neapolitans both became captives and regained their liberty.' All surviving Gothic troops were spared from execution.[29] Belisarius was now ready to advance on Rome.

Within Rome itself, tensions were running high. Theodahad's decision to install a Gothic garrison there—probably after Belisarius' occupation of Syracuse—had sparked off rioting, and the king had written to the senators ordering them to intervene and calling upon the population to desist. Beyond Rome, the leading members of the Gothic nobility and army were increasingly aghast at Belisarius' advance and Theodahad's inability to contain it. They gathered together at Regata, about fifty kilometres south of Rome, to elect a new king, and chose the best warrior from amongst their ranks, the warlord Witigis. Hearing this, Theodahad attempted to flee towards Ravenna, but was hunted down and killed. Witigis now sought to rally the rank-and-file of the Gothic army behind him, reminding them of his 'reputation in war' and declaring that 'he who is able to imitate his [Theoderic's] deeds is he who should be regarded his kinsman'.[30] He also visited Rome in order to stake his claim to authority there.[31]

With Belisarius' army approaching, one might have expected Witigis to stand and fight. Instead, he withdrew with the bulk of his army to Ravenna, entrusting the city of Rome to a garrison of some four thousand troops. The reason was that negotiations between

Constantinople and the Franks had borne fruit, and the Franks were now threatening the Gothic heartlands to the north, which were also vulnerable to Roman attack. Whilst there, he forced Amalasuntha's daughter, Matasuentha, to marry him, so that he could claim a connection by marriage to the dynasty of Theoderic. In order to fend off the Franks, he surrendered to them all remaining Gothic territories in southern Gaul.[32] In Rome, all eyes were now on Belisarius, and with the seemingly enthusiastic encouragement of the recently appointed pope, Silverius (who had succeeded Pope John II in May 535), an envoy was sent to the general inviting him to take possession of the city. As the Roman expeditionary force advanced along the Via Appia, the Gothic garrison melted away. On 10 December 536, Belisarius led his men into Rome via the Porta Asinaria, militarily unopposed.[33] The one Gothic commander who had been left behind was sent to Justinian, in order to present him with the keys to the city. As Procopius would reminisce, 'And so Rome became subject to the Romans again after a space of sixty years.'[34]

THE DOORS OF THE TEMPLE OF JANUS

Belisarius was not a man minded to rest on his laurels. Procopius tells us he immediately set about restoring and improving the circuit walls and defences of the city, anticipating a Gothic counter-attack, directed and perhaps led by Witigis.[35] This was a sensible move, given that the general is reported to have had only 7,000 men with him (many others having been left behind to garrison the cities he had already taken). At the same time, a number of other towns in which Gothic garrisons were notable primarily by virtue of their absence came over to him, the chief of these being Beneventum, so that imperial authority soon extended over Calabria to the south and Apulia to the southeast. A high-ranking Gothic commander in Samnium defected along with his men, giving Belisarius effective control of most of the Italian Peninsula south of Rome. He despatched envoys into Tuscany, where they were welcomed warmly by the inhabitants of Spoletum and Perugia.[36]

To the north, Witigis had managed to secure an uneasy peace with the Franks. His armies in Dalmatia had also successfully contained the imperial advance, pinning down Roman forces at Salona.[37] Now aware of how few men Belisarius actually had with him in Rome, the king rallied his troops in an attempt to retake the city which had been the jewel in the crown of Theoderic's kingdom. On 21 February 537 he made his move, advancing with an army Procopius estimated as comprising some 150,000 cavalry and foot soldiers.[38] The real number of men Witigis mobilised is, of course, unknowable: what Procopius meant to convey was that Belisarius and his troops, holed up in Rome, were massively outnumbered.[39] Frantic efforts were made to concentrate as many imperial troops in Rome as possible without jeopardising the broader territorial gains that had been made. Falling back behind the defences which Belisarius had so recently (and presciently) repaired, his men took up position to resist a siege that would last for over a year, and which Procopius, as one of those defending the city, would narrate in detail.[40]

To Procopius, Belisarius is very much the hero of the tale as he sought to outwit the Goths, prevent his officers from panicking, maintain the morale of both his troops and the civilian population, and stop them from defecting. All able-bodied Roman males were signed up to help man the walls. Despite the huge numerical advantage that the Goths enjoyed, Witigis' troop numbers were not quite sufficient for him to completely surround the circuit defences of the city and thus fully isolate it. Nor did he feel comfortable trying to take Rome by storm, which would have necessitated a very high casualty rate amongst his own men and might have led to a collapse of Gothic morale. Despite seemingly insuperable odds, Belisarius was always careful to display a publicly confident demeanour and to raise the spirits of those who depended on him. Musicians were even instructed to play instruments on the walls at night. Meanwhile, Berber scouts accompanied by guard dogs were sent outside to raise the alarm should there be any sign of a nocturnal assault.

As the Gothic siege tightened, Belisarius managed to send a letter to Justinian informing him that he was desperately short of men and begging for reinforcements: 'Let both arms and soldiers be sent to us in such numbers', Procopius claims he wrote, 'that from now on we may engage with this enemy with an equal strength.'[41] Justinian ordered more troops to be sent, but their progress from Greece towards Italy proved to be painfully slow.[42] In order to preserve supplies, Belisarius ordered that all women and children, and men unable to fight, be evacuated to Naples. Some were sent by ship from Portus, whilst others were allowed to leave the city by land unmolested by the Goths. Pope Silverius and several senators were also escorted out of Rome, after Belisarius became suspicious that they were trying to negotiate with the enemy. The pope was taken off to Greece, presumably 'for his own safety', and was replaced as bishop of Rome by a priest named Vigilius. The psychological pressures resulting from the siege led some of the locals to revive older, pre-Christian traditions, which they evidently hoped would help secure the city's survival. Procopius tells us, for example, that the bronze doors to the Temple of Janus in the forum were secretly levered slightly ajar, thereby reviving the pagan tradition that they should always be left open while Rome was at war.[43]

In early April 537, Roman reinforcements finally reached Rome by boat. Although their numbers were not vast (some 1,600 cavalry, made up of Huns and other barbarians recruited from the Balkans), Belisarius decided to take advantage of the arrival of fresh troops to try to break the siege. He ordered a series of sorties to be made outside the city walls, in which his horseback archers, in particular, inflicted considerable casualties on the Goths. Witigis' forces, however, managed to contain a more sustained attempt on the part of

Belisarius' men, including a major infantry component, to break out of the city. The general concluded that his best bet would be to harry and wear down the attackers with repeated cavalry raids. Within Rome, famine and disease were starting to take their toll. Procopius was spirited out of the city and sent to Naples to try to gather supplies, and the remaining civilian population implored Belisarius to bring the struggle to a head in a decisive encounter. They could take no more. Disease also began to afflict the Gothic camp. Exhaustion was mutual. At this point, Procopius recounts, he managed to return to the city, not only with supplies, but also accompanied by over 5,000 additional Roman troops, who approached both by land and by river. In order to distract the Goths and allow these men a chance to join with the defenders, Belisarius launched a sudden cavalry attack as a diversionary measure. The strategy worked.[44]

Aware that additional Roman troops had successfully reached the city, Witigis finally despaired of victory and entered into negotiations with Belisarius. The Gothic envoys told Belisarius the Romans could have Sicily, 'since without it you cannot possess Africa in security'. Belisarius replied, according to Procopius, 'And we on our side permit the Goths to have the whole of Britain.'[45] There was no point in people offering land they claimed to own but which, in practice, they did not control. The Goths then agreed to surrender all claims to Naples and Campania and to pay an annual tribute. Belisarius said he was not authorized to accept any such deal and would await instructions from the emperor. In late December 537, an exchange of hostages occurred, and a three-month armistice was agreed as Belisarius awaited orders. But in a sudden move to try to catch the general off guard, Witigis made three more attempts to gain entry to the city: through the broken aqueduct, through an adjacent gate, and then by boat. Each of these failed, and Witigis finally withdrew from Rome. The siege ended in mid-March of 538. Additional Roman reinforcements also arrived in the peninsula, led by the general Narses, who had previously helped crush the Nika revolt.

A dispute between Belisarius and Narses soon ensued over how best to proceed, with Belisarius, anxious about the precariousness of the Roman position, favouring the consolidation of territory already held, whilst Narses wanted to take battle to the enemy and expand the sphere of imperial control. This argument revealed simmering tensions and rivalries within the Roman army's officer corps. Belisarius had recently survived an assassination attempt perpetrated by a disgruntled subaltern, and the ambitious Narses was eager to fuel such discontent. When Belisarius was obliged to brandish his official letter of appointment from Justinian granting him plenipotentiary power and ordering all officers and troops 'to follow him in the interest of our state', Narses quibbled that there was no obligation to follow orders if his commands were *not* in fact in the interest of the state but informed by poor strategic thinking. Belisarius eventually reported Narses to Justinian for insubordination, and Justinian ordered that he briefly return to Constantinople.[46]

BELISARIUS EMPEROR OF THE WEST?

Witigis, now convinced that Belisarius was preparing to march on Ravenna, sought to mobilise the empire's potential enemies and rivals on other fronts. According to Procopius, the king sent envoys to the Lombards in the northwestern Balkans only to find that their ruler had negotiated an alliance with Justinian. He then decided to send an embassy to the Persian shah, Khusro, encouraging him to break the 'Endless Peace' that had been negotiated in 532. Witigis used bribes to get two 'priests of Liguria' (the assumption must be that they were Catholics) to travel east and convey his message to the Persian court. One pretended to be a bishop, the other his attendant (thus enabling them to use the *cursus velox*, or imperial transport and relay system). Once in Ctesiphon, Procopius claims, they told Khusro that if he did not strike soon, it would be too late, as Justinian would emerge from victory in Italy too powerful to defeat, and was bound thereafter to direct his armies towards Persia.[47] Khusro appears to have heeded their advice.

Seemingly alert to signs of Persian mobilisation on the eastern front, Justinian 'decided to bring the war in the West to an end as quickly as possible, and to recall Belisarius, in order that he might take the field against the Persians'.[48] Gothic ambassadors whom Witigis had sent to Constantinople to negotiate during the course of the previous armistice were sent back to inform their king that a peace delegation from Constantinople was imminent. In the meantime, Belisarius did indeed set about trying to isolate Ravenna in preparation for an assault on the epicentre of Gothic rule, cutting off its supply route along the river Po. Witigis now offered to share what remained of his kingdom with the Franks, if their leader Theodebert would come to his aid. Belisarius managed to persuade the Frankish ruler, however, that he would have more to gain from a deal with Justinian. As conditions in Ravenna deteriorated, Goths in the surrounding forts and settlements began to desert and come to terms with the Romans.[49]

It was at this point that Justinian's envoys arrived in pursuit of a peace settlement. Again, Procopius recorded the terms in some detail. He remained by Belisarius' side and so is likely to have been well informed as to the nature of the offer conveyed, which may have represented the full extent of Justinian's ambitions with respect to Italy at this moment in time. The ambassadors informed Witigis that Justinian was effectively willing to let the king keep his crown and his capital at Ravenna, and to recognise a rump Gothic state north of the Po. In return, the Goths would be expected to share half of the income of the Gothic royal treasury with Justinian and recognize Roman authority to the south, which Justinian would make 'subject and tributary to himself'.[50] Witigis and his court signalled that these terms were acceptable. A deal seemed to have been struck.

The one stumbling block was Belisarius. Convinced that the prize of Ravenna was within reach, Procopius reports, the general refused to add his signature to the treaty, as the Goths expected him to do. Desperate for peace and sensing an opportunity to avoid having to subject those Gothic communities south of the Po to Justinian's direct rule, members of the Gothic nobility, and then representatives from Witigis himself, came to Belisarius with a new proposal. They would surrender the entirety of Italy to him if he agreed to become emperor in the West, occupying the throne which Romulus Augustulus had been obliged to vacate in 476, and ruling over both Italians and Goths.[51] Belisarius agreed, swearing that he would do the Goths no harm, but indicating that he would not ratify the deal formally until he was within Ravenna and in the presence of Witigis and his leading noblemen. He informed his high command that the Gothic capital would soon be theirs if they did what he told them. Soon thereafter, Belisarius and his army entered the city, whilst also ordering that ships carrying grain dock in the adjacent port of Classe, so as to feed Ravenna's now starving population. The Gothic envoys marched with him, oblivious to the fact that the general had set them up.

After first Carthage, then Syracuse, and most recently Rome, Belisarius now made his fourth great entry into a hitherto enemy-held city essentially unopposed. 'And while I watched the entry of the Roman army into Ravenna at that time,' Procopius would relate, 'it occurred to me that it is not at all by the wisdom of men or by any other sort of excellence on their part that events are brought to fulfilment, but that there is some divine power which is ever warping their purposes. . . . For although the Goths were greatly superior to their opponents in number and in power . . . still they were being made captives by the weaker army.' Moreover, he noted, 'when the women, as they sat at the gate, had seen the whole army (for they had heard from their husbands that the enemy were men of great size and too numerous to be counted), they all spat in the faces of their husbands, and pointing with their hands to the victors, reviled them for their cowardice'.[52]

Once ensconced in Ravenna—and still, according to Procopius, maintaining the pretence that he was about to revive the Western Empire—Belisarius placed Witigis under protective guard, and told those Gothic troops resident there whose families were beyond the Po that they could return home. As Roman troops secured their positions across the city, he took possession of the royal treasury, with a view to sending it on to the emperor. Representatives of the Gothic garrisons in the surrounding towns soon began arriving to pledge loyalty to Belisarius, thus allowing him to extend his authority over Venetia and the Treviso. The only Gothic warlord of any significance who demurred was a certain Ildibad, who commanded the Gothic troops in Verona. It is recorded that he sent envoys to Belisarius (as his children, we are told, were held as diplomatic hostages in Ravenna), but he did not submit to him.[53]

Belisarius was playing a dangerous game. Procopius insists that the general had no real intention of claiming the title of western emperor for himself. But he must have been tempted. The Goths were clearly mostly willing to submit, and many of his troops were devoted to him. What did his wife, Antonina, think? She had followed him the whole campaign through. Belisarius was soon obliged to make up his mind, for reports yet again began to reach the emperor that, for all his professions of loyalty, the general was considering setting himself up as an independent ruler in the West. Given the increasingly serious military situation to the East, Justinian decided that the best course of action was to summon Belisarius home. The Gothic leadership expected him to ignore the summons, 'thinking that Belisarius would never regard the kingdom of Italy as of less account than loyalty to Justinian'.[54] By the time they realised that he was not only intent on returning to Constantinople, but also planning to take the Gothic royal treasury and their captive king with him, it was too late. They had handed their capital over to Belisarius, and through Belisarius, had gifted it, and mastery of Italy, to Justinian.

Before Belisarius departed, the remnants of the Gothic nobility gathered together and after some deliberation decided to offer the crown to Ildibad, the Lord of Verona, who had kept Belisarius at arm's length. It was agreed that first Ildibad should yet again offer to submit on behalf of the Goths, if only Belisarius would consent to remain as emperor. Instead, in 540, Belisarius set sail for Byzantium, taking with him Witigis, other leading Goths, King Ildibad's own children, and the Gothic royal treasury (comprising vast sums of gold, silver, and precious gems). All of these he would present to Justinian, whilst entrusting Ravenna and the rest of Italy beyond the Gothic enclave around Verona to the most loyal of his commanders. It appeared that Italy, too, had now been restored to the empire. As had also been the case with Africa, Roman tax collectors sent out from Constantinople would soon be on their way.[55]

In marked contrast to his arrival in Constantinople in 534, when his achievements had been the occasion for victory celebrations, Belisarius' arrival in the capital in 540 was a relatively muted affair. As Procopius tells us, 'upon receiving the wealth of Theoderic, a notable sight in itself, he [Justinian] merely set it forth for the members of the Senate to view privately in the palace, being jealous of the magnitude and splendour of the achievement; and neither did he bring it out before the people, nor did he accord Belisarius the customary triumph, as he had done when he returned from his victory over Gelimer and the Vandals. However, the name of Belisarius was on the lips of all.' 'Tall and remarkably handsome', 'affable' and humble, 'beloved by both soldiers and peasants', the charismatic general had made a great impression. Everywhere on the streets of Constantinople, Belisarius was followed by adoring crowds, thereby arousing both Justinian's suspicions and Theodora's jealousy. The sooner Justinian could get him away from the capital and back fighting the Persians, the better.[56]

Chapter 10

The Sleepless Emperor

THE EAGLE AND THE SNAKE

In a simple but elegant museum adjacent to a sleepy side street in Sultanahmet, the old town of Istanbul, lie a series of mosaics that once covered the sixth-century 'peristyle' (or cloistered) courtyard of the Great Palace of Constantinople.[1] The scenes they depict are largely of a bucolic or sporting character, perhaps meant to distract, entertain, and raise the spirits of those courtiers, officials, guardsmen, and envoys who would have viewed them on a regular basis. A young boy tends geese; a farmer feeds a donkey; young men enjoy the pleasures of the hunt; while animals fight in the wild or in the circus. One image, however, stands out for its political resonance. It is an eagle, symbolizing the office and person of the emperor, locked in struggle with a snake. The snake is wrapping its body around the eagle, in an evident effort to constrict and crush it. At the same time, the eagle grasps the snake's neck in its ferocious beak, tearing at its writhing body with its talons, eyes fixed purposefully on the serpent, signalling both its clear intent to kill and the imminence of its victory. Although scholars quibble over the precise date of these mosaics, this is an image that perfectly encapsulates how Justinian viewed himself, his enemies, and the nature of his imperial mission.[2] Locked in mortal combat with a slippery and poisonous foe, the emperor could not afford to relax or relent.

This may explain why, as well as a series of foreign campaigns aimed at restoring Roman might abroad, the 530s also saw Justinian engage in a major wave of administrative reform. He overhauled provincial structures of government in order to tighten central control, and maximized tax revenues to help fund his armies, cracking down on tax evasion and lawlessness within the provincial and senatorial aristocracy, his attitude towards many members of these elites marked by hostility and suspicion. The laws he issued to effect these changes and others would be known collectively as his *Novels*, or 'New Laws' (they were 'new' in that they were issued after the codification of imperial constitutions contained in the code). The contents of these laws (the first full and annotated English translation of which I published with my friend and collaborator David Miller) reveal more clearly than any other source the emperor's personal 'voice' and concerns.[3] At one point, we even catch the emperor making a joke, albeit with respect to the serious issue of the grounds on which a wife was allowed to divorce her husband. She could do so, the emperor declared, if, amongst other things, he took up sorcery, brought other women into the family home, hid bandits, or started robbing tombs and stealing livestock—'Of course,' Justinian adds, 'she would not have to prove all these grounds at once!' The wife, by contrast, could be divorced for 'engaging in witchcraft', 'spending the night out against her husband's wishes', 'enjoying herself by attending the races against his will', or merely 'visiting theatres'.[4]

In other instances, the laws are composed in the florid style of his learned chief legal officer, Tribonian.[5] But the policy agenda and mindset that they reveal are unmistakably those of the emperor. Justinian represented himself in them as the 'sleepless emperor', ever alert to the needs of his subjects and the business of state (a motif which, as we have seen, he had previously deployed in the inscription celebrating the construction of the Church of Saints Sergius and Bacchus).[6] The legislation reveals a remarkable concern for detail and an obsession with the minutiae of government, down to the fine detail of the level of remuneration to be assigned to junior officials serving governors on the distant fringes of empire in Palestine, Egypt, and Arabia.[7] Indeed, some have even drawn comparison in this regard between Justinian and Stalin.[8] Across this legislation, we also see the emperor taking Roman law in new directions, breaking away from the more traditional modes of thought that had informed—and constrained—the legal thinking of his predecessors.[9] Justinian's *Novels* effectively mark the beginning of Byzantine law.

The emperor clearly understood that a measure of his authority had to be delegated to those who served under him, and he frequently complained of the volume of petitions and appeals from the provinces that came to him, in person, at court.[10] Yet, psychologically, he evidently had great difficulty in letting go. He was particularly furious when he discovered that cases and appeals that he had assigned to other judges and officials to hear on his behalf were being conducted *as if* the emperor were present, and that 'litigants, their representatives, their advocates and all those serving on such cases were using apparel, footwear and language before our officials that befit only those entering [into the presence of] the Sovereign'.

As his laws reveal, Justinian had a superabundant sense of his own dignity. The legislation also reveals the active role that the empress Theodora played in the business of government. In a measure prohibiting the purchase of governmental office, for example, Justinian informs John the Cappadocian, his chief finance minister, that it was only after first considering the matter himself, and then referring it to 'our God-given and most pious consort' Theodora, that he had put it before John and taken some of his views into account.[11] The sequencing of the consultation was telling.

Purging the Senate in the immediate aftermath of the Nika riots had allowed Justinian to rid himself of those senators whom he most distrusted or whose popularity and appeal he most feared. He also took advantage of the weakness of his opponents in the aftermath of the revolt, and the goodwill generated towards the regime by the seemingly easy victories in Africa, Sicily, and Rome, to fundamentally recast political conditions in Constantinople. Henceforth, whilst senatorial *status* would remain hereditary, active membership of the Senate would increasingly be limited to those holding the highest senatorial grades, which only came by virtue of holding office, to which Justinian had a monopoly on appointment. The sons of the highest-ranking senators (*illustres*) did not automatically inherit that rank (although they could petition the emperor to award it to them). Justinian also charged this reconfigured Senate with enhanced judicial authority, turning the assembly into more of a branch of government than an element of the constitution.[12]

Although he and Theodora remained childless, Justinian also tightened his grip on power by appointing members of his own extended family to high military office (such as his cousin Germanus, whom he had sent to Africa to help contain discontent amongst the troops). Justinian appointed more members of his family to high office than any other emperor of the sixth century. To the one nephew whom he did not make a general, he granted the politically important position at court of *curopalates* ('one who takes care of the palace').[13] It was this nephew, Justin, who would eventually succeed him on the throne, although there is no indication that Justinian was attempting to line him up for it. It seems likely that Justinian surrounded himself with family in this manner to insulate and protect himself from his enemies and rivals.

ORDER ON THE STREETS

In the aftermath of the Nika insurrection, Justinian was determined to impose law and order on the streets of Constantinople. He also wanted to stem what he saw as the unrestrained and potentially politically destabilizing flow of economic migrants and petitioners from the provinces into the city. In 535 he created the new office of the 'praetor of the people', with special responsibility to 'quell public disorder'. This praetor would have an extensive staff at his disposal. These officials would help the praetor in 'detaining the disorderly whenever necessary and putting the civic administration into proper shape'. The praetor himself was to be answerable not only to the urban prefect of Constantinople (who was traditionally responsible for law and order in the city), but also to the emperor in person. Justinian wanted direct assurance that the streets of his capital were under control. As he informed his subjects in the law establishing this post, 'We will leave nothing undone which is in your interests. . . . Your individual concerns are our concerns. . . . [We] maintain a paternal care for you all.'[14]

In 539 Justinian also created the office of *quaesitor*. As well as assisting the praetor in the task of supervising and policing the population of Constantinople, this official was given special responsibility for what we might think of as immigration control. Provincial petitioners with genuine legal grievances, which they had a right to take before the emperor or his representatives, were to have their cases expedited. Economic migrants were to be refused entry, and all able-bodied beggars were to be either removed from the city, if they were not native to it, or forced to work if they were. Leniency was only to be shown to those beggars described as 'physically handicapped, or grey or infirm', who were 'by our command to remain in this city unmolested' and to receive support from its charitable institutions. Officials were also to be posted at the main maritime approaches to the capital to prevent undesirables from arriving by ship.[15]

In this legislation, Justinian draws a novel distinction between those 'native' to the city (the 'Byzantines' of Constantinople) as a separate and distinct people, or *ethnos*, and those who, though Roman, were outsiders, who should 'avoid abandoning their homelands and leading a wretched life over here, perhaps dying deprived of what is theirs, and without even the benefit of their ancestral burial-grounds'.[16] As the adopted son of an economic migrant who had come to the city to make a better life, Justinian might have been expected to show greater sympathy towards others who wished to do the same. But as emperor, his overriding priority was to maintain social order. He was also determined to maintain economic order, as the steady flow of tax revenues to the capital depended upon it. The same law reveals, for example, that one of the main factors drawing petitioners to Constantinople was a desire on the part of agricultural and estate workers to petition and even sue their landowning employers, who were presumably resident members of the Constantinopolitan aristocracy. Bands of such peasants were only to be allowed to send one representative at a time (rather than be admitted en masse), and they were to be sent home again as soon as possible, as 'their time away from work on the land' was, Justinian declared, 'injurious both to themselves and to their masters'.[17]

'OUR FACE GOES RED WHEN WE HEAR OF SUCH LAWLESSNESS'

The emperor had only ever regarded the codification of the inherited body of the law as the first phase in a much broader programme of reform intended to make the law much more accessible to his subjects: 'Greater justice closer to home' would accurately sum up Justinian's core legal objective subsequent to the promulgation of the *Digest* in 534. His next step, therefore, was to strengthen the writ of imperial law in the provincial world beyond Constantinople. Indeed, this was a necessary precursor to limiting the flow of petitioners into the capital, where, he claimed, they were clogging up the courts.

Possibly as early as January 535, Justinian issued a law reinvigorating the courts of provincial governors.[18] In August that same year, he went to great lengths to strengthen the office of 'civic defender' (*defensor civitatis*). These were civic officials charged with defending the interests of poorer provincials against the powerful, and who, by Justinian's day, served as the lowest rung of the judiciary.[19] Until then, such 'defenders' had only been allowed to hear cases dealing with disputes worth up to fifty *solidi*. Justinian increased that sum to three hundred, making the civic tribunal presided over by the *defensor* the court of first instance for the overwhelming majority of his subjects.[20] Appeals against the judgements issued by such *defensores* were to go before the local provincial governor in person, and the *defensor* of each city had the right to report the governor of their province to the praetorian prefect in Constantinople if he thought he was up to no good. Amongst other responsibilities, the *defensor* was charged with the maintenance of local archives to preserve legal and fiscal documents. He also had responsibility for prosecuting pagans and heretics. 'These provisions', Justinian declared, 'are to be in force for all time, since we have devised them, with all unsleeping earnestness and zeal towards God, as a gift for our subjects.'[21]

Justinian then proceeded to further limit the flow of appeals to the imperial capital (and, ultimately, to the imperial court) by clustering provinces together and designating within each cluster a higher-ranking governor who was entitled to hear appeals on the emperor's behalf. Such appeal-court judges were entitled, however, to refer cases upwards to Constantinople if they were deemed to be especially complicated or of particular legal significance. The reformed procedures could be remarkably speedy in operation: in 543, for example, an important case pertaining to inheritance rights would be fast-tracked from the court of first instance in Antioch all the way through to the emperor in Constantinople in barely eighteen months.[22]

Justinian's insistence that the civic defenders keep a careful eye on their governors and report any suspicions that they harboured directly to Constantinople was telling. Similar instructions were issued to bishops urging them to act as the emperor's 'eyes and ears' in the provinces, observing the governors' every move.[23] The provincial governor was the linchpin in the Roman system of administration, and indolence or—worse—corruption on his part threatened the legal, political, and fiscal stability of the entire realm. Local corruption generated legal complaints and petitions to the capital; occasioned discontent and insubordination in the provinces; and could lead to the siphoning off of the vital tax revenues on which the state depended for its administrative cohesion and military effectiveness. The same was true of tax evasion by wealthy and well-connected landowners in the provinces, facilitated by corrupt governors. Fewer taxes meant fewer soldiers, and at a time of mounting warfare, Justinian wanted more of both (he complained in one of his laws that the state was beset by 'heavy expenditure and large-scale wars').[24] Accordingly, from 534, he unleashed a remarkable wave of legislation to address the problem of corruption on the part of governors whilst simultaneously strengthening their authority over their subordinates, as well as seeking to disentangle them from what had become increasingly powerful networks of local patronage and aristocratic control by dramatically improving their levels of pay. Through these measures, he hoped to focus the loyalty of provincial governors more directly on the person of the emperor and his court.

The flagship piece of legislation was issued on 15 April 535.[25] In it, the emperor prohibited the purchase of governorships, which had become standard practice since the late fourth century (and the acceptability of which Justinian had taken for granted just a year earlier, when issuing the second version of his code).[26] The sale of provincial governorships might have had initial 'up-front' benefits to the government, but in the long term, Justinian had concluded (in consultation with Theodora) that it was counterproductive, as it effectively incentivised recently appointed governors to seek to recoup their costs by illicitly extorting money from their newly acquired provincial subjects.[27] Newly appointed governors were still expected to pay an 'entry fee' when coming into office, but it was to be proportionate and carefully regulated.

In justification of the legislation, Justinian painted a vivid picture of provincial lawlessness: 'People are deserting their provinces,' he declared, 'and all of them—priests, city councillors, civil servants, property-owners, townsfolk, agricultural workers—come pouring over here in distress, quite rightly complaining of the officeholders' thefts and injustices. Nor is that all: riots in cities, and civil disturbances, are in large part caused from start to finish by money. In sum, all the troubles stem from one and the same cause: the officeholders' demands for money are the beginning and end of every iniquity.' The cupidity of his governors and administrators demonstrated, the emperor continued, the 'complete truth of the saying in divine scriptures: "Love of money is the mother of all evils."' 'No one in the past', he complained, 'has had the courage to rebuke them openly.'[28] No one, that is, until Justinian.

The fine detail of the law that ensues is highly revealing. The emperor can be observed cracking down on illicit fees and bribes charged by government officials; regularizing the procedures for appointing provincial governors (who would have to swear before God to 'keep their hands clean'); ensuring that new governors both understood and recognized the importance of collecting taxes; making it easier for provincials to sue or denounce former governors after they had left office; and ordering military units stationed in the provinces to help the governors when asked.[29] In the schedule attached to the law, he set out in fine detail what entry fees were to be payable by governors across the entirety of the empire, and precisely what allowances his officers were entitled to receive by way of pay.[30]

Justinian also assured his subjects that so long as taxes were paid in full, and the tax revenues properly and fully forwarded to Constantinople, no increase in the level of provincial taxation would be necessary. Increased rates of taxation, he feared, 'would destroy our subjects' entire livelihood'. Maintaining taxes at a reasonable level required everyone to play by the rules: 'For our part, what we regard as sufficient revenue for the Sovereign is simply the bringing in of the public taxes in full.' 'Therefore,' Justinian concluded, 'let all people alike send up hymns of praise to our great God and saviour Jesus Christ for this very law, which will grant them safe residence in their homelands and secure possession of their property, in enjoyment of justice from their rulers.' He was keen to convey to his subjects that he would not allow 'any unjust treatment of the people whom God has entrusted to us'. The language of imperial law thus morphed into that of the 'Divine Liturgy' celebrated in the empire's churches. This legislation, moreover, was to be proclaimed and advertised not only in Constantinople but throughout the cities of the empire.[31]

Importantly, Justinian's legislation of 535 ordained that upon taking office all governors were henceforth to swear an oath 'by Almighty God and his only-begotten son Jesus Christ our God, by the Holy Spirit, by the holy, glorious Mother of God and ever-virgin

Mary, by the four gospels . . . and by the holy archangels Michael and Gabriel' to attend 'vigilantly to the tax revenues', and to perform 'true service to our most divine and pious lords Justinian and Theodora, consort in the same Majesty'. The stridently Christian tone of the oath is unsurprising. Non-Christians had been excluded from holding official posts for a number of years now, and new governors also had to swear that they were 'in communion with God's holy catholic and apostolic church' and would 'in no way and at no time oppose it'. What was striking, however, was the obligation to swear personal loyalty and devotion to both Justinian and his wife, the empress Theodora (presenting her, to all intents and purposes, as a co-ruler). This sort of duty of absolute loyalty not to the state, but rather to the person of the ruler as one's individual lord, was characteristic of the increasingly lord- and king-focused societies that had emerged under barbarian rule in the fifth- and sixth-century West.[32] But many of a more conservative frame of mind would have regarded it as deeply un-Roman.

At the same time, Justinian issued a set of instructions reiterating what he regarded to be the most pressing causes of disorder at a provincial level to which he expected his governors to attend. Given the military context—and the fiscal pressures the emperor and his praetorian prefect, John the Cappadocian, believed were likely to arise as a result—there is an understandable emphasis on tax evasion and making sure governors did not pocket tax revenues for themselves. Rioting by Circus Factions and others in the cities of the empire was also to be put down. Legal proceedings were to be settled swiftly, and appeals to Constantinople kept to a minimum. Officials were not to make unauthorised or unnecessary demands of the emperor's subjects, and even when 'hunting down heresy', they were to maintain order and observe property rights.[33]

In particular, governors were to keep a careful eye on members of the provincial (and largely senatorial) landowning elite. Such men and their families were not to be permitted to engage in 'unjust patronage', not only by withholding taxes but also by trying to assert ownership of lands which were not really theirs, including property that belonged to the Crown and the imperial government. They were to be prevented from forcing peasants to work on their estates as tied agricultural labourers (*coloni adscripticii*), or poaching *coloni* owned by others. Civilians were to be prohibited from carrying arms. The governors' terms of appointment were also to be widely disseminated: 'As soon as you set foot in the province,' Justinian declared, 'you will call a meeting of all those with a position of authority in the main city there (we mean the most God-beloved bishop, the holy clergy and the civic authorities). You will make these divine orders of ours known to them with an entry in the public records; and you will post a copy of them publicly, not just in the main city [*metropolis*] but also in the other cities of the province . . . for all to know the terms upon which you have taken up your office, and to see whether you are observing them, and proving yourself worthy of our choice.'[34] Yet again, Justinian emphasised encouraging mutual surveillance and supervision on the part of his subjects, urging them to inform on one another. As a result of this strategy (and possibly satirising it), Procopius would later complain that during Justinian's reign 'it was not possible to elude the vigilance of multitudes of spies, nor, if detected, to escape a most cruel death'. 'Indeed,' he added, 'I was unable to keep confidence even in the most intimate of my kinsmen.'[35]

The broad concerns set out by Justinian in his general instructions to governors were soon followed by a series of wide-ranging but interconnected laws concerned with individual provinces. From 535 to 539, the emperor set about overhauling the fiscal and administrative structures of no fewer than nineteen provinces in a concerted move to upgrade the fiscal and administrative cohesion of the East Roman state. That these efforts were primarily the result of perceived financial pressures arising from the superpower rivalry with Persia is strongly indicated by the fact that the Sasanian shah, Khusro, simultaneously engaged in a series of largely parallel reforms.[36]

Justinian sought to bolster the governors' authority by uniting both military and civil responsibilities in their hands (thus dismantling the system introduced by Diocletian, which was predicated on their separation). Only in those frontier provinces most bedevilled by military insecurity or internal unrest (such as Armenia, Palestine, and Arabia) was the distinction preserved. On 18 May 535, for example, Justinian issued a law reforming the administration of Pisidia in southern Anatolia, which was renowned for the lawlessness of its inhabitants, who had been able to avoid the full reach of imperial government due to the region's intractable and mountainous landscape. This territory, Justinian declared, 'needs a higher and more powerful governor, as there are very large, heavily populated settlements in it, often actually in revolt against the public taxes. We have found, too, that this governorship includes under its authority the bandit-ridden, murderous regions situated on the mountain ridge called the Wolf's Head, known as the homeland of the "Wolfheads", and that it is campaigning against this area in a hit-and-run sort of style, instead of in a proper military fashion.' The newly appointed governor of the redrawn province, henceforth to be known as the 'Justinianic praetor', or *praetor Justinianus*, was to banish from it 'murders, adulteries, abductions of virgins, and all crime' and to 'uphold justice throughout, with regard to our laws, and try cases in accordance with them'. He was to prevent the onward flow of petitioners to Constantinople 'coming here and troubling us with minor cases', and was not 'to permit the cities to riot nor the population outside of them to defy the public treasury'.[37]

This legislation on Pisidia was only one of a bundle of laws concerned with provincial reform issued on the same day. Justinian also released legislation on Lycaonia and Isauria (which stretched over an extensive area of the interior of Asia Minor), where the emperor denounced the inhabitants as both tax-shy and violent, and Thrace (encompassing the region in the vicinity of Constantinople on the European side). Two months later, on 16 July, further laws were issued overhauling the provinces of Helenopontus (on the Black Sea coast) and the adjacent territory of Paphlagonia. With respect to the former, Justinian declared, 'It seems to us that, by the gift of God, it was reserved to ourselves not merely to bestow freedom on Africa, and the nations there, but also to free those in the very heart of our realm', by stopping corruption amongst governors and tax collectors. The governor was obliged to 'keep his hands clean' (a phrase the emperor deployed repeatedly), whilst simultaneously making sure to 'enrich the public treasury, taking every care for its interests and refraining from accepting anything for himself'.[38]

In the legislation on Paphlagonia, Justinian again sought rhetorically to connect his western campaigns of reconquest and his efforts to restore imperial authority within the provinces of the empire: 'We, who have liberated those who had been our taxpayers from barbarians and restored to them their ancient freedom, will not let those who are our own be slaves to others.' In several of these laws, too, he renamed the reformed governorships after himself: the *praetores Justiniani* of Lycaonia, Thrace, and Paphlagonia, and the *moderator Justinianus* of Helenopontus.[39] He also named new military regiments in his own honour, typically units made up of recruits from the newly occupied territories (such as the 'Vandals of Justinian', or *Vandali Justiniani*).[40] It was perhaps with some reason that Procopius would later criticise Justinian for megalomania, berating him for his obsession that 'everything should be new and should bear his name'.[41]

Another major piece of legislation was issued in March 536 concerned with the administration of Cappadocia, at the heart of the Anatolian Plateau. This was a crucial region for a number of reasons, not least because it was home to a large number of estates which belonged to the imperial household. These were treated as the private property of the emperor and would appear to have been centres of textile production, from which major profits could be derived. The law reveals that Justinian had assigned a significant proportion of the revenue from these estates to the empress Theodora, thereby providing her with a very substantial private income of some 3,600 *solidi* a year. This, of course, represented just a fraction of her wealth, as we know that Justinian also granted his wife similar estates elsewhere in the empire, such as in Egypt.[42] Cappadocia was also prime horse-rearing country, and the imperial estates appear to have provided mounts for the cavalry.[43] The emperor thus had good reason to take a keen interest in the administration of the province, where he granted the new governorship the lofty title of *proconsul Justinianus Cappadociae* ('Justinianic proconsul of Cappadocia').[44]

The picture the legislation paints of conditions in the region was not a pretty one: 'The properties of the crown treasury [i.e., the imperial estates]', Justinian tells us, 'have fallen into such a terribly run-down state and have been sold off in every direction, such that they are practically valueless', whilst 'the managers of landholdings belonging to powerful personages . . . have bodyguards protecting them . . . all committing barefaced banditry.' As a result, the emperor continues, 'every day, both when we are at prayer and when we are occupied in public affairs, there is a throng of wronged Cappadocians petitioning us—priests, many of them, and women, in extremely large numbers—all with tearful complaints of having been robbed of their possessions, because there is no one at hand to put a stop to this kind of thing.' He further bemoaned the fact that 'practically every holding of the crown treasury has fallen into private hands through being broken up and seized, along with their stock of horses; and no one at all has been raising a voice in opposition, because their mouths have been stuffed with gold.' 'Our face goes red', Justinian fulminated, 'when we hear of such lawlessness.' The new governor was to return imperial estates to the imperial household; collect the much neglected public taxes in full; mobilise the army to 'suppress the bodyguards of the powerful'; and 'not allow villages to be plundered and forcibly expropriated'. At the same time, he was to investigate 'adultery, the abduction of virgins, robbery with violence, murder and any similar offence'. The proconsul was encouraged to punish wrongdoers harshly and to be 'a severe chastiser of offenders'. Such harshness, Justinian argued, 'was not inhumane, but rather the highest form of humaneness, in that as a result of it many will be saved through the correction of a few'.[45]

The abuses Justinian sought to address in the frontier provinces—and others where he decided it was best to keep civil and military commands separated, such as in Palestine—were broadly similar, reflecting empire-wide social and economic trends. Notable amongst these were the emergence and enrichment of an imperial aristocracy, the leading members of which had previously dominated the Senate of Constantinople.[46] In May 536, for example, the emperor legislated on the province of Arabia (in southern Syria), where 'powerful houses' (meaning aristocratic households), as well as government officials, were to be prevented from 'inflicting any harm on our taxpayers'. Here, rioting by members of the Circus Factions was also a concern: 'Neither in Bostra nor anywhere else', the emperor declared, 'are people to abandon themselves to rioting and civil disorder, or to turn what in ancient times were occasions for relaxation and entertainment into bouts of murderous insanity.' In Palestine, the authorities had to ensure 'good order in the cities and good order among the country-dwellers, as well as the exaction of taxes', whilst simultaneously cracking down on 'religious dissension'.[47] In the province of Phoenice Libanensis, governed from the city of Emesa (modern Homs), the new *moderator* was again to ensure that 'powerful households', as well as imperial officials and other officeholders, were prevented from inflicting 'any loss whatsoever on our taxpayers'. He was to be provided with a personal military retinue to assist him 'in the collection of taxes and in the conduct of fiscal affairs, and also in keeping the cities free from hardships'.[48]

These reforms—which were also associated with significant reconfiguration of the geographical boundaries of the provinces concerned—were all issued in less than two years. In 539 Justinian turned his attention to Egypt, the wealthiest province in the Roman world. Constantinople, many other cities of the East, and even the imperial army on campaign depended on its grain for much of their food supply. As Justinian put it, in a preface to the law addressed to his praetorian prefect, John the Cappadocian, 'While the taxpayers were insisting that they were definitely having the whole assessment demanded of them in full, the pagarchs [members of the landowning elite charged with organizing the collection of taxes, both from their own estates and from neighbouring communities], city councillors, and tax collectors, and in particular the governors at the time, have hitherto arranged the business in such a way that no one can find out anything about it, and that only they can profit.' 'We have been surprised at the disorder', the emperor commented, but, he added, returning to the theme of his own sense of providential mission, 'God has granted this too has been kept for our times and your excellency's ministrations.'[49]

To counter these problems, Egypt was broken up into a series of smaller provinces where civil and military responsibilities were merged to ensure closer cooperation between the two arms of provincial administration. Not only governmental but also ecclesiastical officials (such as representatives of the patriarch of Alexandria) were to be prohibited from granting licenses of tax exemption, which had clearly become a significant abuse. Governors, tax collectors, pagarchs, and their heirs were to bear full personal liability for any taxes in coin or kind which they failed to collect. Pagarchs who failed to collect taxes that were assigned to them, or who were caught embezzling government revenues, risked having their estates confiscated. Failure to secure the grain supply to Constantinople was to be punished especially harshly. Likewise, soldiers who failed to assist with the collection of taxes when ordered to do so faced being reposted and forced to serve along the empire's dangerous and inhospitable Danubian frontier. They were even liable to the death penalty.[50]

Justinian's repeated threats towards pagarchs and others made it clear that he deemed the connivance of such individuals in tax evasion and fraud to be the main structural problem in the administration of Egypt. It was an inevitable feature of a society in which those with the greatest vested interest in the evasion of taxes (such as great landowners) were also those to whom governmental responsibilities were often entrusted. Justinian attempted to break this vicious cycle by emphasising the personal liability of such officials for any debts they incurred, and by enhancing the pay of governors to render them more loyal to the emperor and less prone to the blandishments of local networks of aristocratic influence.[51] He also sought to remind his subjects of their moral duty to the empire, to the emperor, and through him to God.

'THAT EVERYTHING SHOULD BEAR HIS NAME'

As the naming of many of the newly reformed governorships and regiments after himself made clear, Justinian was keen to convey to his subjects the extent to which his reign was witnessing a new era of uniquely active rulership, driven by his personal sense of God-given mission. The message was not just that the empire was being strengthened and revived, after years of torpor, but that he (aided by his wife) was the person strengthening and reviving it. The self-aggrandising rhetoric of much of the imperial legislation of this period is startling, and it clearly grated with the likes of Procopius. We see throughout Justinian's laws a calculated and concerted effort to build up what we might think of today as a 'personality cult'.

This effort is reflected, for example, in an interesting measure which Justinian issued in 537 concerning the dating formulae to be used on official documents and legal proceedings. East Roman society in the early sixth century was both highly litigious and awash with paperwork. Roman law in this period placed a growing emphasis on the need for written proof for contracts, payments, and receipts, and as a result, the dating and authentication of documents became increasingly important in legal proceedings. The problem of identifying forgeries therefore drew Justinian's attention. On 15 August 537, he decreed that only papyrus derived and issued from official stocks was to be used for official or legal purposes, and ordered that sheets of papyri were to preserve their official authenticating 'protocol', or stamp. Most documents were written on papyrus during this period, and much of it was produced from reeds in Egyptian workshops before being sent to Constantinople. Two weeks later, on 31 August, he issued an important and related law on how such documents were to be dated. Up to this point, different dating systems had been used in an almost haphazard way: many cities had their own dating systems, which often went back to the pre-Roman past, whilst in other contexts people dated documents or events according to who the current consul was or where they stood with respect to the fifteen-year-long fiscal cycle known as the 'indiction': 'Reign of Anastasius, first indiction, year four', and so on. These variations could cause genuine confusion and uncertainty in legal proceedings. Accordingly, Justinian decreed that henceforth all documents were to be dated according to the regnal date of the reigning emperor and had to be written in a clearly legible script. In other words, his name had to come first, plain for all to see.[52]

In one measure, which seemed designed to enhance the office of the emperor by denying others a stage on which to promote themselves, Justinian, in 541, mothballed the ancient institution of the consulship (from which he personally had derived much political benefit prior to his accession to the throne).[53] This move greatly offended the more conservative members of the political classes. Procopius, for example, would complain, with respect to the splendours and largesse associated with the consulship and the consular games, 'Eventually the people never saw that office again even in a dream, and consequently mankind was being most cruelly pinched by a kind of poverty, since the emperor no longer provided his subjects with what they had been accustomed to receive.'[54] John Lydus regarded the ending of the consulship as signalling the final abolition of the 'last vestige of Roman freedom'.[55]

Justinian and his courtiers were, however, aware of the need to appeal to conservative sentiment (particularly within the imperial bureaucracy). This was particularly true of his learned chief legal officer, the *quaestor* Tribonian, who, after the completion of the codification project, put much effort into composing elaborate antiquarian prefaces to Justinian's legislation, intended to justify the provincial reforms, in particular, in terms of ancient precedent.[56] Justinian had spoken in the *Digest* of his 'reverence for antiquity' (*reverentia antiquitatis*), and in these prefaces the case was essentially put forward that his reforms were not innovations; rather, he was restoring institutions and arrangements that had existed in the distant past.

In his legislation on Pisidia, for example, Justinian declared, 'We are convinced that even the ancient Romans could never have built up so great a realm from small, even minimal beginnings, and from that taken over almost the whole world and set it in order, had they not made their grandeur more evident by means of sending governors of relatively high rank out to the provinces, and equipping them with authority over both arms and laws.' By doing the same in Pisidia and elsewhere, the emperor went on to argue, and adopting for them the ancient Roman title of praetor, 'we are restoring antiquity to our realm, in a greater flowering, and are enhancing the grandeur of the Roman name.' 'We wish to begin with the province of Pisidia,' he continued, emphasising his own supposedly active scholarly endeavours, 'as we have found it stated in earlier historians that the whole of that area was previously under the rule of the Pisidian people, and we are sure that this province needs a higher and more powerful governor.' Reforms to the government of the nearby territory of Lycaonia, the emperor claimed, were justified with reference to origin myths 'described to us by historians of antiquity . . . these events to which we are referring going further back in time than even the days of Aeneas and Romulus [the mythical founders of Rome]'.[57]

Justinian was keenly aware of the propagandistic value of law. His newly issued legislation would be advertised throughout the empire, typically in an abbreviated form mediated by his officials and governors, read out by heralds, and displayed in the porticoes of churches and in public inscriptions, some of which survive. Given the varied nature of the audiences to which his laws were addressed, the power of the emperor's message did not necessarily depend on the accuracy of the claims made. Many of the antiquarian justifications for Justinian's provincial reforms were largely spurious, but they sounded convincing, and the number of those in a position to question them would have been relatively small.[58] At times in Justinian's *Novels* we find earlier laws being attributed to the wrong emperor, or emperors getting confused. At one point, for example, Justinian refers to the emperor Antoninus Pius (r. 138–161) when he means the emperor Caracalla (r. 188–217).[59] Were these errors based on genuine misconceptions? Did contemporaries not really care about this sort of historical detail? Or were Justinian and those around him just perhaps in too much of a hurry to check? These explanations are plausible, but it was the *veneer* of knowledge that arguably counted the most.

The intensity, range, and scope of Justinian's legal activity in the years between the promulgation of the *Digest* in 534 and his mothballing of the consulship in 541 are little short of breathtaking. The 'sleepless emperor' just did not stop. Whilst preparing to restructure provincial administration (and sending armies to the West), Justinian nevertheless found time, for example, to codify and Christianise the entire inherited body of Roman law on marriage.[60] This remarkably detailed and exhaustive piece of legislation—in which it is possible to discern the influence of the empress Theodora—was issued on the same day as his first tranche of provincial reforms (18 March 536). We also have important legislation concerning inheritance and wills; monasteries and ecclesiastical administration and property; prostitution; debt-bondage; public funeral arrangements in Constantinople; regulations for legal proceedings; the status of agricultural workers tied to estates; heresy; horticulture; credit arrangements and maritime loans; city councils; and divorce.[61] Town and country, rich and poor, high and low—there was barely an aspect of East Roman society on which Justinian did not legislate at this time, or with respect to which he did not respond to petitions, despite all his grumbling.

Indeed, as well as an obsessive eye for detail, Justinian and those around him had a remarkably 'joined-up' view of how the empire worked as an interconnected whole and how it could be made to operate more cohesively. Concerted efforts were made, for example, to extend the writ of Roman law to the empire's Armenian territories, where hitherto local custom had prevailed.[62] In 536, the tax revenues of the wealthy island and coastal territories of Cyprus, the Cyclades, and Caria (in Asia Minor) were assigned to support the troubled Balkan regions of Scythia and Moesia.[63] Likewise, tax revenues from Egypt were used to maintain military garrisons along the region's distant frontier with the Libyan desert, some 290 kilometres west of Alexandria.[64] The laws also confirm that Justinian seized upon the opportunities presented by his conquests in the West to enrich the imperial household and to dramatically expand the resources directly at his disposal. In 537, for example, he declared that the entirety of Sicily was to be regarded as the 'personal fund' (*peculium*) of the emperor, although he went out of his way to reassure the papal authorities in Rome that their extensive estates there would be safe.[65]

THE RECEPTION OF THE LAW

Legislation was only half the battle: the law had to be applied and used. So how far did knowledge of Justinian's legislation really percolate beyond the world of the court and the imperial bureaucracy? The short answer is far more than is commonly thought. Justinian's legislation on dating formulae in contracts appeared in documentary practice almost immediately: the new regnal dating system is attested in private documents that survive from Palestine which are almost coterminous with the legislation. It is even found on large public inscriptions put up in the vicinity of Constantinople, in Bithynia, Asia Minor, and Thrace, a monumental context in which Justinian had not in fact demanded that it be used. Clearly, some of the emperor's subjects were keen to be seen to express their loyalty to him by going well beyond the letter of the law.[66]

Justinian believed in advertising his laws, but he did not necessarily expect familiarity with the fine detail of them to spread much beyond the ranks of officialdom, or the confines of landowning society. A law of 538 that sought to prevent men of the highest senatorial rank from taking wives without dowries provided a pen portrait of the different rungs of contemporary East Roman society and how the emperor expected each group to relate and respond to imperial law. He refers to 'men of the higher ranks, at the level of senators', 'those in the upper service appointments, or in business, and in the more respectable professions', and lastly, those 'of the least regarded station in life, owning little property, and down at the lowest level of society . . . agricultural workers and undistinguished soldiers under arms'. Of the latter, Justinian commented, 'Their ignorance of public affairs and lack of desire for anything other than tilling the land or warfare is something highly desirable and praiseworthy.'[67] Such men, evidently, were not expected to show much interest in the emperor's legislation.

It is clear, however, that some of these men exhibited far more curiosity in the law than Justinian either expected or liked, especially when it pertained to their own station in life. Agricultural workers tied to great estates (known in Latin as *coloni adscripticii*, or in Greek as *enapographoi georgoi*), for example, were an important feature of the rural economy, and by the sixth century such workers could be found from Illyricum to Palestine and from Egypt to Thrace. These *coloni* were obliged to serve their landowning employer, as were their children and heirs.[68] But what happened if a tied peasant from one estate produced children with a partner from another? Which of the landowners could claim the offspring? Or what happened if a 'free' woman—whose labour was not owned by a landowner—gave birth to a child whose father was a *colonus adscripticius*? Could the father's employer claim authority and effective ownership over the infant, or did it inherit the free status of the mother? Justinian wrestled with these important issues as petitioners brought cases to his attention.

In 533 he issued a law establishing that children fathered by a *colonus adscripticius*, but born to a free mother, were to inherit the free status of the mother's 'womb', and hence could not be forced to become *adscripticii*, tied as labourers to the estate on which their father toiled. In a law of 537, the emperor tells us, estate workers whose mothers had been free, upon hearing of this law, had simply abandoned their estates, not realising that the legislation was *not* intended to apply retrospectively. Such peasants, Justinian fulminated, were interpreting his legislation in 'a stupid and criminal way', and were engaged in 'criminal schemes . . . to the detriment of the owners of estates'.[69] That they knew of and were acting upon his legislation at all, however, is striking, providing vivid testimony as to the circulation and significance of law in Justinian's empire. This was a world where the law really did matter.

Chapter 11

A New Kind of Power

THE GLORIOUS HOUSEHOLD

Justinian's reign transformed how imperial power operated and was expressed in the Roman world. Compared to his predecessors, he favoured a much more court-based, personality-driven style of rule focused on himself as emperor and his wife as co-ruler. Conservative observers of the regime were highly suspicious of this shift in emphasis. Procopius complained, for example, of how Justinian and Theodora insisted 'that they be consulted on each and every matter' and 'forced everyone to court them in the most servile way'.[1] 'Almost every day,' Procopius continued, 'it was possible to see the law courts virtually empty of people, but in the imperial court there was a vulgar mob, pushing, shoving, and always debasing itself.' Forced to attend upon the workaholic emperor, the courtiers 'had to stand continuously throughout the day and then during a long part

261

of every night', such that they were deprived of food and sleep and their health inevitably deteriorated.[2]

Justinian justified this concentration of power by emphasising the chaos rampant in the empire, asserting that he had a moral duty to crack down on the lawlessness and confound those who opposed him, for the glory of God and the good of his other subjects. The emperor's provincial legislation paints a vivid picture of tax evasion and disorder in East Roman society, much of it associated with the burgeoning influence of the 'powerful households' of the imperial aristocracy. The members of this elite class were able to take advantage of their political connections and social and economic clout at a local level to effectively pick and choose which imperial laws they observed and which they found more convenient to ignore. Their cooperation was vital to the smooth running of the empire, but their determination to play by their own rules was a potential threat to its stability. Or was it? To what extent was this simply a rhetorical posture on Justinian's part? Was this struggle against the ruses of the 'mighty' real? Or was it simply a figment of the emperor's overly suspicious imagination and a useful excuse for an increasingly interventionist form of imperial government?

To answer this question we have to turn to Egypt. As noted earlier, the overwhelming majority of documentary and other texts written in the sixth century, including literary works, were written on sheets of papyrus, which were mass-produced in Egypt—the only region of the Roman world where papyrus reeds grew—before being exported elsewhere. Papyrus was light, portable, and comparatively easy to write on and store, which was why it had long been the favoured medium for documentation in the ancient world. The one problem with papyrus, however, is that it decays and rots if not kept dry. As a result, despite the hundreds of thousands of papyrus documents that must have been produced every year in the age of Justinian, very few have survived to the modern day, save in Egypt, where the dry sands and arid climate have preserved thousands of documentary texts that enable us to re-create the social and economic conditions in what was economically and fiscally the most important region in the empire.

Justinian's legislation also reveals Egypt to have been a place where he believed the problems caused by corruption, tax evasion, and fraud were especially severe. The papyrus documents from the region thus enable us to contextualise Justinian's provincial reforms in a way that no other body of evidence can, and to ascertain whether or not the abuses which Justinian claimed to be current actually existed on the ground. It was for this reason that I chose to focus on them when writing my doctoral dissertation in Oxford in the 1990s, using the documentary papyri to attempt to re-create a picture of economy and society in the age of Justinian that did not simply depend on the emperor's own assertions.[3] As a result, I learned to read and transcribe these often heavily damaged and almost indecipherable texts. Amongst the fragments I had the chance to examine was a section of Justinian's law overhauling the administration of Egypt.[4]

For our purposes there are two particularly important collections of documentary papyri that survive. The first of these is the so-called Apion archive, initially discovered between 1896 and 1907 in rubbish tips adjacent to the ancient city of Oxyrhynchus (modern al-Bahnasa) in 'Middle Egypt'. Two British scholars, B. P. Grenfell and A. S. Hunt, found them while in search of fragments of biblical texts and lost works of classical literature.[5] The quantity of documentary material that they discovered was such that scholars today are still piecing together and editing papyri that Grenfell and Hunt initially sent back to the Egypt Exploration Society in London. Indeed, some of the most revealing documents from the archive were only published in 2019.[6] What makes the documents so important is that they appear to record the origin, expansion, and operation of precisely the sort of 'powerful household' Justinian frequently complains about in his provincial legislation. The bulk of the documents originate from an estate office which oversaw the administration of extensive properties belonging to what is termed the 'Glorious Household' of the wealthy and politically well-connected Apion family.

On the basis of the papyri that survive from Oxyrhynchus, we can see that the Apion family first rose to prominence in their local society in Middle Egypt (the central part of the Nile Valley, south of Alexandria and the Delta) in the very early fifth century. One of the earliest members of the dynasty affirmed in the documents was a landowner and a city councillor with special responsibility for the administration of imperial estates around the city of Oxyrhynchus. This gave the family an especially close connection to the imperial household and its representatives which they would harness to their advantage. We can then trace members of the family advancing up the imperial career ladder as the estates of the Glorious Household around Oxyrhynchus began to expand. They acquired land from their social equals and rivals, probably from local peasants and farmers, and even from the imperial household itself.[7]

By the middle of the sixth century, the papyri reveal, the Apion family had come to own somewhere in the region of 30 to 40 percent of all agricultural land in the vicinity of Oxyrhynchus and its neighbouring city of Cynopolis (amounting to some forty-eight thousand acres). But that was only one source of the family's regional influence and power, for the papyri reveal that members of the family had also come to hold, seemingly by hereditary right, the title of 'pagarch', which gave them responsibility for collecting taxes from a still broader section of Oxyrhynchite society. This would have greatly increased their powers of patronage and authority, and we can trace land they managed as pagarchs passing into their ownership as well as their control. There are also indications that along with owning land around Oxyrhynchus, the Apion family acquired land elsewhere in Egypt, and possibly elsewhere in the empire too. The family had estate offices in Alexandria and in Constantinople.

But on the basis of the recently published papyri, we can conclude that simply in terms of estates and fiscal responsibilities around Oxyrhynchus and Cynopolis, the Apion family had a hand in processing over three and a half million kilograms of grain a year, essential supplies that were sent from Egypt to feed Constantinople and the cities of the East more generally. The Apiones were important not only on a local and regional level, but also in terms of their role in the political economy of the empire as a whole.[8]

Like other landowners, in Egypt and throughout the empire, the Apion family had a portfolio comprising urban property in Oxyrhynchus, a villa in the suburbs, and extensive stretches of agricultural land. In some villages, the Apiones' estate managers operated cheek-by-jowl alongside other landowners great and small, whilst the family also owned other estate settlements (known as *epoikia*) in their entirety. These rural properties were typically inhabited by families of agricultural labourers who bore the legal designation of *coloni adscripticii* and were tied to the estate. The estates were overseen by stewards, who were issued with production targets for the lands assigned to them. Oxyrhynchus was a major ecclesiastical centre, and many of those employed as managers on the estates were connected to the Church. The household also owned some slaves, who were employed in both productive and administrative capacities.

The reality of life for the Apion family's *coloni adscripticii* could be harsh, and the documents, and Justinian's laws, enable us to see why many such *coloni* might have contemplated flight from the estates to which they were bound. One of the texts that survives, for example, is a petition addressed to the head of the household on the part of a fugitive *colonus*, named Pieous, who begs forgiveness for his attempted flight. He ascribes it to the injustices he had been forced to endure at the hands of the local estate manager, who had seized his belongings after he had fallen into arrears. Pieous goes on to request that he be permitted to return to his holding: 'Formerly,' he declares, 'I sowed so that in turn I would be able to work on the holding and bring up my poor children.'[9] All he asked was to be allowed to do so again.

At the same time, there is evidence that the managers of the Apion estates (as well as their colleagues on similar estates, for which we possess rather less extensive archives) managed the land in a highly efficient manner that would have contributed to the agrarian expansion and growing commercialisation that are discernible at this time. The overseers, for example, made considerable use of wage labour. Their accounts reveal a high degree of monetisation on the estates, and commercial properties and warehouses owned by the family were rented out in the local town.[10] The Apion household also entered into credit relations with local farmers and peasants, sustaining the broader development of the agrarian economy through investment and patronage. The net economic effect of the emergence and consolidation of great estates such as that owned by the 'Glorious Household' was probably a positive one. The challenge from the perspective of the imperial government was how to harness and tax the economic prosperity that such estates helped to generate.

But perhaps more importantly, the testimony of the Apion archive serves to remind us that relations between Justinian and members of the provincial aristocracy were not uniformly antagonistic. The Apiones themselves were strong supporters of Justinian and his regime, and the emperor clearly trusted them. The family had emerged, as we have seen, in Middle Egypt around the early fifth century. By the early sixth century, both the papyri and literary sources reveal, members of the dynasty were sufficiently wealthy and well connected to forge successful careers for themselves in Constantinople, where some of them served in the Senate. From there, they were able to maintain contact with their estate managers in Oxyrhynchus, periodically intervening in estate business and affairs.[11]

The Apion family was not given to originality when it came to the names it gave to its eldest sons. The dynasty maintained a tradition of naming the firstborn sons after their grandfathers, which meant that as head of the family, a Flavius Apion would tend to be succeeded by a Flavius Strategius, who would then in turn be succeeded by a Flavius Apion, who would be followed by another Strategius ('Flavius' was an inheritable title granted to members of the social elite). They resolutely stuck to this pattern from the early fifth through the early seventh centuries, when the family disappears from the historical record amid troubled political and military conditions in both Constantinople and Egypt. The head of the family at the start of the sixth century (Flavius Apion) had been one of a coterie of Egyptians who had prospered at court under the patronage of the emperor Anastasius.[12] Procopius describes him as 'an extremely efficacious man of eminence amongst the patricians', and Anastasius appointed him to oversee the grain supply that fed and sustained the imperial army on campaign during the course of the Persian War of 502–506.[13] Given the role played by Egyptian grain in feeding the imperial army, the choice of an Egyptian landowner to fill this post made good sense.[14]

From 508 to 510, Flavius Apion is recorded to have been present in Constantinople, where the hardline anti-Chalcedonian churchman Severus of Antioch dedicated a theological tract to him, signifying that his theological sympathies (like those of many of his fellow Egyptians) put him in opposition to the Council of 451. Suddenly, in 510, Apion and one of his younger sons fell from favour at court. Apion was exiled to Nicaea and denounced by Anastasius as a 'pederast and heretic'. In 518, Flavius Apion was rehabilitated and summoned back to Constantinople by the new emperor, Justin. By this point he would seem to have shifted to a pro-Chalcedonian theological stance: according to one source, he was convinced to change sides theologically in direct response to a personal intervention by the emperor Justin himself, backed up by the future emperor

Justinian.[15] Clearly, Flavius Apion was known personally to both, and Justin appointed him to serve as praetorian prefect of the East. Perhaps not coincidentally, Flavius Apion's eldest son, Flavius Strategius, also advanced rapidly up the ranks of imperial service at this time. It would be under Justinian, however, that Flavius Strategius' career reached its zenith. In the lengthy edict on the administration of Egypt that he issued in 539, Justinian praised Strategius for the efficiency with which he had organised the annual grain shipment to Constantinople during his period of office as 'Augustal prefect' (or governor) of Egypt and Alexandria. Indeed, a fragment of this edict survives from the family archive in Oxyrhynchus.[16] Appointed to the rank of general (*magister militum*), as well as 'patrician', he was sent by Justinian to negotiate with the Persians in 531 and 532. In 532 he also presided over a session of the discussions between the pro- and anti-Chalcedonian bishops that Justinian had convened in Constantinople.[17]

By 535, Strategius was 'Count of the Sacred Largesse' (*comes sacrarum largitionum*), one of the two highest-ranking financial officers of state, with responsibility for minting money, running the state monopolies (such as papyrus production), and other financial issues not assigned to the praetorian prefecture.[18] In that capacity, he is recorded to have played an active role in assisting Justinian in the construction of Hagia Sophia. So close were they that a later somewhat fantastical account of the construction of the Great Church (which nevertheless includes significant factual information) would claim that Strategius was Justinian's 'spiritual brother', a recognised category of intimate friendship and adopted kinship within ancient and eastern Christianity.[19] In the 1990s, it was even argued by the pioneering historian of homosexuality, John Boswell, that such consecrated ties of spiritual brotherhood were effectively a form of same-sex marriage.[20] One wonders what Theodora would have made of that. Strategius would appear to have died in the early

Justinian and Theodora accompanied by their entourages. The emperor favoured a court-focused style of rule.

These statues of the Tetrarchs stood in the heart of Constantinople. The future emperor Justin I probably marched past them as a young recruit.

Ivory diptych announcing Justinian's appointment as consul. He used the consulship to buy up public support

A gold coin showing Justinian alongside Justin I. Such coinage advertised his appointment as co-ruler.

The soldier saints Sergius and Bacchus. This is a modern reproduction of an original icon from St Catherine's Monastery, Sinai.

Justinian's Great Church of Hagia Sophia. It would long be remembered as the emperor's most magnificent monument.

Contemporaries regarded Hagia Sophia as a space where heaven and earth met. Later visitors regarded it as the dwelling place of God.

Gold medallion celebrating the Gothic king Theoderic. He is accorded imperial titles on it, but sports a very Teutonic moustache.

Justinian's Basilica Cistern would be the largest underground reservoir in the city. It redeployed and hid pagan statues that had previously adorned the capital.

Mosaic from the Great Palace in Constantinople. It depicts an eagle (representing the emperor) overpowering a snake (representing his foes).

The Madaba Map provided pilgrims with a visual guide to the Holy Land. It focused on the city of Jerusalem, including Justinian's New Church.

The Virgin Mary was regarded as Constantinople's divine patron. This icon is from St Catherine's Monastery in Sinai, which Justinian founded.

A silk fragment showing men wrestling with lions. Silk was one of the most prized commodities of the ancient world, and Justinian's agents acquired the secret of its production.

Tenth-century mosaic of Justinian from the vestibule of Hagia Sophia. It depicts him presenting the cathedral to the Virgin Mary.

Justinian as represented on a fourteenth-century manuscript of the *Digest*. His legal legacy to the medieval West would be immense.

A sixteenth-century Ottoman manuscript showing Justinian's equestrian statue (as imagined after its destruction). It stands adjacent to the Hippodrome and Hagia Sophia.

540s, but his eldest son, whom he had named Flavius Apion, served as consul in 539 (just before Justinian mothballed the institution). The chronicler John Malalas described this Apion as a leading figure in the Senate of Constantinople. He goes on to record how the servants attached to Apion's residence in the imperial capital hurled insults at members of the Green Faction. Under Justinian, he would also hold high military rank, commanding the palace guards as *comes domesticorum*. Later appointed general, he would return to Egypt around the year 550 to serve as governor (*dux*) of the province of the Thebaid.[21]

From this evidence it would seem that members of the Apion family were highly cooperative with Justinian, enjoying his patronage, friendship, and support, and that they helped the emperor advance his agenda by implementing his laws. As we can see from the papyri, the Apion family's managers were rigorous in the collection of taxes and in conveying them to the imperial authorities. Whether the 'Glorious Household' paid all the taxes that it was expected to pay in full, or off-loaded some of its tax burden onto the shoulders of others, it is impossible to tell. But certainly, the papyri that have emerged to date have revealed little sign of large-scale embezzlement of the type Justinian complains of in his legislation with respect to other pagarchs.

The papyri that survive from Oxyrhynchus illustrate the extent to which provincial society in the age of Justinian had indeed become increasingly dominated by members of the landed elite. But as long as such landowners showed loyalty to the emperor and exhibited a general willingness to support the regime (above all by paying taxes) this was not necessarily a problem. The Apion family provides a clear example of how the relationship between Justinian and the imperial aristocracy could work to the benefit of both sides if due reverence towards the emperor were shown. But what of those who refused to cooperate? They were a very real problem.

'THE INTRIGUES OF THEODOSIUS'

The activities of these 'others' are recorded for us in a second and perhaps still more fascinating collection of documentary papyri that survive from the sixth century, in this case from the personal archive of a small-town lawyer, Dioscorus.²² Again, we largely owe our knowledge of these documents to chance discovery, and to a brilliant young French scholar, Jean Maspero, whose imagination was caught by them, but who died tragically young during the First World War.²³ Dioscorus came from the settlement of Aphrodito (the 'village of Aphrodite' in Greek) in the Fayyum. Although Aphrodito did not possess the formal status of a city, it was effectively a large rural town with an economically and socially diverse population. In addition to tenant farmers, peasants, and shepherds, the papyri reveal the presence in the town of teachers of Greek grammar (the native language of the local population was Coptic), public officials, skilled artisans, and textile workers. It was dominated, however, by a clearly designated elite comprising members of the local landowning gentry alongside representatives of the Church. In a copy of a report that would be sent to the empress Theodora on behalf of the inhabitants of the town, for example, we find that the letter was signed by the village headman (*protokometes*), twenty-two landowners (*ktetores*), the collector of the public taxes, eleven priests and three other churchmen, two legal notaries, a wine dealer, and six guild masters.²⁴ Its total cultivated area would appear to have been somewhere in the region of four thousand acres, and its population probably amounted to some seven thousand people.²⁵

Dioscorus was born around the year 520, and his father, Apollos, is described in the documentary papyri as one of the leading villagers. Much of the town's fiscal administration had been entrusted to the village leadership after Aphrodito was granted a right known as *autopragia*. This designation gave the townsfolk the right to collect and pay their own taxes to the imperial authorities without any involvement from the local pagarchs whose extensive estates abutted their smallholdings. The origins of the family were rather humble. Although Dioscorus and Apollos were descended from a certain Psimanobet, which, in Coptic, meant 'the Goose-herd's son', Apollos had clearly done well. He ended his days founding and retiring to a small monastery, in which the family would long maintain an active interest even after Apollos' death in 545. While his father was alive, Dioscorus had received an education in Greek grammar and rhetoric, and ultimately in law, possibly going off to Alexandria to study at the law school there. Returning to Aphrodito, Dioscorus built up a legal practice drafting documents, organising dispute resolutions, and presenting cases at the court of the local governor. He attempted to remain abreast of changes in imperial law (no easy matter under Justinian), and by 543 had been accorded the honorary title of *scholastikos*, indicating that he was held in high professional esteem. With the death of his father, Dioscorus assumed leadership of the family, stepping into Apollos' shoes as a headman and helping to run the settlement and represent its interests to the outside world.

The documents that survive from sixth-century Aphrodito largely consist of Dioscorus' personal and professional papers. As a result, we have draft legal contracts, letters, accounts of proceedings, and even an extensive number of poems by Dioscorus himself on mythological and religious themes, or addressed to officials and magnates in order to curry favour with them. These poems have not always met with critical approval—a fastidious classical scholar once described the unfortunate Dioscorus as perhaps the worst poet whose poems have survived from antiquity, 'the McGonagall of the ancient world'.[26] Dioscorus' archive nevertheless preserves an extraordinary assemblage of material that casts fresh light on almost every aspect of life as it was actually lived in the sixth century. Importantly, it also reveals how the inhabitants of the town got on with their aristocratic neighbours.

Aphrodito, a large and independent settlement, less a village and more a town, had been granted fiscal autonomy with respect to imperial taxes during the reign of the emperor Leo (r. 457–474). But living alongside the 'powerful households' of great landowners necessarily meant that their influence was keenly felt there. Apollos, for example, had been employed as an overseer by a local landowner named Ammonius.[27] Described in the documents of the archive as 'the most glorious Count [comes]', and 'the most magnificent', Ammonius was a former provincial governor who owned land not only around Aphrodito and the neighbouring city of Antaeopolis, but also around Hermopolis (where the Apiones also owned land). The honorifics accorded to him would suggest that he was a member of the inner circle known as the 'sacred consistory' (sacrum consistorium), which effectively served as the executive branch of the Senate in Constantinople.[28] Other great landowners, such as 'the most magnificent Theodosius' and the 'most glorious and most magnificent' former prefect (or ex-governor) Julian, also appear in the papyri.[29] Often, it would appear, playing these great landowners off against one another was the key to maintaining Aphrodito's independence from aristocratic ownership and control.[30]

Modern historians of the sixth century have often assumed that forcing great landowners in Egypt such as the Apiones to serve as pagarchs and collect taxes from neighbouring communities was a great burden imposed upon them by the state. The Aphrodito papyri reveal how far this assumption is from the truth. Great landowners in Egypt liked to collect other people's taxes, because tax collection could be profitable (it was always tempting to take a cut, and at different moments in time the imperial authorities would even encourage this or build it into the tax calculation by way of incentive). It also allowed aristocratic households to establish and project their authority over others, often with a view to acquiring their neighbours' land for themselves if they fell into debt. The autonomy of Aphrodito, for example, clearly grated with the local landowners and pagarchs, to the extent that they repeatedly attempted to deny and ignore it, sending men in to collect taxes by force.[31] The result was a series of disputes between villagers and pagarchs, recorded in detail in the Aphrodito papyri of Dioscorus.

By the late 530s, the archive suggests, relations between Aphrodito and the local pagarchs had deteriorated to such an extent that in around 540 Dioscorus' father led a delegation to Constantinople to bring the complaints of the townsfolk before Justinian, and, significantly, to have the village placed within the protective embrace of the imperial household. The local landowner Theodosius took advantage of the absence of the village leaders, however, to turn up in Aphrodito and forcibly collect its taxes. He pocketed the proceeds in precisely the manner Justinian had complained about in his recent legislation on Egypt. The staff of the local governor then appeared and made the inhabitants pay the taxes all over again. Justinian himself wrote about the incident in an official letter to the local governor in 551, complaining about the injustice and brutality to which the villagers had been subjected by 'those holding office at the time', such that they had 'submitted to our household and placed themselves under its patronage'.[32]

The dispute over Aphrodito's fiscal status continued into the early 540s, by which point, as the papyri reveal, certain of the villagers had begun to conspire with the local officials and magnates against their neighbours. The conflict appears to have been exacerbated by a series of brutal murders. At trial, a local landowner, Sarapammon, was forced to answer for his actions after a priest, Victor, had been beaten to death by a soldier named Menas. The latter had then proceeded to kill another villager with the active connivance of the local village guild masters, who had got their victim drunk before Menas put him to the sword and a botched attempt was made to burn the body. The charred remains had then been disposed of, and the deceased's widow, Maria, complained to the court that she did not 'know where they have laid them'. The implication is that Menas was acting on Sarapammon's orders. In his testimony, the landowner claimed that 'some men from the village of Aphrodito' were engaged 'in a conspiracy to separate the village', possibly a reference to its disputed fiscal status. The fragmentary court proceedings also allude to grain taxes owed to the imperial authorities, and the possibility of the case being sent on to Constantinople.[33]

While this was going on, Dioscorus continued to pursue his father's complaints against the landowner Theodosius. It was now Dioscorus' turn to petition Justinian on the village's behalf. In his letter to the governor in 551, Justinian noted, 'He [Dioscorus] . . . procured an imperial ordinance from us concerning this, addressed to your excellence, but the intrigues of Theodosius proved stronger than our commands.' In 547, the villagers petitioned the empress Theodora, under whose personal patronage Aphrodito had now been placed, complaining that another local magnate, one Julian, was attempting to 'add the village to his pagarchy'.[34] Around the year 551, Dioscorus led another delegation to Constantinople, where he was obliged to navigate and flatter his way through the corridors of power in order to present his case.[35] We see him writing poems, for example, addressed to high-ranking officials in the capital or dedicated to their kin, such as the court usher (*silentarius*) Dorotheus, or the son of a high-ranking official within the praetorian prefecture, Domninus.[36] In his letter of 551, Justinian ordered the governor to investigate Julian's activities. This would appear to have been sufficient to persuade Julian to leave Aphrodito alone, at least for the time being, although in the late 560s Dioscorus was still petitioning and flattering high officials in an attempt to fend off the designs of the locally powerful on his hometown. After the death of Justinian in 565, however, there would be no more embassies to Constantinople. Instead, Dioscorus was reduced to trying to pit one local magnate against the other, whilst constantly trying to convince the governor to intervene.[37]

THE ACCESSIBLE EMPEROR

Dioscorus and Apollos clearly had sufficient faith in Justinian for them to think it worthwhile to make the arduous and expensive journey to Constantinople to petition the emperor in person. Likewise, for all his complaints concerning the number of such petitioners turning up at his court, Justinian cared sufficiently for the population of Aphrodito and their concerns to place the settlement under imperial patronage, and to write to their governor (the 'duke of the Thebaid') pressing their case. The impression that Justinian attempted to convey of the sleepless emperor, constantly worrying about his subjects, was not entirely fictitious, nor were the provincial abuses he tried to stop. Theodosius' purloining of the tax revenues of Aphrodito, and his refusal to act in accordance with the commands sent from Constantinople, chime precisely with Justinian's complaints in his lengthy edict of 539. If Justinian's legislation on Egypt was an accurate depiction of and response to objective social, economic, and administrative conditions on the ground, we have no reason to assume that the same was not also true of the rest of his provincial legislation.

Justinian had an enormously elevated sense of the dignity of the imperial office and his responsibilities to God and to those over whom he ruled. This both fed into and was reflected in his attempts to recast the Roman state along more centralised lines, maximising the power of the palace just as he had already recast Roman law in order to maximise the authority of the emperor. In doing so, Justinian was ultimately laying the ideological foundations for the medieval empire of Byzantium, with its much more court-focused, palace-based, political culture.[38]

Procopius tells us that under Justinian, it was the emperor who now read out responses to petitions from his subjects, rather than his chief legal officer, or *quaestor*, which hitherto had been the norm. Likewise, the Senate of Constantinople was increasingly sidelined in the development of policy, its members reduced to sitting passively, 'as if in a picture', as Procopius put it.[39] Active membership of the Senate itself was increasingly limited to high-ranking officeholders, who owed their place there primarily to the emperor, rather than to their inherited status and wealth. Power was increasingly concentrated at court, where ceremonial meant to elevate the person of the emperor, and to emphasise his unique superiority over all mankind, took on an increasingly elaborate and Christian form. The emperor and empress began surrounding themselves with images (or 'icons') of Christ, the Virgin Mary, and the saints, whom they evidently regarded as appropriately lofty and august company.[40] Yet, as the letter from Justinian written on behalf of the villagers of Aphrodito reminds us, this court remained potentially accessible to provincial petitioners and litigants, sometimes including those of surprisingly humble background and origin. Justinian's critics and opponents may have been 'snobs', but there is little evidence that the emperor himself was one. He felt morally obliged to serve the interests of even the lowliest of his subjects. To borrow the words of Scripture, through his laws, Justinian not only 'put down the mighty from their seat', but also 'exalted the humble and meek'.[41]

Chapter 12

The 'Orthodox Republic'

THE PROMISED LAND

Late on a Sunday morning in September 2015, I found myself squeezed into the Greek Orthodox Church of Saint George in a picturesque Jordanian town, Madaba, one of the few settlements outside the capital of Amman that still has a sizeable Christian population. Members of the local congregation made their way out into the courtyard to chat and smoke, clutching pieces of consecrated bread to take home to relatives who had been unable to make it to the weekly 'Divine Service', which had just finished. Instead of following them outside, I approached the railing, where the priests and curators were in the process of revealing to camera-clutching tourists one of the finest examples anywhere of sixth-century Byzantine religious art. This is the so-called Madaba Map, a stunning mosaic depiction of the biblical Holy Land, showing pilgrims how to pass from the Jordan Valley and Mount Nebo (where God had revealed to Moses the Promised Land, rich with milk and honey) to Jerusalem, and on to Bethlehem.[1] This mosaic map, probably dating from between the early 540s and the end of Justinian's reign, is striking testimony to the expansion of the pilgrimage trade, focused on Palestine, which was a marked feature of the era.[2] Our sources record how pious visitors would venture to remote monasteries in the Judaean desert to experience a taste of the spiritual life. At the same time, wealthy aristocrats bought up residential property in Jerusalem at a massive markup to guarantee close proximity to the Holy Sepulchre, built by the emperor Constantine and his mother Helena on the traditional site of Christ's tomb, or the recently constructed *Nea Ekklesia*, or 'New Church', built by Justinian and dedicated to Mary, the Mother of God (Greek *Theotokos*), in 543, which appears on the Madaba Map.[3]

When, later that same day, I made my own way up to Mount Nebo, the view over Jerusalem and the Holy Land was obscured by a ferocious sandstorm: had the Lord led Moses there in similar conditions, the history of mankind might have been rather different. But the magnificent Church of the Nea (as scholars often refer to it) and the throngs of pilgrims converging on the Holy Land, which a sixth-century visitor would have been able to observe from that vantage point, were both products of an expansive religious agenda which, from the 540s onwards, Justinian pursued with a vehemence arguably even greater than that with which he had conducted his military campaigns.

PIETY AND PERSECUTION

Justinian had been determined from the start to press ahead with the full-blown Christianisation of the Roman state, targeting religious dissidents and anyone else who met with the disapproval of the imperial Church. He issued and enforced laws against them with unprecedented fervour. While previous emperors had sought to prohibit acts of pagan sacrifice or worship, Justinian made it illegal even to be a pagan. Those who refused to convert to Christianity were to be exiled, while those who converted but then backtracked would be killed. Particularly severe waves of persecution directed at pagans are recorded in Constantinople in the years 528–529, 545–546, and 562, and throughout the empire, bishops and other representatives of the imperial government took inspiration from the emperor's initiatives to press ahead with purges in the provinces.[4] An inscription from the city of Sardis, for example, which has been dated to the mid-sixth century, records a list of the inhabitants of the city who had been put on trial and found guilty of paganism by the local judge.[5] In around 540, when a number of members of the illegal 'Manichaean' sect, a religion of Persian origin, were discovered in Constantinople, the emperor ordered that they be burned to death. The anti-pagan crackdown of 545–546 was supposedly inspired by the clergyman John of Ephesus: 'In the nineteenth year of the emperor Justinian,' he wrote in his *Ecclesiastical History*, 'by encouragement of our humble self the affair of the pagans was investigated. There were found in the capital famous persons, nobles and others . . . and when they were exposed, on being tortured, they denounced each other. They were arrested, scourged and imprisoned. Then these patricians and nobles were sent into churches to learn the faith of the Christians as befitted pagans.'[6]

As John hints, many of the pagans (and Manichaeans) targeted in the purges of the 520s and 540s were members of the upper classes, and it is likely that a number of the denunciations were politically motivated. Members of the Senate who were accused of paganism had their estates automatically confiscated by the Crown, and paganism was an easy charge to level against any man of classical education, whose literary tastes would have been regarded as profoundly suspect by hardline elements within the Church, due to the pre-Christian origins of the texts they studied. While the narrator of Justinian's wars, Procopius, for example, viewed the world around him through the lens of his essentially secular, classical literary training, his contemporary John Malalas believed that 'Bible learning' was all one really needed to make sense of the world.[7] Procopius decried Justinian's persecutory instincts, whereas Malalas went out of his way to praise the 'divine fear' which the emperor's policies instilled in the minds of his subjects. Malalas' hardline perspective chimed with the instincts of clergymen such as John of Ephesus, or the Constantinopolitan hymn-writer Romanos, whose pro-regime compositions were chanted on the streets of the capital during night vigils, egging the emperor on in what John termed his 'severe zealousness'.[8]

Accusing a high-ranking senator or an official of paganism was an easy way to get rid of them and played well politically with a key component of the emperor's support base. Many members of the Church hierarchy, the Circus Factions, and the urban population of the great cities of the empire appear to have been convinced that the governing classes were riddled with crypto-pagans, even if the actual evidence for such suspicions was slight.[9] From Egypt, we possess a letter from an influential abbot accusing a local landowner of paganism: his proof consisted of little more than the fact that the notable concerned had statues in his garden modelled on pagan mythological themes. In the eyes of the abbot, the landowner's classical tastes were enough to damn him.[10] Likewise, Romanos derided as pagan those whose only apparent 'crime' was a devotion to the poetry of Homer, or an admiration for the philosophy of Plato.[11] Such attacks by Christian militants reveal the existence across the empire of a sixth-century 'culture war' which the most aggressive elements within the Church lobbied the emperor to help them pursue with ever greater resolve. At court, important figures attempted to counter such demands.[12] One of Justinian's chief legal officers,

Junillus, for example, continued to argue publicly for the essential compatibility of Christian faith and the traditional inherited intellectual culture, and Justinian's own laws combined biblical allusions with occasional references to the works of classical authors.[13] The hardliners did not have things entirely their own way, but they clearly felt they were in the ascendant.

There is also likely to have been a political dimension to Justinian's persecution of men accused of homosexuality, of which the emperor and his supporters in the Church strenuously disapproved. Acts 'contrary to nature', as Justinian described them in his laws, were believed to incite divine wrath, and to be partly responsible for the earthquakes and diseases that seemed to be ravaging the empire with increasing frequency.[14] Procopius, highly critical of the emperor's policy, describes how those who were arrested and charged with 'pederasty' were castrated and paraded through the streets in an act of carefully calibrated humiliation.[15] Yet, as the brilliant historian John Boswell noted, the only individuals known by name to have been condemned for homosexuality under Justinian were bishops. It is possible the emperor wanted to be rid of these churchmen for other reasons, and their unmarried status would have rendered them uniquely vulnerable to this sort of accusation.[16]

Justinian also lent his support to efforts to extend the reach of Christianity into the countryside and even to regions adjacent to but outside of the empire where it had not yet spread. Again, he seems to have been motivated by a mixture of piety and politics. In the Caucasus and southern Arabia, the imperial authorities in the early sixth century had learned to 'weaponise' Christianity, using it as means of drawing the inhabitants of the region into the political orbit of Constantinople. Around the year 543, missionaries were sent to the African kingdom of Nubia, south of Egypt, close to the strategically vital East African kingdom of Axum.[17] At around the same time, Justinian helped to finance a major missionary drive amongst the rural population of Asia Minor, led by John of

Ephesus. Consequently, the prelate declared, 'God's grace visited the countries of Asia, Caria, Lydia, and Phrygia by the zealousness of the victorious Justinian. It proceeded from him abundantly by the mediation of our humble self . . . to the effect that by the power of the Holy Spirit 70,000 souls were instructed in the faith and turned away from the error of paganism.' John's claim is lent credence by the fact that he provides concrete numbers over and above those for the souls saved: 'The sign of the cross of salvation', he reports, 'was set up everywhere among them, and God's churches were consecrated with much zealousness and care in every place . . . where paganism had disappeared. As many as ninety-six of them were built and erected, and twelve monasteries. . . . Where the word "Christianity" had never been pronounced . . . there fifty-five churches were built with money from the public treasury, but the new Christians built forty-one at their own expense, whereas the victorious emperor through our humble self abundantly gave silver and linen garments, books and brass vessels gladly and willingly.'[18]

As well as cracking down on pagans, Justinian had from the beginning of his reign targeted Samaritans, Jews, and those Christians who departed from the officially sanctioned definition of the faith and were deemed heretics. Many Samaritan places of worship were destroyed after the Samaritan uprising of 529, and tens of thousands had been killed or sold off into slavery. Like pagans, Samaritans, heretics, and Jews, Justinian decreed, were banned from holding any post in the imperial administration or army.[19] Ominously for his Jewish subjects, in the *Codex Iustinianus*, Justinian dropped the provision in imperial law which had granted Judaism the status of a legally permitted religion (or 'lawful sect').[20] Previous Roman rulers could be viciously anti-Jewish: when, in the late fifth century, for example, the emperor Zeno had been informed that the Green Faction in Antioch had burned down the Jewish synagogue there, he had supposedly responded, to demands that those behind the pogrom be punished, 'Why did they not burn all the Jews, the living along with the dead?'[21] But on paper, at least, Roman law had protected the emperor's Jewish subjects. Justinian now removed that protection, and his subsequent laws included measures aimed at sowing discord within the Jewish community and destabilizing relations between its members.[22]

Across his legislation, Justinian effectively transformed the Roman Empire into what historians today would call a 'confessional state'. The opening volume of the *Codex Iustinianus* (in marked contrast to the fifth-century *Codex Theodosianus*) gave pride of place to laws concerned with 'the most exalted Trinity and the Catholic Faith' and began with the emperor Theodosius I's proclamation of imperial Christianity as the official religion of the Roman state.[23] It was only once the rights and concerns of the Church had been addressed that the code proceeded to detail those of the government more generally. Justinian sought to transform the empire into a state that was officially Christian, not only in its ideology and official pronouncements, but also in terms of its interactions with its citizens. He progressively advanced the rights of those 'most lawful' of the emperor's subjects who upheld the imperially sanctioned definition of Christianity, whilst curtailing and applying steady downward pressure on the rights of religious and other minorities who were to be regarded as outsiders in his 'Orthodox Republic' (*orthodoxos politeia*).[24] Under Justinian, the legal rights of the empire's citizens were increasingly determined by their officially reckoned degree of religious conformity.

Deliberate efforts were made to marginalize the heterodox and to treat heretics, Samaritans, and Jews as a sort of undifferentiated mass of second-class citizens, increasingly burdened with obligations rather than bearing rights. In 529 the emperor had banned Samaritans from making wills. The right to make a will and choose how to divide an estate after one's death was highly prized by the Roman elite, and this prohibition had been meant as a deliberate act of degradation. In a major consolidation and extension of legislation against all heterodox groups, he had also decreed that only orthodox Christians had a right to inherit property under the full protection of the law, and in the absence of orthodox Christian heirs, estates could be seized by the imperial government and become property of the Crown (known as the *res privata*), under the direct control of the imperial household (*domus divina*). This would have had the twin advantage, from Justinian's perspective, of both punishing religious nonconformity and potentially increasing the resources at his own disposal. In the law of 537 describing the empire as an 'Orthodox Republic', upper-class heretics, Samaritans, and Jews were uniformly branded as living in a state of publicly declared shame known as 'infamy' (*infamia*). The penalties against infamy effectively stripped them of their social status and turned them into outcasts from respectable society. As a result of this legislation, such heretics, Samaritans, and Jews were henceforth to be subject to physical punishments previously reserved for members of the lower classes. Justinian declared, 'The law allows city councillors numerous privileged exemptions, such as from being beaten, produced for punishment or deported to another province, and innumerable others; these people are to enjoy none of them. . . . Their status is to be one of disgrace, which is what they have desired for their souls as well.'[25]

The ecclesiastical officials known as *defensores ecclesiae* ('defenders of the Church') were empowered to arrest, cross-examine, and torture individuals suspected of paganism, heresy, and immorality.[26] A law concerned with provincial administration from 535 alludes to such 'heretic hunting' in passing as a now entirely standard feature of life within the empire, and local purges are described in detail in a number of contemporary accounts.[27] These heresy hunters were, in effect, the forerunners of the Inquisition, their activities anticipating (and perhaps in a sense inspiring) the 'heresy trials' that would characterize the world of later medieval Europe. In many ways Justinian effectively established and defined the ideological foundations of the

Christian state on which subsequent medieval rulers would build, delineating through his laws an overarching vision of a Christian society, presided over and disciplined by a pious monarch, in which deviance and error were to be ruthlessly identified, extirpated, and suppressed. Perhaps most striking, however, is the way the emperor sought to target the domestic roots of nonconformist belief. By dramatically advancing the claims of orthodox Christian heirs to inherit the property of their non-orthodox or non-Christian relatives, he sought to encourage conversion and set father against son and sibling against sibling. The final victory of Christianity, Justinian evidently believed, was to be secured not at the level of the state, but rather at the level of the household and the family within each and every town and village of his realm.

THE SUFFERING OF GOD

How often were such laws actually put into effect? The inscription from Sardis detailing the prosecution of pagans and the casual reference to 'heretic hunting' in Justinian's provincial legislation would suggest that both the rhetoric and the reality of persecution intensified during his reign. Where local governors and bishops most enthusiastically supported the emperor's religious agenda, the seizure of property, physical assaults, and arrests are likely to have become increasingly common features of daily life. Perhaps not surprisingly, from the reign of Justinian onwards, we begin to see evidence for a growing reassertion of Jewish religious and cultural identity. The emperor's Jewish subjects began to feel alienated from the empire and increasingly hostile to its ever more exclusivist Christian ideology.[28]

But when circumstances demanded it, Justinian was also willing to be pragmatic. In 551, for example, he agreed to formally restore a number of legal rights to the sizeable Samaritan population of the city of Caesarea in Palestine—namely, the ability to inherit, make wills, and leave property to heirs of their choice. He had been petitioned to grant this concession, the emperor relates, by the local bishop, in recognition of improved relations between the Samaritans and the representatives of the imperial government in the town. Interestingly, he adds that in Caesarea, at least, the legislation removing such rights had never in fact been fully implemented: no Samaritan estates had yet been seized by his officers, as the law permitted. This perhaps suggests that the primary goal of the legislation had been to humiliate the Samaritan elite and inculcate a sense of legal insecurity within its ranks. Likewise, in an earlier measure, he had granted an exemption from recent marriage legislation to the Jewish inhabitants in and around the city of Tyre. The legislation had sought to ban matrimony between cousins, which was common practice amongst Jews and Samaritans in Palestine and elsewhere.[29] It is likely that this concession was made in recognition of the important role these Jewish subjects played in the local imperial textile factories, which Justinian was trying to build up into a major source of revenue.[30]

The emperor had to be especially careful when his moralising and Christianising agenda potentially impinged upon the empire's economic and fiscal interests. It is striking that despite the fact that Christian theologians and spokesmen had long been critical of usury (the lending out of money at interest), Justinian never made a serious attempt to legislate against it. The empire's commercial and fiscal economy in general (and that of Constantinople in particular) was simply too dependent on the workings of bankers and moneylenders for such legislation to be politically or economically viable. Many of the emperor's subjects had to routinely borrow money in order to meet their tax debts. Indeed, later in his reign Justinian himself would resort to a series of loans from the banking community to help address a perceived shortfall in income. The only 'professional' groups that he expressly targeted in his legislation on moral grounds were pimps and dealers in eunuchs, those who castrated Roman boys before selling them on.[31]

Likewise, despite regarding Arian Christians as heretics, Justinian and his uncle Justin had initially permitted barbarian troops posted in Constantinople to maintain Arian places of worship. The concession was only rescinded in 538, when the emperor may have perceived that he no longer needed these men.[32] The imperial authorities were also notably cautious when it came to applying the full letter of the law to communities of religious nonconformists concentrated in militarily sensitive locations or regions. It has long been suggested that a significant pagan community may have been allowed to survive in the Syrian city of Harran, for one. The town was perched on the cusp of the Roman-Persian frontier, and it has been argued that Justinian's regime could not afford to alienate its inhabitants, for fear they would go over to the enemy.[33]

Certainly, there are signs that the emperor's non-Christian subjects remained capable of resistance to the increasingly persecutory state. In 556, Jewish and Samaritan rioters yet again rose up in Caesarea in Palestine, where, we are told, they 'attacked the Christians of the city and killed many of them', 'plundered the churches', and killed the governor. Justinian, incensed, dispatched an investigating officer, who 'searched for and found those who had committed the murders. He hanged some, beheaded others or cut off their right hands, and confiscated others' property.' As a result, 'there was great fear in the city of Caesarea and the eastern regions'.[34] The emperor may well have regretted the concessions he had made to the Samaritans in 551.

Justinian's willingness to be flexible and pragmatic when it was in his interest, even when it came to matters of faith, was at its most apparent in his handling of those churchmen opposed to the definition of the relationship between the human and divine in the person of Christ that had been established at the great council of the imperial Church held at Chalcedon in 451. Justinian was almost unique amongst emperors in terms of his personal interest in religious policy and in his direct engagement with the minutiae of Christian doctrine. Only law and legal reform were of comparable interest to him, and the only two previous emperors whom he seemed to regard as his near equals were Theodosius II (who had previously attempted to codify the law) and Constantine the Great.[35] The emperor would bequeath to posterity not only legal texts through which we hear his voice, but also theological treatises and hymns, through which he attempted to comprehend and resolve the doctrinal disputes of his day.

Long before his accession to the throne, as we have seen, Justinian had corresponded on matters of theology with Pope Hormisdas, and in 532 he had personally convened discussions between pro- and anti-Chalcedonian clerics. Justinian's interest in these topics was obvious, and his commitment to the resolution of disputes within the Church was absolute and formed a key component of his strong sense of personal providential mission. It was also central to his vision of a Christian empire, in which the prayers of monks and priests, the piety and orthodoxy of his subjects, and the vigilance and interventionism of the emperor himself would combine harmoniously to ensure divine favour and imperial success both at home and abroad.[36] But from his perspective, there were two problems: too many of his subjects were morally weak, and too few of the empire's prelates and clergy sufficiently committed to Church unity, for his vision of empire to be fully realised. He was constantly willing, however, to improvise and adjust policy in pursuit of his overarching goals.

Following the accession of the emperor Justin to power in 518, there had been a renewed commitment to Chalcedonian orthodoxy on the part of the imperial authorities. Justin had removed from office those bishops and heads of monasteries in Syria who opposed the Chalcedonian formula. Chief amongst these had been the patriarch of Antioch, Severus, the most intellectually brilliant of these critics, who had been forced to flee to Egypt, where the strength of anti-Chalcedonian feeling on the ground made it politically impossible for Justin to move against him.

In his correspondence with Pope Hormisdas, Justinian had been strongly supportive of his uncle's hardline stance, and eager to convey a perhaps exaggerated sense of his personal importance and influence at court. But whereas Justin appears to have regarded acceptance of Chalcedon primarily as a matter of Church discipline, and a key to rebuilding relations with the papal authorities in Rome, Justinian appreciated the intricacies of the dispute from a more theological perspective. In particular, he was keen to find ways of moving the debate forward, aware that in terms of actual belief, the differences between the conflicting parties were not nearly as great as they had been made to sound. Getting to grips with Justinian's Christological policy can be tough going. But it is essential to any proper understanding of both the man and his reign.

For Justinian, the key to restoring unity to the imperial Church lay in convincing the conflicting parties to move beyond their fixed positions and come to a deeper understanding of the beliefs they held in common. During the negotiations under his uncle Justin which had ultimately led to the restoration of ecclesiastical relations between Rome and Constantinople, Justinian had initially been highly suspicious of a group of so-called 'Scythian monks' who had travelled to Rome proposing a novel doctrine known as 'Theopaschism' (from Greek *theos*, meaning 'god', and *paschein*, 'to suffer'). His potential rival for the throne, the popular general Vitalian, actively supported them, and Justinian had written to the pope warning him of their theological machinations.[37] On closer inspection of their doctrine, however, Justinian believed it potentially offered a solution. The novel Theopaschite doctrine, which the Scythian monks proposed as an addition to the Chalcedonian formula, emphasised that the Jesus who had suffered on the cross was not only Jesus the man, but also Jesus the Son of God (also referred to as the 'Divine Word', or, in Greek, the *Logos*) who had preexisted within the Holy Trinity prior to Christ's incarnation and was both consubstantial and coeternal with God the Father.[38] In particular, the emphasis on personhood, individuality, and suffering that Theopaschite teaching proposed offered a means of moving beyond the abstract and increasingly sterile consideration of 'natures' that had come to dominate the theological debate. It made both the divinity and humanity of Christ more tangible, by focusing on him in a more personal and emotive way. Pope Hormisdas was not interested: the Chalcedonian definition was sufficient for him. But an important seed had been sown in Justinian's mind.

CARROTS AND STICKS

Upon his accession to the throne, Justinian had made a determined effort to ease tensions with the leaders of the anti-Chalcedonian elements within the imperial Church. There are indications that anti-Chalcedonian abbots and their followers were permitted to return to their monasteries, and the emperor moved to establish genuine theological dialogue.[39] It is likely that he was encouraged in this direction by his wife, as a range of contemporary authors across the theological spectrum describe Theodora as having been sympathetic to the anti-Chalcedonian cause.[40] The pro-Chalcedonian Church historian Evagrius wrote that, 'whereas Justinian most resolutely supported those who had gathered at Chalcedon and what had been expounded by them, his consort Theodora upheld those who speak of one nature'.[41] Evagrius (along with Procopius) believed that the imperial couple might have been tempted to adopt these conflicting stances for political purposes, allowing the regime to maintain points of contact and support across the Christological divide.[42] But Theodora's religious convictions were not doubted by

John of Ephesus or by a number of other churchmen associated with opposition to the council. John records that she provided accommodation in the Palace of Hormisdas for as many as five hundred dissident clergymen and monks 'from all quarters of the East and of the West'.[43]

Theodora extended her hospitality and patronage even to individuals who were far from deferential to her and Justinian. Since the fourth century, the Christian imagination had become preoccupied with 'holy men'—individuals who had chosen to separate themselves from society and live a life of pious contemplation, drawing ever closer to God through cycles of prayer, fasting, and mortification of the flesh. The first such figure was Saint Antony, who had retreated to the desert to pursue this path. His spiritual journey had been popularised in a biography (a 'hagiography', or *Life*) of him by the fourth-century patriarch of Alexandria, Athanasius. Antony was revered both as the first Christian hermit and as the founder of monasticism, as others had sought to emulate his devotion to God by coming to live in proximity to him. As Antony's fame had spread (not least through the circulation of Athanasius' *Life*), so, too, had a growing number of pious Christians responded to it by also adopting an ascetic lifestyle.[44] This potentially caused problems: legislation had to be issued to prevent slaves or agricultural workers from simply abandoning their toils to become holy men or monks without the permission of their masters. At the Council of Chalcedon in 451, monasteries and individual hermits had been placed under the supervision of bishops to make sure they did not spread or sponsor heresy.

Such holy men came to possess enormous spiritual authority, and petitioners and pilgrims would visit them to seek advice or in search of miracles. Indeed, by the sixth century, spending time as a holy man or monk was increasingly considered a prerequisite for appointment to episcopal office, such experience being regarded as crucial to securing the respect of the laity.[45] Their spiritual authority meant they were able to speak truth to power, and some of them began to emerge as potentially significant political players.

In the aftermath of the Nika riots, Justinian had redoubled his efforts to regain divine favour by healing the rift within the Church, inviting the leaders of the anti-Chalcedonian faction to Constantinople to negotiate with him and with the pro-Chalcedonian leadership in person. At Theodora's prompting, the emperor urged Severus to join these discussions, but Severus demurred, pleading ill health.[46] One of those who did visit was a diminutive Syrian monk, Zoora ('shorty' in Syriac), who had attracted great fame for his piety. Upon arriving in Constantinople and being introduced to Justinian, he is recorded to have unleashed a torrent of abuse upon the emperor (to which Justinian responded in kind). The empress nevertheless provided accommodation for the holy man in the suburbs of Sycae (Galata). When she received another holy man, a famous ascetic from Syria named Mare, in the palace, she offered him a large sum of money for his own needs and those of the poor. He apparently threw it across the room and told Theodora to get stuffed. But Theodora put him up, too, in Galata at her own expense. The sense we derive from the sources is that the empress was more interested in performing acts of charity than in parsing the abstruse theological concepts which so fascinated her husband. Nevertheless, a number of important anti-Chalcedonian theologians and churchmen composed Christological treatises and pamphlets addressed to her at around this time in recognition of her importance to their community.[47]

At the discussions of 532, Justinian had made it clear to the opponents of the council that he did not regard them as heretics, but simply believed they were guilty of 'excessive scruples over detail', which prevented them from entering into communion with the defenders of Chalcedon.[48] In a remarkable concession, the emperor had offered to restore the dissident bishops to their sees if they would acknowledge the disciplinary provisions of the Council of Chalcedon while simply agreeing to differ over its Christological ones; he also wanted them to rescind their condemnation of the writings of the fifth-century Pope Leo and the statement of faith (known as the *libellus*) that had been issued by the sixth-century Pope Hormisdas.[49] The fact that the latter had condemned those heroes of the anti-Chalcedonian party who had led resistance to the council, however, had meant that this proposal was condemned to failure.

But Justinian did not give up. Instead he attempted to take a different tack, refloating the doctrine of Theopaschism. In March 533 he issued an edict declaring that 'Jesus Christ, God's son and our God, incarnate, taking nature and crucified, is one of the holy and consubstantial Trinity'.[50] The edict contained no explicit reference to Chalcedon, although the emperor confirmed in private correspondence, with both the patriarch of Constantinople and the pope, that he still stood by the council.[51] Soon thereafter the emperor composed a strongly Theopaschite hymn (based on one, in fact, which had originally been written by the anti-Chalcedonian Severus) and introduced it into the liturgy of the Great Church. Praising the 'Only-begotten Son and Word of God', the hymn celebrated how 'Christ the God', 'crucified', 'crushed death with death'.[52] The following year (534), Justinian extracted an acknowledgement from Pope John II in Rome that 'God suffered in the flesh', finally marking papal acceptance of the Theopaschite doctrine.[53] Justinian had become committed to this view: both sides, it seemed, could agree that the 'crucified Christ' should be clearly defined as God.[54]

In 535 Severus finally journeyed to Constantinople, where the empress Theodora received him and his followers and provided accommodations for them. Her influence on her husband's religious policy was now at its height (perhaps as a result of her having helped to stiffen his resolve in the face of the Nika riots).[55] Once in the capital, Severus entered into discussion with the newly appointed patriarch, Anthimus (who had participated as a pro-Chalcedonian spokesman in the negotiations of 532). In Egypt, Justinian had recently supported the appointment of a follower of Severus, one Theodosius, as patriarch of Alexandria. Later sources sympathetic to the anti-Chalcedonian cause record that, as a result of a three-way exchange between Anthimus, Severus, and Theodosius, a joint 'declaration of the faith' was negotiated and agreed. This set out as a common position the belief that each of Christ's natures had 'remained without confusion in its sphere of manifestation'. This sounded essentially dyophysite. But it also asserted the essentially miaphysite position that 'out of the two natures' had been formed 'one Son, one Lord, one Christ, and one nature of the incarnate Word [Logos]'. Anthimus had not agreed to revoke Chalcedon, but he had agreed to supplement it along lines acceptable to Severus.[56]

It seems almost inconceivable that Anthimus would have made this concession without Justinian's consent. The fact that Justinian did not broker or sign off on the deal himself, however, might suggest that he wanted to see how it would be received before he put his name to it. As news of the theological concordat spread, a furious reaction ensued from the council's supporters both in the provinces and on the streets of Constantinople.[57] Opposition to the deal was given leadership and focus by the recently appointed pope, Agapitus, whom the Gothic king, Theodahad, had sent to Constantinople to try to negotiate peace in Italy on his behalf. After the pope's arrival, according to our chief papal source (the Book of the Pontiffs), 'a disputation occurred between the emperor and Agapitus. Justinian told him: "Either you will agree with us or I will have you sent off into exile." Then the blessed Pope made this reply joyfully to the emperor: "Sinner that I am, I have long wanted to come to the most Christian Emperor Justinian—but now I have encountered Diocletian!" . . . The most holy Pope Agapitus convinced him [Justinian] of his error and was honoured by all the Christians.'[58] Confronted by the pope, the emperor had backed down.

Whatever one thinks of the details of this account, the arrival of the pope in Constantinople had left Anthimus dangerously exposed politically, and Justinian had little choice but to hang him out to dry. Faced with a wave of opposition to the deal, and perhaps anxious not to jeopardise the military campaign in Italy by turning the leadership of the Catholic Church against him, Justinian agreed to depose Anthimus and renounce the 'Definition of the Faith' the patriarch had just negotiated on his behalf. The newly appointed patriarch of Constantinople, Menas, speedily convened a synod which denounced his predecessor along with Severus of Antioch and other miaphysite leaders. Only the personal intervention of the empress Theodora prevented Severus from being arrested. In 537, Justinian dispatched troops to Alexandria to depose the patriarch Theodosius (who was sent into exile) and forcibly replace him with a pro-Chalcedonian.[59] This move was clearly part of a broader effort to remove all remaining anti-Chalcedonian bishops from their posts.[60] Justinian was careful not to declare theological opposition to the Council of Chalcedon itself to be a heresy.[61] But he did now declare Severus and his followers to be heretics, and therefore subject to the same legal penalties as Arians, Samaritans, and Jews. Scribes caught making copies of the writings of Severus, Justinian decreed, were henceforth to have their hands chopped off.[62] In a later move, the decrees of the Council of Chalcedon were granted the status of imperial law, such that the emperor thereby branded its opponents as criminals.[63]

What did Justinian hope to achieve with these suddenly aggressive policies? As with his measures against pagans, the new anti-miaphysite legislation was applied more stringently in some areas than in others. In Syria, for example, the stridently pro-Chalcedonian patriarch of Antioch, Ephraem, is reported to have unleashed a vicious persecution that attempted to employ the law to maximum effect.[64] Taking advantage of a period of peace in Roman-Persian relations, Ephraem even secured the arrest and extradition of a leading anti-Chalcedonian clergyman, the former bishop John of Tella, from Persian territory. The bishop had been deposed from office previously, but had continued to ordain new anti-Chalcedonian clergy in breach of canon law. He was taken to Antioch, where he died in prison. Only the revival of warfare between Rome and Persia in 539–540, we are told, enabled the 'monks of the East', who had been 'driven from their monasteries', to come out of hiding 'in the various places in the wilderness' in which they had taken refuge.[65]

The patriarchate of Antioch was perhaps a special case. Ephraem had been one of those who had orchestrated opposition to Anthimus' proposed deal and he was clearly determined to make the most of his moment of triumph.[66] Justinian may initially have meant his rebranding of Severus and his supporters as heretics as a stick with which to chastise and intimidate them, in the hope of inducing a more cooperative attitude. If so, it was a dangerous strategy: by redesignating fellow Christians as heretics even though he had so recently acknowledged their orthodoxy, he risked making future dialogue almost impossible. One suspects that it may also have caused problems at home. As Evagrius put it, writing of Justinian's and Theodora's respective religious positions, 'Neither made any concession to the other.'[67]

Despite Justinian's condemnation of Severus and his followers, Theodora continued to maintain contact with leading figures amongst the anti-Chalcedonian factions and even secretly provided the deposed patriarch, Anthimus, with sanctuary in her palace, where he would be discovered after her death. She is also recorded to have lent her patronage to missionary activity by anti-Chalcedonian priests directed to Nubia and Arabia in the early 540s.[68] After Pope Agapitus scuppered Justinian's attempted rapprochement with Severus and his disciples, Theodora clearly took over patronage of the remaining Severan party, perhaps in the hope that moderates amongst them could still be persuaded to work with Justinian, as, of course, she herself did.[69] It may be significant that a considerable amount of imperial patronage was directed towards the city of Antioch—where strong anti-Chalcedonian sentiment persisted—specifically in the empress' name, possibly as a means of reaching out to the city's otherwise dangerously alienated nonconformist congregations.[70]

There are indications that any such policy was not without success. It was *after* Justinian had denounced Severus, after all, that the anti-Chalcedonian (but clearly pragmatic) John of Ephesus agreed to accept Justinian's support in his conversion drive amongst the peasants of Asia Minor.[71] A detailed theological discourse, in the form of a letter written by Justinian in around the year 542–543, survives from Egypt in which he addressed himself to a body of monks from the Ennaton monastery near Alexandria. This institution had formerly been a hotbed of resistance to Chalcedon. In the letter, the emperor congratulates the monks concerned on having seen the light and submitted to the Chalcedonian authorities.[72] There clearly remained a party of moderate anti-Chalcedonians with whom progress could still be made, and Justinian was more than willing to work with such moderates to spread Christianity within and beyond Roman territory. His efforts to restore unity to the Church and realise his vision of empire could not be abandoned. As the manifestation of a great plague in Constantinople in 542 had recently demonstrated, God remained angry, and constant effort was needed to secure divine favour.[73]

THE 'THREE CHAPTERS'

Justinian interpreted the arrival of the plague in fundamentally religious terms, as a punishment for sin and a call to moral and spiritual renewal. Confronted by the pandemic, he attempted to rally the spirits of his subjects and unite them in prayer. In the plague year of 542, for example, Justinian moved the date of the feast day known as the *Hypapante* (referred to in the West as Candlemas) and transformed it into a celebration of the city of Constantinople's divine patron, the Virgin Mary, who was believed to be able to ward off disease. The construction of the 'New Church' dedicated to the Virgin in Jerusalem the following year, and his institutionalisation of the Feast of the Annunciation (Greek *Evangelismos*), should also probably be understood in this context.[74] Justinian's public religious statements to date had already placed a strong emphasis on the importance of devotion to the *Theotokos*, which, like a proper understanding of Christ's suffering on the cross, offered a means of focusing the minds of Chalcedonian and anti-Chalcedonian Christians alike on the deeper truths and mysteries of the faith they shared. In the years that followed, this emphasis would become still more pronounced as churches dedicated to the Virgin continued to proliferate throughout the empire.[75]

The emperor also sought to mobilise holy relics and images, or icons, of Christ, Mary, and the saints to rally the faithful and communicate with the divine. Holy images have been found in all of the earliest places of Christian worship that survive, and stunning examples of sixth-century icons can be seen to this day in Saint Catherine's Monastery in Sinai, which Justinian founded. In the year 544, what was believed to be a miraculous image of Christ kept in the city of Edessa was credited with responsibility for a Roman victory over Persian forces nearby, and that same year a famous icon of Christ was sent by the emperor on a tour of the East to raise money for pious causes and as a focus for prayer.[76] Such images began to play an ever more important and visible role in official imperial ceremonial, both on the streets of the capital and at court, where, significantly, images of the emperor were placed alongside those of Christ.[77] Any distinction between the heavenly court of God and the earthly court of the emperor became increasingly blurred as imperial ceremonial, in the words of a pioneering historian of Byzantine culture, became 'intricately interwoven with the religious calendar'.[78] When, in 559, for example, Justinian celebrated a triumphal entry (or *adventus*) into Constantinople to mark the recent defeat of bands of Huns known as Kutrigurs, he did so not with the traditional ceremony, stretching back to the days of the Roman Republic, with which he had celebrated Belisarius' defeat of the Vandals in 534. Rather, he rode into the city on horseback, dismounting at the Church of the Holy Apostles to light candles and pray at the tomb of his beloved wife Theodora, who had died several years earlier.[79]

In the 540s, Justinian pressed ahead with his efforts to find a theological solution to the divisions within the Church. His attitude in his dealings with Severus and his followers took on an unremittingly harsh tone: in the letter to the Alexandrian monks who had changed sides, for example, he repeatedly refers to the Severans as 'heretics' and 'enemies of the truth'; at one point he even compares them to 'demons'.[80] Such rhetoric would have gone down well with the most enthusiastic pro-Chalcedonian elements within the Church whose support he had been within an ace of losing in 535. In 543 Justinian also authorised a purge of seemingly highly intellectual (and thus perhaps dangerously free-thinking) elements within the monastic communities of Palestine which had been demanded by his supporters there.[81] Securing and consolidating his credentials amongst the most hardline advocates of Chalcedon was vital: for the emperor was about to press ahead with yet another initiative that would risk provoking a major backlash amongst them.

Justinian's advocacy of Theopaschite doctrine remained central to his understanding of how Chalcedonian orthodoxy could be clarified and made more tangible so as to widen its appeal. In his 'Edict on the True Faith', which he would promulgate in 551, he conveyed that doctrine in its purest and most compelling form: 'Confessing therefore that he [Christ] is God, we do not deny that he is also man, and when we say that he is man, we do not deny that he is also God. For if he was God alone, how could he suffer, how could he be crucified, and how could he die as these things are alien to God? But if he was a mere man, how could he conquer through suffering, how could he save, how could he bring life? . . . So then the same one has suffered; the same saves and conquers through his suffering; the same is God, the same is man, the two natures exist together as one.'[82]

In order to clarify the orthodoxy of Chalcedon, however, still more needed to be done. Justinian believed that the teachings of Cyril of Alexandria, who had led resistance to the Council of 451, were entirely consistent with the definition of the faith established at Chalcedon, despite the patriarch's strident opposition to it. The problems that had arisen, Justinian and his court theologians believed, were partly a matter of semantics. Cyril had been regrettably loose in his usage of the Greek word for 'nature' (*physis*), sometimes using it in contexts where others would have used the term for 'substance' or 'essence' (*hypostasis*). When the decrees of the Council of Chalcedon spoke of Christ having one *hypostasis*, or 'substance', comprising both the human and the divine, this was actually the same thing that Cyril had meant when he had insisted on Christ having one 'nature'.[83] This was a point Justinian sought to convey through his 'Edict on the True Faith' as he condemned those who fixated on and demanded the use of specific words without grasping their actual meaning. As the emperor declared in the work's concluding salvo, 'Therefore, if after this orthodox confession which condemns the heretics, one separates oneself from the holy church by disputing over names or syllables or phrases rather than by preserving a pious understanding, then his piety exists in name only and not in deed, and such a one delights in schism. He will render an account of himself and of those whom he has deceived or will deceive to our great God and Saviour Jesus Christ at the Day of Judgment.'[84]

Proving to followers of Cyril of Alexandria that his teachings, if properly understood, were actually consistent with Chalcedonian orthodoxy faced one additional doctrinal stumbling block. At the

300

discussions which the emperor had convened in 532, the miaphysite party had objected to the fact that the Council of Chalcedon had failed to condemn the writings of three fifth-century theologians who had sympathised to varying degrees with the hated Nestorius: Ibas, Theodore of Mopsuestia, and Theodoret of Cyrrhus. Indeed, the council had expressly admitted Ibas and Theodoret back into the Church after their earlier expulsion, but they had remained controversial figures even amongst the Chalcedonians. Under Justin, troops had been sent to Cyrrhus to destroy an icon of Theodoret which the locals there had come to venerate. Justinian clearly thought the miaphysites had a point, and in 544–545, he decided that in order to remove the taint of Nestorianism from the council, the writings of these three deceased churchmen had to be condemned. The 'True Faith' of the empire had to be beyond reproach. Accordingly, in that year he issued a denunciation of all three authors and their works—known as the 'Three Chapters'. He repeated it in his 'Edict on the True Faith' of 551.[85]

Justinian's condemnation of the 'Three Chapters' was met with deep unease amongst the Council of Chalcedon's most uncompromising supporters in the East. The patriarch of Constantinople, Menas, initially claimed that he could not subscribe to it without first hearing the views of the recently appointed pope, Vigilius. When Justinian obliged him to sign up to it anyway, the patriarch informed the papal ambassador resident in the city that he would withdraw his support if the pope objected. The strongly pro-Chalcedonian patriarchs Ephraem in Antioch, Zoilus in Alexandria, and Peter in Jerusalem all accepted the emperor's decree, but made it clear to those around them that they had done so under duress.[86]

Predictably, the most vehement resistance came from the western parts of the empire. After consulting with representatives of the western churches in Syracuse in Sicily in 546 (where he had escaped to avoid capture by the Goths), Pope Vigilius made his opposition clear.[87] He and the emperor's other critics argued that by acknowledging that its treatment of Ibas, Theodoret, and Theodore had been erroneous, and that those the council had deemed orthodox were now heretical, Justinian was potentially opening the door to those who believed that the council's treatment of Jesus Christ had been flawed. Chalcedon had to be accepted in its entirety or it would have no legitimacy; basic issues, including the 'primacy of honour' of the bishop of Rome, would once more be up for grabs. Justinian responded by summoning the pope to Constantinople.

Once in the capital, Justinian clearly expected Vigilius to bend to his will, as the patriarchs of Constantinople, Antioch, Jerusalem, and Alexandria had done. This was to be no rerun of Agapitus' visit of ten years earlier: then Justinian had needed the pope more than the pope had needed Justinian, so that East Roman armies could press ahead with the early phases of the conquest of Italy. Now the military situation on the ground was completely different, and the new pope owed his position entirely to Justinian's patronage.[88] Everything seemed to be in place for Justinian to obtain the final signature he needed: once the bishop of Rome was on board, his new policy could claim the support of all five of the patriarchs of the Church, those to whom the spiritual and religious authority of Christ's apostles was believed to have been transmitted.

EMPEROR AND PRIEST

Vigilius finally arrived in Constantinople on 25 January 547, but upon his arrival he proved far less accommodating than Justinian would have hoped. Instead of heeding the emperor, the pope excommunicated all the bishops who had signed Justinian's condemnation of the 'Three Chapters', including the patriarch of Constantinople, and ordered them to withdraw their signatures. In a series of tense encounters with the emperor, the pope was subjected to mounting pressure. His allies would later claim that he had declared to Justinian, 'I swear that even if you keep me a prisoner, you cannot make the blessed apostle Peter a prisoner!' By June, he had begun to relent and agreed to rescind his excommunication of Patriarch Menas. He also gave private written statements to both Justinian and Theodora condemning the 'Three Chapters'. In April 548, Vigilius sent a 'Judgement' (known as the *Iudicatum*) to Patriarch Menas in which he again condemned the 'Three Chapters', but this time openly.[89]

News of the pope's surrender to Justinian was met with fury in the West. Faced with a crumbling of papal authority there, Justinian allowed the pope to withdraw his statement. He only did so in return for Vigilius agreeing to take a solemn oath, sworn over the Gospels and a sacred relic (one of the nails thought to be from Christ's crucifixion), that he would strain every nerve to secure the condemnation of the 'Three Chapters'. Vigilius swore the oath on 15 August 550. It was further agreed that the matter would be settled once and for all by yet another great Ecumenical Council, to be held in Constantinople, which a significant number of western bishops would attend. For the first time ever, all the patriarchs of the Church would gather in person in the imperial city to perfect the faith at the instigation of the emperor.[90]

The western reaction was predictably unenthusiastic, and the summons to Constantinople was met with a combination of blank refusal, foot-dragging, and excuses of varying plausibility. Justinian had never been known for his patience, and it was in this context that in July 551 he issued his 'Edict on the True Faith', perfecting his Theopaschite doctrine and damning the 'Three Chapters'. The pope was presented with a copy of the edict at the papal ambassador's residence in the capital (known as the Placidia Palace), where he had been based since his arrival. He would later claim to have replied, 'Ask the most pious prince to remove his edict, which he has ordered to be posted, and remind him that he is obliged to wait for a common resolution to be reached.' The issue could not be settled, the pope insisted, without the agreement of an Ecumenical Council with a strong western presence. Those who accepted the edict were to be excommunicated—including Justinian's chief theological adviser—Bishop Theodore Ascidas (who may at this point have played a role in the emperor's theological writings comparable to that played by Tribonian in his legal output earlier in the reign). A month later, Vigilius expressly broke off communion with the patriarch of Constantinople and ordered that Theodore be expelled from the priesthood. Fearing arrest, the pope took refuge in the Church of Saint Peter, which Justinian had dedicated over thirty years earlier.[91]

Soldiers were soon sent in pursuit of the pontiff, who would later recount how in a mutually undignified and unedifying episode, with soldiers grabbing at him, he had almost pulled down the entire high altar in the church as he clung to it for dear life. Eventually, the officers sent in pursuit of the pope—headed by Justinian's nephew, the high-ranking courtier Justin—promised to ensure his physical security, and he was returned to effective house arrest at the ambassadorial residence. There, all his correspondence with the outside world was censored; it would even be claimed that fake letters supposedly written by the pope were put into circulation by imperial agents in Italy so as to discredit him. The drama, however, was not over: on 23 December 551, the pope and his closest advisers took advantage of some building work to sneak through a hole in the wall of the Placidia Palace and escape by boat to the Church of Saint Euphemia in Chalcedon, where the Ecumenical Council of 451 had been held. Vigilius informed Justinian that he would remain there until the emperor accepted his condemnation of Theodore Ascidas and those bishops who had signed up to the 'Edict on the True Faith', which the bishop of Rome was careful to blame on the emperor's chief adviser rather than on the emperor himself.[92]

Over the course of his career, Justinian had dealt with several popes, but none exasperated him more than Vigilius. On 31 January

552, the emperor responded to the pontiff's grandstanding in terms so abusive that the pope thought it best to presume that the letter concerned had been written by somebody else—'for it proved to be packed with matters so far removed from the truth and with such insults that the mildness of the imperial mouth could never be believed to have dictated it'.[93]

After several months of further bickering, an uneasy compromise was reached: Vigilius agreed to retract his condemnation of the patriarch and Justinian's theological adviser. In return, Theodore, Menas, and the other eastern bishops with whom the pope had severed relations issued a written statement saying they would uphold Chalcedon and the other Ecumenical Councils 'without any addition or change' and would not issue any further statements concerning the 'Three Chapters' without prior papal approval. The pope was also issued an apology for his unceremonious treatment. In the West, it was reported that the emperor ('our pious master') had repented.[94] Still, the fact remained that Justinian's 'Edict on the True Faith' had not been rescinded and thus remained law. The emperor had every intention of pressing ahead with his condemnation of the 'Three Chapters' at the Ecumenical Council that had been agreed.

Vigilius' strategy was now reduced to trying to find excuses to postpone the convocation of the council. Justinian was not, however, one to hang about, and he made it clear that the council had to proceed. Patriarch Menas had died in August 552. In January 553, his successor, Eutychius, wrote to Vigilius asking him to preside over the imminent assembly. Reluctantly, the pope consented, agreeing to provide a list of western bishops he thought should attend. When the council finally opened on 5 May 553, only 16 bishops from the West appeared out of a total of over 160 attendees, and most significantly, Vigilius himself failed to turn up. Instead, he remained ensconced within the Placidia Palace in the company of an additional 15 bishops from Italy, Africa, and Illyricum, as well as two high-ranking bishops from Asia Minor of western origin.[95] The opening of the council was no doubt intended to be a great statement of religious and imperial unity, but Vigilius had rained on Justinian's parade. Accordingly, the emperor transferred the honour of presiding over the council to his patriarch, Eutychius.

Vigilius once again played for time. He asked Justinian for a twenty-day break so he could compose his thoughts on the 'Three Chapters'. Justinian does not appear to have replied, and the bishops who had gathered for the council agreed to proceed without the pope. They began with a series of sessions which had clearly been carefully choreographed in advance by Justinian's advisers, at which lengthy, pre-prepared speeches were read out. The event had all the spontaneity of a 'party congress' in a modern totalitarian state. Justinian sent instructions to the bishops ordering them, in characteristic style, to hurry up and get on with it.[96]

In the papal ambassadorial residence, Vigilius, meanwhile, was busy presiding over what amounted to a mini council of his own. On 14 May the pontiff issued a 'Constitution' (*Constitutum*) which was meant to be his final word on the 'Three Chapters' controversy. It was a direct refutation of both Justinian and the gathering he had convened.[97] In response, the emperor publicly humiliated and discredited the pope in the most dramatic of ways. What had begun as a loyalist 'party congress' was about to morph into a show trial of the hapless Vigilius.

As the seventh session of the Ecumenical Council got underway, it was suddenly interrupted by officers sent by Justinian. To the assembled patriarchs and bishops, they revealed a series of documents dating from 547 to 550 proving the pope to be a liar, a perjurer, and a traitor even to his own side. The evidence included copies of his private correspondence with Justinian and Theodora, in which he had promised that he would condemn the 'Three Chapters'; details of the oath he had sworn on the Gospels to persuade others to do the same; and a statement he had made pledging to secretly denounce anyone he heard attempting to defend the 'Three

Chapters' or their authors, and to pass on their details to the emperor.[98] As those in attendance digested and responded to the extraordinary exposé, another delegation arrived from the imperial palace bringing a decree from Justinian: he had ordered that Vigilius be suspended from office. On 2 June, when the eighth and final session of the Council of Constantinople convened, it upheld the refined (or 'Neo-Chalcedonian') definition of the faith, the one that Justinian and his court theologians had been working on for the past twenty years, and formally condemned the 'Three Chapters'. The council was over, but could Vigilius finally be persuaded to sign up to its concluding statements?

Eventually, after enduring several months of considerable psychological and physical duress, the pope cracked. He signed a letter to Patriarch Eutychius which amounted to an abject and humiliating self-denunciation. A broken man, Vigilius once more agreed to condemn the 'Three Chapters'. He would subscribe to the decrees of the Council of Constantinople. He even went so far as to proclaim that his earlier opposition to it had been prompted by the workings of the devil. On Justinian's explicit orders, the pope then issued a longer and more detailed critique of the writings which the council had condemned. His statement reads as a work of desperate and verbose insincerity, but Vigilius had given the emperor what he wanted, and he was finally allowed to leave Constantinople and return to Italy. The unfortunate pontiff then died before he was able to reach home. As a recent commentator has noted, 'Vigilius suffered the posthumous humiliation of being the only pope of the sixth century not to be buried in St Peter's and since then he has excited more contempt down the centuries than any of his predecessors on the papal throne. A more distant and more charitable look may recognize in him a man who was not by nature duplicitous and unprincipled but who was placed in circumstances that required gifts he did not possess—self-confidence, a thick skin, and an iron will.'[99] Whilst nobody would ever have credited Justinian with having a thick skin, perhaps Vigilius' greatest misfortune was that he was obliged to contend up close with an emperor whose self-confidence and iron will were rarely in doubt.

DOCTRINE AND DISSENT

In the years that followed, opposition to Justinian's condemnation of the 'Three Chapters' would continue to flare up on occasion. But by the end of the sixth century, the most revered of the early medieval bishops of Rome, Pope Gregory the Great, would be a firm exponent of Justinian's Neo-Chalcedonian doctrine. The council was also widely accepted within the imperial Church to the East, although some hardline opponents of Chalcedon, such as the brilliant miaphysite theologian and philosopher John Philoponus of Alexandria, argued that in condemning the 'Three Chapters', supporters of Chalcedon had merely condemned themselves.[100]

In his own mind, Justinian had achieved his goal, which was to place Chalcedonian orthodoxy beyond theological reproach. Through the measures which he and his uncle Justin had taken against Severus and his supporters, he had managed to effectively purge the imperial episcopacy of its most troublesome elements. This would be true even in Egypt, where resistance to Chalcedon had been at its strongest.[101]

What Justinian had not managed to do, however, was to exercise a comparable degree of control over the laity—the broader body of his Christian subjects, whose prayers the empire needed if it was to secure divine favour and prosper. Severus and his supporters may have effectively been driven out of the structures of the imperial Church, but in response a separate miaphysite Church began to emerge in the countryside of Syria and Egypt. Drawing on the example of John of Tella, opponents of the Council of Chalcedon began to ordain their own bishops and priests, free of imperial control, and to compete for congregations with representatives of the imperial ecclesiastical establishment.[102]

The prayers and souls of these humble believers mattered to Justinian, and he never ceased to consider new ways of trying to persuade opponents of imperial orthodoxy to return to the fold. John of Ephesus records, for example, how in 559–560, the emperor gave orders that 'the lawyers, teachers, monks and shipowners of Alexandria, Lower and Upper Egypt should gather in the capital for a discussion concerning the faith. Now, as all the shipowners who transported wheat for the state were (true) believers [i.e., opponents of Chalcedon], they appeared together before the emperor Justinian, who, knowing that they opposed the Council, discussed the faith with them.'[103]

Likewise, around the year 561, Justinian invited representatives of the strongly 'two-nature' Church of the East (representatives of the Christian Church in Persia) to come to Constantinople and engage in a theological debate, records of which survive.[104] In diplomatic negotiations with the Persians, he demanded guarantees for the religious liberties of Christians living under the shah that he would not have accorded them within the Roman Empire itself, given that he would have regarded the theological stance of many of their leaders to be 'Nestorian', and hence heretical.[105] Justinian evidently expected a higher degree of religious conformity from those Christians who were fortunate enough to live within his 'Orthodox Republic' than from those who dwelled beyond it. For all his growing intolerance of dissent, he also remained willing to engage with non-Chalcedonian Christians in strategically sensitive regions such as the Caucasus, East Africa, and Arabia, and even to provide them with military assistance. He seems to have felt that although imperial orthodoxy represented Christianity in its purest form, all those who accepted the Christian faith as defined under the emperor Constantine at the Council of Nicaea in 325 were, in a sense, part of a broader Christian family. They could be mobilised, for example, against non-Christian rivals such as the Zoroastrian empire of Persia, should circumstances permit. To members of what has been termed this 'Christian Commonwealth' of late antiquity, the pathway to salvation remained open.[106] As late as 564, Justinian was still exploring theological avenues that he thought might offer interesting and creative ways to resolve the divisions remaining in the imperial Church. His interest in one such doctrine (known as 'Aphthartism') led to complaints from the patriarch of Antioch, and it would later be claimed that further opposition to this creed led Justinian to sack the patriarch of Constantinople, Eutychius, despite the fact that the bishop had been such a firm supporter of the emperor's at the Council of Constantinople in 553.[107] These ongoing efforts reveal Justinian's deep personal interest in matters of theology, which could prove exhausting and dangerous even to those most inclined to agree with him.

THE BLENDING OF COLOURS

Contemporary perspectives on the reign of Justinian were inevitably strongly coloured by how the emperor's policies impacted the lives of his subjects. When it came to matters of religion, for those who did not conform, the 'Age of Justinian' was a time of growing persecution, intolerance, and fear. There can be no doubt that the emperor's 'Orthodox Republic' was for many an increasingly dangerous place to live. Justinian pressed ahead with his programme to undermine the legal and social status of Jews, Samaritans, and an increasingly broad cross section of Christian society that he deemed heretical. At the same time, he sought to expunge the empire of pagans and crack down in the cruellest of manners on those whose choices and sexual proclivities he deemed immoral. The explicit exemptions that

Justinian granted to groups such as the Jews of Tyre, or the Samaritans of Caesarea, only make sense, after all, if understood against a broader background of active persecution.

Yet to concentrate simply on those who were penalized as a result of Justinian's ever more exclusivist vision of empire would be to give a misleadingly lopsided sense of the complexity of imperial legislation and the evolution of political and religious culture which he oversaw. While the emperor was responsible for many laws which persecuted religious and moral nonconformity, he also issued laws which improved the lot of vulnerable women, slaves, orphans, and the destitute.[108] Justinian cared deeply about the lives of his subjects and the salvation of their souls, even if he was not too concerned about the manner in which he ensured that salvation. He seems to have been a strong believer in the idea that his ends justified his means. His religious and religiously inspired measures were an often disorientating combination of cruelty and charity, light and shade. As Procopius put it, the emperor's policies seemed to epitomize the claims of sixth-century philosophers that 'exactly opposite qualities may be combined in the nature of Man, just as in the blending of colours'.[109] Living under so paradoxical an emperor was no easy matter.

PART 4

The Great Unravelling

Chapter 13

The Four Horsemen of the Apocalypse

'A MOST DREAD PORTENT'

By the year 540, Justinian's attempts to restore Roman rule to the West and to reassert the authority of the emperor at home had been startlingly successful. From that point on, however, his increasing preoccupation with theology and his ever more urgent efforts to elicit divine favour for his empire coincided with (and were probably intensified by) a series of military and natural catastrophes. An unprecedented combination of warfare, climate change, and disease interacted with the inner tensions at the heart of sixth-century society to shake Justinian's regime to its very core.

The empire was dealt a devastating blow in the East in June 540, when the Persian shah, Khusro (encouraged by the Goths), successfully struck at Antioch, sacking one of the greatest cities in the Roman world. He had succeeded by marching around and behind the recently upgraded Roman defences in Syria, advancing with his Arab allies along the desert frontier. As the churchman John of Ephesus recorded, 'Powerful Persian troops, coming together with their king Khusro, approached and conquered the city of Antioch. They burned it with fire and destroyed it. They stripped it and removed even the marble slabs with which the walls (of the buildings) were overlaid, and took them away to their country.'[1] To celebrate his triumph, the shah forcibly resettled much of the city's surviving population within his own realm in a new city bearing a deliberately provocative name: Weh Antiok Khosrow— 'Better than Antioch, Built by Khusro'. His armies then proceeded to rampage through Syria, exacting tribute and targeting other major cities. In a symbolically charged episode, after entering the port town of Seleucia, Khusro had even washed his warboots in the waters of the Mediterranean, and whilst at Apamaea he presided over a series of races and games in the city's hippodrome after the manner of a Roman emperor. The impact of these events on contemporary political opinion should not be underestimated. When attempting to narrate the fall of Antioch, Procopius would write, 'I become dizzy as I write of so great a calamity and transmit it to future times, and I am unable to understand why indeed it should be the will of God to exalt on high the fortunes of a man or of a place and to cast them down for what appears to us no cause whatsoever.'[2]

The impact of simultaneous warfare to East and West on the empire's military and fiscal resources must have been considerable. Antioch had to be rebuilt at great expense.[3] The implications for the civilian populations of the affected regions were, of course, still more severe. In the cities of Syria and Italy, Persian, Gothic, and Frankish armies, we are told, deliberately targeted the civilian populations, often selling off survivors as slaves. Church authorities made strenuous efforts to reclaim and buy back as many Roman captives as they could. In the countryside, the inevitable damage and disruption caused by warfare, as well as the forced requisitioning and plundering of supplies by armies on the march, frequently led to widespread famine. Procopius was horrified at the suffering he witnessed as he passed through Italy with Belisarius' forces. He describes the skeletal appearance of men, women, and children who were reduced to eating grass, and corpses left to rot in the open air, as no one had the strength to bury them. The bodies of the dead, he tells us, had so little flesh on them that the crows did not even bother trying to strip it from their bones.[4]

The great hunger which gripped much of Italy and other regions in the late 530s was not simply the result of warfare. Writing in 536, the Roman aristocrat and courtier Cassiodorus sent out orders that emergency food supplies be set aside, due to poor harvests. A mysterious climate phenomenon had caused the sun itself to darken during the crucial summer months. For almost a year, Cassiodorus complained, it had been as if there were an eclipse: 'We still perceive', he wrote, 'a kind of sea-coloured sun; we marvel that physical bodies lack shadows at midday and that the strength of the sun's fullest exposure attains only the dullness of a cooling tepidness. . . . What a terror it is, to endure daily what usually frightens people only for a passing moment! . . . What may produce fertility, if the earth does not warm?'[5] Procopius wrote, of Africa, how 'it came about during this year that a most dread portent took place. For the sun gave forth its light without brightness, like the moon, during the whole year, and it seemed exceedingly like the sun in eclipse, for the beams it shed were not such as it is accustomed to give out.'[6] Writing in Constantinople, the scholar and bureaucrat John Lydus, too, commented on the situation: for nearly a whole year, what he perceived to be moisture had 'gathered into clouds dimming the light of the sun, so that it did not come into our sight or pierce this dense substance'.[7] Across the global Northern Hemisphere, from Ireland to Japan, contemporary chronicles record a blocking out of the sun's rays and other climate anomalies, leading to localised harvest failure and severe famine, all around the year 536–537.[8] In Ireland, we hear of 'a failure of bread' and an associated wave of starvation. The Chinese sources describe yellow dust or ashes raining down from the sky and bitter frosts ruining crops, and in Japan, an edict attributed to the 'great king' Senka declared, 'Food is the basis of empire. Yellow gold and ten thousand strings of cash cannot cure hunger. What avail a thousand boxes of pearls to him who is starving due to the cold?'[9]

It is conceivable, as some have argued, that these sources all describe unrelated phenomena that just happened to take place at around the same time. It is not, however, very likely. Indeed, over the course of the past thirty years or so there has been mounting scientific evidence—based on studies of trees rings, ice cores, and other geological 'proxy data'—that one of the most sudden and severe temperature drops in human and global history took place across the Northern Hemisphere in the second half of the 530s. As a result, some scholars have even referred to this period as a 'Late Antique Little Ice Age'.[10] This precipitous decline in temperatures, estimated by some to have reached about two degrees Celsius, may have had far-reaching societal implications.[11] In North America, the period of climate instability and associated famine appears to have sparked off widespread migration and the emergence of new types of villages and settlements, which archaeologists and anthropologists have come to regard as the origin of the 'Pueblo societies' that would henceforth dominate much of the region until the era of European settlement and conquest.[12] In Scandinavia, a major shift in religious culture took place, whereby the local population abandoned the traditional worship of the sun and moon, and instead turned to what we now know as the 'Norse' pantheon (comprising gods and goddesses such as Thor, Odin, and Freya).[13] In the East Roman Empire and the societies that surrounded it, the phenomenon was taken by some as confirmation that the 'End of the World' was nigh.

That there was a sudden period of climatic instability at this time is not to be doubted. However, with respect to the Mediterranean, at least, talk of an 'Ice Age' is to be treated with some caution. The literary sources, such as Procopius, Cassiodorus, and John Lydus, suggest a sudden drop in temperatures and a series of catastrophic harvests from around the year 536. There is good reason to believe that the period of maximum disruption may have lasted some ten years.[14] But as Justinian's armies attempted to consolidate their control over Africa and extend it over Italy, and as his administrators strained every nerve to maximise the flow of tax revenues into the coffers of the Roman state, these were ten crucial years when the fortunes of the emperor's efforts at imperial renewal hung in the balance.

What could possibly have caused so sudden a drop in temperatures? The answer would appear to lie in an extraordinary series of volcanic eruptions, from Central America to Iceland, which geologists have been able to date to this period, which stands out from the geological record as an era of 'unparalleled volcanic violence'.[15] These eruptions (in about 536 and 540) cast vast amounts of dust and debris into the air, creating an enormous sulphuric acid aerosol veil in the stratosphere, with effects that were clearly discernible as far afield as Constantinople and beyond.[16] The result was to block out the sun's light and warmth, with devastating consequences in terms of poor harvests and famine. The phenomenon—sometimes referred to as the 'dust-veil event'—would thus have significant consequences. It was perhaps with good reason that Procopius would write that 'from the time when this thing happened, men were free neither from war nor pestilence nor any other thing leading to death'.[17] For the great hunger of the late 530s was not the only natural disaster that would befall the empire at this time and put Justinian to the test.

DISASTER AND DISEASE

The village of Barrington, in Cambridgeshire, presents the visitor with a quintessentially idyllic rural scene: with its thatched cottages and village pub, and one of the best preserved and extensive village greens in the country, it could not feel further removed in place or time from the Mediterranean world in the age of Justinian. Yet nearby at a site called Edix Hill (about half an hour's walk from my home), archaeologists and geneticists have discovered startling evidence for a series of convulsions that would ultimately transform not just England, but much of western Eurasia at this time. In the late 1980s, a team of archaeologists led by Tim Malim and Professor John Hines from the University of Cardiff excavated an extensive Anglo-Saxon cemetery at Edix Hill dating back to the sixth century.[18] In 2018, a study of the DNA preserved in the human skeletal remains that had been found there revealed that many of those interred (including a woman and child buried in the same grave) had died of bubonic plague, which the literary sources reveal had arrived in the Mediterranean, in the Eastern Roman Empire of Justinian, by the year 541.[19]

The origins of bubonic plague can be traced back around seven thousand years, when it split off from a disease known to medical scientists and geneticists as 'pseudo-tuberculosis'.[20] By the Bronze Age, it was established in Central Asia, where it evolved a highly lethal and virulent strain that would become 'endemic' to the rodent population of the region (including marmots, which were and remain present across the grasslands of the Eurasian steppe). The causative agent of the plague (the bacterium known to science as *Yersinia pestis*) fatally infects the blood and can be easily transmitted to other mammals through fleas and similar bloodsucking parasites, which become desperate for new sources of nutrition after the disease or some other factor—such as starvation—has killed off their initial host. The bacterium can also be transmitted via soil, through aerosol droplets, or by eating infected animals. Bubonic plague is thus capable of sudden 'spillover events', whereby it can leap between species, including, crucially, to human beings.[21]

Indeed, patterns of human behaviour may have rendered human communities in the sixth century particularly vulnerable to outbreaks of the disease. The nomads of Central Asia (such as the Huns) placed great value on animal skins and especially furs, including those of marmots. The practice of hunting, skinning, and eating such animals, which we know to have been widespread, could have placed them at considerable risk.[22] Many sedentary human communities—both in town and countryside—lived with rats and other rodents in their midst, the vermin attracted by their leftovers, waste, and stores of food. The ancient remains of black rats (*Rattus rattus*) have been found at the site of Justiniana Prima, and increasingly sophisticated archaeological techniques have revealed that they were common in sixth-century Italy and, by inference, elsewhere in the Mediterranean.[23] These small mammals were highly susceptible to plague and could easily pass it on to their human neighbours, via their fleas.[24] Reduced levels of sunlight (leading to vitamin D deficiency) and weakened immunity resultant from hunger would also have rendered people in the 540s especially vulnerable to disease.[25]

In its most common form, the bubonic plague is capable of killing a human victim in just five to ten days, with over half of those who contract the disease likely to die of it. It is also capable of developing a 'pneumonic' strain, which can be passed on by breath droplets between human carriers. The pneumonic plague kills almost everyone who contracts it and does so with even greater rapidity.

The plague is capable of burning through and wiping out isolated communities that come into contact with it, and can spread like wildfire between connected ones. Until the development of modern medicine (and especially antibiotics) it was probably the most deadly and terrifying disease known to man, its signature being the painful black tumour or pustule (known as a 'bubo') that typically swells up in the armpit, neck, or groin of its victim as the lymph nodes become infected prior to recovery or death.[26]

Bubonic plague may have made its way to the Mediterranean from Central Asia in the centuries before the Age of Justinian. One Roman medical author, Rufus of Ephesus, describes what sounds like a very similar disease in Syria and North Africa (Libya) around the first century CE.[27] Thereafter, there is reason to believe that the plague may have 'focalized', establishing a 'plague reservoir' amongst the rodent population somewhere in East Africa, circulating at low rates without causing excessive rodent die-off. Certainly, a number of contemporary sources would expressly associate the plague that suddenly emerged in the sixth century with territory ruled by the Ethiopian kings of Axum, who were in frequent contact with the authorities in Constantinople through political, military, and economic channels as a result of the struggle with the Persians over control of Arabia.[28] The 'Plague of Justinian', as it is commonly referred to in scholarship, was the result of a characteristically late antique form of globalization and connectivity.

The dimming of the sun and the precipitous drop in temperatures that occurred in around 536, along with the advent of the bubonic plague in around 541, transformed the climatic and epidemiological circumstances in which Justinian, his officials, and millions of his increasingly beleaguered subjects found themselves. The arrival of bubonic plague, in particular, was probably the single most important event of the entire sixth century.[29] Since the 1990s, historians and archaeologists have increasingly raised the question of whether the climate disruption and the plague were connected. It seems highly likely that they were, although the exact nature of the connection is not yet entirely clear.

The first person to seriously examine this possibility was an archaeology correspondent attached to the UK-based newspaper *The Independent*, David Keys. By reading the latest scientific literature, Keys had become aware of the mounting evidence for a dramatic drop in global temperatures (or at least temperatures in the Northern Hemisphere) in around 536. Through his knowledge of more recent periods of history, he was also aware that such dramatic drops in temperature were often associated with volcanic eruptions (such as that which occurred on the Indonesian island of Krakatau in 1883). He began to go in search of evidence for sixth-century volcanic activity. At the same time, he came across the literary evidence for the bubonic plague. Coincidentally, I had recently given my first seminar paper as a graduate student in Oxford on that topic, so Keys got in touch with me.[30] I became an adviser and consultant to him for his research on the Justinianic plague, which culminated in 1999 with the publication of his book *Catastrophe: An Investigation into the Origins of the Modern World.*

According to Keys' model, the ecological disruption caused by climate change in the 530s is likely to have led to altered patterns of foraging on the part of plague-bearing rodents, who may have come into closer contact with human populations at that time, whether in East Africa or elsewhere. The plague then made one of its fatal leaps from one species to another. For the transmission of the plague via the Red Sea to the Mediterranean, Keys' model remains the best hypothesis that we have. In the later Middle Ages, it has been noted, periods of poor harvest were often followed by outbreaks of bubonic plague.[31] The inference is that a decline in vegetation or food supplies forced rats to move closer to human settlements or even killed off many of the rodents, obliging the plague-bearing fleas that fed on them to suddenly seek out human hosts. A similar sequence of events may have transpired in the sixth century. It is possible that a high degree of person-to-person transmission of the plague then ensued.[32] But whether the sudden climate disruption of the late 530s—which led to severe famine—and the plague of the 540s were directly connected or not, the effects of each would have compounded the problems caused by the other.

'THIS TERRIBLE AND MIGHTY SCOURGE'

According to Procopius, the plague first manifested itself in the summer of 541 at the Egyptian port town of Pelusium, which connected the Mediterranean to the Red Sea via an important canal. From there it quickly spread east along the coastal road to Gaza and west to the city of Alexandria. By the spring of 542, it had arrived in Constantinople, extending its reach into Syria, Anatolia, Greece, Italy, and North Africa. By 543 the plague had struck both Armenia and Frankish-ruled territory in Gaul (modern France). In the former, it obliged the Roman and Persian armies to disengage from military operations. The following year it is recorded to have reached Ireland.[33] In the most densely populated of these regions the plague would establish reservoirs amongst the local rodent population, thereby facilitating future outbreaks (which would recur down to at least the middle of the eighth century). As Procopius would write, 'It did not just come into one part of the world nor just upon certain men, nor did it confine itself to any one season of the year . . . but it embraced the entire world, and blighted the lives of men.'[34] Not for the first time, Procopius was well placed to make this observation, for he was present in the imperial capital of Constantinople when the disease first struck there.

Procopius' account of the advent of the plague conveys a vivid and harrowing sense of the terror and confusion that it occasioned amongst the population of the city. Rumours circulated that the disease was spread by ghostly apparitions, and as a result many citizens began to congregate at the churches and shrines of the capital in the hope of divine protection. Yet 'even in the sanctuaries where many of them fled for refuge', Procopius wrote, 'they were dying constantly'. Others holed themselves up in their own homes, refusing to answer the door even to friends or loved ones, 'fearing that the person calling was in fact one of the demons'. Most of those struck by the disease were 'seized by a sudden fever', which many initially assumed they would overcome. A couple of days or so later, however, ominous bubonic swellings would appear. Some would then slip into comas, while others were seized by delirium. The doctors of the city, Procopius relates, were at a loss either to explain the disease or to know how to deal with it (a fact confirmed by the medical literature which survives from this time). Some victims would die immediately, others a number of days later, frequently covered in black pustules or vomiting blood. Many with doctors and families who tried to care for them died, whilst others who had been entirely neglected somehow managed to survive. In the case of pregnant women, sometimes the mother survived, sometimes the child. Those whose buboes tended to swell up and then burst were the most likely to pull through. Many of these survivors, Procopius tells us, were nevertheless left with withered limbs and speech impediments. The first wave of the pandemic, he reports, lasted in the capital for four months, killing at its height somewhere in the region of five thousand to ten thousand victims a day.[35] If these figures are to be believed, roughly half the population of the city may have been wiped out.[36]

Procopius' testimony is largely confirmed by that of another eyewitness to these horrific events. At around the same time that the plague was making its way to Constantinople from Egypt, via Palestine and Syria, the clergyman John of Ephesus was making the same journey. John would subsequently collate his memories in a 'Book of the Plague', which he later integrated into a longer work of ecclesiastical history. John interpreted the plague as a punishment sent from

God: 'a terrible and mighty scourge with which the whole world was lashed', whereby 'God's wrath was turned into a wine-press, which piteously trampled and squeezed' all those caught within it 'like fine grapes'. He describes corpses lying unburied on the streets, ships drifting in from sea on which entire crews had perished, and villages and small towns that appeared to have been wiped out in their entirety. 'Thus it was told about one city on the Egyptian border', he related, 'that it perished totally and completely with only seven men and one small boy ten years old remaining in it.'[37]

As John travelled from Palestine and Syria into Asia Minor on his way to Constantinople at what he describes as the height of the plague, he and his companions felt as if they were constantly 'knocking at the gate of the tomb', anticipating death at any moment. 'In these countries,' he wrote, 'we saw desolate and groaning villages and corpses spread out on the earth' as well as cattle, pigs, sheep, and goats 'roaming scattered . . . with nobody to look after them'. Harvests remained rotting in the fields and vines untended. News of the plague, he tells us, reached Constantinople even sooner than the plague itself. Its impact on the imperial capital when it reached there was devastating: 'When thus the scourge weighed heavy upon this city,' John recorded, 'first it eagerly began to assault the class of the poor, who lay around on the streets. It happened that 5000 and 7000, or even 12,000 and as many as 16,000 of them departed from this world in a single day.' Government officials who were charged with counting the number of the dead gave up once the figure reached 230,000, and attempts to provide the dead with proper burials were increasingly abandoned in favour of mass graves, or simply casting the bodies into the sea (also described by Procopius). 'Not only those who died', John relates, 'but also those who escaped sudden death were struck by this plague of swelling in their groins, with this disease which they called *boubones*. . . . Both servants and masters were smitten together, nobles and common people impartially. They were struck down one opposite another, groaning.' So high was the rate of death and so sudden its onset that—in the hope of avoiding being buried in an unmarked grave or dying without one's loved ones knowing of one's demise—'nobody would go out of doors without a tag bearing his name and which hung on his neck or arm'. So common were funerals as a result of the mass mortality that 'there was no more weeping. . . . People were smitten in their hearts and became numb.'[38]

There is sometimes a tendency for historians to be dismissive of the accounts of the plague provided by Procopius and John of Ephesus: our authors are often accused of providing deliberately inflated or fantastical numbers, or of exaggerating the impact of the disease on Constantinople for rhetorical or moralizing purposes. Such criticisms, however, are largely unfounded and reveal a startling lack of empathy. Each author was attempting to describe an epidemiological horror that would have been on an unprecedented and entirely unfamiliar scale, and which would continue to recur down to the late sixth century and well beyond. Probably writing in the 580s, John emphasised how 'the eastern regions were overwhelmed by these horrors, which have not yet come to an end'.[39] Both authors attempted to truthfully convey the trauma they had personally witnessed and felt. Moreover, statistical analysis has revealed that the rates of sudden mass mortality that Procopius and John describe are entirely consistent with the sort of death toll we know to have been associated with later, better recorded outbreaks of bubonic plague from the fourteenth to seventeenth centuries (especially if the sixth-century plague developed a pneumonic strain, which there are indications it had).[40] Procopius, in particular, is likely to have had access to official governmental records when writing his *History*. Given what we know from John about the imperial government initially attempting to keep track of the number of dead in Constantinople, it is entirely possible that Procopius derived his figures from an official source. The contemporary accounts we have of the plague are emotive because they are authentic. As survivors of the pandemic, Procopius and John should be read and treated with respect, and spared the misplaced condescension of posterity.

'GOD'S RIGHTEOUS ANGER'

How were Justinian and his court meant to respond to a crisis of such unparalleled severity? As John of Ephesus intimated, the period between the initial identification of the plague in the summer of 541 and its arrival in Constantinople in the spring of 542 provided the emperor and those around him with at least some time to reflect and to begin to plan ahead as news of the mounting cataclysm came in from the provinces. John of Ephesus and Procopius concur that the task of dealing with the consequences of the plague once it struck Constantinople was entrusted to a close confidant of Justinian's by the name of Theodore. Theodore's official post hitherto had been that of *referendarius*, acting as an interlocutor between the emperor and those who wished to petition him.[41] With respect to the plague, he should probably be thought of as a sort of roving 'minister without portfolio', charged with responding directly to the immediate impact of the plague on the streets of Constantinople. There are hints that he may have been the nephew of a famous holy man known as John the Hesychast, who was the object of great devotion and admiration within the Church.[42] He may therefore have been particularly well placed to mobilise support and call in assistance from the patriarch of Constantinople and the many priests, monks, and other employees at his disposal in the imperial city. Justinian's legislation reveals that the patriarchate had long been responsible for organising burials in the capital, providing gravediggers, funeral cortèges, and even troupes of nuns acting as professional mourners to see off the dead.[43] Given the fact that, as John put it, the city increasingly 'stank with corpses', assistance from the Church was going to be vital.[44]

It is striking that none of our sources describe any concerted effort on the part of the imperial government to provide care for the sick and dying. In terms of what we would now think of as 'public health', the overriding priority was simply disposing of the bodies of the dead as rapidly as possible. This was the task on which Theodore concentrated. With assistance from the Church, speedy burials were organized, and when these became impossible the mass graves and other emergency measures which both John of Ephesus and Procopius describe were put into effect. John records that Justinian instructed Theodore 'to take and spend as much gold as was necessary for supervising these matters'. He was to persuade 'people with great gifts not to be negligent but to dig large ditches' for the corpses. Many people joined him in this effort, but he had to pay them exorbitant wages to persuade them to help. Bubonic plague reduces its victims to a wretched condition, and handling the cadavers would not have been a pleasant task. Acting on Justinian's orders, Theodore 'had very large pits dug, in every one of which 70,000 corpses were put'. By the pits, he posted 'men holding gold and encouraging the workmen and the common people with gifts to carry and to bring up corpses, giving five, six and even seven and ten gold coins for each load. He also personally walked around the city urging people to bring out the dead. . . . Thus, by his application the city was gradually rid of the corpses.' Other officials, such as the urban prefect, would have been busy trying to address a plague-induced crisis in the city's food supply as well as its entire system of provisioning. According to John, 'buying and selling ceased and the shops with all their worldly riches . . . closed. The entire city came to a standstill . . . with the result that food vanished from the markets and great tribulation ensued.'[45]

Theodore was clearly a public servant of remarkable commitment and devotion. Procopius tells us that he even paid for many of the funerals and burials in the capital out of his own pocket.[46] While he was busy on the streets of Constantinople, John relates, 'the imperial palace was overwhelmed and overcome by sorrow. The emperor and empress to whom myriads and thousands of commanders and the whole great senate had bowed and paid honour every day, now were miserable, and like everybody else sank into grief, being served only by a few.'[47] Indeed, Procopius tells us, despite being enclosed within the walls of the palace, even Justinian was struck by the plague. The emperor, however, was fortunate enough to recover, possibly crediting his survival to the miraculous intervention of the medical saints Cosmas and Damian, who were highly revered in the capital. His right-hand man in the project of legal reform, the *quaestor* Tribonian, was not so lucky: Procopius reported that he died of disease at around this time.[48]

Despite Tribonian's death and the emperor's illness, the imperial authorities responded to the arrival and impact of the plague with a series of carefully targeted administrative and legal measures aimed at limiting and containing the disease's social, economic, and fiscal impact. Certain of these measures were clearly planned and prepared before the disease had managed to reach the capital, revealing a remarkable capacity on the part of the court to analyse and respond to a fast-changing situation. In March 542, in a law that Justinian describes as having been written amid 'the encircling presence of death' (which, he adds, had 'spread to every region'), the emperor attempted to prop up the 'banking sector' of the imperial economy, which played an important role in the fiscal operations of the state. In this law, Justinian made it easier for bankers and moneylenders to pursue the heirs of debtors who had suddenly died, and gave the banking community fast-tracked access to a special court to pursue their claims.[49] Likewise, in 543, Justinian legislated to resolve difficulties caused by people who had died without having made proper wills (a phenomenon which John of Ephesus expressly associates with the plague).[50] In a law issued the following year,

Justinian addressed the inheritance rights of children, in response to a case that had arisen in Antioch in Syria after first a mother and then her daughter had died in quick succession 'in the recent epidemic of plague'.[51]

In a 544 law of great significance, Justinian attempted to impose price and wage controls as labourers, artisans, and agricultural workers who had survived the first bout of disease sought to take advantage of localised labour shortages to obtain higher wages or extract higher prices for goods or services. As the emperor declared, 'This chastening sent by God's goodness ought to have made those following occupations and trades . . . into better people, but it has come to our notice that instead, as a result of it, they have turned to avarice, and are demanding prices double or triple what was formerly customary.' New procedures were put into place to forcibly assign abandoned agricultural land, or land in areas that had been depopulated, to neighbouring landowners or communities. Those who had such properties foisted upon them consequently became responsible for the associated taxes. The pandemic appears to be referenced in a piece of legislation concerned with 'blasphemy', in which Justinian explained to his subjects that it was because of their immorality that 'famines, earthquakes, and plagues occur', and that unless they changed their ways, they risked being 'destroyed by God's righteous anger'.[52] Justinian evidently agreed with John of Ephesus that the cause of the plague was sin.

Justinian and those around him were very worried that the plague signalled that God had turned against the empire, and was punishing the emperor's subjects for their moral failings and once more calling them to repentance. The emperor and his court were no less worried by the impact of the disease on the empire's tax revenues: mass mortality meant fewer taxpayers; fewer taxpayers meant lower tax revenues; and lower tax revenues would make it harder to fund warfare to both East and West as well as to meet the costs of the daily operations of the state. Procopius would complain that

Justinian was so cruel that he refused to write off tax debts owed by landowners, despite the fact that most of their agricultural workers had been wiped out by the disease.[53] Likewise, documentary evidence from Egypt reveals that in the aftermath of the plague, levels of taxation would dramatically increase, conceivably to make up for the fiscal impact of depopulation.[54] This was despite Justinian's earlier assurances that tax hikes would not be necessary if everybody paid their way.

The impact of the plague is discernible on the empire's monetary system. Probably in order to help stabilise the empire's finances, the minister charged with minting and distributing coinage (a former banker, Peter Barsymes) issued a series of lighter-weight gold *solidi*. At around the same time that Justinian issued his emergency banking legislation, the weight of the copper coinage of Constantinople had also been reduced. The implication is that the state may have made payments to its employees and others in these lighter-weight coins, while demanding that taxes be paid in full-weight currency. The aim would have been to stretch the empire's suddenly constrained reserves of both cash and metal. As for the latter, copper mining, a heavily labour-intensive industry, appears to have started to go into decline from around this time, probably as a result of shortages of manpower. This was especially evident in Cyprus, where the empire's main copper mines were located.[55]

As in the 520s, during the plague years Justinian sought to put his coinage to propagandistic use: at precisely the period when Procopius suggests the emperor is likely to have been suffering from bubonic plague, for example, the authorities in Constantinople minted a series of copper coins that appear to depict Justinian either with a bubo in his neck or under his chin, or, on one of the coins, possibly wearing a mask covering such a bubo. These features disappear from the coinage soon thereafter.[56] The emperor's miraculous recovery, these coins may have been meant to signal to the surviving inhabitants of Constantinople, would also be that of the empire itself, especially if his subjects attended to matters not just human, but also divine.

THE VICISSITUDES OF WAR

The misery caused by the plague and climate disruption was further exacerbated by warfare. Christian authors in the Middle Ages expounded the biblical concept of the 'Four Horsemen of the Apocalypse', who were given power to inflict the horrors of warfare, famine, and disease on mankind.[57] From the 540s onwards, the empire of Justinian would increasingly find itself racked by each of these woes, usually simultaneously.

As we saw in the aftermath of the Persian sack of Antioch in 540, Khusro and his armies had rampaged across northern Syria, exacting tribute and humiliating the imperial authorities in the eyes of Justinian's subjects. In response, Justinian once more sent Belisarius east. Mustering Roman forces and their Arab allies at Dara, the general led a retaliatory attack on the Persian-held city of Nisibis and captured and destroyed an important enemy fortress before retreating into Roman territory and being recalled to Constantinople.[58] He was then sent back to the Syrian frontier in 542 to contain renewed aggression on the part of Khusro. Hearing news that Justinian had fallen ill with the plague, he reportedly stated that he would refuse to acknowledge any new emperor appointed in Constantinople in his absence.[59] Procopius emphasises that Belisarius had repeatedly promised Justinian that he would not make a bid for the throne during the emperor's lifetime. The indications are that he and those around him were now beginning to consider the options open to them in a world without Justinian. News of these discussions supposedly reached Theodora, and accordingly, Belisarius was once more summoned back to the capital and subjected to an investigative enquiry. During the course of the investigation, his private fortune was confiscated, and he is reported to have lived in fear of assassination. The general was eventually cleared of misconduct and had most of his fortune restored to him. Despite his request to once more be sent out against the Persians, Belisarius was kept in Constantinople until Justinian decided that his services were needed again in the West.[60]

In 545, Justinian's ambassadors persuaded the shah to agree to an armistice and then to accept a peace settlement. The price of peace was high: Justinian was obliged to send Khusro 144,000 *solidi* as well as a well-known physician (possibly attached to his court) who, Procopius tells us, had previously helped cure the shah of 'a severe disease'. Two years earlier, Persian troops had retreated from Armenia for fear of contracting the plague, and it is conceivable that Khusro, fearful of this disease, credited the doctor (rather than Saints Cosmas and Damian) with responsibility for Justinian's recent recovery from the pestilence, and hence may have wanted him close to hand. Justinian, we are told, immediately sent both the medic and the money.[61]

The truce negotiated between Justinian and Khusro in 545, however, only appears to have applied to Syria, as warfare continued in the Caucasus. It was in this zone of superpower rivalry that during the 520s and 530s the Romans had made their most significant advances, securing the defection of the king of Lazica, extending control over Tzanica, and placing the Roman territories of Armenia more firmly under the imperial yoke. Khusro was determined to roll back these Roman gains, taking advantage of growing hostility towards Justinian's overbearing rule on the part of the nobility in both Lazica and Armenia. Here warfare would continue unremittingly, with the Persians coming to dominate the river valleys, cities, and lowland zones, and the Romans and their allies increasingly having to resort to ambushes and other techniques of guerrilla warfare in the highlands and mountain passes. A truce would not be finally agreed with respect to this northern front for another twelve years, by which point the two empires had essentially fought themselves to a standstill. Relations along the Syrian or 'Mesopotamian' frontier also remained tense: in 547 Khusro launched an unprovoked (and unsuccessful) assault on the Roman fortifications at Dara, and clashes continued to occur between the two empires' Arab client kings.[62] For many of the inhabitants of Constantinople's easternmost provinces, the truce of 545 had brought peace, but not security.

'SO SAD A SOUND OF DEATH...'

The military situation in Africa also remained challenging. In 536, attempts by the Roman commander there, Solomon, to extend imperial authority over the troublesome Berber warlords of the region had been thrown into disarray by a major mutiny led by the Herul general Stotzas. Only the arrival of Belisarius in Carthage had helped to salvage the situation. The period from 536 to 539 would nevertheless be characterised by ongoing military unrest, further undermining Justinian's ability to consolidate his rule over the territory that had once been at the core of the Vandal realm. Indeed, at times, imperial authority in the region extended little further than Carthage itself, as what effectively amounted to a civil war between elements of the Roman field army repeatedly flared up. In the aftermath of the failed revolt of 536, a purge of officers and troops deemed treacherous or unreliable was undertaken. No new troops, however, were sent out from Constantinople to take their place, as the Italian campaign was now underway. The net result was an inevitable decline in overall military effectiveness, which allowed the Berber warlords of the African hinterland beyond the coastal zone to strengthen their position. There are signs that from the 530s to the late 540s, the Berbers—perhaps aided by opposition to the Roman imperial presence—would acquire ever greater political and military cohesion. Consequently, they came to pose an increasingly significant threat to those areas that remained under imperial control.[63]

The main causes of military unrest remained religious and economic, with many of Justinian's barbarian troops bristling at the anti-Arian measures which were being introduced in the province and increasingly resentful at mounting arrears in pay.[64] In August 535, Justinian had prohibited Jews, pagans, Arians, and other heretics from conducting religious ceremonies or possessing places of worship in Africa: 'The ungodly', Justinian declared, 'are to be excluded altogether from services and from churches. No licence at all is to be allowed to them to appoint either bishops or clergy, or to baptise any persons whatever and drag them into their own madness. Such sects have been condemned not only by us, but also by previous laws; their adherents are utterly criminal, and depraved as well.'[65] Encouraged by the Catholic bishops of Africa, Justinian had ordained that all Jewish synagogues were to be demolished and rebuilt as churches, and all Arian churches and property confiscated and assigned to the Catholic Church, as 'the performance of sacred rites by the impious is quite unacceptable'.[66] Likewise, Procopius remarked, 'Justinian was tardy in the payment of his military forces, and in other ways became a grievance to the soldiers. From these causes arose the insurrections which resulted in great destruction.'[67]

Belisarius had managed to drive Stotzas and his rebels from the walls of Carthage. He had not, however, been able to capture him. When he arrived in Carthage, Justinian's cousin Germanus had found that 'a third of the army was in Carthage and the cities, while all the rest were arrayed with the tyrant [Stotzas] against the Romans'.[68] Finding himself significantly outnumbered, Germanus made the rational decision not to risk a frontal assault on Stotzas, but to attempt to win over hearts and minds amongst the disaffected

troops. He offered a general amnesty to the mutineers and promised to honour all pay that was owed, even for periods during which
the soldiers concerned had served under the usurper.[69] This effort,
we are told, met with considerable success, and Germanus readied
his forces to go on the offensive. Stotzas decided to preempt him by
once more marching on Carthage.[70]

As Germanus rallied his troops for battle, Procopius claimed,
he attempted to bolster their sense of obligation by reminding them of what they owed to Justinian: 'That there is nothing,
fellow-soldiers, with which you can justly reproach the emperor,
and no fault which you can find with what he has done to you,
this, I think, not one of you could deny; for it was he who took you
as you came from the fields with your wallets and one small gar-
ment apiece and brought you together in Byzantium, and who has
caused you to be so powerful that the Roman state now depends on
you.'[71] Confronted with a larger and more resolute army than he
had anticipated, Stotzas lost his nerve and retreated to Numidia,
pursued by Germanus and his men.

At a site known as Scalae Veteres ('The Old Stairs'), the two
armies finally clashed. Procopius describes a battle scene of chaos,
confusion, and mayhem: with troops on both sides speaking the
same languages and wearing the same uniforms, it became very hard
for the combatants to distinguish friend from foe. Germanus himself fell from his horse and would probably have died had his guards
not immediately clustered around him.[72] In the end, the superior
discipline and tighter battle formation of Germanus' troops won
out, and Stotzas, forced to abandon the field of battle, fled to Mauretania with a handful of Vandal retainers.[73] A period of relative peace
ensued, but tensions within the Roman military remained high.
An attempted coup orchestrated by an officer named Maximinus
was now uncovered, and Germanus had him impaled outside the
city walls. Many of Maximinus' conspirators were executed in the

hippodrome of Carthage. By 539, the situation was deemed sufficiently stable for Justinian to recall his cousin to Constantinople,
entrusting Africa once more to the prefect Solomon.

The imperial authorities in Carthage, however, had not heard the
last of Stotzas. The Berber warlords of the African hinterland clearly
took the rebel general very seriously. While holed up in Mauretania, he is reported to have married the daughter of a local ruler,
and he would later reemerge in 544 to lead troops under the overall
command of Antalas, the dominant Berber warlord in Byzacena.[74]
Antalas had taken advantage of the Roman civil war to intensify
pressure on imperially controlled territory, taking vengeance on
the Roman authorities for having executed his brother and denying him the customary payments with which they had hitherto
secured his cooperation. Solomon led his troops out of Carthage to
Teveste (Tébessa) accompanied by two of his nephews—Cyrus and
Sergius—whom Justinian had appointed to govern Pentapolis and
Tripolitania. In the battle that ensued, Solomon and his men were
put to flight, and the emperor's commander-in-chief in Africa was
ultimately killed after falling from his horse and into the hands of
the enemy. Sergius was appointed to replace his uncle. This decision
was met with almost universal dismay, owing to his unfailing ability
to irritate and alienate both subordinate and subject alike. Antalas,
we are told, even wrote to Justinian offering to make peace if the
emperor would just appoint someone better.[75]

It was at this point that Antalas was joined by Stotzas. The two
men managed to secure the capture of an important coastal city,
Hadrumetum (modern Sousse), which was plundered and briefly
occupied.[76] Justinian now looked once more to members of his
own family to help restore imperial fortunes in the region, sending
Areobindus, a general who was married to his niece Praeiecta, to
Carthage.[77] Sergius was left in command of the forces in Numidia,
while Areobindus took battle to the enemy in Byzacena. Sergius
was finally dismissed after failing to send troops to assist in an

important encounter against the enemy. He was replaced as chief military commander in Numidia by a certain Gunthar (the name would suggest a Germanic origin), who had previously served as a private armed retainer (*buccellarius*) to the late Solomon. In 546, Gunthar repaid Justinian for his kindness by launching a successful coup against Areobindus, whom he killed and decapitated. He sent his head to Antalas, with whom he had promised to share control of the former Vandal kingdom. Both Antalas and Gunthar were in turn outmanoeuvred by an Armenian general loyal to Justinian named Artabanes, who had defected to the Romans from the Persian army during the course of the recent war in the Caucasus. Carthage had been held by the usurper for just over a month. Artabanes had not defeated Gunthar in open battle, but had instead promised to support him, and then slain both the general and his leading supporters at a banquet.[78] The restoration of imperial control in Africa was an eye-wateringly close-run thing.

In 546, Artabanes asked to be recalled to Constantinople. Accordingly, he was replaced by a certain John Trogolita, who, having previously served in Africa under both Belisarius and Solomon, knew the region well. His subsequent campaigns against the Berbers would be celebrated by a Latin poet from Carthage, Flavius Cresconius Corippus, who composed a 4,700-line, eight-book epic poem in his honour titled the *Iohannid*. There is good reason to believe that Corippus' enthusiasm for John was genuine and fully justified: the general would appear to have decided to take war to the enemy almost immediately upon arriving in the territory, advancing into Byzacena and sending letters to Antalas soon thereafter demanding his submission. A series of struggles between imperial forces and the Berbers then ensued (punctuated, yet again, by a mutiny alluded to by the poet).[79] Finally, at some time around the middle of the year 548, John inflicted a decisive defeat on the empire's foes at a site known as the Plains of Cato. Eighteen leading Berber warlords were killed, and Antalas was forced to submit.[80] 'Thus it came to pass', as Procopius put it, 'that those of the Libyans who survived, few as they were in number and exceedingly poor, at last and after great toil found some peace.'[81] That peace was not absolute, for, as Corippus also noted, at the same time that warfare was raging across Africa, so too was the plague. In a description which chimes very closely with the accounts we have of the impact of the disease in Constantinople, he relates how a terrible pestilence arrived by sea, as a result of which death was so ubiquitous that survivors became desensitized to it, no longer mourning for their loved ones or observing the customary funerary rites. Society and public morality appeared to Corippus to be on the verge of collapse: 'Piety', he wrote, 'withdrew entirely', with the plague destroying 'both men and women and the tottering world around them'.[82] 'Never before', he declared, 'had so sad a sound of death been heard.'[83]

SHIFTING FRONTIERS

In the decades ahead, it would become clear that the settled and urbanised population of the Roman Empire was far more susceptible to the impact of the bubonic plague than its more dispersed and often nomadic 'barbarian' opponents. This problem repeatedly came to haunt the imperial authorities. As a result of the plague's disproportionate effects, the balance of power along the empire's frontiers in Africa and Arabia, as well as in the Balkans and northern Italy, would begin to shift—sometimes decisively—against the empire. The authorities were in a sense fortunate that in the 550s the plague would also spread to the most urbanised parts of the Sasanian Empire in Assyria (modern Iraq).[84] As a result, the disease is likely to have sapped the strength of both great empires simultaneously, rather than destabilising the balance of power between the two of them to the disadvantage of Constantinople.[85]

By 548, Procopius felt that a fundamental change had occurred in the nature of the relationship between the empire and its rivals and foes, especially in Europe. Narrating a series of military reversals to which we shall return, he would write of how, 'at about this point, the barbarians became unquestionably masters of the whole West'. 'For the Romans', he continued, 'had been at first decisively victorious in the Gothic war, as I have previously said, but the end result for them was that not only had they consumed money and lives in prodigal fashion to no advantage, but they also managed to lose Italy all over again, and had to look on while practically all the Illyrians and Thracians [in the Balkans] were being ravaged and destroyed in a pitiable manner by the barbarians, seeing that they had now become their neighbours.' Ominously, he noted, even the Franks, who had once been allied to the empire but who were now intervening in Italy in pursuit of their own territorial gains, were openly challenging imperial claims to authority with brazen insouciance. This was epitomized, Procopius felt, by the fact that the Frankish kings had taken the outrageous step of beginning to mint gold coins bearing their own image on them, rather than that of the emperor in Constantinople (the minting of such coins, as we have seen, was traditionally regarded as an imperial prerogative). Barbarian envoys, he complained, were increasingly sent to the imperial capital to demand and receive payments from the emperor, while simultaneously plundering his subjects in the provinces.[86] It is telling that these searing criticisms were made in Procopius' publicly circulated *History of the Wars*, which, as we shall see, would attract a significant and well-connected readership. Buffeted by plague and exhausted by warfare, Justinian and his regime were now subject to increasingly public and negative critiques.

Chapter 14

Propaganda
and Dissent

INTRIGUE AT COURT

'Now the plague, which was described by me in my earlier writings, fell upon the whole world, yet just as many people escaped it as had the misfortune to succumb—either because they avoided the infection altogether, or because they got over it if they happened to be infected. But this man not a single person in the whole Roman Empire could escape. Like any other visitation from heaven falling on the entire human race, he left no one completely untouched.'[1] With these startling words, the historian Procopius sought to compare the impact of the bubonic plague of the 540s with the initial ambition and reach of the emperor Justinian and his policies.

Had Justinian died of the plague when it laid him low in 542, his reputation in the eyes of posterity would have been that of an emperor of unprecedented energy and success. The early years of his reign witnessed remarkable legal creativity and the effective imposition of order upon the sprawling mass of legal texts upon which the system of justice within the empire depended. The administration of the empire itself had been drastically overhauled. Africa and Italy had been rapidly conquered, and the empire now stretched once more from the Pillars of Hercules (adjacent to the Strait of Gibraltar) to the Euphrates and beyond. Within Constantinople itself, the emperor had transformed the imperial capital and effectively rebuilt it in honour of its divine patron, the Virgin Mary, God, and, of course, the emperor himself and his divinely appointed consort, Theodora.

Through his laws, Justinian had made strenuous efforts to convey to his subjects his unique concern for their interests. Such imperial propaganda had then been further disseminated across the realm, through great inscriptions placed on the walls of the cities of the empire, and outside their cathedrals and churches, where pro-regime sermons and speeches were delivered by clergymen and bishops sympathetic to the regime. Justinian's military campaigns had also clearly done much to restore Roman prestige abroad, and as far away as Britain we have evidence for the maintenance of contacts with the imperial capital. From the site of Penmachno in Wales, for example, we possess a sixth-century stone inscription seemingly dated according to the period in office of the then consul in Constantinople. Meanwhile, trading vessels from the empire continued to reach the coastline of Cornwall, where, at places such as Tintagel, they exchanged imperial gold for local tin.[2]

Despite these seeming demonstrations of imperial power and control, from the late 530s onwards there had been considerable intrigue in and around the imperial court as future potential claimants to the throne jockeyed for position around the emperor, who had remained childless, but who, unlike his uncle, had failed to adopt.[3] Theodora had kept a careful eye on the highest officers of state and the emperor's closest kin: according to Procopius, she was particularly suspicious of Justinian's cousin, Germanus (who had helped restore order in Africa), and mistrustful and envious of Belisarius. It is also recorded that she secured the dismissal and exile of several officials whom she had come to distrust or with whom she had clashed. Procopius was bitterly critical of her active involvement in both imperial policy and court politics, but to Justinian her vigilance was a source of security. She was not universally mistrustful: one official whom she held in the highest regard was the finance minister Peter Barsymes, who as 'Count of the Sacred Largesses' had done much to stabilise imperial finances in the context of the first ravages of the bubonic plague.[4]

Justinian and Theodora had never really seen eye to eye, however, on one key figure: John the Cappadocian, who, along with Tribonian, had spearheaded the emperor's programme of internal reforms from 534 to 540. John was reputed to be the only person Justinian allowed both to disagree with his wife and to criticize her to his face, to the extent that the imperial couple almost fell out over it.[5] In May 541, John fell into a trap. Procopius relates in his *History of the Wars* (likely repeating what may have been a widely known version of this sensitive event) that Theodora—assisted by Belisarius' wife, Antonina, who resented the Cappadocian for what she regarded as his hostility to her husband—had hatched a plot to bring John down. Encouraged by Theodora, Antonina let slip to John the Cappadocian's daughter, Euphemia, that Belisarius was increasingly disenchanted with Justinian owing to the emperor's supposed lack of gratitude for his military achievements and the general direction of imperial policy. When Euphemia responded by pointing out that Belisarius and Antonina had it within their power to bring down Justinian and his regime, Antonina indicated that they would be willing to do so if John were to agree to join them.

Euphemia promised to convey this message to her father.[6] At this point, Belisarius's reputation was at its height and John at the zenith of his authority. The proposed coup d'état was thus by no means unrealistic.

Accordingly, Euphemia passed on the proposal to John the Cappadocian, who, Procopius claims, 'assented without any hesitation and instructed his child to arrange a meeting with Antonina for the following day, at which pledges would be made'. Antonina claimed that she was about to head to the eastern front (where Justinian had recently sent Belisarius to face down Khusro), and proposed that they confer at midnight outside Belisarius' villa on the outskirts of the city. Theodora, informed of the plan, gave it her approval. Rumours that something was afoot would also appear to have reached the ears of Justinian, who passed on a message to John that he should avoid Antonina. The prefect did not take the hint. Meeting Belisarius' wife at the agreed time and place, he made the mistake of openly agreeing to bring down Justinian, 'binding himself with the most dread oaths'. A coterie of troops, led by the general Narses and another officer, one Marcellus, who had been lying in wait, suddenly sprung out to arrest him. As John's bodyguards fought them off, John fled to a church, where he took sanctuary. Had he immediately made his way to the emperor to put across his version of events, Procopius suggests, John might have got away with it. Instead, he had played straight into Theodora's hands. His property was confiscated, and John was dismissed from office and exiled to Egypt.[7] It was a sign of Justinian's lingering devotion to the man that he escaped with his life. This was to the great irritation of the empress, who never ceased machinating against him.[8]

As a result of the fall of John the Cappadocian in 541 and the sudden death of Tribonian in 542, therefore, Justinian was in quick succession denied the services of the two men on whom he had most relied in the business of government and the pressing ahead of reform. From that point on there occurred a noticeable and precipitous decline in the legal output of the court. Between Justinian's accession to the throne in 527 and 541 (when John fell and the bubonic plague arrived), the emperor had issued around 530 laws (of which we still have copies), so roughly thirty-five a year. Setting aside the emergency plague-driven legislation of 542–545, from 546 onwards the emperor is known to have issued just 19 new laws.[9] With the court sapped of its most brilliant members, and the machinery of the state as a whole knocked seriously off kilter by the ongoing ramifications of the plague, Justinian's government increasingly seemed to be sinking into a state of torpor.

From the mid-540s—and especially from 548, when his beloved Theodora died—Justinian found himself increasingly isolated politically. Buffeted by the cumulative effects of financial crisis and plague, as well as greater military resistance to the West, and enemy incursions in the Balkans and to the East, the emperor and his regime risked losing control of both the overarching military situation and the political narrative. Within Constantinople, public criticism of the regime and hostility towards the emperor were once more on the rise. Indeed, in 549 a plot to assassinate Justinian was uncovered when the conspirators attempted to draw a young relative of the emperor into their plans.[10]

As the events surrounding the Nika riots had demonstrated, opinions about Justinian had always been divided within Constantinopolitan society. Some hardline Christian contemporaries were appreciative of the emperor's efforts to crack down on religious minorities, and encouraged him to purge and persecute still more aggressively. Yet others of a more conservative and traditionalist mindset had long been critical of what they regarded as Justinian's excessively autocratic tendencies. In 537, for example, Justinian had lashed out in one of his laws against opponents of his regime who criticised him for issuing too much legislation and thereby spreading legal confusion.[11] From the late 540s onwards, the emperor's critics became increasingly vocal, expressing their opposition to the regime in ever more trenchant terms. Such criticism would be most famously preserved for posterity through a perhaps somewhat surprising source.

SECRET HISTORIES

Four hundred years ago, in 1623, an Italian Catholic priest and scholar of Greek descent, Niccolò Alemanni, caused something of a publishing sensation.[12] Alemanni was a renowned classical scholar, and, as a result of the booming interest in the subject in Italy at the time, a much sought-after teacher of Greek. By virtue of his talent as a scholar and teacher, Alemanni had been appointed secretary to Cardinal Borghese, and was then made custodian of the Vatican Library in Rome, giving him ready access to one of the finest book collections in the world. There, he had made a startling discovery. In the 530s and early 540s, as we have seen, Justinian's favoured general, Belisarius, had been accompanied on campaign by his secretary, Procopius, who had taken advantage of his wealth of personal experience and contacts to write an eight-volume history of Justinian's wars against the Vandals, Goths, and Persians. At face value this work seemed to glorify both Belisarius and Justinian. Procopius had then written an additional work (*Buildings*) celebrating Justinian's architectural achievements, including the construction of Hagia Sophia, the erection of Justinian's equestrian statue, and the foundation of Justiniana Prima. Procopius' *Wars* had quickly become something of a classic in their own right. In the preface to Book Eight, for example, the author had noted with evident satisfaction that copies of his preceding volumes were already in circulation and had been read 'in every corner of the Roman Empire'.[13] Historians of the following generation would regard him as a towering figure. In the late sixth century, the diplomatic historian Menander would praise what he described as the 'eternal light' of Procopius, who to this day is regarded by many as one of the finest historians ever to have written in the Greek language.[14]

It had long been known in Byzantium, however, that Procopius had also written, but never, it would seem, got round to publicly circulating, a ninth, additional volume to his *Wars* in which he had turned on both Belisarius and Justinian. It was a manuscript copy of these 'unpublished materials' (known in Greek as *Anekdota*) that Alemanni had discovered in the Vatican Library, and which, in 1623, he published, alongside a Latin translation, under the title of the *Secret History* (Latin *Historia Arcana*). In this shocking work, Belisarius was depicted as a clueless cuckold, whose wife had spent much of her time sleeping with their adopted son. Justinian, in turn, was denounced as a 'demon king', or the 'lord of the demons', bent on the destruction of mankind, whose head would detach from his body and float around the palace late at night. Whilst the emperor claimed to be restoring Roman law and the Roman Empire, Procopius claimed, in reality he was hell-bent on transforming it into an instrument of his own tyranny, driven primarily by bloodlust and greed. He also lambasted the empress Theodora for her cruelty and—in highly graphic terms—her supposed sexual excess prior to her childless marriage to Justinian.[15] Procopius claimed that during her time on the stage, the empress had repeatedly got pregnant and procured abortions: the one (illegitimate) son of hers who had survived into adulthood, he reported, she had then had murdered. She had also been, Procopius went on to assert, notorious for her penchant for group sex, and renowned for a party trick which involved a goose being induced to eat grain from between her legs (probably a burlesque performance based on the classical myth of 'Leda and the Swan').[16]

In particular, Procopius presented Justinian as the exact opposite of what a good emperor was meant to be. Justinian was vulgar instead of noble, he said, capricious instead of just, and as close to Satan as he claimed to be close to God. Theodora, likewise (whom the emperor was of course known to consult on matters of policy), was for Procopius the inversion of the ideal Roman matron, sexually immodest instead of chaste, and murderous instead of maternal. By attacking her, Procopius was able to redouble his assault on the emperor.[17] 'These two people', the author declared, 'never seemed to me to be human beings, but rather avenging demons . . . engaged in the joint venture of ascertaining how they might be able most easily and most quickly to destroy all races of men and their works.' In this, he noted, the pair were assisted by the earthquakes, plagues, and other natural cataclysms that characterised what Procopius understood to be their period of joint rule.[18]

Alemanni's edition of the *Secret History*—which carefully excluded the most sexually explicit passages—convulsed, fascinated, and scandalized the intellectual world of seventeenth-century Europe, transforming forever the way in which Justinian would be viewed.[19] But, more importantly, the full text of the *Secret History* reveals the intensity of contemporary opposition to the emperor. For many of the criticisms Procopius levelled at Justinian and those around him were also echoed by other figures writing at the time, or were conveyed by Procopius in his publicly circulated works in slightly more subtle or circumspect ways. Taken together, these sources reveal an increasingly lively culture of dissidence and debate in sixth-century Constantinople, arguably fuelled and funded by the emperor's enemies in the capital and the Senate, who never relented in their opposition to what they regarded as his upstart dynasty and regime, and who once more regarded Justinian as politically vulnerable.

THE HISTORIAN AND HIS WORKS

Procopius and his writings have already featured prominently in the pages of this book: for many of the military aspects of

Justinian's reign, he is sometimes not only our best but our only source. By virtue of his experience on the front line with Belisarius, or in Constantinople during the Nika riots, and in the capital again for the arrival of the plague, he emerged as an author possessed of unrivalled knowledge and rare historical vision. But it is perhaps worth pausing to consider what we both know—and do not know—of the man and his literary works.[20] Procopius tells us that he came from the city of Caesarea in Palestine. In the sixth century, this was an important and thriving port town, locked into broader networks of Mediterranean trade (hence Procopius' encounter with his merchant schoolfriend upon his arrival in Syracuse during Belisarius' advance on Africa). It was also a religiously diverse and culturally sophisticated place. A significant proportion (perhaps a third) of its population was made up of Samaritans, whom the imperial authorities had come to view with mounting hostility and suspicion. It was home to both an important school of rhetoric and, it would appear, a law school, where the young Procopius may have trained prior to entering government service.[21] Certainly, his knowledge of the law would shine through in his works, and particularly in his criticisms of Justinian. In his so-called *Secret History*, for example, Procopius pointedly attacks specific laws of the emperor's that we still possess.

Procopius' evidently high level of education suggests that he probably came from the city's prosperous landowning elite—his father is likely to have been one of the city councillors to whom much of the day-to-day administration of the town would have been entrusted, with pockets deep enough to be able to send his son to a good school. Although, as we have seen with respect to his vivid description of the starving peasantry of Italy, Procopius was capable of feeling compassion and empathy for men and women of all backgrounds, his political sympathies were largely aristocratic and conservative. The best rulers, he felt, were those who left the laws and long-established customs intact. He was a proud Roman, who bristled with indignation at the presumptuousness of the empire's 'barbarian' neighbours, and who felt deeply the blow of military catastrophes such as that which befell the city of Antioch in 540.

In religious terms, Procopius' worldview would appear to have been broadly Christian, but his historical imagination and literary tastes were primarily informed by the glories of classical Greece and Rome. Perhaps by virtue of his upbringing in the religiously diverse melting pot of Caesarea, he bore his faith relatively lightly, evincing a suspicion of religious fanaticism in all its forms. When, for example, Justinian unleashed a wave of persecution against the Samaritan population, which was so strongly represented in and around his hometown, Procopius criticised not just those Samaritans who chose to cling to their 'mindless dogma', but also the emperor for persecuting them for it.[22] Likewise, he told his reader, he would refrain from engaging in detailed discussion of Justinian's efforts to resolve the theological disputes of the day, as to him it was 'an insane folly to investigate the nature of God'.[23] People, he argued, should be left to believe what they wanted. Procopius' religious attitude was essentially that of a liberal sceptic: he accepted the broad outline of the Christian faith without really seeming to be that interested in it.[24]

Apart from that, we can establish little beyond where he was and when. He served as legal secretary to Belisarius on the eastern front in 529–531, was probably with the general in Constantinople during the Nika riots in 532, and sailed with him via Sicily to Africa in 533. He is likely to have returned to Constantinople for Belisarius' 'triumph' in 534, and participated in the opening phases of the Italian campaign in 535. He then served under the general Solomon in Africa for a year before rejoining Belisarius, who sent him to Naples to obtain fresh troops and supplies during the drawn-out siege of Rome in 537–538; and he was back in Constantinople in 542 (possibly after accompanying Belisarius to the eastern frontier in 541).[25] He would then appear to have returned to the army in Italy in about

546.[26] Thereafter he is likely to have made his way back to Constanti-nople, where he remained. A slightly garbled seventh-century source (which survives only in Old Ethiopic) refers to a writer and official by the name of Procopius who resided in Constantinople under Jus-tinian 'whose work is well known'. Likewise, the *Chronicle* of John Malalas refers to a certain Procopius who held the high-ranking administrative and legal position of urban prefect of Constantino-ple in 562, who presided over an important treason trial.[27] He, too, may have been our historian, although we cannot be sure.

We have no idea at precisely what point Procopius decided to write his *History of the Wars*. The accounts of those campaigns in which he was personally involved may suggest that he had conceived the idea at an early stage and had begun to take notes. He almost certainly set about writing it, however, in Constantinople in the sec-ond half of the 540s, given that almost every historian we know to have written in this period did so in the capital, where much of the readership for their works would have been concentrated, and where additional archival sources and oral testimony would have been available.[28] There are indications that in writing his account of mil-itary operations in which he was not himself personally involved, Procopius took advice from veterans who were known to him, as well as making use of official records detailing the heroic exploits of men who had been 'mentioned in dispatches' and rewarded by the emperor.[29]

Procopius arranged his *History* campaign by campaign rather than as a single seamless narrative. The events covered in each of the resulting volumes, on Justinian's Persian, Vandal, and Gothic wars, thus enable us to ascertain the date by which each of them was completed. He wrote two volumes on Justinian's eastern campaigns, which take the reader down to 548–549; two volumes on the Afri-can campaigns, up to 548; and three volumes on the Italian cam-paigns, to around 551. He then wrote an eighth volume, but here he abandoned the geographical arrangement to provide an integrated narrative covering all fronts down to about 553–554. He explains in the preface to that volume that he was obliged to do so, as his earlier books had already 'appeared before the public', and hence he was 'no longer able to add to each the events which happened afterwards'.[30] So volumes one to seven of *History of the Wars* were completed and put into circulation between 548 and 551 and were then updated by 554.

Importantly, the *Secret History* appears to have been written at about the same time (*c.* 550–551), and seems to have been conceived of as a ninth, concluding volume, to be circulated after the death of Justinian, setting out 'not only those things which have hitherto remained undivulged, but also the [true] causes of those occurrences which have already been narrated'.[31] 'In the case of many of the events described in the previous narrative,' meaning the *Wars*, Procopius wrote, 'I was compelled to conceal the causes which led up to them.' The reason for this, he claimed, was that 'it was not possible, as long as the actors were still alive, for these things to be recorded in the way they should have been. For neither was it possible to elude the vigilance of multitudes of spies, nor, if detected, to escape a most cruel death.' With Theodora now dead, we might infer, the historian may have felt emboldened, though he remained understandably anxious: 'As I turn, however, to this new endeavour which is fraught with difficulty and is, in fact, extraordinarily hard to cope with, being concerned, as it is, with the lives lived by Justinian and Theodora, I find myself stammering and recoiling as far from it as possible, as I weigh the chances that such things now to be written by me will seem neither credible nor probable to men of a later generation.'[32] Certainly, in contrast to the polished prose of his *History of the Wars*, Procopius' *Secret History* is a messy and possibly rushed text, which survives only in an incomplete form. It is possible that the author never got round to finishing or editing it. Procopius' *Buildings* also appears unfinished: in places it simply consists of lists of construction projects.[33]

LANGUAGE AND MODELS

If Procopius wrote his works in Constantinople, he would have found a readership for the type of book he was writing within the city. His work was concerned with contemporary military affairs and high politics, so it would have been of obvious interest to high-ranking civil servants, officials, senators, and generals, who usually either lived in the city or had to visit it frequently. In the late sixth century, the general and future emperor Maurice, for example, enjoyed reading historical works, perhaps hoping to derive strategic lessons from them. There are indications that Constantinople at this time was home to a thriving network of literary *salons*, at which authors would read out extracts from their 'work in progress', and perhaps refashion it in the light of the criticism or feedback they received.[34] We should imagine Procopius trying out and performing his compositions (including, perhaps, extracts from the *Secret History*) at these sorts of private gatherings. All of his works, we should note, were written in an identical form of rhythmic prose, possibly geared towards such oral performance. Procopius wrote in a highly polished form of classical Greek based on the language of the ancient authors of the fifth century BCE, such as the Athenian historian Thucydides. This language was far removed from the Greek spoken on the streets of the empire (which was much closer to the Modern Greek of today). But members of the social and political elite were obliged to study it at school, and it was required for entry into the civil service. In Constantinople, there is likely to have been a critical mass of readers capable of actually appreciating and admiring what Procopius had written.

Importantly, Procopius not only wrote in a highly antiquated form of Greek, but also modelled the shape and narrative of his *History* on the writings of the classical authors. While much of his vocabulary was derived from Thucydides, his decision to describe Justinian's wars front by front may have been modelled on the

History of the campaigns of Alexander the Great written in the second century CE by the Greek historian Arrian. The influence of authors such as Herodotus and Plutarch is also discernible, and allusions to the epic poems attributed to Homer similarly appear. By drawing on these earlier models, Procopius was able not only to show off his own learning, but also to convey to his readers that his own age was no less significant than any era of the past. His record of it was therefore just as important as previous histories: just as Thucydides had been witness to the Peloponnesian War of the fifth century BCE, so, too, had Procopius been an eyewitness to the greatest events of his own day. He was determined to make the most of the opportunity for literary fame that his privileged perspective had afforded him.

Like Thucydides, Procopius put elaborate speeches into the mouths of his characters, and, like Herodotus, he interspersed his narrative with lengthy digressions concerned with geography, ethnography, and tales of a seemingly mythological character. These were meant to entertain, but they were also meant to inform. Many of the speeches Procopius composed and attributed to his cast of historical actors have something of the character of 'briefing notes', meant to alert the reader to the significance of the events that were about to ensue, or to place them in a broader analytical context.[35] Procopius leads his reader into the history of Justinian's Persian wars, for example, by means of a detailed excursus drawing on legends describing the humiliation of the Sasanian monarchy at the hands of the Huns in the preceding century. A proper understanding of what had gone before, the author was attempting to convey, was vital to an appreciation of how and why warfare had broken out between Rome and Persia in his own day. This is not how any historian would write today, but Procopius' contemporaries would have known how to read a work such as this.

In writing his *History*, Procopius drew on 'classical' models, but he did so in a highly creative and original way, drawing on the inspiration of different classical authors for his purposes. In his two other works, his creativity was even more pronounced. At school, he and his readers would have been trained in rhetorical exercises, such as the composition of standardised speeches or poems of praise (known as 'panegyrics' or 'encomia'). At the same time, they learned how to write invectives (known as *psogoi*) demolishing the reputation of an imaginary or anticipated rival or foe. It would have been a standard exercise to compose both a speech of praise and a speech of denunciation directed at the same individual (praising Helen of Troy, for example, for her beauty, but then denouncing her for her immorality).[36] Procopius' *Buildings* combined an extended form of the panegyric, outwardly praising the emperor, but with *virtuoso* architectural descriptions of individual buildings after a manner that was seemingly unprecedented in Greek literature. Likewise, Procopius' *Secret History* was primarily an extended invective, inverting the norms and expectations of the panegyric to present Justinian as the 'ideal type' of anti-emperor and Theodora as the ideal anti-woman.

The *Secret History* is unlike any other literary work that survives from the ancient world. It brilliantly turns imperial propaganda on its head and uses it as a stick with which to beat the emperor. In his legislation, for example, as well as in public inscriptions (like that which adorned the Church of Saints Sergius and Bacchus), Justinian had depicted himself as the 'sleepless emperor', staying awake deep into the night as he wrestled with the concerns of his subjects, and often fasting as a sign of his deeply felt Christian piety.[37] In his *Secret History*, Procopius skilfully parodies Justinian's self-representation to convey the emperor's supposedly true demonic character: 'And how', he wrote, 'could this man fail to be some wicked demon, who never had a sufficiency of food or drink or sleep, but instead . . . walked about the palace at unseasonable hours of the night?'[38] Likewise, Justinian had sought to present himself as the real power behind the throne during the reign of his uncle Justin. Procopius ran with this idea, dating Justinian's reign back to the accession of Justin so that he could blame him for every misfortune that had befallen the empire during his uncle's period of office. Though perhaps rushed, the *Secret History* was a veritable tour de force.

CRITICISING THE EMPEROR

Modern readers have often been confused as to how Procopius could have appeared to praise Justinian in one work, and then denounce him in another. Sixth-century readers trained in the schools of rhetoric, by contrast, might simply have admired his versatility. If the Justinian of Procopius' *Secret History* was a caricature of a bad emperor, the Justinian quite literally praised to the heavens in the preface to his *Buildings* was no less the caricature of a good one.[39] Either way, what would have shone through was the author's artistry and skill. There are indications across all three of Procopius' works, however, that his core attitude towards Justinian was essentially a hostile one, and that his opposition to the regime intensified over time. Although nowhere in his *Wars* or *Buildings* does Procopius scale the vitriolic heights to which he aspires in the *Secret History*, criticism of the regime is palpable in both of these works, even though they were intended for public circulation. Such criticism would have been perfectly apparent to his contemporary readership.

Explicit criticism of both the emperor and his chief ministers (above all, but not only, John the Cappadocian) is clearly discernible in Procopius' *History of the Wars*. This is particularly evident in his coverage of events after 540 and the Persian sack of Antioch, which left a deep impression on him. By the late 540s, we see Procopius despairing, along with Justinian's generals, that the emperor was now too preoccupied with religious and other affairs to pay due attention to the military situation in the West. Although he tells us, in his account of the year 548, that the emperor 'promised to concern himself with Italy', he points out in the next breath that 'still he devoted himself for the most part to the doctrines of the Christians'. Indeed, in many respects the tone of the final volume (Book Eight) of his *History of the Wars* is strikingly similar in its critique to that found in the *Secret History*. In this concluding book of his military narrative, it is the Goths who emerge as the real heroes, as they fight nobly for their liberty.[40]

Negative commentary on Justinian and his regime is also discernible in the earlier sections of Procopius' *History of the Wars*.[41] There is a sense that he was responsive to the broad thrust of Justinian's policy agenda of restoring Roman might abroad to East and West, and restoring Roman law to its pristine glory, but that from the start he was profoundly suspicious of what he regarded as Justinian's megalomaniac tendencies and his reformatory and religious zeal. In essence, his perspective would appear to have been quite similar to that of one of his contemporaries, the scholar and bureaucrat John Lydus. Both of these men despised John the Cappadocian and criticised him for the very policies that Justinian had encouraged and approved.

Procopius' criticism of Justinian and his entourage was fairly consistent: what varied across his writings was the means through which it was expressed. In particular, criticisms that are made in the author's own voice in the *Secret History* tend to be presented in his *History of the Wars* through a series of set-piece speeches lambasting the emperor and his policies, typically put into the mouths of foreigners. One can imagine the contemporary piquancy of such speeches—if Procopius tested them out in the setting of a private literary salon by reading them aloud, his audience would have understood what he was trying to do. Such speeches would have allowed him to give voice to some of his most trenchant criticisms whilst also allowing him to distance himself from them ('I would never have said that! It was those dreadful barbarians!'). The statue of the great Athenian historian Thucydides that stood in Constantinople depicted him declaiming his *History of the Peloponnesian War*.[42] We should imagine Procopius doing the same with choice extracts of his great narrative of Justinian's campaigns.

In particular, Procopius presents us in his *History of the Wars* with three speeches which go to the heart of his critique of the regime, supposedly delivered by ambassadors speaking on behalf of the Goths, the Armenians, and the Caucasian principality of Lazica. The Gothic envoys are depicted as warning the Persian court that Justinian 'is by nature a meddler and a lover of those things which in no way belong to him', and that 'he is not able to abide by the settled order of things': 'He has conceived the desire of seizing upon the whole earth, and has become eager to acquire for himself each and every state.'[43] The Armenian delegation likewise complains, saying that Justinian has 'turned everything in the world upside down, and wrought utter confusion', imposing hitherto unheard-of levels of taxation, for example. 'The whole earth', they warn Khusro, 'is not large enough for this man', who is constantly even 'gazing into the heavens', 'wishing to gain for himself some other world'. The Laz similarly complain of Justinian's 'cruel tyranny'.[44] Procopius' narrative, it has been noted, contains no countervailing speeches *in defence* of the regime.[45] This absence is telling.

Criticism of Justinian and his advisers is also conveyed implicitly in the author's public works through literary and historical allusion.[46] The most often cited example is to be found in a speech Procopius puts into the mouth of the empress Theodora during the Nika riots, when, Procopius claimed, she had supposedly steeled Justinian's nerves and dissuaded him from fleeing the palace by reminding him of 'an old saying' that 'kingship is a good burial shroud'.[47] As many of Procopius' readers would have known, the original saying was actually '*tyranny* is a good burial shroud'—a comment first attributed to the figure of Dionysius of Syracuse (one of the most notorious tyrants of antiquity), when his long-suffering subjects finally rose up against him in revolt.[48] The historian, some have argued, was inviting his readership to make the connection and draw the appropriate inference.[49]

Likewise, it has been suggested that Procopius' description of Justinian's equestrian statue contained in his *Buildings* is far from entirely positive. Procopius compares Justinian to the figure of Achilles in Homer's *Iliad* (a work with which many of Procopius' readers would have been deeply familiar). Justinian, like Achilles in the original poem, is described as 'that autumn star'.[50] In the *Iliad*, however, the verse continues, 'which is the brightest among the stars, and yet is wrought as a sign of evil and brings on the great fever for unfortunate mortals'. Procopius' description also subtly suggests that the emperor was guilty of megalomania, that he had a desire to obliterate the past, and a tendency to make grandiose military claims for himself which stood in marked contrast to his relative lack of actual frontline military experience.[51] Thus, although the statue depicted the emperor facing east, towards the Persians, and commanding the barbarians to advance no further, 'yet he has neither sword nor spear nor any other weapon, but a cross [alone] stands upon the globe that he carries, the only emblem by which he has obtained both his empire and his victory in war. . . . So much, then, for this statue.'[52]

On closer inspection, even Procopius' description of the building of Hagia Sophia looks a bit suspect. Procopius relates that during the course of construction the eastern arch that supported the dome began to crack and seemed on the verge of giving way. In despair, the emperor's chief architects (Isidore and Anthemius) supposedly took news of this to Justinian. 'And straightaway', Procopius writes, 'the emperor, impelled I know not by what, but I suppose by God (for he is not himself a master-architect) commanded them to carry the curve of the arch to its final completion. "For when it rests upon itself", he said, "it will no longer need the props beneath it."' When further problems developed in the masonry between other arches and the dome, Justinian again intervened. 'These instructions', Procopius notes, 'were carried out, and thereafter the structure stood secure. And the emperor in this way enjoys a kind of testimonial from the work.'[53] On the face of it, this episode reflects well on the emperor. But in 558, the 'divinely inspired' eastern arch gave way, as the result of an earthquake the previous year. The entire dome was brought down and had to be rebuilt. Given what Procopius had written of Justinian in his other works, it is tempting to conclude that the author had narrated his account of the construction of the emperor's 'testimonial dome' in the full knowledge that it would eventually collapse.[54] Procopius was subtly lampooning Justinian and his grandiose but ultimately doomed ambitions.

All of this has implications for how we should think about Justinian and the nature of his government. In his legislation, and in particular in the provincial reforms, in which he took on members of the aristocracy, Justinian frequently adopted a rhetorical posture of autocratic omnipotence that was meant to instil fear in the hearts and minds of his opponents. In his *Secret History*, Procopius effectively inverts this imperial rhetoric, casting it back at Justinian with the accusation of tyranny. It is true that the reign of Justinian would witness mounting persecution and periodic purges, but the popularity and widespread circulation of Procopius' *History of the Wars*, in which criticism of Justinian, his generals, and his chief ministers was pretty palpable, would suggest that it was possible to get away with much more public criticism of Justinian and his policies than either Procopius or the emperor wanted people to think.

POLITICAL DEBATE

Procopius was not alone in his criticisms of the regime. With every passing year, as speculation began to mount as to when the emperor would die, there is also likely to have been growing discussion of how imperial policy should be directed after him—and by whom. As a result of reversals in Italy, enthusiasm for Belisarius as a potential successor apparently waned, and the unexpected death in 550 of Justinian's talented and militarily successful cousin, Germanus, removed another highly popular potential successor from the scene. Eyes would increasingly begin to turn to Germanus' son (who had followed his father into the army) and one of Justinian's nephews via his sister, a courtier well liked by members of the Senate: both men were named Justin.[55]

Contemporary anxiety as to the nature and direction of imperial policy is revealed by a fascinating anonymous text known as the *Dialogue on Political Science*. Two books of this work survive: the first is largely concerned with strategy and military affairs, the second with the nature of imperial rule and the ideal emperor. The intended readership of the treatise evidently consisted of members of the military and political elite, and its overarching political perspective was essentially aristocratic. The author of the text took the legitimacy of imperial rule and the office of emperor entirely for granted: a well-ordered society was a society presided over by an emperor, who was expected to rule 'in imitation of God', motivated by concern for his subjects and devoid of personal ambition or greed. This was what the author of the work understood by the term 'providential' or 'philanthropic' rule (each of which was also a theme in contemporary propaganda disseminated on behalf of the regime). For such rule to be genuinely beneficial to society at large, moreover, the ruler had to conform to concepts of lawfulness and hierarchy. He was to live in accordance with and uphold the inherited body of laws and leave them intact, and he was to work cooperatively with his leading citizens (by inference, members of the senatorial elite, referred to as the *optimates*), who stood directly beneath the emperor in the political hierarchy and from whose ranks he should be appointed. It was then the task of this aristocratic social stratum to interact with and mediate imperial rule to the classes that stood beneath it in the hierarchical pecking order. The ideal emperor thus understood that he was dependent on the support and cooperation of the elite and that he should listen to their concerns.[56]

Much of this would have sounded highly critical of Justinian and his regime. The emperor and his wife had been accused from the start of taking advantage of the imperial office to feather their own nests. The emperor's legal interventionism was arguably the very opposite of the conservative and restrained 'lawful rule' favoured by the author of the text. Justinian's attitude towards many members of the elite, as revealed by much of his provincial legislation, had been highly antagonistic, using fear and intimidation as a political tool rather than persuasion or debate. The emperor had repeatedly interfered in areas that, according to the *Dialogue*, should have been left to the *optimates* to sort out. Moreover, Justinian's family had long been resented as opportunistic parvenus, totally bereft of either breeding or legitimacy. As the *Dialogue* put it, 'No citizen should exercise power of his own initiative . . . grasp it by force or deceitful scheming . . . or appropriate power by a preemptive use of fear—for this is the way of a tyrant.' In what reads as a highly pointed criticism, the author also argued that a genuinely public-spirited and altruistic emperor would retire at the age of fifty-seven or if debilitated by illness.[57] As such, Justinian should have stood down around the year 539 (a clear sign that the work was written at some point thereafter).

The *Dialogue* also alludes to a range of contemporary abuses and what the author regarded as social ills. In particular, he rails against foreigners, layabouts, and immigrants on the streets of the capital; members of the Circus Factions; and corrupt priests and especially monks, who he thought should be doing useful work rather than being supported by others. The author favoured compulsory military service and was critical of excessive taxation and the contemporary practice of assigning tax debts owed on abandoned land to other landowners.[58] The latter, as we have seen, had been a lynchpin of Justinian's response to the plague.

There also existed, of course, pro-regime literature or texts more supportive of the ideological underpinnings of imperial policy which were put into circulation, and which tended to be associated with authors of a more militantly Christian viewpoint than would have appealed to the likes of Procopius. Whilst both Procopius and the author of the *Dialogue* decried the use of fear as an imperial tactic, the hardline Christian chronicler John Malalas, their contemporary, cheered on the emperor's deployment of terror tactics against his foes. In recounting the emperor's persecution of homosexuals, for example, John had noted supportively that as a result 'there was great fear and [consequently] security'.[59] Likewise, the author of an ecclesiastical chronicle would look back approvingly on the 'great imperial terror' that Justinian had inspired in the minds of his opponents in the immediate aftermath of the Nika riots.[60]

Perhaps most interestingly, early in Justinian's reign a churchman named Agapetus composed what would prove to be a highly influential treatise, *Advice to the Emperor*, setting out seventy-two precepts by which he hoped Justinian would rule. In contrast to the *Dialogue on Political Science*, the author of this text actively encouraged the emperor to tax the rich to give to the poor. 'Inequality', he declared, 'must be changed to equality.' No man, Agapetus insisted, should take pride in his nobility of birth, and no matter was to be regarded as too small or insignificant to merit the emperor's attention. 'You will best administer your good kingship', Agapetus had advised, 'if you strive to oversee everything and allow nothing to escape your notice', for 'even a light word of the emperor's carries great force with everyone'.[61] This would have appealed to Justinian's instinct to micromanage.

Both the pro- and anti-regime literature responded to contemporary events and 'spun' them in a way that served their political agenda. If Procopius' *Buildings* implicitly took advantage of the rhetorical opportunity presented by the collapse of the eastern arch of Hagia Sophia to satirise Justinian, in 562 a courtier known as Paul the Silentiary focused on the restoration and the repair of the same arch and dome to celebrate the regime in a public oration which served to remind Justinian's subjects of the achievements of his reign. In it he listed the emperor's victories against the Vandals, his seemingly miraculous ability to overcome the plague and cheat death, his generosity to the poor, and the piety of both the emperor and his late wife Theodora, who, like the Virgin Mary or the saints, now interceded with God in heaven on the emperor's behalf. 'Who', Paul declares, 'is capable of describing the wise counsel of the wide-ruling emperor?'[62] These sources allow us to catch echoes of what almost amounted to a 'pamphleteering culture' in sixth-century Constantinople, through which imperial policy was argued over through set-piece public speeches such as Paul's, in private literary salons, and even on the streets. The contemporary historian Agathias describes a sort of 'speakers' corner' in Constantinople, where people openly discussed recent history, current affairs, and philosophy and religion. Such conversations apparently continued in the city's bookshops.[63] Likewise, the fundamentally pro-regime John Malalas seems to have felt obliged to respond to claims that, rather than being an agent of divine providence, Justinian was in fact the biblically foretold 'Anti-Christ', whose manifestation many anxious Christians expected to be imminent.[64] All of this suggests a remarkably lively culture of political engagement and debate of the kind not usually associated with authoritarian regimes.[65]

Chapter 15

Opportunistic Imperialism

THE GOTHIC REVIVAL

Justinian was an inveterate schemer, constantly trying to wrong-foot his adversaries at home and abroad. The late sixth-century diplomatic historian Menander relates, for example, how the emperor would carefully consider how best to mobilise and turn the empire's enemies against one another, so as to destroy them 'if not by war, then by wisdom'.[1] Nevertheless, such efforts were not always successful, and unhappiness with his foreign and domestic agendas heightened political hostility towards Justinian and his regime in Constantinople. As Procopius' criticisms reveal, reversals in the field abroad could make the political weather at home.

Belisarius' occupation of Ravenna in 540 and his capture of King Witigis might have been expected to mark the final defeat of the Gothic kingdom which Theoderic had established in Italy half a century earlier. As with Africa, however, imperial control of the peninsula proved to be remarkably fragile. The demands of Justinian's tax collectors had soon begun to alienate the local Roman population, and although Belisarius had tricked his way into their capital and accepted the submission of much of the Gothic nobility, the Gothic army had not been decisively defeated in the field. Growing unrest amongst the military rank-and-file over the payment of wages and disability benefits further compromised the ability of the Roman army to act as an effective force of occupation.[2]

The one Gothic commander of any significance who had refused to submit to Belisarius was Ildibad, the Lord of Verona, whose sense of his own dignity—and prestige in the eyes of his fellow Goths—was no doubt enhanced considerably by the fact that he was a nephew of Theudis, the Visigothic king of Spain. Gradually realising that Belisarius had hoodwinked them, the Gothic nobility set their hopes and ambitions on Ildibad, and soon after the capture of Witigis, he was declared king. When Belisarius departed for Constantinople, Ildibad began to lead operations against Roman forces almost immediately, despite the fact that Belisarius had taken his children with him to the imperial capital as hostages. The following year, in 541, Ildibad was murdered, and the leadership of the military resistance to Roman rule passed to a commander by the name of Erarich.[3] After just five months, he, too, was assassinated, and succeeded by a nephew of Ildibad's named Totila, whom Procopius describes as 'gifted with remarkable judgment, energetic in the extreme, and held in high esteem among the Goths'.[4] Totila's accession to the throne would herald a dramatic revival in Gothic fortunes which would be greeted in Constantinople with considerable foreboding and dismay.

Early in 542, Totila rallied an army of five thousand men. He then led them across the river Po, routing imperial forces near Florence and capturing a series of significant fortresses. He advanced at speed across the Tiber, striking south into Campania and Samnium, seizing the crucial port city of Beneventum, and laying siege to Naples. Probably attracting growing numbers of erstwhile Gothic troops into his service, he ordered his men to fan out across Lucania, Bruttium, Apulia, and Calabria. By the end of 542 he had established his rule over much of Italy and was able to begin to collect tribute and tax revenues in place of the emperor's officials. As Procopius put it, 'He himself [Totila] collected the public taxes and also received the revenues of the land instead of those who owned the estates, and in all other matters he conducted himself as having become master of Italy.' In the spring of 543, Naples surrendered, and Totila wrote to the Senate in Rome inviting its members to recognise his authority. To help concentrate their minds, he began to advance on the city. In 544, he captured the nearby city of Tibur (Tivoli) and put the entirety of its population to death, sending a clear message to the residents of Rome that it would be in their interests to surrender to him and thereby escape a similar fate. He had earlier attempted to circulate leaflets to the citizens of Rome, promising them safety and security if they would come over to him. It was suspected that this propaganda had been distributed on Totila's behalf by Arian priests, whom the imperial officials then proceeded to round up and expel.[5]

Procopius blamed the rapidity of Totila's advance on Justinian's failure to appoint a single commander-in-chief to oversee the defence of Italy after the departure of Belisarius for Constantinople, and the inadequacy and venality of the various officers whom the emperor had left in place. 'Consequently,' he wrote, 'many blunders were committed by them, and the entire fabric of Roman power there was utterly destroyed in a short space of time.' As Totila advanced on Rome, the emperor's commanders in Italy wrote a joint letter to Justinian informing him that they were 'unable to hold out in the war against the Goths' and indicating 'their reluctance to carry on the struggle'. In response, Justinian decided once more to send Belisarius to Italy. Yet again, we are fortunate that he was accompanied there by Procopius.[6]

The empire was now suffering from a shortage of military power, exacerbated by warfare in both East and West and the increasingly pronounced effects of the plague. In 542 Justinian had felt it necessary to issue a law to prevent landowners from illegally maintaining soldiers on their estates, where they probably used them to cajole and intimidate the peasantry. As he headed west, Belisarius had deemed it impossible 'to detach his own troops from the army in Persia'.[7] Instead, he attempted to raise new recruits as he travelled out from Constantinople, 'offering money to gather fresh volunteers' before sailing up the Adriatic with a force of around four thousand men. After reaching Ravenna, Belisarius was able to restore imperial control over the city of Bononia (Bologna) only to find that many of the troops he had so recently recruited had started to desert. Not only had their salaries gone unpaid, but rumours had reached them that their homeland in the Balkans was under barbarian attack. Increasingly despairing of the situation, the general sent an envoy bearing a letter to Justinian, begging him to send men, money, weapons, and horses. It was, he informed the emperor, impossible to raise any tax revenues in Italy to support his troops, as most of the territory was now in the hands of the enemy, and most of the army had deserted due to lack of pay: 'This debt', he told Justinian, 'has deprived us of the right to command.' He implored the emperor to send him his personal military retinue of *buccellarii*, and to set about recruiting barbarian troops as a matter of urgency. As Belisarius waited for a reply, Totila expanded the area under his control. Many cities simply surrendered to him. Crucially, he was now ready to initiate a siege of Rome.[8]

By early 546, the surviving population of Rome was in the grip of a severe famine as the Goths tightened their blockade of the city and prevented any food supplies from reaching it. Belisarius decided to withdraw from Ravenna (entrusting the city to a subordinate) and instead retreat along the Dalmatian coast towards the port town of Dyrrachium (Durres), where he hoped to rendezvous with fresh forces recruited by Constantinople. With these forces, he surmised, he would be able to make the journey by sea across the Adriatic to break the siege of Rome. A combined army made up of 'barbarian and Roman soldiers' duly met him there. Meanwhile, Belisarius' erstwhile rival, the general Narses, was sent to recruit Herul *foederati*, with whom he would march into northern Italy.[9]

In Rome itself, conditions were deteriorating rapidly, with much of the starving civilian population reduced to eating nettles, which, Procopius relates, grew 'in abundance about the walls and among the ruins in all parts of the city'. Many, he would claim, even chose to commit suicide, as 'they could no longer find either dogs or mice or any dead animal of any kind on which to feed'. The Roman commanders permitted civilians with sufficient strength to flee if they wished to do so. Few of the refugees made it to safety: those who did not simply collapse and die by the roadside were captured and executed by Gothic troops.[10] Belisarius headed there as speedily as he could, attempting to sail up the river Tiber with an advance guard and some two hundred vessels. Before he was able to break through to the city, however, it was betrayed to the enemy by a dispirited band of Isaurian troops. On 17 December 546, Totila's army entered Rome. Much of what remained of the imperial garrison fled, accompanied by members of the Senate, whilst other senators took refuge in Saint Peter's Basilica. The pope had long ago relocated to Sicily. The surviving civilian population sought sanctuary in the city's churches, and Totila agreed to prohibit his men from slaughtering the Romans. When envoys were sent to Justinian to negotiate a peace treaty, the emperor responded that Belisarius had full authority to negotiate on his behalf. Fighting between Roman and Gothic forces continued elsewhere, especially in Apulia and the south.[11]

Throughout 547 the armies of Belisarius and Totila crisscrossed the peninsula, fighting over a landscape ravaged by warfare, famine, and plague. The pandemic had arrived in Italy by 543 (a chronicler describes how in that year 'a great mortality laid waste the land of Italy'), and it would appear to have reached the city of Rome by 545.[12] As Totila advanced into Lucania, attempting to seize Ravenna, Belisarius took advantage of his absence to strike out from Portus (the artificial harbour of Rome), which his forces had infiltrated, to once more occupy the city. Totila had ordered the destruction of Rome's defensive walls, and accordingly Belisarius ordered his men to construct new defences made from the rubble. He also rapidly set about amassing provisions and supplies. To Totila's evident surprise, Belisarius' men managed to fight off a spirited Gothic assault. As a result, the king was upbraided by his nobles for not having razed Rome to the ground when he had the chance.[13]

Now that fighting to the East had ceased in Syria (but not the Caucasus), Justinian decided it was possible to send more reinforcements to Italy to help restore imperial fortunes there, and Belisarius was ordered to head south to receive them. Disappointed at the number of soldiers who arrived (in early 548 Belisarius' men were joined by an additional two thousand infantry in Sicily), Belisarius instructed his wife, Antonina, who had insisted on accompanying him on campaign for all of this time, to head to Constantinople, to plead with Theodora to persuade Justinian to send yet more troops. He then returned to Rome, where he found that the men of the garrison had lynched their commanding officer, accusing him of profiteering. The troops demanded that Justinian issue them a blanket amnesty for this act, and ensure that they be immediately provided with the back pay they were owed. If he failed to agree to this, they warned, they would simply defect to Totila and serve him instead. It was not a sign of strength on Justinian's part that, according to Procopius, 'he immediately complied with their request'.[14] The combined effects of warfare and plague were seriously sapping the empire's military and financial resources as well as the emperor's political credibility. His decision shortly thereafter to summon Belisarius back to Constantinople (for reasons to be recounted in the following chapter) may have led to a further deterioration in the military position to the West.

THE BATTLE OF BUSTA GALLORUM

By 548 the Goths, under Totila's leadership, were once more in control of much of the Italian Peninsula, although the city of Rome itself remained in the hands of its restless and almost mutinous imperial garrison. But it was not just the Goths who had benefited from the weakening of the imperial position in the West. The Franks had taken advantage of the Roman-Gothic wars to occupy the area around modern Venice (the Veneto) and expand their sphere of influence there, while the Gepids had seized for themselves the strategically crucial city of Sirmium (their earlier pact with the empire was clearly no longer in place). At the same time, another Germanic group, the Lombards, was ravaging the emperor's homeland in the western Balkans. Eventually, in January 550, Totila's forces managed to once more enter Rome after it was betrayed to him by a band of imperial troops fed up with the ongoing arrears in their pay.[15] Totila then led his troops into Sicily, much of which his army ravaged.

Faced with the imminent collapse of what remained of the imperial position in Italy, Justinian was forced to commit more manpower and resources. He sent reinforcements to Sicily and appointed his cousin Germanus as overall commander. Germanus, who by now had married a granddaughter of Theoderic's, Matasuentha, had gone on an extensive recruitment drive in the Balkans. There are signs that leading Roman figures from Italy (such as the courtier Cassiodorus) had high hopes that Germanus would appeal to Goths and Romans alike, and restore a semblance of order to the peninsula.[16] Germanus' sudden death in 550 was thus a major blow. The emperor entrusted leadership of the army that was advancing from the Balkans into Italy to a son and son-in-law of the late general. The Roman advance was further hindered by Slav raiders from across the Danube, who had evidently entered into an alliance with Totila.[17]

At the start of 552, Justinian renewed efforts to bring the Italian campaign to a conclusion, ordering the general Narses to march there with a substantial army of some thirty thousand men, made up of much of the remaining imperial field army in the Balkans, but mostly consisting of barbarian mercenary and allied troops.[18] As Procopius put it in his *History*, 'Though the emperor Justinian had previously conducted the war very negligently, he now finally made the most notable preparation for it.'[19] Circumventing both Frankish garrisons and Gothic defences, and overcoming the marshy terrain of the Veneto by means of portable pontoon bridges, Narses led the army against Ravenna, which on 6 June 552 was once more prised from the grip of the Goths. The sudden presence of a large Roman army in the Gothic heartlands north of the Po obliged Totila to lead his men out of Rome to face what was now, finally, a numerically preponderant Roman foe.

In late June or early July 552, the armies met on the plain of Busta Gallorum. Totila attempted to fortify his men's spirits by riding out before his warriors to perform the ritualised horseback war dance that the Gothic elite had learned from the Huns. The scene is vividly described by Procopius, who seems to have drawn on eyewitness accounts on the part of veterans returning to Constantinople: 'The armour in which he [Totila] was clad was abundantly plated with gold, and the ample adornments which hung from his cheek plates as well as from his helmet and spear were not only of purple but in other respects too befitting a king, marvellous in their abundance. And he himself, sitting upon a very large horse, began to perform the dance under arms skilfully between the armies,' Procopius reported. 'For he wheeled his horse round in a circle and then turned him again to the other side and so made him run round and round. And as he rode he hurled his javelin into the air and caught it again as it quivered above him, and then passed it rapidly from hand to hand, shifting it with consummate skill, and he gloried in his practice in such matters, falling back on his shoulders, spreading his legs, and leaning from side to side, as one who had been instructed with precision in this art since boyhood.'[20] This image of military vigour was perhaps meant to contrast in the mind of Procopius' readers with the emperor's military posturing, epitomised by the equestrian statue of Justinian in Constantinople.

Totila now ordered his cavalry to charge the imperial lines, spears prepared for the engagement with Roman troops. Before they could make contact with the enemy, however, the bulk of the Gothic cavalry was cut down or broken by wave upon wave of Roman arrows.[21] As the remaining Gothic horsemen turned in flight, they trampled the Gothic infantry in their rear and the entire army was routed. Some six thousand Gothic warriors were killed, and many more were then captured and executed. The body of the dying king was believed to have been rushed from the battlefield by a small band of loyal retainers, who accompanied it to Caprae (Caprara), where it was buried. The remaining Gothic commander at Verona, Teias, now attempted to rally the remnants of Gothic resistance, but in vain, and within three months he, too, was dead, despite the fact that Procopius regarded his heroism to have been equal to that of all the 'heroes of legend'.[22] At Busta Gallorum, Narses and the Roman forces had managed to kill not only Totila, but also the cream of the Gothic nobility: with them out of the way, victory in Italy was now finally Justinian's. Narses led his army from there to Rome. It was the fifth time the city had been militarily occupied in fifteen years.[23]

'MEN WHO HAVE BEEN DOOMED TO SUFFER ILL'

To Procopius, Justinian's final triumph in Italy represented the hollowest of all victories, one which demonstrated the extent to which even the leading citizens of the city of Rome itself were 'doomed to suffer ill': 'For', he wrote, 'this victory turned out to be for the Senate and people a cause of far greater destruction.' As the Gothic forces had abandoned Rome and withdrawn from southern Italy and the territory of Campania, where many members of the Senate had taken refuge on their extensive estates, they had taken retaliatory action against Roman civilians and especially members of the senatorial elite. Totila had taken hostage three hundred children from aristocratic Roman households. As the Gothic kingdom collapsed around him, Teias had then executed the lot. The 'barbarians of the Roman army', as Procopius describes them, 'treated as enemies all those whom they happened to encounter as they entered the city'.[24] Teias had also attempted to revive Gothic fortunes by further encouraging the Franks to mobilise against the Romans. After his death, the Franks continued to challenge imperial authority in the north of the peninsula, and military campaigns directed against them would rumble on for the remainder of Justinian's reign.[25]

The members of the Roman Senate had managed to preserve their families, their estates, and the city of Rome itself across an extraordinarily turbulent period that, by the reign of Justinian, stretched back almost three hundred years, to the civil wars and military crisis of the third century.[26] Ironically, it would appear to have been the Roman reconquest of Rome, completed by Narses in 552, that effectively marked the final death knell of the institution. In 554, Justinian issued a lengthy and detailed edict, known as the 'Pragmatic Sanction', which set out how Italy was to be reincorporated into the empire. He promised to return estates (as well as slaves and tied peasants) to their rightful owners, to regulate taxes fairly, and to ensure the writ of imperial law.[27] But there was to be no new western emperor and no true restoration of the Roman world of old.[28] Rather, new laws and tax officials were to be sent out from Constantinople, to which tax revenues would then be sent back. Given the extent to which Italy had been racked by warfare, famine, and plague, such revenues were perhaps unlikely to have amounted to much, but the emperor nevertheless regarded them as his. Moreover, these arrangements were issued not in response to a request from the Senate of Rome, as would have been the case in the past, but rather from the bishop of Rome, the 'pope'—that is, the already humiliated Vigilius. Only he, for all his faults, was regarded by Justinian as an appropriate interlocutor, although individual senators were to be allowed to travel to Constantinople if they wished to petition the emperor in person.

The Senate of Rome itself had no real role to play in Justinian's vision of empire, and within a generation the institution would effectively disappear from the historical record.[29] Instead, the pope was now regarded as the spokesman for both the city of Rome and, interestingly, those whom the law of 554 describes as 'all known inhabitants of the West'. By virtue of the final conquest of Italy, Justinian now felt able to legislate for the former territories of the Western Roman Empire as a whole. Across the West, the pope was to be the emperor's representative.[30]

'THE GREATEST AND THE MOST POWERFUL OF THE TRIBES'

The late 540s and early 550s also witnessed mounting military pressure on imperial territory in the Balkans. Groups of Slavs resident north of the Danube (whose raids Justinian's Balkan defences had been designed to counter) began to form larger tribal confederations and groups that were increasingly able to challenge

Roman mastery of the frontier zone and to strike well beyond it. Justinian had sought to disincentivise such attacks by providing Rome's Balkan provinces with greater 'defence-in-depth'. The new Slav raiding parties were now becoming large enough to render that strategy less and less effective.[31] Combined with ongoing attacks from bands of Huns and the serious threat posed by groups such as the Lombards and the Gepids, this made for an ominous situation. Justinian responded by attempting to play off different barbarian groups against one another, his ability to respond militarily severely curtailed by the need to send troops to Italy and the ongoing effects of the plague, which was making it more and more difficult for him to raise new troops. Prior to Narses' march west to confront Totila, a major military offensive had been launched, and in 552 a significant defeat was inflicted on the Gepids, thereby securing the land route to Italy, but after that there were few troops to spare.[32] It must have been becoming clear that, with the emergence of larger barbarian groups, the nature of the military threat posed to imperial control in the Balkans was evolving in a direction that Roman strategy had not anticipated, and that Roman force of arms alone would not be sufficient for the authorities in Constantinople to maintain control of the region.

This fact was brought home in 559, when bands of Kutrigur Huns crossed the frozen Lower Danube, struck into Thrace, and broke through the so-called Long Walls, which the emperor Anastasius had constructed to defend the suburbs of Constantinople from enemy attack. These Huns were joined in their depredations by Slavs whom they had subjected to their authority. In Constantinople, the rapid Kutrigur advance sparked off considerable panic as the outskirts of the city now lay vulnerable to attack.[33] According to the historian Agathias, Justinian ordered that priceless treasures belonging to the Church be shipped across the Bosphorus to prevent them from falling into enemy hands. General Belisarius, meanwhile, was appointed to lead troops against the raiders. He and his men caught some four thousand of them in an ambush and slaughtered them.[34]

Even prior to the Hunnic assault on Constantinople in 559 Justinian had been considering how to address the evolving nature of the threat that confronted his commanders along and beyond the Danube frontier. In around 557, news had reached him of a major reconfiguration of power amongst the nomadic empires of the Eurasian steppe, and he was determined to turn it to the empire's advantage. The dramatic period of climate instability inaugurated by the unprecedented volcanic activity of the late 530s had carried with it significant implications for societies and states across the Northern Hemisphere, from North and Central America to Japan. In Central Asia, it had contributed to a sudden change in the balance of power between the competing nomadic confederations that had come to dominate the region.[35]

These nomadic powers were dependent militarily on cavalry warfare and hence on the maintenance of vast herds of horses as well as other livestock. The horses needed pasture, which, on the eastern steppe, in particular, could sometimes be hard to come by. Any sudden shift in climate which had an adverse effect on the availability of pasture or which altered its distribution could lead to a major reconfiguration of power relations amongst the nomadic peoples. The 530s would appear to have inaugurated such a transformation across the Eurasian steppe impacting first the Chinese, then the Persians, and finally Constantinople. In the early sixth century, the dominant nomadic power on the eastern steppe, along the Chinese frontier zone, had been the so-called Northern Wei, whose rulers had even received envoys from Constantinople. In the mid-530s, this confederacy had entered a period of sustained political crisis and split apart. Their power was increasingly contested and supplanted by groups known to the Romans as the Avars and their rivals, the Turks.[36] A period of crisis may also be discernible on the part of the Hephthalite or White Huns to the East of Persia at this time. The ability of Khusro to commit significant military manpower to attacking Roman positions in Syria and the Caucasus in the 540s suggests that he no longer faced much of a Hunnic threat. Containing military challenges from the steppe had long been the chief Sasanian priority, and such anti-Roman aggression would have been inconceivable had the Central Asian Huns been in a position of strength.[37]

By around 552, the Turks had emerged as the dominant power on the East Eurasian steppe and begun a rapid advance west, pursuing their defeated Avar rivals and forging an alliance with the Persians against the White Huns.[38] By 560, the Turks had destroyed the Hunnic kingdom of Central Asia in its entirety, establishing an empire that stretched from the borders of Iran to those of China.[39] It was the greatest nomadic empire that the Eurasian world had ever witnessed—or would witness again, until the advent of the Mongols in the thirteenth century.[40]

The first that the imperial authorities in Constantinople knew of these dramatic developments was in 557, when a group of Avar fugitives from the Turk expansion made their presence known to Roman commanders in the northern Caucasus. The diplomatic historian Menander (who seems to have had access to official records) comments, 'Concerning the Avars: after many wanderings they came to the Alans and begged . . . the leader of the Alans, that he bring them to the attention of the Romans. [He] informed Germanus' son, Justin, who was at that time the general of the forces in Lazica, about the Avars. Justin told Justinian, and the emperor ordered the general to send the embassy of the tribe to Byzantium. One Kandikh by name was chosen be the first envoy of the Avars, and when he came to the palace, he told the emperor of the arrival of the greatest and the most powerful of the tribes.' Kandikh went on to declare that 'the Avars were invincible and could easily crush and destroy those who stood in their path'. 'The emperor', he advised, 'should make an alliance with them and enjoy their efficient protection. But they would only be well disposed to the Roman state in exchange for the most valuable of gifts, yearly payments, and very fertile lands to inhabit.[41]

The arrival of the Avars north of the Caucasus posed a considerable threat to Justinian, but it also presented him with a great opportunity. The Romans knew from bitter experience that there was little they could do to prevent the Avars from heading further west, towards imperial territory in the Balkans, where the land was comparatively rich, and their enemies, the Turks, would have felt a reassuringly long way away. It was to observe and report back on movements and migrations precisely such as this that Justinian had been careful to establish imperial 'listening posts' in the Caucasus and along the northern coast of the Black Sea in the first place. If, however, the offer of an Avar alliance was accepted, then their military could be harnessed against the Slavs and other barbarian groups from beyond the Danube, who were now menacing imperial territory. If the Avars could distract and defeat the Slavs, the empire potentially had much to gain, whereas if the Slavs, Gepids, and Kutrigurs ended up liquidating the Avars, what did the empire have to lose?

According to Menander, Justinian proposed an Avar alliance to the Senate in Constantinople and then committed to it. As the historian would record, 'The emperor put the matter up for discussion, and when the holy Senate had praised his shrewdness, he immediately sent the gifts, cords worked with gold, couches, silken garments, and a great many other objects which would mollify the arrogant spirits of the Avars.' By 562 at the latest, the Avars appear to have overcome most of the Kutrigurs and the other nomadic tribes that had been attacking Roman territory and had reached the Danube. The emperor then persuaded them to focus their energies against the Gepids.[42] His strategy appeared vindicated: he seemed to be not only weathering the mounting storm of uncertainty blowing westwards from the realm of the steppe, but also harnessing it to his and the empire's advantage. Justinian's instincts and skill as an opportunist evidently remained undimmed.

The ability of the emperor to extract maximum diplomatic and political advantage from a fast-changing situation would soon also become apparent in relations with Persia. By the early 550s, the two great empires had effectively fought themselves to a stalemate in the Caucasus, and as a result the Romans had attempted to engage Sasanian representatives in discussion of a truce. The Sasanian authorities had proven largely resistant to such overtures: after all, they had done well in the region, clawing back many of the Roman gains of the 520s and 530s. In 557, the Persians nevertheless suddenly indicated that they were willing to talk, and an armistice was agreed, whereby each empire was left in possession of such territory as it then held. An extensive series of negotiations ensued, ultimately culminating in a detailed peace treaty also recorded for us by Menander. This treaty, which was formally ratified in 561–562, represented a remarkable success for Justinian. For although he accepted Persian demands that the empire make substantial and regular payments of gold to Khusro (which the shah would be able to represent to his subjects as 'Roman tribute'), the Persians, in return, effectively acknowledged Roman overlordship of the strategically vital territory of Lazica, where the Persians had committed significant military manpower, with great success, for the past twenty years. The treaty therefore delivered a major expansion of the Roman Empire's sphere of influence in the western Caucasus and consolidated its grip on the Black Sea.[43]

This was an extraordinary climb down on the part of Khusro and his advisers. But the timing of it was telling. The dramatic Persian offer of an armistice in 557 appears to have been tied very closely to the arrival of the Avars north of the Caucasus, bringing with them news of the Turk advance. Likewise, the surrender of Lazica coincided with the final destruction of the Hephthalite or White Huns and the sudden establishment of the expansionist

Turk empire along Persia's frontiers. Justinian and his diplomats had apparently been able to play upon the long-standing and deeply rooted Sasanian sense of insecurity with respect to the empires of the steppe to exercise maximum diplomatic leverage. Faced with the advent of a new and aggressive nomadic power, Justinian realised that for Khusro and his court, the overwhelming instinct would be to disengage from warfare with Constantinople. The price of peace would be Lazica. He thus managed to secure for the empire diplomatically what he had failed to secure for it militarily.

NEW HORIZONS

Despite the periodic reversals the empire had suffered in both Africa and Italy, Justinian remained alert to opportunities to expand its frontiers elsewhere. In each of these kingdoms, he had taken advantage of succession disputes within the reigning Vandal and Gothic dynasties to intervene militarily and begin the process of returning these territories to what he regarded as rightful Roman rule. In 551, a similar opportunity had arisen in Spain, when a pretender to the Visigothic throne, Athanagild, operating from his base in the city of Seville, had requested military assistance from Constantinople.[44]

An imperial expeditionary force was sent out led by Liberius, who had served Odoacer and Theoderic in Italy before defecting to the imperial authorities in Constantinople and governing Sicily on Justinian's behalf.[45] He must, by this point, have been a very old man, but is likely to have been well regarded by members of the Roman elite in southern Spain. The region remained the Visigothic kingdom's most Romanised territory, locked as it was into broader patterns of Mediterranean commerce and culture.[46] Certainly, there are signs that the East Roman army received widespread support from members of the Hispano-Roman aristocracy, and, as in Africa, East Roman merchants may have operated as agents of imperial influence. Interestingly, we have no evidence of any attempt to try to justify the imperial intervention in Spain in religious or legal terms, as there had been with Africa and Italy, despite the fact that here, too, 'Catholic' Christians were being freed from the rule of supposedly 'heretical' Arian kings.[47] Having witnessed his campaigns in other locations, contemporaries probably now recognised and appreciated Justinian's opportunistic imperialism for what it was.

It is not clear how far the zone of direct Roman occupation established at Justinian's command extended into the Spanish hinterland. The priorities are likely to have been extending Roman control over the coastal zone and securing the lines of communication that connected the Visigothic kingdom to Africa. Consequently, the significance of the territory occupied is likely to have been primarily strategic. Unlike in the immediate aftermath of Belisarius' campaign of conquest in Africa, the imperial authorities in the newly established province of *Spania* are likely to have had very few resources made available to them with which to invest in defences or fortifications: the empire was now too cash-strapped for that.[48] Whatever frontier was established is likely to have been a highly porous one.[49] Only at Cartagena do we have archaeological evidence for substantial military investment by the imperial authorities. But with southern Spain, Africa, Sicily, and Italy now conquered, the only substantial stretch of the Mediterranean coastline that remained outside direct imperial rule was the area extending from southern Gaul (France) down along the eastern coast of Spain (Map 3). Given the fact that Corsica and the Balearic Islands were now firmly under imperial control, there was little here for the government in Constantinople to worry about.[50] From Justinian's perspective, the Mediterranean was once again what it had last been in the age of Constantine: a 'Roman lake' subject to the authority of a sole emperor.

Nor was the emperor's opportunism in the 550s limited to the diplomatic and military spheres. There was a strong commercial dimension to the ties that bound together the Eurasian world of the sixth century. The route from China, via Central Asia to Persia and Constantinople, was traversed by traders as well as by armies and ambassadors. In particular, since the first century BCE there had existed a considerable trade in luxury goods originating in India or China that made their way onto Roman markets, including black pepper, cinnamon, and other aromatics and spices from the former, and, above all, silk from the latter. For centuries, the Chinese had maintained an effective monopoly on silk production, closely guarding the secret of how to raise silkworms and extract the delicate fibres from them that were then spun into raw silk. As a result of their rarity and elegance, silk garments had come to be prized by both Persian and Roman elites. Merchants could make vast profits conveying bolts of raw silk to Persian and Roman markets, where they were then made into luxurious garments and tapestries in the workshops of the Near East. In the Roman Empire, high-grade dress silks, dyed purple with pigments made from the crushed shells of sea snails, were produced in state-regulated factories in Syria and Palestine. These were primarily for the use of the imperial court and the political and religious elite, but they were also sold or given as diplomatic gifts to courts or elites abroad. In the Sasanian Empire, the royal authorities invested in state-owned workshops producing not only elaborate silks, but also silverware and other luxurious commodities, which were then trafficked by networks of merchants who had commercial alliances with the Sasanian monarchy.[51] Procopius describes the silk trade as permeating all the markets of the Near East. Importers and merchants who made a living from it plied their wares 'in Byzantium, and all the other cities', he said, 'whether operating on land or sea'.[52]

Until the fourth century, silk, aromatics, and spices had reached the Sasanian and Roman Empires primarily by sea. They were first conveyed by land on routes through Bactria (which spanned Central Asia, Afghanistan, and the Hindu Kush) before being shipped to Roman or Persian territory across the Indian Ocean via the Persian Gulf or the Red Sea. This maritime trade had persisted into the sixth century, with the Persians often seeking to prevent Roman merchants and their partners from gaining access to the goods by blockading Indian ports and trying to force the trade up the Gulf, in order to render the Romans dependent on Persian sources of supply.[53] According to Procopius, who had a keen interest in maritime commerce, one of the reasons the two empires had come to vie for control of Himyar (the Yemen) in southern Arabia was the crucial role Himyarite merchants played in East-West trade.[54] A sixth-century author, known as Cosmas—a merchant from Alexandria with strong religious beliefs—would relate an account of Roman and Sasanian merchants competing for favour at the court of one of the rulers of Taprobane (modern Sri Lanka), arguing about whose empire was the greatest and which of them possessed the finest and most prestigious currency.[55]

From the late fourth century onwards, however, the sea routes between East and West would appear to have entered a phase of relative economic decline. The new nomad empires of Central Asia, such as the Huns and the Turks who would come in their wake, attempted to maximise the profits they could derive from such commerce by forcing as much of it as possible across the Eurasian landmass which they controlled.[56] Indeed, there are signs that the knowledge of how to produce silk had seeped out into Central Asia (the Chinese having long used bolts of silk as a form of currency with which to trade or to buy off foreigners, such as their troublesome nomadic neighbours). By the time Procopius was writing, most of the commerce was land-based, with Persia at the centre of the networks of exchange, and Roman merchants increasingly obliged to buy silk off their Persian counterparts at cities and trading posts in Syria.[57] In one of his laws, Justinian would try to legislate to prevent state officials from buying silk off the Persians at what he regarded as exorbitant rates, or then selling it on to Roman traders at more than what he thought to be a fair price.[58] Silk thus stood at the heart not only of the life of the imperial court, but also of the empire's commercial economy.

Justinian regarded Khusro as a rival and an enemy, but he was also ready to learn from his Sasanian foe. It is striking in this context that from the 540s onwards we arguably see Justinian and his officials emulating Sasanian economic policy, trying to build up state monopolies and networks of preferred producers and traders after a manner that stood in marked contrast to earlier Roman practice (Roman law in the Eastern Empire, for example, had long been hostile to monopolistic practices).[59] Procopius associates these policies with the figure of Peter Barsymes, the finance minister who had played a crucial role in coordinating the empire's fiscal and economic response to the bubonic plague, and it may be that circumstances associated with the pandemic pushed the Roman authorities further down this more interventionist route. But one of the areas of economic activity which the emperor and his entourage were clearly most determined to turn into a major source of revenue was the textile industry, and particularly the silk trade.

These efforts came to a head in the late 540s and the years that followed. First, in around 547 or 548, dealing in silk was established as a government monopoly.[60] Second, in a fascinating act of industrial espionage which Procopius dates to the early 550s, Justinian's agents managed to acquire the secret of silk production and establish a homegrown industry, after silkworm eggs had been smuggled into the empire by eastern monks employed for that purpose on Justinian's behalf.[61]

Procopius records that, 'at about this time, certain monks coming from India, and learning that the emperor Justinian entertained the desire that the Romans should no longer purchase their silk from the Persians, came before the emperor and promised to settle the silk question . . . for they had learned accurately by what means it was possible for silk to be produced in the land of the Romans'.

The emperor, he continued, 'promised to reward them with large gifts', and as a result they made their way to the land 'situated north of the numerous nations of India' and smuggled back silkworm eggs feeding on mulberry leaves.[62] When, in the 560s, the Turks offered to sell raw silk directly to the Romans, obviating the Persians (with whom they had fallen out), they were horrified to discover that the imperial authorities were not interested, as they had acquired the necessary technology for themselves.[63]

Thereafter, 'Byzantine' silk would form an important part of the empire's economic arsenal, as traders from throughout Europe flocked to Constantinople in pursuit of this precious commodity.[64] The 'demon king' lambasted by Procopius for his constant meddling and all-consuming ambition had clearly lost none of his cunning: the events of the 550s and early 560s demonstrated that, contrary to the hopes of many, there was life in the old dog yet. As Paul the Silentiary declared before Justinian in 562, 'Victory is inherent to your labours like an emblem. Is it not true that, to the West, we must traverse the whole earth . . . to find the boundary to your power? While to the East do you not now make all men yours?' 'Against all expectation,' Paul proclaimed, 'you escape serenely from disease . . . protected not by spears or shields, but by the very hand of God.'[65]

Chapter 16

Death and Decline

END DAYS

Justinian's longevity was a cause of amazement to some and a source of profound irritation to others. His beloved Theodora, by contrast, had died on 28 June 548, after what may have been a struggle with cancer. We have no contemporary account of her last moments or her burial. Procopius relates simply that she 'had fallen sick and passed from the world'.[1] To opponents of the Council of Chalcedon she would be remembered as 'the rightly believing empress'.[2] Even supporters of the council acknowledged that Theodora had 'died piously'.[3] The emperor had her buried in the Church of the Holy Apostles in a mausoleum he had built for her and for himself.[4]

The psychological and emotional impact on Justinian of the death of the woman he had fallen in love with and then married despite the censures of his aunt, and who had been his constant companion, most stalwart supporter, and even co-ruler for over twenty-five years, can scarcely be imagined. Certainly, the cumulative effect of the events of the late 530s and 540s (climate change, plague, military reversals, and the death of his beloved) had led to an increasingly pronounced turn to religion on the part of an emperor who had always been theologically highly engaged. He had also turned to close relatives and old allies. As we have seen, Belisarius' wife, Antonina, had been sent to Constantinople to plead with Theodora to persuade Justinian to send more troops to the West. Arriving to find that the empress was dead, she had instead suggested to Justinian that he recall her husband to Constantinople, which he had duly done. The emperor even recalled John the Cappadocian, although, in order to remove him from the political fray (and scupper any ambitions John may have harboured for the throne), he had him forcibly ordained as a priest. Justinian's growing preoccupation with religion and the recall of Belisarius had initially left his remaining commanders in Italy worrying that he had lost interest in his western campaigns.[5] Many must have been wondering whether the regime had perhaps run out of steam, or how long Justinian himself had before he, too, died. As the emperor and those around him regained something of their focus and composure, however, the 550s had witnessed a number of important initiatives and interventions.

These final years would reveal a remarkable consistency and circularity in the themes and preoccupations of Justinian's reign. When in 559, for example, he reentered the city to pray at the Church of the Holy Apostles and light candles at Theodora's tomb, he would probably have taken in essentially the same view that he 'had encountered when he had first set foot inside [Constantinople]' some seventy years earlier.[6] Thereafter, he had spent almost his entire life within a stone's throw of the Great Palace or ensconced within its walls. Prior to this ceremony, Justinian had been residing for several months outside the capital—he and his entourage had travelled some sixty-five miles along the coast of the Sea of Marmara to

Selymbria (modern Silivri), where the emperor was reported to have overseen the restoration of defences damaged by a combination of earthquakes and Hunnic attacks.[7] Attempting to contain barbarian aggression, refortify the empire, and restore the damage wrought by sudden natural calamities had, of course, been long-standing themes of Justinian's reign. But travel was unusual for him. It is entirely possible that the elderly and perhaps ailing emperor had been taken to the coastal resort for reasons of health, and that a story had been concocted to explain his absence and justify it (including to the workaholic emperor himself). After his return, news that the emperor was suffering from headaches and was refusing to receive senators sparked off rumours that he had died, which led to panic buying on the streets of Constantinople. Only a decision on the part of the authorities 'to have lights lit throughout the city to show that the emperor was well' had calmed the nerves of the populace.[8]

Likewise, from his correspondence with Pope Hormisdas in 518 down to his discussion of 'Aphthartism' in 564, Justinian had demonstrated an unswerving interest in the details of the Christian faith and a keen sense of personal piety. He is likely to have remained celibate after the death of his wife (he encouraged celibacy for widowers in a law issued just three months after Theodora had passed away), and he may well have been chaste long before that.[9] In 563, Justinian made another departure from the city, but this time his absence was justified as a pilgrimage to the shrine of the Archangel Michael and the Holy Angels in Germia (modern Yürme), which, we are told, he made 'in fulfilment of a vow'.[10] This site was also famous for its natural bath waters, which were believed to possess therapeutic properties.[11] Again, medical reasons for the emperor's absence from Constantinople, as well as the officially stated ones, may reasonably be inferred.

A concerted effort appears to have been made to convey to the emperor's subjects that Justinian remained healthy, active, and in charge of affairs. Those of our sources that draw primarily on official proclamations and statements (such as the contemporary *Chronicle* of John Malalas and later works derived from his account) continued to emphasise the emperor's military vigilance and building projects: in around 559, for example, he ordered the construction of a bridge over the river Sangarios, which was celebrated by the court poet Paul the Silentiary.[12] Others began to infer that the emperor was now fading and his grip on power finally loosening. Describing the Hunnic attacks of 559, and complaining of mounting troop shortages within the army, the contemporary historian Agathias opined that although in earlier days 'the emperor had reduced Africa and the whole of Italy, becoming as a result of those epoch-making campaigns almost the first of the rulers of Byzantium to be *autokrator* [sole ruler] of the Romans in fact as well as in name, he had accomplished these and similar feats when he was still in the full vigour of his youth, but now in his declining years when old age was upon him, he seemed to have wearied of vigorous policies and to prefer to play off his enemies against one another'. As a result, Agathias continued, the officials who served around and under the emperor 'seized the opportunity afforded by this mood of apathy' to once more ignore imperial commands and begin to line their pockets at the empire's expense.[13]

The emperor's final years on the throne seem to have been marked by growing isolation, a tendency to rely on the advice of a small circle of old men, many of whom he had brought with him into the palace almost forty years earlier, and ever more pronounced religious fixations and intolerance.[14] As Procopius had realised, the emperor had always been willing to engage in slaughter to secure his place on the throne or in pursuit of dreams of imperial glory that were not necessarily shared by many of those he claimed to be 'liberating'. He fervently believed that such bloodshed was justified by the higher cause that he served, and he had a strong sense of personal providential mission. In his mind, he was motivated by piety and 'philanthropy' (although his enemies thought him more motivated by personal ambition and demonic forces). He had continued to secure his position against plots and conspiracies by ensuring that there was no clear favourite or heir to the throne, around whom hopes of regime change could coalesce. In many ways, he was the epitome not just of a Christian emperor, but also of the modern autocrat. What Justinian perhaps lacked—at least after the death of Theodora and towards the end of his reign—was the modern dictator's ruthlessness when it came to those suspected of conspiring against him. Only rarely were such individuals actually executed, perhaps by virtue of the emperor's determination to make a public display of the principles of Christian charity and forgiveness from which his late wife might well have dissuaded him. The emperor increasingly comported himself after the manner of the Christian holy men who had periodically frequented his court and sometimes berated him. In the aftermath of the major earthquake in 557, for example, we are told that 'the emperor did not wear his crown for forty days, and even on the holy birth of Christ he processed to Church without it. He stopped the customary luncheons in the Hall of the Nineteen Couches [the ceremonial dining hall in the Great Palace] and gave the money saved from this to the poor.'[15]

Justinian's reliance on elderly generals is particularly striking. Narses was well into his seventies when he secured and consolidated imperial control over Italy. Liberius must have been in his late eighties when he led an imperial expeditionary force to Spain. Belisarius was probably around sixty when Justinian called him out of retirement in 559 to help drive the Kutrigur Huns from Thrace. As a recent commentator has noted, 'Older men were both within Justinian's generation and thus more familiar to him, as well as too old to think about trying to supplant him,' although Belisarius remained younger in the 560s than Justin I had been when he had ascended the throne in 518, and so probably still needed to be watched. The emperor had attempted to insulate himself politically by favouring members of his own family: by the early 560s, two sons of Justinian's deceased cousin Germanus—named Justin and Justinian—and a nephew of the emperor's via his sister, Vigilantia, named Marcellus, were amongst the few generals of any significance from the younger generation. Another son of Vigilantia's—also named Justin—had been appointed to the important position at court of *curopalates* and was one of those despatched to arrest the unfortunate Pope Vigilius in 551.[16] Justin the general appears to have been especially highly regarded. Justinian's determination to appoint relatives to positions of influence and power did not necessarily mean that he had entirely lost his eye for talent.

Justinian had managed to outlive many of his fiercest critics and most stalwart opponents. It is clear, however, that many had grown tired of his austere and autocratic ways, and that manoeuvring was underway at court in anticipation of the emperor's death. It had to occur at some point, be it by fair means or foul. In the aftermath of the emperor's recovery from his headaches in 559–560, when rumours of his death had been rife on the streets of Constantinople, George and Aitherius, two high-ranking courtiers and senators, were accused of machinating to secure the throne for a certain Theodore, whose anticipated candidacy was also supported by the city prefect, Gerontius. After an investigation was speedily conducted, the supposed plotters were acquitted, but their chief accuser had his property confiscated and fled the city. The following year a full-blown mutiny by units of the palace guard stationed in Thrace, who had been subject to reductions in their pay, was narrowly averted through the intervention of the same Theodore who had recently been suspected of preparing to make a grab for the throne. Soon after that, a courtier named Zemarchus was denounced by two relatives of the empress Theodora for 'having made many terrible statements against the emperor'. At around the same time, there was a major resurgence of rioting and violence orchestrated by the Circus Factions, often, as we have seen, a sure sign that members of the court or Senate were jockeying for political position, trying to flex their muscles and buy up support on the streets of the capital.[17]

In November 562 a well-connected plot to assassinate the emperor was only thwarted at the last minute. Over the course of the preceding decades, the empire had found itself increasingly short of money. As a result, rates of taxation had risen dramatically from the 540s onwards.[18] By the 560s, even the emperor was beginning to feel the pinch, and he is reported to have extracted a series of forced loans from the banking community of Constantinople, which he used in part to pay for 'a display with lavish illuminations' to celebrate the dedication of a new church to the Holy Martyr Theodora.[19] Grievances over these loans on the part of some of the bankers combined with broader hostility towards the regime and the wish to place a new emperor on the throne. Matters came to a head when three men—a certain Ablabius, described as a 'former musical composer', probably associated with the Hippodrome and Circus Factions; a banker by the name of Marcellus; and Sergius, a nephew of the same Aitherius who had been implicated in the plot of 560—conspired to murder the emperor in the dining hall of the Great Palace at the end of his evening meal, assisted by contacts of theirs who worked there.[20]

One contemporary source reported that Ablabius had been paid the significant sum of 3,600 *solidi* to help execute Marcellus' plot, but had then let news of it slip to two high-ranking acquaintances. One of these men had first forewarned the emperor and then arrested the plotters, who were found to be carrying daggers and swords.[21] Marcellus immediately turned his blade on himself and died. Sergius was interrogated and, we are told, 'persuaded' to name as co-conspirators two other bankers as well as a member of the household of the retired general Belisarius. When these three individuals were arrested and interrogated in turn, they 'testified and gave evidence against the patrician Belisarius'.[22] Interestingly, the official charged with these investigations was a 'prefect' (meaning the urban prefect of Constantinople, which was a partly judicial post) named Procopius. Was this Procopius 'the prefect' the same man as Procopius the historian, who had previously served under but become disenchanted with Belisarius? We cannot know for sure, but it remains an intriguing possibility. We are told that many courtiers fled, and that the emperor announced a purge of the plotters at a meeting of the imperial advisory council, or *silentium*. Belisarius as well as the patriarch of Constantinople, Eutychius, who would appear to have been one of the general's allies, both attended.[23] The emperor ordered the removal of Belisarius' entire staff (probably meaning his military retainers, or *buccellarii*), and the retired general was placed under house arrest.[24]

Unfortunately, we know little about the investigations and manoeuvrings that ensued other than that within a matter of months, Belisarius had been rehabilitated and the urban prefect Procopius sacked. As Procopius left the palace for the last time, his successor was met with a barrage of stones, insults, and abuse, cast at him by members of the Green Faction.[25] Although Belisarius was once more 'received and given back all his honours', he would die less than two years later, with the imperial government once more taking control of his property.[26] It was rumoured that he had only been implicated in the plot to distract attention from the potential role played in it by Aitherius.[27] The latter was evidently an inveterate schemer: prior to the negotiation of peace with Persia in 561, he and a colleague had reputedly attempted to persuade Justinian to hire the services of an expert in black magic, one Masedes, who would be able to cast spells to ensure the destruction of the Persians as well as the emperor's other enemies. Predictably, the pious emperor was not impressed, and Aitherius and his sidekick were assured that imperial victory would be obtained through the aid of Jesus Christ, not Satan. According to one source, in a characteristically Justinianic exercise in 'housekeeping', the emperor then had Masedes burnt at the stake.[28]

There are hints that in the interim Aitherius had become an ally of the *curopalates*, Justin.[29] Had the emperor's own nephew perhaps known something of the plot against him in 562? With the main conspirators caught, it was perhaps in the interests of many of those around Justinian to persuade him to let the matter drop: at the ceremonial rededication of Hagia Sophia after its restoration in 562, the court poet Paul the Silentiary publicly praised Justinian for his clemency towards those who had recently conspired against him. As Paul declared, 'Best of men: you often moisten your gentle eyes with tears, in royal fashion, distressed on our behalf, particularly when you observe lack of self-control. . . . You release everyone from their evil debts, like God, and rush to forgive.'[30]

There can be little doubt, however, that Justinian's nephew, the *curopalates* Justin, tried to line himself up to succeed to the throne in 562. John of Ephesus records that a number of court officials, as well as Justin's wife, Sophia (a niece of Theodora's), made strenuous efforts at that time to persuade the emperor to formally appoint him as his deputy and heir by making him *Caesar*. Sophia is even reputed to have abandoned her previously well-known anti-Chalcedonian sympathies with a view to making herself more acceptable as a future empress.[31] Justinian, however, pointedly declined to do as he was asked (echoing his own uncle's reluctance to appoint him as co-ruler until the very last minute in 527).

As Sophia's tactical defection to the Chalcedonian party would suggest, manoeuvring at court appears to have increasingly involved members of the Church. This culminated on 22 January 565, when those around the emperor persuaded him to depose his hitherto scrupulously loyal patriarch, Eutychius. Supporters of the bishop would later claim that he had been removed from office because of his steadfast refusal to tolerate Justinian's toying with

Aphthartist doctrine, but, as one scholar has recently argued, we have no contemporary evidence to substantiate this claim.[32] Rather, the closer the emperor was perceived to be to death, the more politically sensitive the role of patriarch of Constantinople became, as the bishop was expected to bless and crown any successor to the throne. It may be significant in this context that the party sent to arrest Eutychius was led by the constantly scheming Aitherius, and that the newly appointed patriarch, John, was closely associated with the *curopalates*, Justin.[33]

'A GRIM ANACHRONISM'

On the night of 14 November 565, the emperor Justinian finally passed away, probably in his sleep. News of his demise was rapidly brought to the attention of his nephew, the courtier Justin, who rushed to the palace with his wife and a coterie of senatorial supporters. With Belisarius now dead, his chief rival for the throne was probably his cousin, the general Justin, whom Justinian had appointed as commander-in-chief of the Roman army in the Balkans (*magister militum per Illyriam*). He was currently away from Constantinople, keeping an eye on the Avars, who had recently established themselves north of the Danube.[34] As the accession of Justin I had demonstrated in 518, control of the palace was the key to securing the throne, and as *curopalates*, charged with overseeing its staffing and administration, the late emperor's nephew had both the palace complex and the narrative of Justinian's death firmly in hand. The previous year, he had appointed an ally of his as head of the palace guard (*comes excubitorum*).[35] It was claimed that Justinian had nominated the *curopalates* as heir with his dying breath. With another of his allies, the recently appointed patriarch of Constantinople, rapidly arriving on the scene, Justin was acclaimed as emperor by the guardsmen and senatorial supporters and blessed by

the bishop. He was then rushed to the Hippodrome to be presented
to and acclaimed by those members of the public who had gathered
as news of Justinian's death had spread.[36] The impression one derives
from the sources is of a carefully choreographed and prearranged
power grab on the part of Justin, which was speedily put into effect
before any other claimant could arrive on the scene. The stratagem
proved effective, but just to make sure, the new emperor would soon
arrange for the deaths of both his cousin, the general Justin, and
the slippery operator with whom he had machinated in the past, his
erstwhile ally Aitherius.[37]

We know of the immediate aftermath of Justinian's death
chiefly from an account of the new emperor Justin II's accession
written by the Latin court poet Corippus roughly a year after the
event had taken place. His aim, predictably, was to justify and legit-
imise Justin's new regime, and the author is at pains to emphasise
the fact that Justin and his supporters had secured a peaceful and
relatively straightforward transition of power. This was vital, for
news of the death of Justinian is likely to have caused considerable
anxiety and consternation. Bearing in mind that he had reigned
for almost forty years, many of the late emperor's subjects, both
in Constantinople and beyond, had never known a world without him. Corippus goes so far as to have Justin describe Justinian as 'the glorious father of the world'.[38] By the 560s, Justinian
was in many ways no longer a person, but an institution. In Constantinople, at least, he was the tree trunk that held aloft all the
branches of the imperial court and central administration. Many
must have been doubtful as to whether the system could survive
without him.[39]

There are hints in Corippus' account that the death of Justinian did indeed spark off mass mourning and near hysteria on the
streets of the imperial capital, after a manner highly reminiscent of
what has sometimes occurred in more modern totalitarian regimes
(one is reminded, for example, of the scenes associated with the

death of Stalin or Mao). As Corippus put it, 'The awesome death of the man showed by clear signs that he had conquered the world. He alone, amidst universal lamentations, seemed to rejoice in his pious countenance.' The poet paints a vivid picture of the emperor's funeral cortège making its way along the streets of Constantinople: 'Who', he wrote, 'can enumerate the wonders of so great a procession? On one side a venerable line of singing deacons, on the other a choir of virgins sang: their voices reached the sky. Tears flowed like snow: the clothes of everyone were wet with the rain, and their streaming eyes swam in their own moisture and watered their faces and breasts. . . . Many burned pious incense for his passing. From all sides the sad people came running in their anxiety to look.' As the procession went on, he recounted, 'All [were united in] one love, in all one rightful grief increased their tears . . . until they came to the halls of the Church of the Holy Apostles and had laid his honoured limbs in the holy tomb which the emperor had himself earlier built from pure gold.'[40] Within the church where he had prayed at the tomb of Theodora some six years earlier, the emperor was now once more united with his beloved wife.

Corippus' description of both the body and the burial of Justinian is fascinating on many levels, for just as the emperor had increasingly adopted the persona of a Christian 'holy man', so, too, was his body described as if it were a miraculous and saintly relic.[41] The poet writes of how Justinian's corpse kept 'the last marks of his life, not changing his colour in death, but shining with his accustomed brightness'. Later, he describes how it seemed 'changed by death into an angelic form'. Justin is depicted as declaring to his late uncle, 'We weep from sorrow, and grieve with all the force of our mind. You, father, are happy, most holy one, amid the holy throng of angels, and having left your body behind you, you now see God.' At the same time, the court propagandist is eager to convey that the felling of the great Roman oak that was Justinian had not brought the rest of the imperial canopy crashing down: rather, the emperor's body was 'like a tree in the middle of the meadows, a welcome haunt of birds', around which, after it had fallen down due to its age, 'all around the chattering birds fly and perch, mourning and grieving that they have lost their former seat', until they 'decide that they must find another tree for their new nests'.[42]

Justinian's funeral was also a celebration of the late emperor's military achievements. Corippus narrates how the new empress, Sophia, brought a fine shroud to the event which she must have had made some time in advance. It was 'interwoven with precious purple, where the whole series of Justinian's achievement was picked out in woven gold and glittered with gems. On one side the artist had cleverly depicted with his sharp needle barbarian phalanxes bending their necks, slaughtered kings and subject peoples in order. And he had made the yellow gold stand out from the colours, so that everyone looking at it thought they were real bodies. The faces were in gold, the blood in purple.' Justinian was depicted on the shroud 'as a victor in the midst of his court, trampling on the bold neck of the Vandal king'. A female figure meant to personify the city of Rome was represented 'holding out her arms and displaying her naked breast, her bosom bared, the ancient parent of empire and liberty'. According to the poet, 'The energetic Sophia ordered this to be made so that at the time of death they might take to the imperial tomb a royal funeral procession adorned with its own triumphs.'[43]

As a great expert on the Age of Justinian has commented of this depiction: 'Although ecstatic and hopeful early in his reign, the mood at Constantinople had changed by the end of Justinian's life to one of angry frustration. Justinian's funeral pall . . . embroidered with scenes of his military triumphs in the 530s . . . must have seemed a grim anachronism to the mourners who laid him to rest.'[44] Certainly, news of Justinian's death was far from uniformly received with the 'one rightful grief', claimed by Corippus. Nor was it universally accepted that he would end up in heaven.

Writing in Antioch, the late sixth-century Church historian Evagrius (an admiring reader of Procopius) noted: 'Thus indeed Justinian, after filling absolutely everywhere with confusion and
turmoil, and collecting the wages for this at the conclusion to his
life, passed over to the lowest places of punishment.'[45] To Evagrius,
Justinian had quite rightly ended up in hell.

THE PRICE OF SUCCESS?

Justinian's reign had been one of breathtaking ambition and considerable achievement. He and his advisers had restored direct Roman
rule over much of the Mediterranean, significantly advanced Roman
interests in the Caucasus, overhauled the structures of government,
and imposed order on Roman law. The emperor had rebuilt the
monumental heart of the capital, and had helped give much greater
theological clarity and definition to imperial orthodoxy. From his
family's modest background in the war-torn landscape of Illyricum,
Justinian had not only secured his place on the throne, but held
on to it for longer than any Roman emperor before him except for
Augustus (r. 31 BCE–14 CE) and Theodosius II (r. 402–450 CE).[46]
This, as we have seen, was not for want of efforts to depose him. He
and his court had also managed the notable feat of steadying the
ship of the Roman state and holding it together when it was buffeted
by a series of extraordinary natural cataclysms and disasters: sudden climate change, earthquakes, and, of course, plague. But at what
price had this success come?

In the half century that followed Justinian's death, the empire
would suffer a series of near-fatal blows. To the West, many of the
emperor's reconquests would prove to be remarkably short-lived.
In around 568, bands of Lombards began to migrate into northern Italy to settle. There are hints that Justinian's commander in
the region, Narses, initially welcomed them, hoping to make use of

their military skill. But before the imperial authorities knew what was happening, much of the peninsula had once more slipped out of the empire's control. Autonomous Lombard 'duchies' emerged from the old Gothic heartlands in the north, spreading as far south as Beneventum. In Spain, the Visigoths once more united behind their kings, and by around 625 Roman forces had been driven out. As the contemporary Spanish author Isidore of Seville wrote, 'Subjected, the Roman soldier now serves the Goths.'[47]

Likewise, by the 580s the empire had lost control over much of the Balkan Peninsula.[48] Late in his reign, Justinian had made contact with the Avars, who were fleeing the dramatic expansion of the Turk Empire to the East. By the 560s, they had established themselves north of the Danube, and upon Justinian's death an Avar embassy arrived in Constantinople demanding payments and subsidies from the new ruler.[49] As relations between the Romans and Avars deteriorated, the nomads began to apply massive pressure on Roman territory in the northern Balkan zone, seizing and sacking cities such as Sirmium, and besieging Thessalonica. At the same time, growing numbers of Slavs began to strike ever further south, even reaching Greece and the Peloponnese. Ominously for the Romans, they were now doing so not just to raid, but increasingly to settle.[50] Across the Balkan Peninsula as a whole, by the end of the sixth century a chronic state of military insecurity had come to prevail. This can be seen from the archaeological evidence that survives from Justiniana Prima. The city built to celebrate the site of Justinian's birth was reduced to ash and rubble at some point in the late sixth or early seventh century. On the foundations of the structures that once stood alongside the city's episcopal complex, it is still possible to discern the scorch marks probably left when the city was put to flame by the invaders. These 'burn layers' (as archaeologists describe them) provide vivid testimony to the 'reversal of fortunes' to which Justinian's empire would ultimately be subject.[51]

Further east, collapse would come later, but would prove to

be equally dramatic. A sudden revival of warfare with Persia in the 570s would lead to the Roman loss of Dara, which had been the 'jewel in the crown' of Justinian's eastern defences. In response, the emperor Justin II is reported to have suffered a mental break-down, and the reins of power had to be passed to General Tiberius (whom Justin had appointed head of the palace guard prior to Justinian's death). A civil war which broke out in the empire in 602 would then open the way to full-blown invasion; as a result, the armies of the Persian shah, Khusro II, were able to attack and conquer Roman Syria, Palestine, and Egypt. In 626, the Persians and Avars even joined forces, to launch a joint assault on Constantinople itself. Although this effort failed, and the Roman emperor at that time, Heraclius (r. 610–641), was able to reverse the Persian gains through a remarkable feat of generalship, the empire was much weakened. In the 630s, Syria, Egypt, and Palestine would be conquered once more, this time by the Arabs, who had been united in the nascent faith of Islam by the Prophet Muhammad. They not only drove the Romans back into Anatolia but also destroyed the ancient empire of Persia. By the late 690s the Arabs managed to drive the Romans out of North Africa, capturing Carthage in 698. In any case, much of the hinterland of the territory had long since come under the control of the local Berber tribes.[52]

Within roughly a century of Justinian's accession to the throne, therefore, much of the Eastern Roman Empire had unravelled. The issue that historians have long debated is whether Justinian's programme of imperial renewal was in some sense responsible for the empire's subsequent crisis and contraction. In particular, had the emperor's western forays led to a dangerous overexpansion? As my essay question at Oxford in 1991 had asked, 'Did Justinian ruin the empire he set out to restore?' My tutor at the time had probably been asked to answer the same question twenty years earlier. I still pose it to students of my own more than three decades on.

'BURDENED WITH INNUMERABLE DEBTS'

In order to come to terms with Justinian's legacy, it is worth considering what his immediate successor made of his reign. Despite the protestations of filial sorrow upon news of the emperor's death, the new ruler, Justin II, adopted a tone that was highly critical of his late uncle. In particular, he claimed that Justinian had left the imperial government teetering on the verge of bankruptcy. As such, his criticisms chimed with those which had been made earlier by the likes of Procopius and Agathias. According to Corippus' account, Justin declared to the senators who had assembled for his coronation, 'Many things were too much neglected while my father [Justinian] was still alive and as a result the exhausted treasury contracted many debts. . . . The old man no longer cared. He was altogether cold and only grew warm with love of another life. All his mind was fixed on heaven . . . and . . . he emptied the resources of the exhausted treasury.'[53] In one of his earliest laws, Justin II declared that upon his accession to the throne he had found 'the treasury burdened with innumerable debts and heading towards utter destitution'. He bemoaned the impact of such fiscal exhaustion on the army and on the empire's ability to withstand the enemy: 'For lack of necessities', he asserted, 'it [the army] has reached the point of collapse, with the result that the state is suffering from innumerable attacks and incursions by barbarians.'[54]

At the same time, the new emperor attempted to rebuild bridges with members of the senatorial and provincial aristocracy, towards whom Justinian had been consistently antagonistic.[55] Justin II reversed a number of Justinian's legislative measures. Repealing one of his predecessor's more austere pieces of marriage legislation (which had effectively made it impossible for couples to separate by mutual consent), Justin II included in his law what amounted to a critique of the Justinianic project as a whole. Justinian, he declared, had 'in piety and virtue surpassed all previous sovereigns'. But he had been incapable of appreciating the weakness and frailty of the human condition, and as a result had simply demanded too much of people. This was a criticism, interestingly, that Justinian had momentarily levelled against himself. In a law issued in 553, he had reversed one of his own earlier provincial reforms on the grounds that petitions from the locals had convinced him that 'they could not bear the burden of the government devised by us'.[56]

It would be unwise to dismiss Justin's claims that the empire was in a precarious financial situation by the second half of the sixth century as mere self-serving rhetoric. There had been signs of growing fiscal instability on the part of the East Roman state from the 540s onwards, and these financial difficulties were bound in the end to have a negative impact both on military fortunes along the empire's frontiers and on political conditions in the capital. The civil war of 602 would break out after the reigning emperor, Maurice (r. 582–602), was deposed and murdered by soldiers furious at his efforts to cut military pay and restrain expenditure.[57] But can we blame Justinian for this fiscal frailty and its military and political consequences? The answer is clearly no. Justinian and his financial officials (such as John the Cappadocian and Peter Barsymes) had strained every nerve to maximise the tax revenues that accrued to the imperial coffers in Constantinople. Initially they had sought to achieve this by cracking down on corruption, then by increasing tax rates.[58] If the empire was short of funds by the late sixth century, it was probably largely due to the repeated bouts of bubonic plague the empire experienced from the 540s onwards. As a result of the plague, the number of taxpayers on whom the state could rely is likely to have been dramatically reduced, whilst the demands made of the state remained at least constant. That serious difficulties ensued should not, therefore, surprise us. Justinian and Peter Barsymes were arguably responsible for the fact that what had followed the initial impact of the plague was a fiscal crisis rather than a total financial collapse.[59] Justin II, by contrast, would make the empire's financial predicament considerably worse, by abandoning many of Justinian's anti-corruption measures and giving tax handouts to his senatorial friends.[60]

Nor can Justinian reasonably be accused of having engaged in military overreach to the West, and thereby having weakened the defences of the East. The armies sent West with Belisarius in the 530s were not particularly large, and only a small number of the troops deployed there had been redeployed from the East. At no point, in other words, had the needs of the eastern frontier ever been neglected for the sake of Justinian's western adventures. The East was always the chief priority, as it was from that direction that the Romans faced their most prestigious and dangerous foe in the form of the Sasanian Empire of Persia. It was to the East, one should note, that Justinian's great equestrian statue in Constantinople faced, and it was against the Persians that the emperor was depicted in that statue raising his hand, ordering the barbarians to advance no further.[61] Procopius' complaint was not that Justinian had committed too many resources to the West, but too few.

The territories that the empire conquered in North Africa, Sicily, Italy, and southern Spain, moreover, were amongst the wealthiest that had dropped out of direct Roman rule in the fifth century. These were of course highly taxable, and it was not an unrealistic expectation that they would make a net contribution to imperial coffers in the future (indeed, in the mid-seventh century, the emperor Constans II would base himself in Sicily precisely so as to harness the economic resources of the empire's remaining African and Italian possessions against the Arabs).[62] If the empire was faced with troop shortages in the late sixth century (as, for example, Agathias claimed), then the bubonic plague is again likely to have been the main cause.[63]

It has also sometimes been suggested that Justinian's failure to heal the rift with the miaphysites was partly responsible for
the later crisis of the empire in the seventh century, as alienated
anti-Chalcedonian communities would end up welcoming first
Persian and then Arab invaders as liberators, freeing them from
the rule of heretical emperors.[64] This argument, too, needs to be
handled with caution. No emperor made as concerted an effort as
Justinian to find a theological resolution to the Chalcedonian dispute. It is true that by driving the followers of Severus and other
anti-Chalcedonian factions out of the episcopacy, he forced the
miaphysites to press ahead with creating their own independent and
separate Church hierarchies. But the fact remains that the emperor
Heraclius received enthusiastic support against the Persians from
many miaphysites in Armenia and the Caucasus in the 620s, and
a good number of them subsequently also allied themselves with
Constantinople against the Arabs.[65]

Nowhere in the Roman Near East could it be said that the con-
quering Arab armies of the seventh century enjoyed widespread
Christian support. It is true that Justinian's religious policies probably did turn many of his Jewish subjects against the empire, and
that this did have military consequences in the seventh century, but
these were not sufficient to explain the Arab conquests as a whole.[66]
Nor, of course, did Justinian play any direct role in the emergence
of Islam, although the rivalry between Rome and Persia that characterised much of the sixth century did play a vital role in creating
the religious and political conditions in southern and central Arabia
out of which Islam would emerge.[67]

Ultimately, Justinian's ability to fully realise his vision of empire
was severely constrained by a number of factors which simply could
not be overcome. These were determined primarily by the inherent
limitations of autocracy in a premodern society and the core internal
paradoxes of imperial power.[68] In terms of tax and administration,

for example, Justinian was never able to surmount the fundamental problem that the same officials, administrators, and landowners on whom he was dependent for the implementation of his policies at a local level were frequently precisely the same people his legislation was seeking to target. The residents of Aphrodito in Egypt had repeatedly petitioned Justinian to intervene on their behalf, to protect their village against the depredations of local landowners. But as the emperor himself admitted, the ruses of the locally powerful proved stronger than his commands, and the imperial officials on the ground could not be persuaded to act. Likewise, when it came to matters of faith, he could force individual bishops out of the Church, but he could not force people to think as he wished them to. Perhaps he would have done well to listen to the words of the Gothic king Theoderic, whose realm he destroyed, who had famously declared that 'nobody can be made to believe against his will'.[69]

Beyond that, the great unravelling that the empire would experience from the second half of the sixth century was largely the result of circumstances that were entirely beyond the emperor's control: an initial period of climate disruption, followed by plague, and—crucially—the renewed era of instability across the Eurasian steppe that had led to the westward flight of the Avars. There was nothing that Justinian could have done to prevent the Avars (like the Huns before them) from heading westwards to the lands north of the Danube. Once it was clear that they were on the move, it was entirely sensible for him to attempt to forge an alliance with them against the Slavs, who posed a burgeoning threat to Roman positions. It was primarily the consolidation of Avar power north of the Danube in the 560s that served to undermine the Roman position in northern Italy, as the Lombards appear to have made their way into Roman territory there to escape Avar domination.[70] The same 'push factor' is likely to have informed the decision of many Slavs to begin to settle in Roman territory in the Balkans from the 580s onwards.

In both the Balkans and Italy, dramatically changed circumstances combined to undo many of Justinian's military achievements. As the emperor had remarked in a law issued in 538, 'Virtually nothing on earth remains the same, but nature is constantly flowing in numerous irresistible twists and turns that cannot easily be foreseen or foretold.'[71]

Chapter 17

Imperial Legacies

LIFE AND AFTERLIFE

Throughout his reign Justinian had elicited strong and contradictory emotions, and the same would be true of his legacy after his death. Predictably, many of his greatest admirers were to be found in the Church. In the late seventh century, Pope Agatho in Rome wrote of how 'the blessed memory of Justinian is to this day honoured by all nations. He was the king who more than any other kings became a zealot of the truth. . . . His orthodox faith, which has been spread to the whole world through his respected edicts is glorified. . . . This great Justinian [was] the last but the greatest of all [emperors], whose virtue and piety renewed all things for the better.'[1] Others, however, would long continue to criticise the consequences of the emperor's constant interfering and meddling. The Byzantine emperor Leo VI (r. 886–912) censured Justinian for having issued so much legislation (in the form of his *Novels*) after his codification of Roman law was supposedly complete. The result, he argued, had been to sow confusion rather than bring clarity.[2]

What difference did Justinian as an individual actually make to the world in which he lived? Probably as much of a difference as any emperor could.[3] It is true that in foreign affairs (the empire's relations with Persia, the Caucasus, and the kingdoms of the West), there were deep-rooted continuities between his policies and those of Anastasius and Justin I. His investment in the defensive infrastructure of the Balkans and the Roman Near East clearly followed in the footsteps of those who had gone before him. Moreover, given the sudden revival of warfare with Persia, almost any emperor would have felt obliged to overhaul the fiscal and military infrastructure of the Roman state, just as other emperors might have been tempted to take advantage of dynastic disputes in the barbarian kingdoms of Africa, Italy, and Spain to restore imperial control. Justinian was not the first emperor to try to unite the Church and advance its interests, nor would he be the last. Emperors both before and after him supported the promulgation of the Christian faith beyond the empire's frontiers, as well as reform of the law at home.[4]

But Justinian pursued these policies with unmatched intensity and determination, harnessing the talent of his generals in the field and his advisers at court (Belisarius, Tribonian, John the Cappadocian, Theodore Ascidas, and others). For the most active period of his reign, his was also effectively a joint rule sustained, supported, and often given direction and focus by the indomitable Theodora. If we can speak of an 'Age of Justinian', then it was her 'Age' too.[5] But, above all, Justinian's fascination with law and theology inspired and sustained many of the policies that would contribute to his most lasting legacies—ones that would prove to be far more enduring than any of the emperor's military achievements. Under his patronage, we see the last (and perhaps greatest) efflorescence of Roman legal thought, and a brilliant distillation of a thousand years of jurisprudence which would determine the form in which Roman legal culture would be transmitted to posterity, not only within the empire but far beyond. The emperor also stimulated and contributed to one of the most creative moments in the history of Christian religious thinking, drawing upon the rich intellectual heritage of the Greek philosophical tradition to give greater conceptual complexity and nuance to the faith, and defining how Christian orthodoxy would be received in the Middle Ages to both East and West. He encouraged his architects in the construction of what would prove to be the greatest church building in the medieval Christian world, and one which would change architecture forever. And the events of his reign gave rise to some of the finest literature that would ever be written in the Greek language. The historian Procopius of Caesarea may have been a bitter and disillusioned critic of the emperor, but without the wars which Justinian initiated, what would the author have had to work with? For good or ill, Procopius ultimately owed his inspiration to Justinian.

It is often assumed that the sixth century witnessed a narrowing of intellectual horizons. On the contrary, the literature produced in Constantinople under Justinian and in response to his policies would suggest that the emperor presided over and galvanized an era of remarkable originality and creativity which would continue after his reign. What brought this wave of creativity to an end was not Justinian's supposed totalitarian tendencies, but the cultural dislocation and damage caused by first Persian and then Arab invaders in the seventh, eighth, and ninth centuries. Justinian had encouraged the Christianisation of the empire's intellectual culture, just as through his church-building he had made a fundamental contribution to the more full-blown Christianisation of the 'townscape' of Constantinople. But at the same time, other individuals attached to his court sought to protect and defend core elements of the empire's inherited intellectual high culture from the criticism of the most extreme Christian hardliners, who believed that only

'Bible learning' was true learning.[6] Justinian may have been a zealot, but he was not a narrow-minded one, and his court embraced individuals of diverse opinion and background. The emperor liked to discuss and debate topics ranging from the divine to the mundane and surrounded himself with people whose ideas he thought were interesting and worthwhile.[7]

MEMORY AND IMAGINATION

It is easy for us to assume that subsequent medieval rulers, both of Byzantium and elsewhere, were profoundly influenced by Justinian, and that they took him as a model of how to rule. Many of them undoubtedly were and did, regarding him as the epitome of the active and pious emperor. Yet, perhaps ironically, given how much propaganda Justinian's court had promulgated, and how determined the emperor had been to advertise his own name, even in Constantinople this was not always the case.[8] Rather, in Byzantium, as elsewhere, Justinian's legacy would be mediated primarily through his works rather than through an immutable memory of him as a man. The fact that the emperor had died still at odds with elements of the imperial Church would complicate his memory. There are hints that he was regarded as a saint as early as the seventh century (and both he and Theodora are venerated within the Eastern Orthodox tradition today), but that status was highly contested.[9] As we have seen, many who had lived through Justinian's reign had learned to hate him: one man's saint remained another man's demon.

Devotion to the memory of Justinian would, understandably, be at its most intense in Constantinople. The medieval city that pilgrims and other visitors would have encountered for almost the next one thousand years was substantially the city as it stood after Justinian's reconstruction of it, with the magnificent dome of Hagia Sophia and Justinian's towering equestrian statue dominating its skyline.[10] It is clear that an appreciation of these lasting works informed the manner in which some, at least, thought the emperor should be viewed. In the tenth century, a fine mosaic was erected above an arch in the vestibule of Hagia Sophia. The image is still visible today. In the main panel, it depicts the Virgin Mary (the 'Theotokos'), who since the fifth century had come to be regarded as the divine patron of the imperial capital. To her left, the emperor Constantine can be seen, bowing his head and presenting the Virgin with the city as a gift. To her right stands an elderly Justinian, his hair and beard shaggy and grey, his head similarly inclined, the Church of Hagia Sophia depicted in his hands, being offered up to the Mother of God. By putting Justinian in the place of honour to the Virgin's right, the mosaic artist conveyed the message that Justinian was greater even than Constantine (who was universally regarded as a saint 'equal to the Apostles').[11]

Justinian would be remembered in Byzantium for his monuments and building work, for his devotion to the faith and contribution to Christian doctrine, and as a legislator. Indeed, the legislation which the emperor issued and his codification of Roman law (soon translated in its entirety into Greek) would constitute not just the bedrock and foundation, but the main body, of both Byzantine secular and canon (or ecclesiastical) law for the rest of the empire's history.[12] Subsequent emperors added to or further condensed it, but Justinian's legal achievement was never supplanted. It would be transmitted from Constantinople to the world of the Orthodox Slavs as they progressively adopted Christianity in the centuries that followed.[13]

The emperor would also, to some extent, be remembered as a conqueror. But it is interesting that Justinian's wars of western reconquest (which feature so prominently in modern assessments of his reign) received relatively little attention from the sixth-century chronicler John Malalas, who wrote in a more accessible form of Greek than Procopius did and thus could inform a larger, though perhaps politically less well-connected, readership. The campaigns featured in the ninth century in an influential chronicle written by the monk Theophanes, which drew upon the writings of Procopius, but thereafter Byzantine authors (largely under this Procopian influence), tended to ascribe Justinian's victories to Belisarius, around whom a body of sometimes highly imaginative romantic literature would develop.[14] Justinian's wars had mattered to Procopius because he had participated in them, and because they offered him an opportunity to display his remarkable literary talent. It is conceivable that many of Justinian's subjects and their descendants were far less interested in the emperor's military achievements than has sometimes been supposed. Later generations of Byzantines tended to read Procopius not because they were interested in what he wrote about, but primarily because of how he wrote it. He was regarded as a master of style.[15]

The memory of Justinian was embedded in the minds of many of the emperors who ruled in Constantinople in the centuries that followed. To them, as Cyril Mango put it, the Christian empire of Justinian came to serve as a 'mirage . . . an ideal to be striven for but never attained'.[16] For their subjects, it was probably a different matter. It is striking, for example, that an eighth-century guide to the monuments of the city, full of antiquarian detail and lore, seems poorly informed on the emperor (though the author does name him alongside Constantine as a 'new Apostle'). There were moments in the thirteenth and fifteenth centuries when viewers of the emperor's equestrian statue seemed unsure whether the figure depicted on horseback on top of the column was Justinian, Heraclius, or Constantine.[17] At times even popular memory of the emperor's patronage of Hagia Sophia appeared to be on the verge of oblivion: in the ninth century, after the dissolute emperor Michael III (r. 866–867) was heard boasting that he would be eternally remembered because of an especially fine set of stables he had had built, he was reminded by a member of his entourage that 'Justinian built the Great Church embellishing it with gold, silver, and precious pearls but now his memory does not exist any longer, and you, emperor, having built a place for the dung and a repose of horses claim to be remembered for it?'[18]

Most of the inhabitants of medieval Constantinople probably had better things to do than worry about who had built what, and the literary tastes and historical interests of even members of the better-educated classes were almost certainly far more lowbrow than is sometimes imagined. It puts the long-term effectiveness of some of Justinian's efforts at self-aggrandizement into perspective that one of the episodes dating from his reign that would most often be repeated in subsequent Byzantine chronicles, from the sixth century onwards, was not Belisarius' conquest of Africa, or the emperor's codification of Roman law, but rather the arrival in Antioch in the year 530 of a performing dog.[19] Amongst the clever canine's tricks was the ability to identify coins issued by different emperors, and to spot and point out pregnant women, and adulterers, from amongst its highly entertained but no doubt somewhat nervous audience.

To whatever extent memories of Justinian in Constantinople and the broader Byzantine world beyond the capital would wax and wane between the sixth century and the fifteenth, the monuments he built in the 'sovereign city' (as he had referred to it in his laws) would remain central to the identity and morale of its inhabitants and hold an especially totemic status in the minds of Orthodox Christians (both Greek-speaking and Slavonic). When, in the fourteenth century, the orb (by that point thought to be an apple) was reported to have fallen from the hand of Justinian's equestrian statue, this was interpreted by many commentators as a sign of impending doom.[20] On 29 May 1453, as Ottoman troops broke through the walls of the city, many of its inhabitants took refuge within the walls of Justinian's Great Church of Hagia Sophia, where it was believed by some that they would be saved by angels. The angels never came, however. After the invaders successfully stormed the building (and slaughtered those inside), the twenty-one-year-old Ottoman sultan Mehmed II made his way to the Great Church and decreed that it was to be immediately turned into a mosque—as it is again today. As his *muezzin* issued the Islamic declaration of faith from the pulpit, the sultan clambered onto the stripped altar to lead prayers. After giving due thanks to Allah for his victory, Mehmed is reported to have paid a visit to the ruined halls of the old palace complex nearby, where Justinian had once stalked the corridors. There he whispered the words of a Persian poet: 'The spider weaves the curtains in the palace of the Caesars; the owl calls the watches in Afrasiab's towers.'[21]

Even before the Ottoman conquest of the city, Justinian's legacy to the Islamic world was already a significant one. Scholars of early Islamic history have become increasingly aware in recent years of the fundamental contributions of Justinianic law to the ideological and legal development of the Umayyad Caliphate of the seventh and eighth centuries. Ideas derived from Justinian's legislation influenced the caliphate as it consolidated Islamic rule over the lands of the Near East and as Islam itself continued to take shape as a religion.[22] In the world of the caliphate, for example, the Muslims effectively ruled as a privileged caste over communities of non-Muslims granted the status of *dhimmi*—subject peoples accorded rights, but fewer than those that Muslims enjoyed, and excluded from certain privileges and professions. It is likely that this system evolved from the 'confessional state' that Justinian had established in many of the lands that the Arabs had now come to rule (in Syria, Palestine, and Egypt). The difference was that Orthodox Christians were now numbered amongst the subjugated rather than the privileged. When, in the sixteenth century, the Ottoman sultan Suleiman 'the Magnificent' codified Ottoman law after a manner reminiscent of the codification of Justinian, he was accorded the epithet *kanuni* (lawgiver), ultimately derived from a Byzantine Greek word for 'rule' or 'law' (*kanon*).[23]

Within the Ottoman Empire, Mehmed's decision to turn Hagia Sophia into a mosque—even (uniquely) preserving its original Christian name—would have far-reaching consequences.[24] It meant that the architectural style that Justinian and his engineers had pioneered was established as the prestige style for mosque decoration throughout the Ottoman Empire thereafter. Mehmed II himself copied it in the great mosque (known as the Fatih Cami) that he built on the site of the Church of the Holy Apostles, which he flattened. Likewise, Suleiman *kanuni* deliberately sought to emulate the internal appearance of Hagia Sophia by collecting different marble columns from across the empire for the new mosque he constructed. Through his Great Church, therefore, Justinian's influence lived on in Constantinople despite the end of the empire to which he had been so devoted. His equestrian statue and its column, however, were torn down. According to a legend in circulation amongst the surviving Greek population of Constantinople in the sixteenth century, Mehmed II personally destroyed the statue with his own mace. After he had done so, Greek onlookers pointed out to him that the statue had acted as a talisman, protecting the city against plague. That very year, pestilence struck, and the sultan fled to Bursa.[25] Given that Justinian's statue had been put up in the city just after the bubonic plague had first arrived in Constantinople in the early 540s, the idea that it had provided the population with protection against disease may well have been rooted in a genuine folk memory.[26]

THE VIEW FROM THE WEST

The memory of Justinian in the early medieval West would initially prove to be both patchy and mixed. Our chief witness to sixth-century Frankish history—Gregory of Tours—has relatively little to say about him, whilst the seventh-century Spanish historian Isidore of Seville is positively hostile. This is not perhaps surprising. Isidore was strongly opposed to the imperial presence in Hispania and celebrated its liquidation in the 620s (despite his own family probably being of eastern origin).[27] Likewise, at the end of Justinian's reign the empire had been locked in military conflict with the Franks in northern Italy, so Gregory would hardly have been inclined to go out of his way to praise the late ruler.[28] The eighth-century English historian Bede barely mentions him.[29]

The most fulsome early medieval western account of his reign is to be found in the writings of the eighth-century Italian historian Paul the Deacon. Paul's enthusiasm for Justinian is especially noteworthy, not least because he regarded himself to be of Lombard descent. In Paul's view, Justinian had guided the Roman Empire 'with good fortune. For he was prosperous in waging wars and admirable in civil matters.' Summarizing Justinian's military victories, he wrote, 'For by Belisarius, the patrician, he vigorously subdued the Persians and by the same Belisarius he reduced to utter destruction the nation of the Vandals, captured their king Gelimer, and restored Africa to the Roman Empire after ninety-six years. Again, by the power of Belisarius, he overcame the nation of the Goths in Italy and took captive Witigis their king. He subdued the Moors who afterwards infested Africa. . . . In like manner too, he subjugated other nations by right of war.' For these achievements, Paul believed Justinian 'deserved to have his surnames, and be called *Alamanicus, Gothicus, Francicus, Germanicus, Anticus, Alanicus, Vandalicus,* and *Africanus*'.[30]

Paul went on to praise Justinian for his legal reforms, and noted approvingly that 'the same Emperor also built within the city of Constantinople to Christ our Lord, who is the wisdom of God the Father, a church which is called by the Greek name *Hagia Sophia,* that is "Divine Wisdom". The workmanship of this so far excels that of all other buildings that in all the regions of the earth its like cannot be found. This Emperor in fact was Catholic in faith, upright in his deeds, just in his judgements, and therefore to him all things came together for good.'³¹ Essentially the same assessment of Justinian would be repeated in the twelfth century by the polymathic Austrian bishop Otto of Freising, who narrated in his chronicle how 'this most zealous Christian monarch resurrected his domain, as it were, from the dead'.³²

Given the fact that he had humiliated Pope Vigilius and forced his condemnation of the 'Three Chapters' on the Church in the West, Justinian was also surprisingly well regarded by the *Liber Pontificalis* (*Book of the Pontiffs*), our chief source from the city of Rome. Here, he is described as 'a devout man with the highest of love for the Christian religion' and 'a most pious emperor'. In the seventh century and thereafter, Frankish sources would relate a series of legends concerning Justinian's close friendship with Belisarius, including an account repeating the claim that they had met their future wives, Theodora and Antonina, jointly on a night out in a brothel. The women, in one version, supposedly belonged to the gigantic race of the Amazons.³³ In that sense, the fable probably caught something of Theodora's character, if not quite her diminutive physical stature.

Justinian's building works and other sites associated with him would exercise considerable fascination in the West across the Middle Ages. It has been argued that the palace of the first Frankish emperor, Charlemagne, built in Aachen in the 790s, was modelled on the Church of San Vitale in Ravenna, with its magnificent and still luminous mosaics of Justinian and Theodora.³⁴ Pilgrims and Crusaders who passed through Constantinople, or western knights who spent time serving under Byzantine emperors there, would bring back memories and descriptions of the monuments built by Justinian. The author of the fourteenth-century *Travels of Sir John Mandeville*, for example, one of the most popular and fantastical pieces of late medieval 'travel literature' (supposedly penned by a knight from my hometown of St Albans), contains a fascinating description of Constantinople that was clearly composed after

Justinian's equestrian statue had dropped its *globus cruciger*: 'There [in Constantinople] is the best kirk [church] of the world and the fairest, and it is of Saint Sophia. And before the kirk of Saint Sophia is an image of Justinian the emperor, well over-gilded; and it is made sitting upon a horse and crowned. This image was wont to hold in its hand a round apple of gold; but it is long since it fell out of the hand. And men say that the falling out of the apple is a token that the emperor has lost a great part of his lordship.'[35] But in the West, as in the East, the most important aspects of Justinian's legacy would be mediated through politics, culture, and law rather than through direct memory.

Paradoxically, one of Justinian's most significant contributions to the development of the medieval West was his role in the creation of the papacy. Despite having humiliated Pope Vigilius and forced his theological will on Italy and Africa, in his so-called 'Pragmatic Sanction', the emperor had treated the pope, and not the Senate, as the main point of contact between the city of Rome and the imperial authorities.[36] Many senators, of course, had fled the city, but they would have returned had it been worth their while. Justinian had also confirmed the pope's status as the primary interlocutor between Constantinople and what Justinian had referred to as 'all known inhabitants of the West'.[37] The medieval papacy, which would reach the height of its powers as a 'papal monarchy' in the eleventh century, could ultimately be seen as a product of Justinian's political and religious agenda. The greatest of early medieval popes, Gregory I, who would do much at the end of the sixth century to develop the institutional reach of the papacy and who was its finest theologian, was a committed advocate of Justinian's 'Neo-Chalcedonian' doctrine.[38]

Justinian's legal contribution to the West was also immense. The emperor had intended that his reformed body of law should apply to the empire as a whole. As a result, just as efforts had to be made to translate the *Digest* and *Institutes* into Greek, for the benefit of

Greek-speaking students, so, too, did legal scholars in Constantinople translate Justinian's *Novels* (which had mostly been written in Greek) into Latin.[39] In the late 550s, a scholar known as Julian, who was described as 'a most illustrious professor from Constantinople', produced a Latin epitome of Justinian's legislation covering the period from 534 to about 557.[40] This text would appear to have then made its way to Rome, where, along with another translation of the *Novels*, known as the *Authenticum* ('The Real Thing'), it seems to have formed the basis of a programme of legal education at a functioning school of Justinianic Roman law that operated in the city down to the eighth century, presumably with papal support.[41] From there, knowledge of Justinianic Roman law radiated westwards, mediated by the papacy and through canon law. Until the eleventh century, it was primarily through Julian's *Epitome* of Justinian's *Novels* that Roman law would be known there.[42]

Justinianic Roman law was thus never completely lost in the medieval West. Indeed, a unique sixth-century manuscript of Justinian's *Digest*, which probably originated in Ravenna and then made its way to Amalfi, has revealed that the emperor's great distillation of Roman legal science remained in continuous circulation in southern Italy from the sixth to twelfth centuries, and knowledge of it would continue to spread from there.[43] The text of the *Authenticum*, however, would appear to have dropped out of use until it was rediscovered in Bologna in about 1100, and from the eleventh and twelfth centuries onwards the Justinianic legal texts—including the Latin constitutions that had been included in Justinian's code—would be the focus of renewed and intensive study as surviving manuscripts were tracked down and copied.[44] First in Italy, and then across the world of Latin Christendom, these works would be appropriated and used by a new class of legal scribes and scholars to help describe and regulate the world around them, such that Justinian's legislation and legal compendia would come to form the basis of 'the common law of the continent of Europe'.[45] This would remain the case until the nineteenth century, when Napoleon replaced the inherited body of civil law with a code of his own.[46] Only in England would the indigenous common law prevail, although, even there, Justinian's legislation would exercise a strong influence on legal thinking.[47] As a result of the medieval revival of Roman law, interest in Justinian also increased. It was primarily by virtue of his legal achievement that in the fourteenth century the Italian poet Dante Alighieri chose to place Justinian in the 'second sphere' of Paradise, dedicating to him an entire canto of his own, in which he depicts the emperor declaring:

> 'Caesar I was. Justinian I am.
> Who through the will of the primal love I feel,
> Removed the vain and needless from the laws.'[48]

But what of the actual uses to which secular and ecclesiastical authorities in the West would put Justinian's legislation in the twelfth, thirteenth, and fourteenth centuries? Again, it is here that we see the emperor's greatest impact. Laws that had been framed in the very different world of the late antique East—for example, to control agricultural workers on large estates (*coloni adscripticii*)—would be used in the Latin West to define the legal status of medieval serfs. Justinianic legislation, in other words, would play a vital part in the institutionalisation of what historians have traditionally described as 'feudalism'. Laws and legal concepts derived from Justinian would eventually be carried by the European powers to the 'New World', where they were deployed on the *haciendas* and plantations onto which the indigenous population and imported slaves were corralled. The relative ease with which Justinianic Roman law, with respect to *coloni* and slaves, came to be applied in these contexts arguably reveals much of the social and economic circumstances in which such legislation had originated in the first place.[49]

At the same time, the revival of Justinianic Roman law coincided with what one distinguished historian of medieval Christendom, R. I. Moore, has described as a 'permanent change' in Western society whereby 'persecution became habitual'. 'That is to say', he continues, 'not simply that individuals were subject to violence, but that deliberate and socially sanctioned violence began to be directed, through established governmental, judicial and social institutions, against groups of people defined by general characteristics such as race, religion, or way of life; and that membership of such groups in itself could be regarded as justifying these attacks.' This process was the result of the growth of the state in the eleventh and twelfth centuries and the associated emergence of members of a clerical elite, which used persecution as 'an instrument for consolidating their power over society at large'.[50] The groups targeted consisted of those who were deemed outsiders in the world of Latin Christendom: heretics, dissidents, those regarded as sexual deviants, and Jews. They were essentially the same groups that had been targeted by Justinian, and they were effectively targeted on the basis of legal principles derived from Justinian's laws. Moore has described the eleventh, twelfth, and thirteenth centuries as witnessing 'the formation of a persecuting society' that would ultimately lead to the world of heresy trials and public burnings which the popular imagination associates with the horrors of the Inquisition or the trials of the Cathars and Waldensians.[51] But the origins and legal inspiration for that 'persecuting society' ultimately went back to Justinian.[52]

It was therefore in the world of the Latin West in the eleventh and twelfth centuries, and with the assistance of legal sources shaped in Constantinople in the sixth, that Justinian's vision of a truly Christian society would come to be most fully realised. In one crucial respect, this would prove to be bitterly ironic. For the tomb in which Justinian was laid to rest in the Church of the Holy Apostles was not ransacked, as one might imagine, when Mehmed 'the Conqueror' destroyed the building after his capture of Constantinople in 1453. Rather, it had already been pillaged in 1204, when Crusaders from the West sacked the city. The contemporary Byzantine author Nicetas Choniates would describe the scene as the westerners smashed open the tomb: 'Finding that the corpse of Emperor Justinian had not decomposed through the long centuries, they looked upon the spectacle as a miracle, but this in no way prevented them from laying their hands on the tomb's valuables. In other words, the Western nations spared neither the living nor the dead, but beginning with God and his servants, they displayed complete indifference and irreverence to all.'[53]

End of Empire

Beyond the inheritance of Roman law, modern Western perspectives on Justinian would primarily be shaped by the reading of Procopius. In Byzantium, Procopius had been read mostly for his style, but as manuscripts of his works began to make their way to Italy in the dying days of the empire, he was increasingly read in Western Europe for his content. Prior to Alemanni's discovery of the *Secret History* in the Vatican Library, the best-known and most studied of his works was the *History of the Wars*, which had been of interest to both Italian and German scholars, who had read it to learn about the early medieval history of the Italian Peninsula and the Germanic peoples, respectively. In France, his writings had attracted the attention of legal scholars, whose studies had led them to wrestle with the figures of both Justinian and Tribonian. Many lawyers, in particular, were scandalised by the depiction of Justinian that would emerge from the pages of Alemanni's edition in 1623. One English civil lawyer, Thomas Ryves, suspecting Alemanni of being engaged in a popish plot to discredit secular lay rulers, penned a 'Defence of the Emperor Justinian Against Alemanni'. He was particularly incensed by the accusations of ignorance and boorishness that Procopius levelled at Justin and Justinian, and the impression that Justinian had led his uncle around like an old donkey. Fulminating at the Vatican librarian, Ryves wrote, 'For, what would you say if Justinian were summoned back from the dead to show you not only the corpus of civil law he created in which he seems to exceed the capacity of human knowledge but also the churches, basilicas, public streets, harbours, walls, aqueducts, and other buildings constructed by him, immense in size, countless in number, impressively skilful and admirably beautiful, and to ask whether those appear to be like the works of a stupid beastly man pulling a harness? Surely you would free him by your pronouncement from the notion of stupidity?'[1]

By the eighteenth century, print editions existed of all of Procopius' works, and a number of translations of them into Latin and modern languages had begun to appear. Accordingly, thinkers and historians increasingly began to draw upon them in their study of the history of Rome and Constantinople and their contributions to civilization. The eighteenth century was the 'Age of Reason', 'the Enlightenment', a time when philosophers and authors such as Voltaire directed their ire against what they regarded as the obscurantism and anti-intellectualism of much organised religion. This was not an atmosphere that would prove conducive to a positive assessment of either Byzantium in general or Justinian in particular. Voltaire himself famously dismissed the history of the East Roman Empire as 'a worthless collection of orations and miracles . . . a disgrace to the human mind'.[2] To Voltaire's fellow *philosophe* Montesquieu, Justinian was the epitome of oriental despotism: a tyrant and bigot, dominated by his wife, and wracked with jealousy directed at Belisarius.[3] The influence of Procopius' *Secret History* here is clear.

The writings of Procopius (and especially the *Secret History*) would also profoundly inform the historian Edward Gibbon's view of Justinian. Gibbon's *Decline and Fall of the Roman Empire*, published in six volumes from 1776 to 1788, would do more than any other work to inform how generations of English-speaking readers viewed the emperor and his reign.[4] As Gibbon wrote, 'From his elevation to his death, Justinian governed the Roman empire thirty-eight years, seven months, and thirteen days. The events of his reign, which excite our curious attention by their number, variety, and importance, are diligently related by the secretary of Belisarius, a rhetorician whom eloquence had promoted to the rank of senator and prefect of Constantinople. According to the vicissitudes of courage or servitude, of favour or disgrace, Procopius successively composed the history, the panegyric, and the satire of his own times.'[5]

Gibbon concurred with Montesquieu (and Procopius) as to the tyrannical and bigoted nature of Justinian. He declared, for example, that the emperor 'was regulated not by the prudence of a philosopher, but the superstition of a monk'. Gibbon had to contend with the fact that the history of Justinian's reign in many ways confounded his own overall narrative of decline, at least until the arrival of the plague in the 540s and all of its ramifications, which Gibbon took very seriously. Under Justinian, the empire had expanded. The emperor's legal achievements were significant.[6] Even commerce and industry, Gibbon noted, had thrived.[7] What, he suggested after giving a detailed overview of Justinian's legal reforms, had ultimately hamstrung the emperor and poisoned his legacy was a misplaced nostalgia and an ultimately destructive obsession with the Roman Empire of old. In particular, the emperor's 'reverence for antiquity' had accentuated his own inner lack of 'creative genius'. Gibbon concluded, 'Instead of a statue cast in a single mould by the hand of an artist, the works of Justinian represent a tessellated pavement of antique and costly, but too often of incoherent, fragments.'[8]

But was this assessment fair? Gibbon's accusation against Justinian of incoherence of policy is, to my mind, especially misjudged. It was the result of his trying to make sense of a reign of remarkable achievement, creativity, and reform primarily through the essentially hostile and unsympathetic lens of Procopius. An over-emphasis on Procopius and his military narratives, I would suggest, has long led historians to judge Justinian unfairly by prioritising his wars of reconquest and their relatively short-lived success. Yet Justinian's western forays had always been primarily opportunistic. From the start, what had mattered most to the emperor had been the definition of 'orthodoxy' and reform of the law. In these two spheres of activity his achievements would endure.

This point has been grasped by others.[9] In 1949, whilst actively engaged in Britain's withdrawal from empire, and pondering how the newly rebranded British Commonwealth might yet remain a force for good, the postwar Labour prime minister Clement Attlee was reading Gibbon's *Decline and Fall*. As he wrote to his brother Tom at the time, Attlee did not think Gibbon had quite got Justinian right. Rather, in the words of the prime minister's recent biographer, 'he admired the later emperor's commitment to spreading the values of the Roman Empire—such as the rule of law—to other nations, even as its territory and military strength receded'.[10] The emperor's values are not necessarily our values, but the remarkable extent to which Justinian's influence has been felt across the world in societies both East and West, in the 1,500 years that have passed since he first ascended the throne of Constantinople as sole emperor on that day in August of 527, would suggest that Attlee had a point. Whether viewed as a holy emperor or a demon king, as soldier or saint, Justinian made a fundamental contribution to the world in which we live today, and his legacy is still with us.

ACKNOWLEDGEMENTS

This book is very much a product of COVID-19 and the lockdown that came with it. For many months, my agent at Pew Literary, Doug Young, had been encouraging me to write a book on the emperor Justinian aimed at a general readership. As the world closed down around me, I got to grips with the project, confident that having been studying Justinian since the 1990s I knew what I wanted to say. But while writing it, I found myself obliged to reconsider key aspects of Justinian, his reign, and his broader legacy. As a result, my view of Justinian is now very different to what it was even three years ago.

Much of this book was written at home in rural Cambridgeshire. It also benefitted greatly from a writing retreat to Cromer in Norfolk and a number of solitary trips I undertook to Zakythnthos, Rhodes, Symi, Athens, and Thessaloniki, carrying a suitcase of clothes with one hand and dragging a suitcase of books with the other. The process of writing was given focus and encouragement by my editor Sarah Caro and my publisher Brian Distelberg at Basic Books. They and their assistants (Siam Hatzaw and Alex Cullina), as well as Katie Carruthers-Busser, have helped me to produce a much better book than I otherwise would have done. I am also enormously grateful to my excellent copy editor, Kathy Streckfus.

In addition to my wonderful agent and publishing team, I would also like to thank those who first directed me towards the study of Byzantium in general and Justinian in particular. I was first pointed to Byzantine history by my schoolmaster Nigel Williams, who lent me his copy of George Ostrogorsky's *History of the Byzantine State* (Oxford, 1957) just before I went up to Oxford to start university in 1990. There one of my first tutors, the late and much missed Patrick Wormald, introduced me to Justinian. Crucially, Patrick made me read the extraordinary book *The World of Late Antiquity* (London, 1971), written by his old tutor Peter Brown. As a result, in my final year as an undergraduate, I committed myself fully to Byzantium, studying the period from the sixth to tenth centuries with James Howard-Johnston and attending lectures by the late Cyril Mango, whose knowledge and understanding of Byzantine civilization remain unsurpassed. James then became my doctoral supervisor as I focused on the Age of Justinian for my postgraduate work. He has been a constant source of encouragement and inspiration. I also owe an enormous amount to Turlough Stone, who has had the misfortune of reading in draft almost everything I have written over the past quarter century. It is to James and Turlough that this book is dedicated jointly.

I am also indebted to many of the students I have taught over the years. I would like to thank in particular those doctoral students who have worked with me on sixth-century topics or on aspects of Byzantine imperial ideology and religious culture (especially Phil Booth, Matt Dal Santo, Danielle Donaldson-Verhoef, Matt Hassall, Mike Humphreys, Agostino Minichiello, Silvio Roggo, and Doug Whalin). They (along with my friends and colleagues Jairus Banaji, Caroline Goodson, Geoffrey Greatrex, Monica Green, Peregrine Horden, Michael Maas, Rosamond McKitterick, David Miller, Richard Payne, Alex Sarantis, Teresa Shawcross, Theodore Simitis, Reuben Stanley, Norman Underwood, Chris Wickham, and Philip Wood) have all made significant contributions to how I think about the Byzantine and early medieval world.

This is a book meant for the general reader. It sets out my interpretation of Justinian and his 'Age' and why I think Justinian matters. Many of my colleagues will disagree with my analysis. But this book has not been written for them. Rather, I present this study to the reading public firm in my belief that the world would benefit from knowing more about the emperor Justinian and the era over which he presided. Justinian has long fascinated me. I hope he will fascinate others.

Peter Sarris
Willow Cottage
March 2023

NOTES

INTRODUCTION: JUSTINIAN—THE LIGHT AND THE SHADE

1. B. Stanicek, 'Hagia Sophia: Turkey's Secularism Under Threat', *European Parliamentary Research Service*, July 2020. See also O. Uygun, '"Ghostly and Melancholic": Bustling Istanbul Is Muted by Quarantine', *National Geographic*, 30 April 2020, www.nationalgeographic.co.uk/photography/2020/04/ghostly-and -melancholic-bustling-istanbul-muted-quarantine.

2. D. Obolensky, *The Penguin Book of Russian Verse* (London, 1965), 351–352.

3. P. Sarris, 'New Approaches to the Plague of Justinian', *Past and Present* 254 (2022): 315–346.

4. For an excellent recent survey of the issues concerning Justinian's reign and a collection of sources, see F. Haarer, *Justinian: Empire and Society in the Sixth Century* (Edinburgh, 2022).

5. For this process, see P. Sarris, *Empires of Faith: The Fall of Rome to the Rise of Islam* (Oxford, 2011), 4–82.

6. M. R. Salzman, *The Falls of Rome: Crises, Resilience, and Resurgence in Late Antiquity* (Cambridge, 2021), 243–299.

7. P. Birks and G. McLeod, 'Introduction', in *Justinian's Institutes*, tr. P. Birks and G. McLeod (London, 1987).

8. P. Sarris, 'At the Origins of the "Persecuting Society"? Defining the "Orthodox Republic" in the Age of Justinian', *Travaux et mémoires* 26 (2022): 407–422. For the burning of books, see D. Rohmann, *Christianity, Book-Burning and Censorship in Late Antiquity* (Berlin, 2016), esp. 96–101.

9. See Sarris, 'At the Origins of the "Persecuting Society"', and R. I. Moore, *The Formation of a Persecuting Society* (Oxford, 1987).

10. The best recent studies have been P. Heather, *Rome Resurgent: War and Empire in the Age of Justinian* (Oxford, 2018); P. Maraval, *Justinien: Le rêve d'un empire chrétien universel* (Paris, 2016); and H. Leppin, *Justinian: Das Christliche*

NOTES FOR CHAPTER 1

Experiment (Stuttgart, 2011). See also the excellent studies by M. Meier, *Das andere Zeitalter Justinians* (Göttingen, 2003), and *Justinian: Herrschaft, Reich und Religion* (Munich, 2004).

CHAPTER 1. AN EMPIRE DIVIDED

1. Procopius, *Anecdota* 8.22. Procopius has been the subject of many important studies, of which the most thought-provoking remain A. Cameron, *Procopius and the Sixth Century* (London, 1985), and A. Kaldellis, *Procopius of Caesarea: Tyranny, History, and Philosophy at the End of Antiquity* (Philadelphia, 2004). The Greek text of Procopius' works with facing translations can be found in the Loeb Classical Library series: *Procopius: History of the Wars, Secret History, Buildings*, tr. H. B. Dewing and G. Downey, 7 vols. (Cambridge, Mass., 1914–1940). For an excellent updated version of the Loeb translation of the *History of the Wars*, see Prokopios, *The Wars of Justinian*, tr. H. B. Dewing, with an introduction and notes by A. Kaldellis (Indianapolis, 2014). For the so-called *Secret History* or *Anecdota*, see also Prokopios, *The Secret History with Related Texts*, tr. A. Kaldellis (Indianapolis, 2010), or Procopius, *The Secret History*, tr. G. A. Williamson and P. Sarris (London, 2007). Where Procopius is quoted in this book, I tend to use or modify the versions of Dewing and Downey.

2. J. Griffin, 'Introduction', in Virgil, *The Aeneid*, tr. C. Day Lewis (Oxford, 1986), x.

3. G. Woolf, *Becoming Roman* (Cambridge, 1999).

4. See A. Wallace-Hadrill, '*Civilis Princeps*: Between Citizen and King', *Journal of Roman Studies* 72 (1982): 32–48, and C. Norena, *Imperial Ideals in the Roman West* (Cambridge, 2011).

5. See S. Price, *Rituals and Power: The Roman Imperial Cult in Asia Minor* (Cambridge, 1986), and G. Fowden, *Empire to Commonwealth: Consequences of Monotheism in Late Antiquity* (Princeton, N.J., 1993), 1–36.

6. See discussion in Price, *Rituals and Power*.

7. F. Millar, *A Greek Roman Empire* (Berkeley, Calif., 2006).

8. F. Millar, *The Roman Empire and Her Neighbours* (London, 1967).

9. M. Todd, *The Early Germans* (Oxford, 1992); M. Todd, 'The Germanic Peoples and Germanic Society', in *The Cambridge Ancient History*, vol. 12, *The Crisis of Empire, AD 193–337*, ed. A. Bowman, P. Garnsey, and A. Cameron (Cambridge, 2005), 440–460.

10. M. J. Bonner, *The Last Empire of Iran* (Piscataway, N.J., 2020), 25–54.

11. P. Southern and K. Dixon, *The Late Roman Army* (Guildford, 1996), 4–33; G. Greatrex, 'Roman Frontiers and Foreign Policy in the East', in *Aspects of*

the Roman East: Papers in Honour of Professor Fergus Millar, ed. R. Alston and S. Lieu (Turnhout, 2007), 103–173.

12. J. Drinkwater, 'Maximus to Diocletian and the "Crisis"', in Bowman et al., *Crisis of Empire,* 28–66.

13. Ibid.

14. P. Sarris, 'Is This the Face of Britain's Forgotten Emperor?', *The Times,* 25 February 2004, 1, 4; R. Stoneman, *Palmyra and Its Empire* (Ann Arbor, Mich., 1992).

15. P. Sarris, *Empires of Faith: The Fall of Rome to the Rise of Islam* (Oxford, 2011), 14–17.

16. See Drinkwater, 'Maximus to Diocletian and the "Crisis"'.

17. Ibid., 64. See also S. Williams, *Diocletian and the Roman Recovery* (London, 1985), and R. Rees, *Diocletian and the Tetrarchy* (Edinburgh, 2004).

18. See Southern and Dixon, *The Late Roman Army.*

19. See discussion in W. Treadgold, *Byzantium and Its Army* (Stanford, Calif., 1997), 8–14.

20. M. Corbier, 'Coinage and Taxation: The State's Point of View, AD 193–337', in Bowman et al., *Crisis of Empire,* 327–392.

21. M. R. Salzman, *The Falls of Rome: Crises, Resilience, and Resurgence in Late Antiquity* (Cambridge, 2021), 2–10; S. Mitchell, *A History of the Later Roman Empire, AD 284–641,* 2nd ed. (Chichester, 2015), 165–205.

22. Aurelius Victor, *De Caesaribus* 39.2–4. See Rees, *Diocletian and the Tetrarchy,* 93.

23. H. Mattingly, 'Jovius and Heraclius', *Harvard Theological Review* 45 (1952): 131–134.

24. A. Cameron, 'The Reign of Constantine, A.D. 306–337', in Bowman et al., *Crisis of Empire,* 90–109. See also M. S. Bjornlie, ed., *The Life and Legacy of Constantine* (Abingdon, 2017).

25. Zosimus, *New History* 2.29.

26. For recent scholarship and perspectives on Constantine, see R. Flower, 'Visions of Constantine', *Journal of Roman Studies* 101 (2012): 287–305, and Bjornlie, *The Life and Legacy of Constantine.*

27. See discussion in T. D. Barnes, *Constantine and Eusebius* (Cambridge, Mass., 1981).

28. See H. A. Drake, *In Praise of Constantine: A Historical Study and New Translation of Eusebius' Tricennial Orations* (London, 1975), and H. A. Drake, *Constantine and the Bishops* (London, 2000).

29. N. P. Tanner, ed., *The Decrees of the Ecumenical Councils,* 2 vols. (Washington, D.C., 1990), 1:1–19.

30. P. Brown, 'Christianization and Religious Conflict', in *The New Cambridge Ancient History*, vol. 13, *The Late Empire, AD 337–425*, ed. A. Cameron and P. Garnsey (Cambridge, 1998), 632–664. For the pronouncement of Theodosius I, see *Codex Theodosianus* 16.1.2.

31. H. Chadwick, *East and West: The Making of a Rift in the Church from Apostolic Times to the Council of Florence* (Oxford, 2003), 1–19.

32. H. Chadwick, *The Early Church* (London, 1993), 41–45.

33. See, for example, 2 Peter 3:14–18.

34. See G. E. M. de Ste. Croix, *Christian Persecution, Martyrdom, and Orthodoxy*, ed. M. Whitby and J. Streeter (Oxford, 2006), 201–252.

35. See R. Williams, *Arius: Heresy and Tradition*, 2nd ed. (London, 2001).

36. See *The Acts of the Council of Chalcedon*, vol. 1, tr. and ed. R. Price and M. Gaddis (Liverpool, 2007), 17–75.

37. I owe this analogy to Dermot MacCulloch.

38. Tanner, *The Decrees of the Ecumenical Councils*, 1:85–86 (emphasis added).

39. See discussion in C. Rapp, *Holy Bishops in Late Antiquity: The Nature of Christian Leadership in an Age of Transition* (Berkeley, Calif., 2005), 235–273.

40. See J. Meyendorff, 'Justinian, the Empire, and the Church', *Dumbarton Oaks Papers* 22 (1968): 43–60.

41. See H. J. Kim, *The Huns* (Abingdon, 2016), and N. Di Cosmo, *Ancient China and Its Enemies: The Rise of Nomadic Power in East Asian History* (Cambridge, 2002).

42. M. Meier, *Geschichte der Völkerwanderung: Europa, Asien, und Afrika vom 3 bis zum 8 Jahrhundert n. Chr.* (Munich, 2020), 156–170.

43. Ibid., 171–224.

44. S. Mitchell, *A History of the Later Roman Empire, AD 284–641*, 2nd ed. (Oxford, 2015), 86–102. See also M. McEvoy, *Child Emperor Rule in the Late Roman West, AD 367–455* (Oxford, 2013).

45. Mitchell, *History of the Later Roman Empire*, 97–101.

46. Ibid., 98–118.

47. See Meier, *Geschichte der Völkerwanderung*, 387–544, and H. Börm, *Westrom: Von Honorius bis Justinian* (Stuttgart, 2018), 63–80.

48. Kim, *The Huns*, 92–108.

49. Sarris, *Empires of Faith*, 52–55.

50. A rival claimant to the Western throne—Julius Nepos—remained politically active in Dalmatia until his assassination in 480. He had been recognized by the authorities in Constantinople, but lost power in Italy in 475. See Mitchell, *History of the Later Roman Empire*, 124–125.

51. See P. Sarris, *Byzantium: A Very Short Introduction* (Oxford, 2015), 17.

52. See P. Sarris, 'Economy and Society in the Age of the Sons of Constantine', in *Sons of Constantine*, ed. S. Tougher and N. Baker-Brian (London, 2020), 329–344.

53. See C. Begass, *Die Senatsaristokratie des oströmischen Reiches, ca. 457–518* (Munich, 2018).

54. See R. Pfeilschifter, *Der Kaiser und Konstantinopel: Kommunikation und Konfliktaustrag in einer spätantiken Metropole* (Berlin, 2013), and G. Greatrex, 'The Emperor, the People, and Urban Violence', in *Violence in the Ancient World*, ed. J. Dijkstra and C. Raschle (Cambridge, 2020), 389–405. On the Hippodrome, see E. Akyürek, *The Hippodrome of Constantinople* (Cambridge, 2021).

55. For Illyricum in this period, see A. Sarantis, *Justinian's Balkan Wars: Campaigning, Diplomacy and Development in Illyricum, Thrace and the Northern World, AD 527–565* (Prenton, 2016).

56. C. Mango, *Byzantium: The Empire of New Rome* (London, 1983), 203–204.

57. Sarris, *Empires of Faith*, 133–134, 127–128.

CHAPTER 2. FROM RAGS TO RICHES

1. For an introduction to the site, see V. Ivanišević, 'Carčin Grad (Justiniana Prima): A New-Discovered City for a "New" Society', in *Proceedings of the 23rd International Congress of Byzantine Studies, Belgrade, 2016*, ed. S. Marjanović-Dušanić (Belgrade, 2016).

2. *Justiniani Novellae Constitutiones* (*Novels of Justinian*), 11 pr. (*J.Nov.* hereafter). For an English translation, see *The Novels of Justinian: A Complete Annotated English Translation*, ed. P. Sarris, tr. D. J. D. Miller (Cambridge, 2018).

3. See A. Sarantis, *Justinian's Balkan Wars: Campaigning, Diplomacy, and Development in Illyricum, Thrace, and the Northern World, AD 527–565* (Prenton, 2016), 156.

4. Procopius, *Buildings* 4.1.17.

5. Procopius, *Anecdota* 6.3. For the Via Militaris, see M. Larnach, 'All Roads Lead to Constantinople' (PhD diss., University of Sydney, 2016). The main alternative Roman road—the Via Egnatia—is recorded to have been in a treacherous state by the late fifth century (see ibid., 78). For Vederiana (or Bederiana, as it is also known), see Sarantis, *Justinian's Balkan Wars*, 150. It was evidently in close proximity to the future Justiniana Prima (see Procopius, *Anecdota* 6.2–3, and *Buildings* 4.1.17).

NOTES FOR CHAPTER 2

6. Priscus 11.2.50–55, quoted in Sarantis, *Justinian's Balkan Wars*, 116.

7. See V. Ivanišević, 'Barbarian Settlements in the Interior of Illyricum: The Case of Caričin Grad', in *The Pontic-Danubian Realm in the Period of the Great Migration*, ed. V. Ivanišević and M. Kazanski (Paris, 2012), 57–70.

8. The story is preserved by the twelfth-century historian Zonaras. See discussion and references in A. A. Vasiliev, *Justin the First* (Washington, D.C., 1950), 63.

9. I am extremely grateful to Dr Alexander Sarantis for discussion of this point.

10. See discussion in P. Amory, *People and Identity in Ostrogothic Italy* (Cambridge, 1989), 94, 278–291.

11. Larnach, 'All Roads Lead to Constantinople', 244; C. Mango, 'The Triumphal Way of Constantinople and the Golden Gate', *Dumbarton Oaks Papers* 54 (2000): 173–188, 174–175.

12. Mango, 'Triumphal Way', 175; A. Berger, *The Statues of Constantinople* (Cambridge, 2021), 33–35, 12.

13. Berger, *The Statues of Constantinople*, 7–11.

14. For a plan of Constantinople, see C. Mango, ed., *The Oxford History of Byzantium* (Oxford, 2002), 64, and (in this book) Map 4.

15. Procopius, *Anecdota* 6.3. I concur with the suggestion of Croke that they are likely to have been appointed *scholarii* rather than *excubitores* in the first instance. See B. Croke, 'Leo I and the Palace Guard', *Byzantion* 75 (2005): 117–151, 145.

16. John Malalas, *Chronicle* 17.1. For a translation of this important source, see *The Chronicle of John Malalas*, tr. E. Jeffreys, M. Jeffreys, and R. Scott (Canberra, 1986).

17. Ibid. and Procopius, *Anecdota* 6.18.

18. Malalas, *Chronicle* 17.1. See also Procopius, *Anecdota* 6.12–17.

19. Procopius, *Anecdota* 6.18.

20. For service on crown estates belonging to the imperial household or emperor, see *J.Nov.* 30.

21. Malalas, *Chronicle* 16.3.

22. Procopius, *Anecdota* 6.4–10.

23. B. Croke, 'Justinian Under Justin', *Byzantinische Zeitschrift* 100 (2007): 13–56, 19. For the revolt of Vitalian (which occurred between 514 and 516) and its context, see Sarantis, *Justinian's Balkan Wars*, 130–134. Many of the troops under his charge would have been barbarian *foederati*, including a considerable number of Arians, aggrieved more at the emperor's economic policies than at his religious ones (see ibid., 26). For wider public hostility to aspects of Anastasius'

economic policies, see P. Sarris, *Economy and Society in the Age of Justinian* (Cambridge, 2006), 200–201. See also H. Elton, 'Fighting for Chalcedon: Vitalian's Rebellion Against Anastasius', in *Violence in the Ancient World*, ed. J. Dijkstra and C. Raschle (Cambridge, 2020), 367–388. For the emperor's reign in general, see F. Haarer, *Anastasius I: Politics and Empire in the Late Roman World* (Cambridge, 2006), and M. Meier, *Anastasios I: Die Entstehung des Byzantinisches Reiches* (Stuttgart, 2009).

24. See discussion in Croke, 'Leo I and the Palace Guard'.

25. See discussion in Croke, 'Justinian Under Justin'. For the law, see *Codex Iustinianus* 6.23.31 (dating from 534).

26. Malalas, *Chronicle* 16.11, 16.16.

27. For the complexity of the different factions involved, see discussion in S. Brock, 'The Nestorian Church: A Lamentable Misnomer', *Bulletin of the John Rylands Library* 78 (1996): 23–35.

28. Croke, 'Justinian Under Justin', 19, also notes the strongly Chalcedonian stance of 'Illyrian generals and other military commanders'.

29. Procopius, *Anecdota* 6.17, 9.48 (emphasis added). *Anecdota* 9.49 suggests that the name change occurred when Justin ascended the throne. Her original name meant 'little wolf'. Procopius states that she had previously been the concubine of the man who had bought her: it is possible that man may have been Justin, in which case he would have had to 'emancipate' her to enable them to wed. Alternatively, Lupicina might have been emancipated by a previous owner before her marriage to Justin.

30. Croke, 'Justinian Under Justin', 20–21. The date of the adoption is not clear. For Taurisium, see Procopius, *Buildings* 4.1.17.

31. Agathias, *Histories* 5.21.1–4. For an English translation of this source, see Agathias, *Histories*, tr. J. D. Frendo (Berlin, 1975).

32. For full references, see J. R. Martindale, *The Prosopography of the Later Roman Empire*, vol. 2, *A.D. 395–527* (Cambridge, 1980), 645. Fl. Petrus Sabbatius Iustinianus 7.

33. Agathias, *Histories* 21.1–4.

34. A. M. Honoré, 'Some Constitutions Composed by Justinian', *Journal of Roman Studies* 65 (1975): 107–123.

35. See M. Amelotti and L. M. Zingale, *Scritti teologici ed ecclesiastici di Giustiniano* (Milan, 1977), and E. Schwartz, *Drei dogmatische Schriften Iustinians* (Munich, 1939).

36. For discussion of the educational system at this time, see P. Lemerle, *Byzantine Humanism* (Canberra, 1986), 43–79.

37. Procopius, *Anecdota* 8.12 (*ouk amorphos*); Malalas, *Chronicle* 18.1.

However, see discussion in C. Head, 'The Physical Appearance of the Emperors in Byzantine Historical Writing', *Byzantion* 50 (1980): 226–240, and B. Baldwin, 'Physical Descriptions of Byzantine Emperors', *Byzantion* 51 (1981): 8–21.

38. Croke, 'Justinian Under Justin', 21.

39. Justinian's *buccellarii*—including Belisarius—are recorded to have conducted raiding operations against the Persians in that year, a point I owe to Dr. David Parnell.

40. Malalas, *Chronicle* 16.19.

41. The best discussion from a sociological perspective is to be found in P. Bell, *Social Conflict in the Age of Justinian* (Oxford, 2013), 119–159.

42. Procopius, *Anecdota* 7.1–42.

43. Sarris, *Economy and Society in the Age of Justinian*, 201; John Lydus, *De Magistratibus* 3.46. For a translation of this source, see Ioannes Lydus, *On Powers, or the Magistracies of the Roman State*, ed. A. C. Bandy (Philadelphia, 1983).

44. A. Cameron, *Circus Factions: Blues and Greens at Rome and Byzantium* (Oxford, 1976), 105–125, 261–270.

45. For the evolution of acclamation and coronation ceremonies at this time, however, see discussion in C. Begass, 'Die Rolle des Senats bei den Kaisererhebungen in Konstantinopel von Konstantin bei Justinian', in *Das Zeitalter Diokletians und Konstantins*, ed. A. Goltz and H. Schlange-Schöningen (Vienna, 2022), 325–355.

46. See *Anonymous Valesianus* c. 13 and Vasiliev, *Justin the First*, 88–89. For the *Anonymous Valesianus*, see *Pars Posterior: Historia Theodericiana* in Ammianus Marcellinus, *Res Gestae*, tr. J. C. Rolfe (Cambridge, Mass., 1935).

47. See A. Cameron, 'The Household of Anastasius', *Greek, Roman and Byzantine Studies* 19 (1978): 259–276, and Croke, 'Justinian Under Justin', 16.

48. Malalas, *Chronicle* 16.19.

49. Marcellinus Comes, *Chronicle*, sub anno 520–521. See Marcellinus, *The Chronicle of Marcellinus*, tr. B. Croke (Sydney, 1995), 41.

50. Croke, 'Justinian Under Justin', 16; G. Greatrex, 'The Early Years of Justin I's Reign in the Sources', *Electrum* 12 (2007): 99–113, 99.

51. Constantine Porphyrogenitus, *De Cerimoniis* 1.39. See Constantine Porphyrogennetos, *The Book of Ceremonies*, ed. and tr. A. Moffatt and M. Tall (Leiden, 2017), 426.

52. Croke, 'Justinian Under Justin', 16.

53. Ibid., 17; Lydus, *De Magistratibus* 3.17.3.

54. Constantine Porphyrogennetos, *Book of Ceremonies* (Moffatt and Tall), 427, although I concur with Croke, 'Justinian Under Justin', as to the more appropriate translation of 'world' rather than people in this chant. The emphasis

the crowd placed on an emperor for the army (*exercitus*), given its known pro-Chalcedonian sympathies, would suggest that the Blues were in charge of the chants, just as Peter reveals them to have been more actively involved in the associated melee.

55. Ibid.

56. Ibid., 427–428.

57. Ibid.

58. Ibid., 429–430.

59. Evagrius, *Ecclesiastical History* 4.1–2. For a translation of this source, see *The Ecclesiastical History of Evagrius Scholasticus*, tr. M. Whitby (Liverpool, 2000).

60. *Collectio Avellana*, in *Epistolae Imperatorum Pontificum Aliorum*, vol. 2, ed. O. Güenther (reprint, Cambridge, 2019), letter 141 (586) ('nos licet nolentes ... electos fuisse').

61. Procopius, *Anecdota* 6.11.

62. See *The Chronicle of Pseudo-Zachariah Rhetor*, tr. G. Greatrex, R. Phenix, and C. Horn (Liverpool, 2011), 281. See also discussion in Greatrex, 'The Early Years'.

63. As suggested by Greatrex, 'The Early Years'.

64. See Croke, 'Justinian Under Justin', 24.

65. *Collectio Avellana* letter 197 (657).

66. Ps. Zachariah Rhetor, *Chronicle* 8.1.

CHAPTER 3. SUCCESSION

1. *Anonymous Valesianus* c. 13.

2. V. Menze, *Justinian and the Making of the Syrian Orthodox Church* (Oxford, 2008), 8.

3. See P. Maraval, *Justinien: Le rêve d'un empire chrétien universel* (Paris, 2016), 45–49.

4. Ibid., 46–47; John Malalas, *Chronicle* 17.6.

5. See *The Chronicle of Pseudo-Zachariah Rhetor*, tr. G. Greatrex, R. Phenix, and C. Horn (Liverpool, 2011), 281, and Maraval, *Justinien*, 47.

6. Malalas, *Chronicle* 17.5.

7. See ibid., 17.3, and P. Sarris, *Economy and Society in the Age of Justinian* (Cambridge, 2006), 16.

8. *Collectio Avellana*, in *Epistolae Imperatorum Pontificum Aliorum*, vol. 2, ed. O. Güenther (reprint, Cambridge, 2019), letter 141 (586), 142 (586–588).

9. Maraval, *Justinien*, 50–51, provides an excellent potted account.

10. Ibid., 51.

11. See *The Book of the Popes (Liber Pontificalis)*, tr. L. R. Loomis (New York, 1916), 129.

12. Maraval, *Justinien*, 51, 52.

13. Ibid., 52.

14. See P. Sarris, *Empires of Faith: The Fall of Rome to the Rise of Islam* (Oxford, 2011), 111–112.

15. *The Book of Pontiffs (Liber Pontificalis)*, tr. R. Davis (Liverpool, 1989), 49–50. John had been sent to Constantinople by Theoderic to plead for tolerance for the empire's Arians. Whilst in the capital, he had participated in a ceremony to crown Justin as emperor, but failed to extract any significant concessions from him, thereby exciting Theoderic's wrath.

16. Sarris, *Empires of Faith*, 109–111; J. Moorhead, 'The Last Years of Theoderic', *Historia* 32 (1983): 106–120.

17. *Collectio Avellana* letter 194 (652). For a letter from the pope to Euphemia, see ibid., 156 (603).

18. On Euphemia, see Procopius, *Anecdota* 9.47–49, and the account of John of Ephesus preserved in Pseudo-Zachariah of Tel-Mahre, *Chronicle: Part III*, tr. W. Witakowski (Liverpool, 1996), 18.

19. *Collectio Avellana* letter 182 (637), 152 (600), 174 (630), 164 (615), 147 (592–593). Justin would remove Celer from the post but he clearly remained a significant figure in 519. See B. Croke, 'Justinian Under Justin', *Byzantinische Zeitschrift* 100 (2007): 13–56, 24. Pompey was still in charge of the army in Thrace at this point but would be replaced by Justin's nephew Germanus by 520. See A. Sarantis, *Justinian's Balkan Wars: Campaigning, Diplomacy, and Development in Illyricum, Thrace, and the Northern World, AD 527–565* (Prenton, 2016), 84.

20. For a translation, see F. Haarer, *Justinian: Empire and Society in the Sixth Century* (Edinburgh, 2022), 145.

21. See discussion in A. M. Honoré, 'Some Constitutions Composed by Justinian', *Journal of Roman Studies* 65 (1975): 107–123. For a more sceptical position, see H. Leppin, *Justinian: Das Christliche Experiment* (Stuttgart, 2011).

22. As suggested by Croke, 'Justinian Under Justin', 25.

23. *Collectio Avellana* letter 147 (592–593).

24. Ibid., letter 187 (644), letter 196 (655–656). See also Maraval, *Justinien*, 53, and Menze, *Justinian and the Making of the Syrian Orthodox Church*, 39–40.

25. See *J.Nov.* 111. For Justinian's sudden change of heart with respect to the 'Scythian monks', in the context of the broader consistency of his religious policy, see J. Powell, *Justinian's Indecision: How Social Networks Shaped Imperial Policy* (Piscataway, N.J., 2021).

26. *Collectio Avellana* letter 243 (743).

27. Ibid., letter 211 (669–670), 198 (657–658), 188 (645–646).

28. Ibid., letter 207 (666), 179 (635).

29. Procopius, *Anecdota* 6.11–12, 8.2–3.

30. Here Croke, 'Justinian Under Justin', is fundamental.

31. Croke, 'Justinian Under Justin', 29.

32. *Collectio Avellana* letter 218 (679–680). Saint Peter, of course, would have been regarded as Justinian's patron saint, as his first name was Petrus. The church should thus also be thought of as a token of thanks on his part for his and his family's recent good fortune.

33. Croke, 'Justinian Under Justin', 23–24.

34. Ibid., 25, rejecting the commonly asserted claim that Justinian was appointed *comes domesticorum* in place of a relative of Anastasius. That position appears to have been entrusted to a general, Philoxenus, who had the appropriate military experience for it.

35. Ibid., citing Victor of Tunnuna, who appears to have been well informed on Constantinopolitan affairs.

36. Pseudo-Zachariah, *Chronicle*. See *Chronicle of Pseudo-Zachariah Rhetor*, tr. Greatrex et al., 282.

37. Croke, 'Justinian Under Justin', 33. There were two *magistri militum praesentalis* leading two separate armies stationed outside the capital.

38. Pseudo-Zachariah, *Chronicle*. See *Chronicle of Pseudo-Zachariah Rhetor*, tr. Greatrex et al., 283; Procopius, *Anecdota* 6.27–28.

39. Croke, 'Justinian Under Justin', 34, quoting Victor of Tunnuna. See also discussion in G. Greatrex, 'The Early Years of Justin I's Reign in the Sources', *Electrum* 12 (2007): 99–113, 105.

40. Croke, 'Justinian Under Justin', 35 and note 126.

41. Procopius, *Wars* 3.9.5.

42. Procopius, *Anecdota* 7.6; Malalas, *Chronicle* 18.1 ('He favoured the Blue faction').

43. *J.Nov.* 105 c. 1

44. *J.Nov.* 123 c. 4.

45. See *Codex Iustinianus* 12.3.2: a law of the fifth-century emperor Marcian with which Justinian would say he disagreed (*J.Nov.* 105). For the objects scattered, see *J.Nov.* 105 c. 2.1.

46. See Procopius, *Anecdota* 26.12–15, and C. Morrisson and C. Cheynet, 'Price and Wages in the Byzantine World', in *The Economic History of Byzantium*, vol. 2, ed. A. Laiou (Washington, D.C., 2002), 799–862.

47. A. H. M. Jones, *The Later Roman Empire*, vol. 2 (Oxford, 1964), 1227. See also A. Cameron and D. Schauer, 'The Last Consul', *Journal of Roman Studies* 72 (1982): 126–145, 138.

48. Marcellinus Comes, *Chronicle*, sub anno 521. See *The Chronicle of*

Marcellinus, tr. B. Croke (Sydney, 1995), 41. For his career, see ibid., xix–xx. Marcellinus would have 'regulated audiences and controlled petitions brought before him' (Sarantis, *Justinian's Balkan Wars*, 56).

49. A. Cutler, 'The Making of the Justinian Diptychs', *Byzantion* 54 (1984): 75–115, esp. 78, 81, 83, 75, 111–112.

50. Malalas, *Chronicle* 18.1.

51. For the Syriac sources with respect to Theodora, see S. A. Harvey, 'Theodora the "Believing Queen": A Study in Syriac Historiographical Tradition', *Hugoye: Journal of Syriac Studies* 4 (2001): 209–234. For her probable date of birth, see C. Foss, 'The Empress Theodora', *Byzantion* 72 (2002): 141–176, 164–166. I generally find Foss's analysis of the sources with respect to the empress's life convincing. For a somewhat later date, see D. Potter, *Theodora: Actress, Empress, Saint* (Oxford, 2015), 8. The latter also has Justinian and Theodora in a stable relationship together by about 521.

52. Harvey, 'Theodora the "Believing Queen"', 222.

53. Potter, *Theodora*, 97–98, dates this event to about 523, signalling that it occurred after Justinian and Theodora had married.

54. See Harvey, 'Theodora the "Believing Queen"', 222, and Potter, *Theodora*, 93, for full references (although I disagree with Potter's translation of *porneion* as 'the actress community': 'brothel' is preferred by Foss, 'The Empress Theodora', 143, as well as Harvey). The narrative is preserved in John of Ephesus, *Lives of the Eastern Saints*.

55. See discussion in Foss, 'The Empress Theodora', 143 note 6, *contra* A. A. Vasiliev, *Justin the First* (Washington, D.C., 1950), 97.

56. Foss, 'The Empress Theodora', 160, citing the Frankish *Chronicle of Fredegar*.

57. Procopius, *Anecdota* 9.11.

58. Luke 15:7 (ESV). See discussion in Harvey, 'Theodora the "Believing Queen"'.

59. *J.Nov.* 14.

60. Malalas, *Chronicle* 18.24.

61. Foss, 'The Empress Theodora', 164–165, although Potter, *Theodora*, prefers a date of *c.* 495.

62. Procopius, *Anecdota* 9.2.

63. See discussion in Foss, 'The Empress Theodora', 165.

64. We also have external evidence that Theodora had a sister named Comito. See Foss, 'The Empress Theodora', 160.

65. Procopius, *Anecdota* 9.7, 9.10, 9.11–13, 9.17–19, 9.20–26.

66. Ibid., 9.27–28.

67. Potter, *Theodora*, 53–59.

68. John of Nikiu 90.87, which is rejected by Foss, 'The Empress Theodora', 166–167, and taken rather further by Harvey, 'Theodora the "Believing Queen"', 214.

69. As suggested by Foss, 'The Empress Theodora', 167–168, and Procopius, *Anecdota* 9.33.

70. Procopius, *Anecdota* 12.28–32, 9.29–32.

71. Procopius, *Buildings* 1.11.8.

72. Procopius, *Anecdota* 10.11–12. See also Procopius, *Anecdota* 1.8, which suggests that the unfinished work will contain a postmortem assessment of their rule.

73. Foss, 'The Empress Theodora', 169–170.

74. Procopius, *Anecdota* 9.14. On the sexual politics of her supposed deportment, see L. Brubaker, 'The Age of Justinian: Gender and Society', in *The Cambridge Companion to the Age of Justinian*, ed. M. Maas (Cambridge, 2005), 427–447.

75. Procopius, *Anecdota* 9.47.

76. D. Daube, 'The Marriage of Justinian and Theodora, Legal and Theological Reflections', *Catholic University Law Review* 360 (1966–1967): 380–399, 386 (although his dating of Theodora's elevation to the rank of *patricia*— which has implications for his argument—needs to be emended in the light of Potter, *Theodora*).

77. Unlike Potter, *Theodora*, 240 note 13, I see no reason not to follow Procopius' chronology.

78. *Codex Iustinianus* 5.27.1, 5.5.7.2; *Digest* 23.2.44.

79. Procopius, *Anecdota* 9.50–52.

80. *Codex Iustinianus* 5.4.23. For Justin's inner dialogue with Euphemia, see Daube, 'The Marriage of Justinian and Theodora'. Had Theodora been elevated to patrician status prior to this law (as is sometimes supposed), then Justinian could in fact have married her, but significant legal disadvantages would still have applied to her daughter. This law opened the way to removing the social stigma that applied to both mother and daughter. For its date, see T. C. Lounghis, B. Blysidu, and St. Lampakes, *Regesten der Kaiserurkunden des Oströmischen Reiches von 476 bis 565* (Nicosia, 2005), 138.

81. See *Digest* 40.11. If Justin had been her former owner (which is possible), he would have had to make the application. Justinian would abolish this procedure in 539 (see *J.Nov.* 78).

82. See discussion in Daube, 'The Marriage of Justinian and Theodora'.

83. *Codex Iustinianus* 5.4.23.1.

84. Ibid., 5.4.23.5.

85. Ibid., 1.4.33 (issued in 534).

NOTES FOR CHAPTER 3

86. Ibid., 6.22.8.1b.

87. Procopius, *Anecdota* 9.50.

88. Ibid., 9.35–42.

89. Croke, 'Justinian Under Justin', 39–40, drawing on the testimony of the *Chronicle* of John of Nikiu, which preserves otherwise lost testimony from the *Chronicle* of John Malalas.

90. Procopius, *Anecdota* 9.39–43.

91. Croke, 'Justinian Under Justin', 42. The date of this event is uncertain, and we rely for our knowledge of it on a considerably later source (Zonaras).

92. Ibid., 42.

93. See B. Croke, 'Justinian, Theodora, and the Church of Sergius and Bacchus', *Dumbarton Oaks Papers* 60 (2006): 25–63, 29–30.

94. Procopius, *Wars* 1.11.16. See discussion and references in Croke, 'Justinian Under Justin', 43–44.

95. Croke, 'Justinian Under Justin', 44–45.

96. Ibid., 44, drawing on the testimony of Victor of Tunnuna.

97. Dumbarton Oaks accession number BZC.1960; for full reference to the numismatic literature, see Croke, 'Justinian Under Justin', 52 note 207.

98. Croke, 'Justinian Under Justin', 51; Malalas, *Chronicle* 17.23; *De Cerimoniis* 1.95.

99. For Justinian's 'vulnerability' at this time, see P. Bell, *Social Conflict in the Age of Justinian* (Oxford, 2013), 257–275.

100. J. Bardill, 'A New Temple for Byzantium: Anicia Iuliana, King Solomon, and the Gilded Ceiling of the Church of St. Polyeuktos in Constantinople', in *Late Antique Archaeology 3: Social and Political Life in Late Antiquity*, ed. W. Bowden, A. Gutteridge, and C. Machado (Leiden, 2006), 339–370; C. Mango and I. Sevčenko, 'Remains of the Church of St Polyeuktos at Constantinople', *Dumbarton Oaks Papers* 15 (1961): 243–247.

101. *Anthologia Palatina* 1.10. For a slightly different (but full) translation, see M. Whitby, 'The St. Polyeuktos Epigram (*AP* 1.10): A Literary Perspective', in *Greek Literature in Late Antiquity*, ed. S. F. Johnson (London, 2006), 159–187.

102. A. Cameron, 'The House of Anastasius', *Greek, Roman and Byzantine Studies* 19 (1978): 259–276.

103. See Croke, 'Justinian Under Justin', 51, for references, although unlike Croke I here prioritise the contemporary account of proceedings by Peter the Patrician preserved in *De Cerimoniis*. See *De Cerimoniis* 1.95. As Croke notes, however, the later Byzantine historian Zonaras claims that Justinian was subsequently also acclaimed in the Hippodrome.

104. See Croke, 'Justinian Under Justin', 51. For the *delphax*, see J. Kostenec, 'Observations on the Great Palace at Constantinople: The Sanctuaries of the

448

Archangel Michael, the Daphne Palace, and the Magnaura', *Reading Medieval Studies* 2 (2005): 27–55, 37–38.

105. Malalas, *Chronicle* 17.18.

106. *De Cerimoniis* 1.95. See Constantine Porphyrogennetos, *The Book of Ceremonies*, ed. and tr. A. Moffatt and M. Tall (Leiden, 2017), 432–433.

107. P. Grierson, C. Mango, and I. Sevčenko, 'The Tombs and Obits of the Byzantine Emperors (337–1042) with an Additional Note', *Dumbarton Oaks Papers* 16 (1962): 1–63, esp. 10–11, 27, 46–47.

CHAPTER 4. CONFRONTING THE ENEMY

1. P. Alexander, *The Oracle of Baalbek* (Washington, D.C., 1967), 28–29. This version of the text seems to date from about 502–506.

2. R. Scott, *Byzantine Chronicles and the Sixth Century* (Abingdon, 2012), sec. 19, 6.

3. P. Sarris, *Empires of Faith: The Fall of Rome to the Rise of Islam* (Oxford, 2011), 134–144.

4. John Malalas, *Chronicle* 17.9.

5. Sarris, *Empires of Faith*, 139–140; Procopius, *Wars* 1.12.1–9.

6. Sarris, *Empires of Faith*, 140; G. Bowersock, *The Throne of Adulis: Red Sea Wars on the Eve of Islam* (Oxford, 2013).

7. It has also been suggested that Justinian may have contributed to a change in policy with respect to the restructuring of the imperial army at this time: see C. Koehn, *Justinian und die Armee des frühen Byzanz* (Berlin, 2018), 56–67.

8. G. Greatrex and S. Lieu, *The Roman Eastern Frontier and the Persian Wars: Part 2, 363–630 AD* (London, 2002), 77–84.

9. See Malalas, *Chronicle* 18.2 (sub anno 527), recording the refortification of Palmyra—crucial to the defence of Damascus.

10. *Codex Iustinianus* 1.29.5.

11. See discussion in N. Adontz, *Armenia in the Period of Justinian* (Lisbon, 1971).

12. Malalas, *Chronicle* 18.4, 18.13; *Chronicon Paschale* sub anno 528.

13. Procopius, *Wars* 1.17.46–48.

14. See Sarris, *Empires of Faith*, 143.

15. Malalas, *Chronicle* 18.19, 18.29.

16. Ibid., 18.35. Procopius' claim that one hundred thousand were killed seems hyperbolic in comparison. See *Anecdota* 11.29. For context and history, see K. L. Noethlichs, 'Samaritans in Late Antique Legislation', *Bulletin of the Institute of Classical Studies* 50 (2007): 57–66.

17. *Codex Iustinianus* 1.5.17.

18. Greatrex and Lieu, *The Roman Eastern Frontier and the Persian Wars*, 88–89.

19. See J. R. Martindale, *The Prosopography of the Later Roman Empire*, vol. 3, *A.D. 527–641* (Cambridge, 1990), *PLRE-III-A*, Belisarius 1 (182, 186).

20. Procopius, *Wars* 1.1.

21. Ibid., 1.14.39–42.

22. Ibid., 1.15.1–33.

23. For the Battle of Callinicum, see Greatrex and Lieu, *The Roman Eastern Frontier and the Persian Wars*, 92–93.

24. Greatrex and Lieu, *The Roman Eastern Frontier and the Persian Wars*, 91–97.

25. See Procopius, *Anecdota* 19.13–17.

26. See R. Payne, 'Cosmology and the Expansion of the Iranian Empire', *Past and Present*, 220 (2013): 3–33.

27. Malalas, *Chronicle* 18.14.

28. Ibid. See discussion in A. Sarantis, *Justinian's Balkan Wars: Campaigning, Diplomacy, and Development in Illyricum, Thrace, and the Northern World, AD 527–65* (Prenton, 2016), 33–35.

29. See discussion in Sarris, *Empires of Faith*, 122–124. The formal baptism of Clovis may have taken place around Christmas 508.

30. Malalas, *Chronicle* 18.6.

31. Sarantis, *Justinian's Balkan Wars*, 45, 46.

32. Ibid., 177, 172, 166.

33. Sarris, *Empires of Faith*, 171–176.

34. V. Ivanišević, 'Barbarian Settlements in the Interior of Illyricum: The Case of Caričin Grad', in *The Pontic-Danubian Realm in the Period of the Great Migration*, ed. V. Ivanišević and M. Kazanski (Paris, 2012), 57.

35. Sarantis, *Justinian's Balkan Wars*, 169–170.

36. Ibid., 52–54, 60–61. The inference of Procopius, *Wars* 5.3.15, is that the assault was unsuccessful, but this is not entirely clear.

37. Sarantis, *Justinian's Balkan Wars*, 60–61. Whereas Sirmium was reached from Constantinople via the Via Militaris, Salona was reached by the Via Egnatia, which extended through Thessalonica and Dyrrachium. See M. Larnach, 'All Roads Lead to Constantinople' (PhD diss., University of Sydney, 2016), 78. This road is recorded to have been in poor condition by the late fifth century but may have been recently restored by Justinian.

38. See J. R. Martindale, *The Prosopography of the Later Roman Empire*, vol. 2, *A.D. 395–527* (Cambridge, 1980), 65.

39. See Procopius, *Wars* 5.2.6–18.

40. Jordanes, *Getica* 305. See Jordanes, *Romana and Getica*, tr. P. Van Nuffelen and L. Van Hoof (Liverpool, 2020), 364–365.

41. Sarris, *Empires of Faith*, 113–114.

42. For this line of thinking, see H. Börm, *Westrom: Von Honorius bis Justinian* (Stuttgart, 2018), 143–155. For the existence of a senatorial 'pro-war' party in Constantinople, see T. Lounghis, 'Die kriegisch gesinnte Partei der senatorischen Opposition in den Jahren 526 bis 529', in *Zwischen Polis, Provinz und Peripherie: Beiträge zur byzantinischen Geschichte und Kultur*, ed. H. Hoffman (Wiesbaden, 2005), 25–36.

43. See *The Chronicle of Marcellinus*, tr. B. Croke (Sydney, 1995), 27 (sub anno 476), xix–xxi.

44. Procopius, *Wars* 3.9.1–9.

45. *Codex Iustinianus*, 1.1.5, 1.1.8.7–24.

CHAPTER 5. THE BODY OF THE LAW

1. Procopius, *Buildings* 1.1.11.

2. On the basis of the number of laws from the reign of each emperor preserved in the *Codex Iustinianus*, Anastasius issued just over sixty laws over a period of twenty-six or twenty-seven years, and Justin issued just under thirty in nine years. See T. C. Lounghis, B. Blysidu, and St. Lampakes, *Regesten der Kaiserurkunden des Oströmischen Reiches von 476 bis 565* (Nicosia, 2005), 82–128, 128–151. It is possible that Justinian's commissioners jettisoned more legislation by Anastasius than by Justin when codifying the constitutions of former emperors, but the rate of legislation under the latter as reflected by the code does not seem unusually low.

3. John Malalas, *Chronicle* 17.14, 17.17, 17.22.

4. Procopius, *Anecdota* 6.18.

5. See *Codex Iustinianus* 1.31.5, 1.5.12–15, 1.15.2, 3.1.12, 7.62.36, 4.20.16, 5.3.19, 12.19.15, and Lounghis et al., *Regesten der Kaiserurkunden*, 146–151.

6. Lounghis et al., *Regesten der Kaiserurkunden*, 151–282.

7. *Codex Iustinianus* 5.16.26, 7.37.3, 7.37.4.

8. Ibid., 1.3.41, 1.4.34.1–4.

9. Ibid., 1.5.12.6—a law promulgated jointly by Justin and Justinian.

10. Ibid., 1.5.12. pr., 1.5.14, 1.5.20, 1.5.20.3. For the extent to which Justinian effectively swept away earlier legislation against heretics and other religious nonconformists and replaced it with much more comprehensive and concerted measures, see P. Riedlberger, *Prolegomena zu den spätantiken Konstitutionen: Nebst einer Analyse der erbrechtlichen und verwandten Sanktionen gegen Heterodoxe* (Stuttgart, 2020), esp. 800–801.

11. See discussion in P. Bell, *Social Conflict in the Age of Justinian* (Oxford, 2013), 235–246.

12. See P. Brown, *Power and Persuasion in Late Antiquity* (Madison, Wis., 1992), 128.

13. *Codex Iustinianus* 1.11.10. See discussion in A. Cameron, *Wandering Poets and Other Essays on Late Greek Literature and Philosophy* (Oxford, 2016), 255–286.

14. *Codex Iustinianus* 1.11.10. pr., 1.11.10.1, 1.11.10.6, 1.11.10.2. Again, the phrase used is 'the ultimate punishments', which in Justinianic law is generally a euphemism for the death penalty.

15. See *Codex Iustinianus* 1.11.10.2 and discussion in D. Rohmann, *Christianity, Book-Burning and Censorship in Late Antiquity* (Berlin, 2016), 96–101; Cameron, *Wandering Poets*, 205–246.

16. See N. Underwood, 'Lawyers and Inquisitors: Reassessing the Role of the *Defensor Civitatis*', *Studies in Late Antiquity* (forthcoming).

17. For bribery of both state and ecclesiastical officials in such contexts, see G. E. M. de Ste. Croix, 'Suffragium: From Vote to Patronage', *British Journal of Sociology* 5 (1954): 33–48.

18. Cameron, *Wandering Poets*, 214.

19. Agathias, *Histories* 2.28–32. See discussion in Cameron, *Wandering Poets*, 205–246. This is the most likely interpretation of the claim, based on a highly garbled passage contained in the *Chronicle* of John Malalas, often interpreted to suggest that Justinian ordered the closure of the philosophical academy in Athens: blanket anti-pagan legislation was issued by the emperor, which the governor in Athens then implemented with particular enthusiasm (John Malalas, *Chronicle* 18.47). There is no evidence that Justinian was hostile to philosophy per se.

20. Agathias, *Histories* 2.31; Cameron, *Wandering Poets*, 221–222.

21. Malalas, *Chronicle* 18.18.

22. Procopius, *Anecdota* 11.34–37. The account of Justinian's anti-pagan legislation contained in Malalas (describing punishments similar to those Procopius relates for homosexuality, but with respect to those found guilty of 'blasphemy') seems to splice and confuse it with the emperor's anti-homosexual measures, indicating the persecutions were possibly perceived to be simultaneous. See also *J. Nov.* 77.

23. For English translations of the constituent parts, see *Justinian's Institutes*, tr. P. Birks and G. McLeod (London, 1987); *The Novels of Justinian: A Complete Annotated English Translation*, ed. P. Sarris, tr. D. J. D. Miller (Cambridge, 2018); *The Codex of Justinian: A New Annotated Translation*, ed. B. W. Frier, tr. F. H. Blume (Cambridge, 2016); *The Digest of Justinian*, ed. A. Watson (Philadelphia, 1985).

24. See C. Humfress, 'Law and Legal Practice in the Age of Justinian', in *The Cambridge Companion to the Age of Justinian*, ed. M. Maas (Cambridge, 2005), 161–184, 165; T. Weir, 'Two Great Legislators', *Tulane European and Civil Law Forum* 21 (2006): 35–51, 40.

25. Humfress, 'Law and Legal Practice in the Age of Justinian', 163.

26. As argued by C. P. Wormald, 'Lex Scripta and Verbum Regis', *Early Medieval Kingship*, ed. P. Sawyer and I. Wood (Leeds, 1977), 105–138.

27. See discussion in A. M. Honoré, *Law and the Crisis of Empire* (Oxford, 1998).

28. Humfress, 'Law and Legal Practice in the Age of Justinian', 164.

29. See discussion and references to this issue in A. M. Honoré, *Justinian's Digest: Character and Compilation* (Oxford, 2010), 11, 81. For the number of volumes, see also *C. Tanta* 1. For the history of legal codification in the empire, see D. Liebs, 'The Code System: Reorganizing Roman Law and Legal Literature in the Late Antique Period', in *Jurists and Legal Science in the History of Roman Law*, ed. F. Nasti and A. Schiavone, tr. P. Christie (London, 2021), 261–286.

30. *C. Haec* 2.

31. Ibid., pr., 3.

32. Ibid., 1 details the full membership of the commission.

33. *C. Summa* 2, 3.

34. *C. Cordi* 2, 3.

35. See *P. Oxy* 15 1814.

36. Humfress, 'Law and Legal Practice in the Age of Justinian', 165; *C. Cordi* 1.

37. Procopius, *Wars* 1.24.16; Procopius, *Anecdota* 13.12.

38. For a sceptical appraisal of such claims, see Cameron, *Wandering Poets*, 273–274.

39. *Codex Iustinianus* 1.17.1; *Collectio Avellana*, in *Epistolae Imperatorum Pontificum Aliorum*, vol. 2, ed. O. Güenther (reprint, Cambridge, 2019), letter 147 (593).

40. *Deo Auctore* 2.

41. Ibid., 4, 5, 12, 14. For 'encyclopaedia' as an equivalent, see Birks and McLeod, 'Introduction', in *Justinian's Institutes*, 10. For the resolution of discrepancies, see *Deo Auctore* 7.

42. *C. Tanta* 1. See discussion in A. M. Honoré, *Justinian's Digest: Character and Compilation* (Oxford, 2010), 11. It is conceivable the commissioners only had some 1,600 books of law (or 2.4 million lines) to read, but it was still clearly a formidable task.

43. Honoré, *Justinian's Digest*, 9, 19, 22–26, 29, 10; Birks and McLeod, 'Introduction', 10–11.

44. *Deo Auctore* 4; Honoré, *Justinian's Digest*, 19.

45. Honoré, *Justinian's Digest*, 11.

46. This is the so-called Bluhme hypothesis. See Honoré, *Justinian's Digest*, 12.

47. *Deo Auctore* 6.

48. Honoré, *Justinian's Digest*, 6.

49. Note the suggestion in Cameron, *Wandering Poets*, 273–274, that this allegation may have been originally directed at another lawyer by the same name active in the reign of Justinian. But see also S. Consentino, 'La legislazione di Giustiniano sui banchieri e la carriera di Triboniano', in *Polidoro: Studi offerti ad Antonio Carile*, ed. G. Vespignani (Spoleto, Italy, 2013), 347–362, and discussion in Miller and Sarris, *Novels of Justinian*, 1056. The 'other' Tribonian who appears in the sources seems to be the same Tribonian as Justinian's *quaestor*.

50. Honoré, *Justinian's Digest*, 80–81.

51. Birks and McLeod, 'Introduction', 11; H. F. Jolowicz and B. Nicholas, *Historical Introduction to the Study of Roman Law*, 3rd ed. (Cambridge, 1972), 505.

52. *C. Tanta* 10.

53. *Deo Auctore* 11; Birks and McLeod, 'Introduction', 12–15.

54. See discussion in P. Sarris, 'Law and Custom in the Byzantine Countryside from Justinian I to Basil II', in *Law, Custom and Justice in Late Antiquity and the Early Middle Ages*, ed. A. Rio (London, 2011), 49–62, 51–53.

55. Honoré, *Justinian's Digest*, 5; Birks and McLeod, 'Introduction', 12–13. *C. Imp. Maj.* 3 makes it clear the *Institutes* were commissioned after the *Digest* was complete.

56. T. Honoré, *Tribonian* (London, 1978), 187–211; Birks and McLeod, 'Introduction', 13.

57. *C. Imp. Maj.*

58. Birks and McLeod, 'Introduction', 10–11; *C. Tanta* 23.

59. *C. Tanta* 12.

60. *C. Omnem.*

61. *C. Imp. Maj.* pr. For the new legal curriculum and how it was received and taught, see the excellent publication by D. Penna and R. Meijering, *A Sourcebook on Byzantine Law: Illustrating Byzantine Law Through the Sources* (Leiden, 2022), 22–70.

CHAPTER 6. THE VOICE OF THE PEOPLE

1. *Chronicon Paschale*, tr. M. Whitby and M. Whitby (Liverpool, 1989), 127, 126.

2. John Malalas, *Chronicle* 18.22, 18.43; Procopius, *Anecdota* 16.8–10.

3. *Anthologia Palatina* 1.10, lines 47–49.

4. For discussion of dating, see B. Croke, 'Justinian, Theodora, and the Church of Sergius and Bacchus', *Dumbarton Oaks Papers* 60 (2006): 25–63, whose arguments I largely find convincing. For a strong argument for a somewhat later dating (and for a suggestion that the original construction may not have been domed), see J. Bardill, 'The Date, Dedication, and Design of Sts. Sergius and Bacchus in Constantinople', *Journal of Late Antiquity* 10 (2017): 62–130. It is agreed that the church existed by 536 and hence predated Hagia Sophia. Most would concur that it was built before 532.

5. It was known to Procopius by the 550s as the Church of Saints Sergius and Bacchus. See Procopius, *Buildings* 1.4.1–7.

6. The translation is taken from Croke, 'Justinian, Theodora, and the Church', 245. See also E. Boeck, *The Bronze Horseman of Justinian in Constantinople: The Cross-Cultural Biography of a Mediterranean Monument* (Cambridge, 2021), 36.

7. Ibid., 35.

8. See discussion in P. Brown, *Power and Persuasion in Late Antiquity* (Madison, Wis., 1992), 3–34.

9. Procopius, *Anecdota* 11.24–26, 11.34–36.

10. See P. Brown, *The World of Late Antiquity* (London, 1971), 36.

11. See discussion in P. Sarris, *Economy and Society in the Age of Justinian* (Cambridge, 2006), 158–159.

12. See discussion in C. Wickham, *Framing the Early Middle Ages* (Oxford, 2005), 73–74.

13. See *Codex Iustinianus* 11.1 and Sarris, *Economy and Society in the Age of Justinian*, 200–201.

14. Procopius, *Anecdota* 8.4, 19.4–8.

15. For the economic context of the early sixth century, see J. Banaji, *Agrarian Change in Late Antiquity*, 2nd ed. (Oxford, 2007), and A. Laiou and C. Morrisson, *The Byzantine Economy* (Cambridge, 2007), 23–38. The earthquake-struck region around Antioch was probably one of the few significant exceptions where economic conditions are likely to have been relatively dire. See A. De Giorgi and A. Asa Eger, *Antioch: A History* (Abingdon, 2021), 190–234.

16. Procopius, *Anecdota* 19.4–5, 19.10, 19.1–3.

17. See J. W. Torgerson, *The Chronographia of George the Synkellos and Theophanes* (Leiden, 2022), with respect to the depiction of the emperor Nikephoros I in the Chronicle of Theophanes.

18. See J. R. Martindale, *The Prosopography of the Later Roman Empire*, vol. 3, *A.D. 527–641* (Cambridge, 1990), *PLRE-III-A*, Ioannes 11, 627–635.

19. Procopius, *Wars* 1.25.3, 1.24.12–14.

20. Martindale, *Prosopography, PLRE-III-A*, 627.

21. John Lydus, *De Magistratibus* 3.57. See Ioannes Lydus, *On Powers, or the Magistracies of the Roman State*, ed. A. C. Bandy (Philadelphia, 1983), 221 ('Bandy' hereafter).

22. See A. Kaldellis, 'Identifying Dissident Circles in Sixth-Century Byzantium: The Friendship of Prokopios and Ioannes Lydos', *Florilegium* 21 (2004): 1–17. Alternatively, the same policies may simply have irritated and alienated the same types of people.

23. John Lydus, *De Magistratibus* 3.57 (Bandy, 223), 3.58 (Bandy, 225).

24. Ibid., 3.61 (Bandy, 227–231).

25. See M. Hendy, *Studies in the Byzantine Monetary Economy* (Cambridge, 1986), 603–608; Bandy, 334, note to 228.5.

26. This cutback is described for other locations in the East by Procopius in *Anecdota* 30.1–11, although he ascribes the policy directly to Justinian rather than to John the Cappadocian.

27. See O. Nicholson, ed., *The Oxford Dictionary of Late Antiquity*, vol. 1 (Oxford, 2018), 440.

28. See discussion in Part I of C. Kelly, *Ruling the Later Roman Empire* (Cambridge, Mass., 2004). For Lydus in general, see M. Maas, *John Lydus and the Roman Past* (London, 1992).

29. John Lydus, *De Magistratibus* 3.68 (Bandy, 239–241).

30. *The Novels of Justinian: A Complete Annotated English Translation*, ed. P. Sarris, tr. D. J. D. Miller (Cambridge, 2018), 15.

31. John Lydus, *De Magistratibus* 3.62 (Bandy, 232–233), 3.69 (Bandy, 240–241), 3.70 (Bandy, 243–247).

32. See discussion in P. Bell, *Social Conflict in the Age of Justinian* (Oxford, 2013), 119–160.

33. See especially *J.Nov.* 13 of 535.

34. John Lydus, *De Magistratibus* 3.70 (Bandy, 244–245).

35. See Sarris, *Economy and Society in the Age of Justinian*, 194–195.

36. John Lydus, *De Magistratibus* 3.70 (Bandy, 241–247), 3.68 (Bandy, 239–241).

37. G. Greatrex, 'The Nika Riots: A Reappraisal', *Journal of Hellenic Studies* 117 (1997): 60–86, suggests that the factions limited themselves under Anastasius largely to involvement in doctrinal issues, but note John Lydus, *De Magistratibus*, 3.46 (a verse critical of Anastasius' imperial monetary policy, which was probably composed and advertised by faction members), discussed in Sarris, *Economy and Society in the Age of Justinian*, 201.

38. On Justinian's relationship with the Circus Factions and the tumultuous events of 532 that would result from the breakdown in relations, see Greatrex, 'The Nika Riots', and G. Greatrex, *Procopius of Caesarea: The Persian Wars. A Historical Commentary* (Cambridge, 2022), 334–359.

39. See Malalas, *Chronicle* 17.18, in *The Chronicle of John Malalas*, tr. E. Jeffreys, M. Jeffreys, and R. Scott (Canberra, 1986), 242–243 ('Jeffreys et al.' hereafter).

40. *Codex Iustinianus* 9.47.12; Greatrex, 'The Nika Riots', 81.

41. See *Chronicon Paschale*, tr. Whitby and Whitby, 114, note 345.

42. Theophanes Confessor, *Chronographia* AM 6024 / AD 531–532, in *The Chronicle of Theophanes Confessor*, tr. and ed. C. Mango and R. Scott (Oxford, 1997), 277–279 (see 281 note 8 for discussion of possible date).

43. I largely follow the reconstruction proposed in Greatrex, 'The Nika Riots', with some minor variations of emphasis, but see also R. Pfeilschifter, *Der Kaiser und Konstantinopel* (Berlin, 2013), 178–210, which offers a highly detailed account. For an overview of contrasting interpretations of the event and its significance, see Greatrex, *Procopius of Caesarea*, 334–345.

44. *The Chronicle of Theophanes Confessor*, tr. and ed. Mango and Scott, 279.

45. Malalas, *Chronicle* 18.71 (Jeffreys et al., 275, 276).

46. Ibid. 18.71 (Jeffreys et al., 276).

47. Ibid. 18.71 (Jeffreys et al., 276).

48. See Greatrex, 'The Nika Riots', 50.

49. Malalas, *Chronicle* 18.71 (Jeffreys et al., 277).

50. *Chronicon Paschale*, tr. Whitby and Whitby, 115 (and note 348), 116.

51. *Contra* Greatrex, 'The Nika Riots'. It is true that Procopius, for example, does not expressly attack Justinian for issuing either the *Codex Iustinianus* or *Digest*, but that does not mean the programme of legal reform did not put conservative nerves on edge while it was underway.

52. Martindale, *Prosopography*, *PLRE-III-A*, 186.

53. He was certainly *magister militum per orientem* again by 533 (see ibid., 187). The *Chronicon Paschale* accords him the title of *magister militum* at this point.

54. *Chronicon Paschale*, tr. Whitby and Whitby, 117; Malalas, *Chronicle* 18.71 (Jeffreys et al., 277).

55. *Chronicon Paschale*, tr. Whitby and Whitby, 117.

56. Malalas, *Chronicle* 18.71 (Jeffreys et al., 277–278).

57. See *Chronicon Paschale*, tr. Whitby and Whitby, 117–118 (and note 351).

58. *The Chronicle of Theophanes Confessor*, tr. and ed. Mango and Scott, 279.

59. *Chronicon Paschale*, tr. Whitby and Whitby, 118.

60. Ibid., 118–119 (and note 353), 119–120. See also Greatrex, 'The Nika Riots', 75.

61. *Chronicon Paschale*, tr. Whitby and Whitby, 121 (translation revised).

62. Greatrex, 'The Nika Riots', 76–77.

63. Procopius, *Wars* 1.24.19.

64. Ibid., 1.24.39.

65. In the year 610, according to the *Chronicle of John of Nikiu*, the emperor Phocas would be deposed and assassinated by members of the Senate as forces hostile to him mobilised on the streets outside. See *The Chronicle of John, Bishop of Nikiu*, tr. R. H. Charles (London, 1916), 177–178.

66. Procopius, *Wars* 1.24.19–21.

67. Ibid., 1.24.23–31.

68. Ibid., 1.24.31.

69. *Chronicon Paschale*, tr. Whitby and Whitby, 123.

70. Greatrex, 'The Nika Riots', 77.

71. *Chronicon Paschale*, tr. Whitby and Whitby, 122.

72. *The Chronicle of Theophanes Confessor*, tr. and ed. Mango and Scott, 279.

73. Procopius, *Wars* 1.24.33, 1.24.36.

74. Greatrex, 'The Nika Riots', 78.

75. Procopius, *Wars* 1.24.39–40.

76. For such private military retainers (known as *buccellarii*) see discussion in Sarris, *Economy and Society in the Age of Justinian*, 162–175.

77. *Chronicon Paschale*, tr. Whitby and Whitby, 124.

78. Procopius, *Wars* 1.24.44–50.

79. Ibid., 1.24.50–52, 1.24.54. See also Boeck, *The Bronze Horseman of Justinian in Constantinople*, 17. That Narses joined in with this is suggested by the *Chronicon Paschale*. See *Chronicon Paschale*, tr. Whitby and Whitby, 124.

80. A. Kaldellis, 'The People of Constantinople', in *The Cambridge Companion to Constantinople*, ed. S. Bassett (Cambridge, 2022), 50–66, 50.

81. Procopius, *Wars* 1.24.56–58.

82. Greatrex, 'The Nika Riots', 80.

83. Procopius, *Wars* 1.24.1.

CHAPTER 7. BUILDING HEAVEN ON EARTH

1. *Chronicon Paschale*, tr. M. Whitby and M. Whitby (Liverpool, 1989), 127.

2. *Codex Iustinianus* 1.44.1–2. See T. C. Lounghis, B. Blysidu, and St. Lampakes *Regesten der Kaiserurkunden des Oströmischen Reiches von 476 bis 565*

(Nicosia, 2005), 244–247. Under normal circumstances, a great deal of legislation would have been issued in the late winter. See P. Noailles, *Les collections de novelles de l'empereur Justinien*, vol. 1 (Paris, 1912), 83.

3. *Codex Iustinianus* 1.1.6 (March 533).

4. *Anthologia Palatina* 7.591. See A. Cameron, 'The House of Anastasius', *Greek, Roman and Byzantine Studies* 19 (1978): 259–276, 264.

5. S. Brock, 'The Conversations with the Syrian Orthodox Under Justinian (532)', in *Orientalia Christiana Periodica* 67 (1981): 87–121, reprinted in A. Cameron and R. Hoyland, eds., *Doctrine and Debate in the Christian World* (London, 2011).

6. S. Brock, 'The Orthodox-Oriental Orthodox Conversations of 532', in S. Brock, *Syriac Perspectives on Late Antiquity* (London, 1984), sec. 11, 224.

7. Ibid., 224, 225.

8. *The Acts of the Council of Constantinople of 553*, vol. 1, ed. and tr. R. Price (Liverpool, 2009), 11–12.

9. Brock, 'The Orthodox-Oriental Orthodox Conversations of 532', 226.

10. *Acts of the Council of Constantinople of 553*, ed. and tr. Price, 1:12.

11. See Brock, 'The Orthodox-Oriental Orthodox Conversations of 532', 226, and *Acts of the Council of Constantinople of 553*, ed. and tr. Price, 1:12. The *Akoimetai* were excommunicated by Pope John II, probably on Justinian's request: see *Codex Iustinianus* 1.8.31–34.

12. *Codex Iustinianus* 1.1.6. See *Chronicon Paschale*, tr. Whitby and Whitby, 129.

13. *Chronicon Paschale*, tr. Whitby and Whitby, 127 (emphasis added).

14. J. Koder, 'Imperial Propaganda in the Kontakia of Romanos the Melode', *Dumbarton Oaks Papers* 62 (2008): 275–291, 281.

15. Ibid.

16. John Lydus, *De Magistratibus* 3.71. See Ioannes Lydus, *On Powers, or the Magistracies of the Roman State*, ed. A. C. Bandy (Philadelphia, 1983), 247 ('Bandy' hereafter).

17. *Chronicon Paschale*, tr. Whitby and Whitby, 127.

18. R. Ousterhout, *Eastern Medieval Architecture* (Oxford, 2019), 199–201. On the construction of Hagia Sophia, see also K. Dark and J. Kostenec, *Hagia Sophia in Context: An Archaeological Reconstruction of the Cathedral of Byzantine Constantinople* (Oxford, 2019).

19. John Lydus, *De Magistratibus* 3.71 (Bandy, 247).

20. See C. Mango, *Byzantine Architecture* (London, 1986), 59–68, and Dark and Kostenec, *Hagia Sophia in Context*, 46.

21. B. Pentcheva, *Hagia Sophia: Sound, Space and Spirit in Byzantium* (Philadelphia, 2017). For the mosaics and their interaction with light, see N.

Teteriatnikov, *Justinianic Mosaics of Hagia Sophia and Their Aftermath* (Washington, D.C., 2016).

22. B. Pentcheva, 'Hagia Sophia: Sound, Space, and Spirit in Byzantium', https://hagiasophia.stanford.edu; *The Russian Primary Chronicle*, tr. and ed. S. Hazzard-Cross and O. B. Sherbowitz-Wetzor (Cambridge, Mass., 1953), 110–111.

23. F. Spingou, *Sources for Byzantine Art History*, vol. 3, *The Visual Culture of Late Byzantium, c. 1081–1350* (Cambridge, 2022), 529–536.

24. Mango, *Byzantine Architecture*, 61.

25. E. Boeck, *The Bronze Horseman of Justinian in Constantinople: The Cross-Cultural Biography of a Mediterranean Monument* (Cambridge, 2021), 23.

26. Mango, *Byzantine Architecture*, 59, 61; Ousterhout, *Eastern Medieval Architecture*, 201–206.

27. Boeck, *The Bronze Horseman of Justinian*, 50.

28. Pentcheva, *Hagia Sophia: Sound, Space and Spirit in Byzantium*, 3.

29. Boeck, *The Bronze Horseman of Justinian*, 50–51.

30. Procopius, *Buildings (De Aedificiis)*, translation taken from C. Mango, *The Art of the Byzantine Empire* (Toronto, 1986), 75.

31. Boeck, *The Bronze Horseman of Justinian*, 50.

32. Procopius, *Buildings* 1.1.27; Boeck, *The Bronze Horseman of Justinian*, 51–52.

33. Ousterhout, *Eastern Medieval Architecture*, 210, 199; Boeck, *The Bronze Horseman of Justinian*, 51–52.

34. Mango, *Byzantine Architecture*, 86, 9–11, 59.

35. Procopius, *Buildings* 1.1.66–72.

36. Teteriatnikov, *Justinianic Mosaics*, 243, 245, 295, 237.

37. Ibid., 270; Pentcheva, *Hagia Sophia: Sound, Space and Spirit in Byzantium*, 121–149.

38. Procopius, in Mango, *The Art of the Byzantine Empire*, 74, 75.

39. Pentcheva, *Hagia Sophia: Sound, Space and Spirit in Byzantium*, 3, 73–74, 188. For the staff employed on the payroll of the Great Church, see *J.Nov.* 3 c.1.1, and Teteriatnikov, *Justinianic Mosaics*, 295.

40. Translation taken from Mango, *The Art of the Byzantine Empire*, 76.

41. Teteriatnikov, *Justinianic Mosaics*, 236, 269, citing D. Janes, *God and Gold in Late Antiquity* (Cambridge, 1999), 8–9.

42. Pentcheva, *Hagia Sophia: Sound, Space and Spirit in Byzantium*, 65–75.

43. Ibid., 39, 23–24, 118–119, 150–152, 19–21.

44. F. Stroth, *Monogrammkapitelle: Die justinianische Bauskulptur Konstantinopels als Textträger* (Wiesbaden, 2021), 34.

45. Teteriatnikov, *Justinianic Mosaics*, 275, 274.

46. Mango, *The Art of the Byzantine Empire*, 89.

47. Ibid., 101, 96 (the *Narratio de aedificatione Sanctae Sophiae*, dating from the eighth or ninth century).

48. Teteriatnikov, *Justinianic Mosaics*, 290.

49. Ousterhout, *Eastern Medieval Architecture*, 206.

50. Mango, *Byzantine Architecture*, 65, 64, 59.

51. For the impact on architecture of the change in circumstances of the 540s, see Teteriatnikov, *Justinianic Mosaics*, 289.

52. Mango, *Byzantine Architecture*, 68. The new constructions are enumerated by Procopius in *Buildings* 1.2–11.

53. N. Karydis, 'Justinian's Church of the Holy Apostles', in *The Holy Apostles*, ed. M. Mullett and R. Ousterhout (Washington, D.C., 2020), 99–130.

54. S. Bassett, *The Urban Image of Late Antique Constantinople* (Cambridge, 2004), 123, 124, 135.

55. Ibid., 129, 128, 133. I owe the point about containing demonic powers to Calum Samuelson. See C. Samuelson, 'The *Parastaseis Syntomoi Chronikai* and Eighth-Century Constantinopolitan Perceptions of Antiquity' (MPhil diss., Cambridge University, 2016). See also discussion in E. Maguire and H. Maguire, *Other Icons: Art and Power in Byzantine Secular Culture* (Princeton, N.J., 2007).

56. Bassett, *The Urban Image of Late Antique Constantinople*, 125.

57. Boeck, *The Bronze Horseman of Justinian*, 46.

58. Procopius, *Buildings* 1.2.1–12.

59. I. Nikolajevic, 'La croix dans la decoration architecturale de Caričin Grad', in *Caričin Grad III: L'acropole et ses monuments*, ed. N. Duval and V. Popović (Belgrade, 2010), 422–428.

60. Boeck, *The Bronze Horseman of Justinian*, 1, 21, 53, 56, 57.

61. Mango, *Byzantine Architecture*, 57.

62. Ousterhout, *Eastern Medieval Architecture*, 200.

63. D. A. Parnell, *Justinian's Men* (Basingstoke, 2017), 134–135.

64. See discussion in J. Haldon, 'Economy and Administration', in *The Cambridge Companion to the Age of Justinian*, ed. M. Maas (Cambridge, 2005), 28–59, 39–41.

65. Boeck, *The Bronze Horseman of Justinian*, 30–31. The standard iconography of the imperial coinage (from a three-quarter-facing bust to a fully frontal image) appears to have been transformed in 538.

66. Virgil, *Aeneid* 10.284.

CHAPTER 8. THE AFRICAN CAMPAIGN

1. Salvian, *De Gubernatione Dei* 7.79–80. See discussion in S. Elm, 'New Romans: Salvian of Marseilles on the Governance of God', *Journal of Early Christian Studies* 25 (2017): 1–28.

2. See A. Merrills and R. Miles, *The Vandals* (Oxford, 2010), 184–192, 191. For Roman-Vandal relations, see especially J. Conant, *Staying Roman: Conquest and Identity in Africa and the Mediterranean, 439–700* (Cambridge, 2012), and R. Whelan, *Being Christian in Vandal Africa: The Politics of Orthodoxy in the Post-Imperial West* (Oakland, Calif., 2017). Although Whelan's usage of the terms 'Homoian' and 'Homousian' in place of 'Arian' and 'Catholic' is theologically more precise when discussing the religious identities that existed and took shape in the Vandal kingdom, I have used the traditional terminology for the sake of comprehensibility on the part of nonspecialist readers. In doing so, I also convey how the religious landscape of the post-Roman West was understood from the perspective of Constantinople and hence at Justinian's court.

3. Zacharias Rhetor, *Chronicle* 9.17.

4. Procopius, *Wars* 4.3.26.

5. See M. E. Williams, 'The African Policy of Justinian I' (DPhil, Oxford University, 2015), 92.

6. *Codex Iustinianus* 1.27.1.4.

7. Procopius, *Wars* 3.9.14–25.

8. Ibid., 3.9.24–26.

9. Ibid., 3.10.2–5.

10. Ibid., 3.10.14–17.

11. Ibid., 3.10.18–21.

12. Williams, 'The African Policy of Justinian I', 98.

13. Victor of Tunnuna, *Chronicle*, sub anno 534.

14. Procopius, *Wars* 3.10.22–23, 3.10.25–34.

15. M. Whitby, *The Wars of Justinian* (Barnsley, 2021), 103–104, 178.

16. Procopius, *Wars* 7.1.19–20.

17. General Mundo, for example, had 3,000 men in his retinue in 532. See the testimony of Theophanes in *The Chronicle of Theophanes Confessor*, tr. and ed. C. Mango and R. Scott (Oxford, 1997), 279. In 543, when Belisarius was obliged to leave his *buccellarii* in the East, where he had once more been fighting, he recruited 4,000 replacement troops in the Balkans (Procopius, *Wars* 7.10.2).

18. For the composition of the early sixth-century army, see Whitby, *The Wars of Justinian*, 85–114.

19. Ibid., 102–103. There are indications that, under Justinian, the number

of mobile troops would be increased at the expense of the number of frontier soldiers. This would have made it easier for the emperor to launch aggressive campaigns abroad, such as the African venture of 533. See C. Koehn, *Justinian und die Armee des frühen Byzanz* (Berlin, 2018), 8–145.

20. See J. Pryor and E. Jeffreys, *The Age of the Dromon* (Leiden, 2006).

21. Procopius, *Wars* 3.11.13–16.

22. Ibid., 3.12.1–10. For Belisarius and his relationship with his wife, see D. Parnell, *Belisarius and Antonina: Love and War in the Age of Justinian* (Oxford, 2023). Unfortunately, this study had not yet been published at the time this book was being written.

23. Procopius, *Wars* 3.13.1–7.

24. For 'biscuit boys', see P. Sarris, *Economy and Society in the Age of Justinian* (Cambridge, 2006), 163. See Procopius, *Wars* 3.13.12–20.

25. Procopius, *Wars* 3.13.21–24, 3.14.5–6.

26. Ibid., 3.14.1–4.

27. Ibid., 3.14.7–17.

28. *Codex Iustinianus* 1.1.8.

29. Procopius, *Buildings* 6.6.8–16.

30. Procopius, *Wars* 3.15.1–36, 3.16.1–8.

31. Ibid., 3.16.9–15.

32. Whitby, *The Wars of Justinian*, 181.

33. Williams, 'The African Policy of Justinian I', 31–32.

34. Whitby, *The Wars of Justinian*, 182.

35. Ibid.

36. Williams, 'The African Policy of Justinian I', 32–33.

37. Procopius, *Wars* 3.19.25–29, 3.19.32.

38. Ibid., 3.20.1–2, 3.20.6.

39. Ibid., 3.20.17–21.

40. Ibid., 3.20.21–24, 3.21.8.

41. Ibid., 3.21.10–16, 3.23.19–21, 3.21.19–25.

42. Ibid., 3.23.1–9.

43. Ibid., 3.25.2–7, 3.25.24–26.

44. Williams, 'The African Policy of Justinian I', 33–34.

45. Whitby, *The Wars of Justinian*, 185–186.

46. Williams, 'The African Policy of Justinian I', 34.

47. Procopius, *Wars* 4.6.27, 4.6.21–22.

48. Ibid., 4.7.12–16.

49. Ibid., 4.9.14, 4.9.1–3.

50. John Lydus, *De Magistratibus* 3.55.

51. Procopius, *Wars* 4.9.11–12.

52. Ibid., 4.9.15–16, 6.30.28. See also 6.29.20 (emphasis added).

53. *C. Imp. Maj.*

54. *C. Tanta* 23.

55. *Codex Iustinianus* 1.27.1–2.

56. A. M. Honoré, 'Some Constitutions Composed by Justinian', *Journal of Roman Studies* 65 (1975): 107–123.

57. Williams, 'The African Policy of Justinian I', 134.

58. *Codex Iustinianus* 1.27.1. See excellent discussion in Williams, 'The African Policy of Justinian I', 92.

59. Williams, 'The African Policy of Justinian I', 121–130, 133. For the parallel with the eastern desert frontier, see *J.Edict.* 4 and *J.Nov.* 102. See also M. Williams, 'East Roman Client Management During the Reign of Justinian I', *Travaux et Mémoires* 26 (2022): 209–232.

60. Williams, 'The African Policy of Justinian I', 136–138.

61. Whitby, *The Wars of Justinian*, 188.

62. Williams, 'The African Policy of Justinian I', 134.

63. Ibid., 113–116; Procopius, *Wars* 4.5.11.

64. Williams, 'The African Policy of Justinian I', 145–146; Procopius, *Buildings* 6.5.8–11.

65. Procopius, *Wars* 4.19.3–4; Procopius, *Buildings* 6.2.1–2.

66. Merrills and Miles, *The Vandals*, 236.

67. Procopius, *Buildings*, 6.2.7, 6.5.11, 6.7.1–11.

68. See, for example, E. Castagnino Berlinghieri and Andrea Paribeni, 'Byzantine Merchant Ships and Marble Trade', *Skyllis* 11 (2011): 64–75.

69. *J.Nov.* 37 (dating from 535); *J.Nov.* 36.

70. Merrills and Miles, *The Vandals*, 236.

71. Williams, 'The African Policy of Justinian I', 107.

72. Merrills and Miles, *The Vandals*, 236.

73. Procopius, *Wars* 4.9.9, 4.14.9–11, 4.8.25, 3.5.12–15. The objects purported to be from Jerusalem would be sent by Justinian 'to the sanctuaries of the Christians in Jerusalem'. See discussion in S. Kingsley, *God's Gold: A Quest for the Lost Temple Treasures of Jerusalem* (London, 2007), 280–286.

74. Procopius, *Wars* 4.8.1–2, 4.8.9, 4.11.52–56. See also discussion in Williams, 'The African Policy of Justinian I', 138–142.

75. Procopius, *Wars* 4.12.27.

76. Ibid., 4.12.30, 4.14.7–14.

77. See Williams, 'The African Policy of Justinian I', 201.

78. Procopius, *Wars* 4.16.2–7.

CHAPTER 9. THE BATTLE FOR ITALY

1. For a magisterial account of Theoderic's regime in Ravenna, see J. Herrin, *Ravenna: Capital of Empire, Crucible of Europe* (London, 2020), 96–136.
2. Procopius, *Wars* 5.1.29.
3. Cassiodorus, *Variae* 10.4. For a full translation of this important source, see Cassiodorus, *The Variae: The Complete Translation*, tr. S. Bjornlie (Berkeley, Calif., 2019) ('Bjornlie' hereafter).
4. Procopius, *Wars* 5.3.1–3; Cassiodorus, *Variae* 10.1.
5. Cassiodorus, *Variae* 10.1 (Bjornlie, 390).
6. Procopius' chronology of these machinations does seem confused, however.
7. Procopius, *Wars* 5.2.22–27, 5.3.4.
8. Ibid., 5.3.28–30. Peter is reported by Procopius to have been an Illyrian (thus perhaps inclined towards the anti-barbarian faction at court) and was the author of the most detailed account of the circumstances of Justin I's coronation encountered in Chapter 2. See J. R. Martindale, *The Prosopography of the Later Roman Empire*, vol. 3, *A.D. 527–641* (Cambridge, 1990), PLRE-III-B, 994–998.
9. Jordanes, *Getica* 306. See Jordanes, *Romana and Getica*, tr. P. Van Nuffelen and L. Van Hoof (Liverpool, 2020), 365 ('Van Nuffelen and Van Hoof' hereafter).
10. Procopius, *Wars* 5.4.12–31.
11. Procopius, *Anecdota* 16.1–5; Cassiodorus, *Variae* 10.20–21.
12. Cassiodorus, *Variae* 10.20.4 (Bjornlie, 409).
13. Jordanes, *Getica* 307 (Van Nuffelen and Van Hoof, 365–366).
14. Procopius, *Wars* 5.4.30.
15. Agathias, *Histories* 1 pr. 30. See M. R. Salzman, *The Falls of Rome: Crises, Resilience, and Resurgence in Late Antiquity* (Cambridge, 2021), 258–259.
16. Procopius, *Wars* 5.5.9.
17. M. Whitby, *The Wars of Justinian* (Barnsley, 2021), 210.
18. Procopius, *Wars* 5.5.7, 5.5.11.
19. Whitby, *The Wars of Justinian*, 211.
20. Procopius, *Wars* 5.5.15–16, 5.5.18–19.
21. *J.Nov.* 30 c. 11.2 (18 March 536).
22. Procopius, *Wars* 5.4.22.
23. Ibid., 5.6.1–27.
24. Ibid., 5.7.1–25.
25. Ibid., 5.7.26–37, 5.8.1–4.
26. Ibid., 5.8.7–11, 5.8.13–14, 5.8.16–21, 5.8.27.
27. Ibid., 5.8.29–41.

28. Cassiodorus, *Variae* 2.27 (Bjornlie, 102).
29. Procopius, *Wars* 5.10.29, 5.10.35, 5.10.37.
30. Cassiodorus, *Variae* 10.13–14, 10.18, 10.31.
31. Procopius, *Wars* 5.11.10.
32. Whitby, *The Wars of Justinian*, 215–216.
33. Ibid., 217; *Liber Pontificalis* Silverius 4. See *The Book of Pontiffs (Liber Pontificalis)*, tr. R. Davis (Liverpool, 1989), 54; Procopius, *Wars* 5.14.14–15. Procopius dates Belisarius' entry into Rome to the 9th; our Roman source (the *Liber Pontificalis*) dates it to the 10th.
34. Procopius, *Wars* 5.14.
35. Ibid., 5.14.15–16.
36. See Whitby, *The Wars of Justinian*, 218 note 33, 217.
37. Ibid., 218.
38. Procopius, *Wars* 5.14–16, 24.3.
39. Whitby, *The Wars of Justinian*, 218.
40. Procopius, *Wars* 5.18–6.10.
41. Ibid., 5.24.8.
42. Whitby, *The Wars of Justinian*, 223; Procopius, *Wars* 5.24.18–20.
43. Procopius, *Wars* 5.25.13–14, 5.25.22–25.
44. Ibid., 5.26–29, 6.1–5.
45. Ibid., 6.6.27–28.
46. Ibid., 6.18.10–29, 6.8, 6.22.1–5.
47. Ibid., 6.22.1–13, 6.22.16–22, 2.2.
48. Ibid., 6.22.21.
49. Whitby, *The Wars of Justinian*, 232.
50. Procopius, *Wars* 6.29.1–2.
51. Ibid., 6.29.3–5, 6.29.18–22.
52. Ibid., 6.29.34.
53. Ibid. 6.29.40–41.
54. Ibid., 6.29.40–41, 6.30.1–3.
55. Ibid., 6.30, 7.1.28–30.
56. Ibid., 7.1.1–7.

CHAPTER 10. THE SLEEPLESS EMPEROR

1. See D. Talbot Rice, *The Great Palace of the Byzantine Emperors* (Edinburgh, 1958), and J. Bardill, 'The Great Palace of the Byzantine Emperors and the Walker Trust Excavations', *Journal of Roman Archaeology* 12 (1999): 216–230. For more recent discussion, see P. Magdalino, 'Imperial Constantinople', in *The Cambridge Companion to Constantinople*, ed. S. Bassett

(Cambridge, 2022), 135–149, and J. Bardill, 'Visualizing the Great Palace of the Byzantine Emperors', in *Visualisierung von Herrschaft frühmittelalterlicher Residenzen: Gestalt und Zeremoniell*, ed. F. A. Bauer (Istanbul, 2006), 5–45.

2. See G. Brett, 'The Mosaics of the Great Palace in Constantinople', *Journal of the Warburg and Courtauld Institutes* 5 (1942): 34–43; K. Dark, 'Roman Architecture in the Great Palace of the Byzantine Emperors', *Byzantion* 77 (2008): 87–105; and especially Bardill, 'Visualizing the Great Palace'. There is good reason to believe that the mosaics were installed in about 580 during the reign of the emperor Tiberius II (r. 574–582) or that of his successor, Maurice (r. 582–602). Tiberius II, in particular, sought to present himself as a 'New Justinian' and attempted to reach back to the legislation of the Justinianic era after the disastrous reign of Justin II (r. 565–574). The mosaics may thus have been meant to reflect a broadly 'Justinianic' ideology and aesthetic. See discussion in *The Novels of Justinian: A Complete Annotated English Translation*, ed. P. Sarris, tr. D. J. D. Miller (Cambridge, 2018), 48–50.

3. Miller and Sarris, *Novels of Justinian*. See also A. M. Honoré, 'Some Constitutions Composed by Justinian', *Journal of Roman Studies* 65 (1975): 107–123. For the unusual (and highly 'Justinianic') intrusion of biblical language and motifs into this imperial legislation, see P. Sarris, 'At the Origins of the "Persecuting Society"? Defining the "Orthodox Republic" in the Age of Justinian', *Travaux et mémoires* 26 (2022): 407–422, 414–415.

4. *J.Nov.* 22 c. 15.1–2.

5. T. Honoré, *Tribonian* (London, 1978).

6. See *J.Nov.* 8 pr.; *J.Nov.* 30 c. 11.2. See discussion in B. Croke, 'Justinian: The Sleepless Emperor', in *Basileia*, ed. G. Nathan and L. Garland (Leiden, 2011), 103–108.

7. See, for example, *J.Nov.* 8.

8. Honoré, *Tribonian*, 28.

9. This would be especially true of his treatment in the *Novels* of social issues, such as marriage and inheritance. Justinian would, for example, reverse centuries of Roman marriage law by effectively making it impossible for couples to divorce by mutual consent. See *J.Nov.* 140, in which the emperor Justin II would attempt to rescind this reform. He would also effectively recast how the family was conceived of and defined in Roman law. See P. Sarris, 'Emperor Justinian', in *Christianity and Family Law: An Introduction*, ed. J. Witte Jr. and J. S. Hauk (Cambridge, 2017), 100–116. I am grateful to Mr Agostino Minichiello for discussion of this point.

10. E.g., *J.Nov.* 1 pr. 1. See also *J.Nov.* 23, which sought to introduce strict time limits on such appeals.

11. *J.Nov.* 126 pr.; *J.Nov.* 8 c. 1.

12. See *J.Nov.* 62 (issued in 537), and J. Haldon, 'Economy and Administration', in *The Cambridge Companion to the Age of Justinian*, ed. M. Maas (Cambridge, 2005), 28–59. The inner circle of the reconfigured Senate—known as the *sacrum consistorium*, or 'sacred consistory'—remained politically important as the emperor was expected to consult it on major matters of state.

13. D. Parnell, *Justinian's Men* (Basingstoke, 2017), 134–135, is excellent on this. For the position that Justin held at court, see *The Chronicle of Theophanes Confessor*, tr. and ed. C. Mango and R. Scott (Oxford, 1997), 344 note 21 ('With Justin's appointment the dignity acquired a new importance, raising the holder above the other patricians without formally indicating him as heir apparent.'). See also discussion in S. Lin, 'Justin Under Justinian: The Rise of Emperor Justin II Revisited', *Dumbarton Oaks Papers* 75 (2022): 121–142.

14. *J.Nov.* 13 c. 1–5, conclusion (abridged).

15. *J.Nov.* 80 c. 5, c. 9.

16. *J.Nov.* 80 c. 10 and c. 5 and 9. See discussion in A. Laniado, *Ethnos et droit* (Geneva, 2015), 215–216.

17. *J.Nov.* 80 c. 2.

18. *J.Nov.* 23. On the date, see Honoré, *Tribonian*, 57. A slightly later date is proposed by T. C. Lounghis, B. Blysidu, and St. Lampakes in *Regesten der Kaiserurkunden des Oströmischen Reiches von 476 bis 565* (Nicosia, 2005), 260.

19. *J.Nov.* 15. See discussion in A. H. M. Jones, *The Later Roman Empire*, vol. 1 (Oxford, 1964), 144–145, and Miller and Sarris, *Novels of Justinian*, 185 note 1.

20. Miller and Sarris, *Novels of Justinian*, 188 note 10; *J.Nov.* 15 c. 3.

21. *J.Nov.* 15 c. 5, conclusion.

22. *J.Nov.* 20; *J.Nov.* 8; *J.Nov.* 23; *J.Nov.* 158.

23. *J.Nov.* 8, appendix. See Miller and Sarris, *Novels of Justinian*, 142–144.

24. *J.Nov.* 30 c. 11.2.

25. *J.Nov.* 8.

26. See *Codex Theodosianus* 2.29.2, and *Codex Iustinianus* 4.3.1. The classic study of this topic remains G. E. M. de Ste. Croix, 'Suffragium: From Vote to Patronage', *British Journal of Sociology* 5 (1954): 33–48.

27. *J.Nov.* 8 c. 1. For the permitted fees, see Miller and Sarris, *Novels of Justinian*, 144–150.

28. *J.Nov.* 8 pr. 1.

29. *J.Nov.* 8 c. 1–9, c. 12–13.

30. See Miller and Sarris, *Novels of Justinian*, 144–150, 152–153 (for a map of the provinces).

31. *J.Nov.* 8 c. 11, conclusion and appendix; Miller and Sarris, *Novels of Justinian*, 143, 144.

32. *J.Nov.* 8, appendix. See Miller and Sarris, *Novels of Justinian*, 154–155. See also P. Sarris, *Empires of Faith: The Fall of Rome to the Rise of Islam* (Oxford, 2011), 83–88. For the religious dimensions of this oath, see M. Wuk, 'Constructing Christian Bureaucrats', *Journal of Late Antiquity* 15 (2022): 170–203.

33. *J.Nov.* 17 c. 1–3 and c. 11–12. 'Hunting down heresy' is mentioned in c. 11.

34. *J.Nov.* 17 c. 13–17.

35. Procopius, *Anecdota* 1.2.

36. See Z. Rubin, 'The Reforms of Khusro Anushirwan', in *The Byzantine and Early Islamic Near East*, vol. 3, *States, Resources and Armies*, ed. A. Cameron (Princeton, N.J., 1995), 227–298.

37. *J.Nov.* 24 c. 1–4; Miller and Sarris, *Novels of Justinian*, 277–284.

38. *J.Nov.* 25–29.

39. *J.Nov.* 29 c. 2; *J.Nov.* 25 c. 1; *J.Nov.* 26 c. 2; *J.Nov.* 28 c. 3.

40. C. Whately, *Procopius on Soldiers and Military Institutions in the Sixth-Century Roman Empire* (Leiden, 2021), 201.

41. Procopius, *Anecdota* 11.2.

42. *J.Nov.* 30; *J.Nov.* 30 c. 6. See Miller and Sarris, *Novels of Justinian*, 325 note 22, and G. Azzarello, *Il dossier della 'domus divina' in Egitto* (Berlin, 2012), 29–31.

43. In general, see E. Cooper and M. Decker, *Life and Society in Byzantine Cappadocia* (London, 2012).

44. *J.Nov.* 30 c. 5.

45. *J.Nov.* 30 c. 4–7 (neglect of tax revenues in c. 4), c. 11.

46. See P. Sarris, *Economy and Society in the Age of Justinian* (Cambridge, 2006), 177–202, and C. Begass, *Die Senatsaristokratie des oströmischen Reiches, ca. 457–518* (Munich, 2018).

47. *J.Nov.* 102 c. 1–2; *J.Nov.* 103 c. 2.

48. *J.Edict* 4 c. 2.

49. *J.Edict* 13 pr. See discussion in Sarris, *Economy and Society*, 212–214, and P. Sarris, 'Egypt in the Age of Justinian: Connector or Disconnector?', in *Egypt in the Eastern Mediterranean World*, ed. J. Bruning, J. H. M. de Jong, and P. M. Sijpesteijn (Cambridge, 2022), 19–45.

50. See *J.Edict* 13 c. 2, c. 24–25, c. 9, c. 11.

51. As argued by Sarris, *Economy and Society*, 214.

52. *J.Nov.* 44; *J.Nov.* 47.

53. M. Meier, 'Das Ende des Konsulates im Jahr 541/2', *Zeitschrift für Papyrologie und Epigraphik* 138 (2002): 277–279.

54. Procopius, *Anecdota* 26.15. See also discussion in M. Kruse, 'Justinian's

Laws and Procopius' *Wars*', in *Procopius of Caesarea: Literary and Historical Interpretations*, ed. C. Lillington-Martin and E. Turquois (Basingstoke, 2017), 186–200.

55. Prokopios, *The Secret History with Related Texts*, tr. A. Kaldellis (Indianapolis, 2010), 115 note 98, discussing John Lydus, *De Magistratibus* 2.8.

56. The classic study of these prefaces is to be found in M. Maas, 'Roman History and Christian Ideology in Justinianic Reform Legislation', *Dumbarton Oaks Papers* 40 (1986): 17–31.

57. *J.Nov.* 24 pr.; *J.Nov.* 24 c. 1; *J.Nov.* 25 pr.

58. See Maas, 'Roman History and Christian Ideology'.

59. See *J.Nov.* 43 pr.; *J.Nov.* 59 pr.; *J.Nov.* 109 pr.; *J.Nov.* 78 c. 5.

60. *J.Nov.* 22. See Miller and Sarris, *Novels of Justinian*, 233–272.

61. See Lounghis et al., *Regesten der Kaiserurkunden*, 276–278, which records five very extensive laws all issued on the same day. For a summary of the topics covered by Justinian's legislation issued after the promulgation of the second recension of the code, see Miller and Sarris, *Novels of Justinian*, v–xv.

62. See *J.Edict* 3 and *J.Nov.* 21.

63. *J.Nov.* 50.

64. *J.Edict* 13 c. 18.

65. *J.Nov.* 75.

66. See D. Feissel, *Documents, droit, diplomatique dans l'empire romain tardif* (Paris, 2010), 510, notes 31 and 33, 509–516.

67. *J.Nov.* 74 c. 4.

68. See discussion in B. Sirks, 'The Colonate in Justinian's Reign', *Journal of Roman Studies* 98 (2008): 120–143. For the history of the institution, see B. Sirks, 'The Colonate in the Later Roman Empire', *Tijdschrift voor Rechtsgeschiedenis* 90 (2022): 129–147.

69. *J.Nov.* 54, pr. and c. 1.

CHAPTER 11. A NEW KIND OF POWER

1. Procopius, *Anecdota* 30.30. See Prokopios, *The Secret History with Related Texts*, tr. A. Kaldellis (Indianapolis, 2010), 132.

2. Procopius, *Anecdota* 30.30–31.

3. Published as P. Sarris, *Economy and Society in the Age of Justinian* (Cambridge, 2006).

4. *P.Oxy.* 63 4400.

5. See P. Parsons, *City of the Sharp-Nosed Fish* (London, 2007).

6. *The Oxyrhynchus Papyri*, vol. 84, ed. A. Benaissa and N. Gonis (London, 2019).

7. Sarris, *Economy and Society*, 18, 72.

8. See P. Sarris, 'Egypt in the Age of Justinian: Connector or Disconnector?', in *Egypt in the Eastern Mediterranean World*, ed. J. Bruning, J. H. M. de Jong, and P. M. Sijpesteijn (Cambridge, 2022), 36–37, and Sarris, *Economy and Society*, 11. In the former, I respond to some misfocused attempts to downplay the size of the estates.

9. *P.Oxy.* 27 2479, and lines 16–17.

10. See discussion in J. Banaji, *Agrarian Change in Late Antiquity*, 2nd ed. (Oxford, 2007), and Sarris, *Economy and Society*, 29–80.

11. See, for example, *P.Oxy.* 63 4397.

12. Sarris, *Economy and Society*, 17 (and note 40 for such 'papponymy'), 1–40, 15–16.

13. Procopius, *Wars* 1.8.5.

14. Sarris, *Economy and Society*, 16.

15. Ibid., 17 note 39.

16. *P.Oxy.* 63 4400.

17. Sarris, *Economy and Society*, 18.

18. Ibid., 18.

19. The *Narratio de Aedificatione Sanctae Sophiae*. See J. R. Martindale, *The Prosopography of the Later Roman Empire*, vol. 3, *A.D. 527–641* (Cambridge, 1990), *PLRE-III-B*, 1200–1201.

20. J. Boswell, *The Marriage of Likeness* (London, 1995). For Justinian and Strategius, see ibid., 229. For a recent study of such ties, see C. Rapp, *Brother-Making in Late Antiquity and Byzantium* (Oxford, 2016).

21. Sarris, *Economy and Society*, 19.

22. See ibid., 96–114, and L. S. B. MacCoull, *Dioscorus of Aphrodito and His World* (Berkeley, Calif., 1988), which remains the classic study. An excellent account of economy and society in sixth-century Aphrodito is also to be found in C. Wickham, *Framing the Early Middle Ages* (Oxford, 2005), 411–419. More recent studies have too often failed to appreciate the potential hostility of the social environment in which the villagers of Aphrodito were obliged to operate.

23. See MacCoull, *Dioscorus of Aphrodito*, 2–5.

24. Sarris, *Economy and Society*, 98–99; *P.Cairo.Masp.* 3.67283. See also L. MacCoull, 'Notes on the Social Structure of Late Antique Aphrodito', reprinted as sec. 20 of L. MacCoull, *Coptic Perspectives on Late Antiquity* (Aldershot, 1993).

25. Sarris, *Economy and Society*, 98, with note 12.

26. Ibid., 97 note 7. For a more sympathetic treatment, see C. Kuehn, *Channels of Imperishable Fire: The Beginnings of Christian Mystical Poetry and Dioscorus of Aphrodito* (New York, 1995).

27. Sarris, *Economy and Society*, 100.

28. *P.Ross.Georg.* 3.37; A. H. M. Jones, *The Later Roman Empire*, vol. 1 (Oxford, 1964), 333–341.

29. Sarris, *Economy and Society*, 101.

30. As argued in ibid., 114.

31. Ibid., 103–105. For the importance of great landowners in the vicinity of Aphrodito, see also the excellent study by C. Zuckerman, *Du village à l'empire: Autour du registre fiscal d'Aphroditô (525/526)* (Paris, 2004).

32. *P.Cairo.Masp.* 1 67024; Sarris, *Economy and Society*, 105–106.

33. Sarris, *Economy and Society*, 107. See also L. MacCoull, 'The Aphrodito Murder Mystery', reprinted as sec. 18 in MacCoull, *Coptic Perspectives*.

34. *P.Cairo.Masp.* 1 67024, 3 67283, 1 67019.

35. Sarris, *Economy and Society*, 109.

36. See J.-L. Fournet, *Hellénisme dans l'Égypte du VIe siècle: La bibliothèque et l'oeuvre de Dioscore d'Aphrodité*, 2 vols. (Cairo, 1999), 1:378–389, and Sarris, *Economy and Society*, 109.

37. Sarris, *Economy and Society*, 109–113.

38. See discussion in M. Whittow, *The Making of Orthodox Byzantium* (London, 1996), 106–112.

39. Procopius, *Anecdota* 14.3, 14.8.

40. A. Cameron, 'Images of Authority: Elites and Icons in Late Sixth-Century Byzantium', in *Byzantium and the Classical Tradition*, ed. M. Mullett and R. Scott (Birmingham, 1981), 205–234.

41. Luke 1:46–55 (KJV).

CHAPTER 12. THE 'ORTHODOX REPUBLIC'

1. For discussion, see M. Avi-Yonah, *The Madaba Mosaic Map* (Jerusalem, 1954), and G. Bowersock, *Mosaics as History: The Near East from Late Antiquity to Islam* (Cambridge, Mass., 2006).

2. See J. Binns, *Ascetics and Ambassadors of Christ: The Monasteries of Palestine, 314–631* (Oxford, 1994), and Y. Hirschfeld, *The Judean Desert Monasteries in the Byzantine Period* (New Haven, Conn., 1992).

3. See *J.Nov.* 40 and D. Krueger, 'Christian Piety and Practice in the Age of Justinian', in *The Cambridge Companion to the Age of Justinian*, ed. M. Maas (Cambridge, 2005), 291–315, 302–305. For the 'New Church', see Procopius, *Buildings* 5.6.1–26.

4. See A. Cameron, *Wandering Poets and Other Essays on Late Greek Literature and Philosophy* (Oxford, 2016), 255, and P. Bell, *Social Conflict in the Age of Justinian* (Oxford, 2013), 245.

5. *I. Sardis* 19, discussed in Bell, *Social Conflict*, 245–246.

6. Pseudo-Zachariah of Tel-Mahre, *Chronicle: Part III*, tr. W. Witakowski (Liverpool, 1996), 71.

7. See P. Odorico, 'La Chronique de Malalas entre littérature et philosophie', in *History as Literature in Byzantium*, ed. R. Macrides (Abingdon, 2010), 275–289.

8. Pseudo-Zachariah of Tel-Mahre, *Chronicle: Part III*, tr. Witakowski., 71. For Romanos, see Krueger, 'Christian Piety and Practice', 297–300; J. Koder, 'Imperial Propaganda in the Kontakia of Romanos the Melode', *Dumbarton Oaks Papers* 62 (2008): 275–291; and M. Hassall, 'Political Debate in the Age of Justinian I' (PhD diss., Cambridge University, 2022), 74–80. The latter is forthcoming as a historical monograph with Oxford University Press.

9. See discussion in S. Roggo, 'Church and Crown in the Capital: The Patriarchate of Constantinople Under Eutychios and John Scholastikos (552–582)' (PhD diss., Cambridge University, 2022), 138–141, forthcoming as a historical monograph with Oxford University Press.

10. See A. Cameron, 'Poets and Pagans in Byzantine Egypt', in *Egypt in the Byzantine World*, ed. R. Bagnall (Cambridge, 2007), 21–46. The incident dates from the fifth century.

11. Romanos, *Hymns* 33.16.3–17.9. See Hassall, 'Political Debate', 75. For Christian hostility to classical literature, see also D. Rohmann, *Christianity, Book-Burning and Censorship in Late Antiquity* (Berlin, 2016), 220–230.

12. See P. Sarris, *Byzantium: A Very Short Introduction* (Oxford, 2015), 104–105, and Hassall, 'Political Debate', 85–93.

13. As argued by Hassall, 'Political Debate', 86–87. For classical allusions, see *J.Nov.* 60 c. 1 (Homer) and *J.Nov.* 22 c. 3 and 105 pr. (Aristotle). The Homeric allusion in *J.Nov.* 60, however, is deployed somewhat inappropriately. See *The Novels of Justinian: A Complete Annotated English Translation*, ed. P. Sarris, tr. D. J. D. Miller (Cambridge, 2018), 463 note 11.

14. *J.Nov.* 77; *J.Nov.* 141; John Malalas, *Chronicle* 18.18.

15. Procopius, *Anecdota* 11.34–36.

16. J. Boswell, *Christianity, Social Tolerance, and Homosexuality: Gay People in Western Europe from the Beginning of the Christian Era to the Fourteenth Century* (Chicago, 1980), 172–173.

17. John of Ephesus, *Ecclesiastical History* 4.6. See *The Third Part of the Ecclesiastical History of John, Bishop of Ephesus*, tr. J. R. Payne Smith (Oxford, 1860), 251–253.

18. Pseudo-Zachariah of Tel-Mahre, *Chronicle: Part III*, tr. Witakowski, 72. The figures given by John probably relate to the number of conversions he and his followers were able to secure over the course of several campaigns, drawn

out over a number of decades (a point I owe to Dr. Kyle Harper and Dr. Scott Johnson).

19. *Codex Iustinianus* 1.5.12.6–9, 1.5.12–22; *J.Nov.* 45. The ban on anyone other than orthodox Christians holding official rank or public office had been legislated on during Justinian's period of joint rule with Justin I.

20. *Codex Theodosianus* 16.8.9.

21. Pseudo-Zachariah of Tel-Mahre, *Chronicle: Part III*, tr. Witakowski, 2–3.

22. *J.Nov.* 146.

23. *Codex Iustinianus* 1.1, 1.1.1.

24. *J.Nov.* 45.

25. For discussion of the earlier legislation and its significance, see P. Riedlberger, *Prolegomena zu den spätantiken Konstitutionen: Nebst einer Analyse der erbrechtlichten und verwandten Sanktionen gegen Heterodoxe* (Stuttgart, 2020), esp. 800–809. Note, however, the important critique of this vast, learned, and meandering work to be found in B. Sirks, 'The Imperial Policy Against Heretics of Restricting Succession in the Fourth Century AD, with an Appendix on the Theodosian Code', *Tijdschrift voor Rechtsgeschiedenis* 89 (2021): 536–577. The prohibition on non-Christians inheriting is criticized by Procopius, *Anecdota* 11.14–15, and is attested in *Codex Iustinianus* 1.5.13 and 1.5.17–22. Under Justinian, estates seized or belonging to the Crown (the *res privata*) were increasingly absorbed by the estates of the imperial household (*domus divina*) under the direct control of the emperor and his entourage. All fines levied on the emperor's subjects also went to the Crown. See R. Delmaire, *Largesses sacrées et res privata: L'aerarium imperial et son administration du IVe au VIe siècle* (Rome, 1989): 414–416, 708–709, and *J.Nov.* 117 c. 13. For *infamia*, see *Digest* 3.2, and (for this legislation) *J.Nov.* 45 pr. This legislation intensified that against pagan, heretics, Samaritans, and Jews found in *Codex Iustinianus* 1.5.12.1–21 (jointly issued by Justin and Justinian).

26. N. Underwood, 'Lawyers and Inquisitors: Reassessing the Role of the *Defensor Civitatis*', *Studies in Late Antiquity* (forthcoming).

27. *J.Nov.* 17 c. 11; *J.Edict.* 2 c. 1. For a contemporary account of purges in the vicinity of Antioch, see discussion in Rohmann, *Christianity, Book-Burning and Censorship*, 102–108 (drawing on the anonymous *Life of St Simeon Stylites the Younger*). See also Procopius, *Secret History* 11.14–15 ('and many straightaway went everywhere from place to place and tried to compel such persons as they met to change from their ancestral faith').

28. See the excellent N. de Lange, 'Jews in the Age of Justinian', in Maas, *Cambridge Companion*, 401–426, esp. 418–422.

29. *J.Nov.* 129 (esp. pr.); *J.Nov.* 139. See also the parallel concession made to Samaritan peasants in *J.Nov.* 154 and discussion in A. D. Lee, 'Close-Kin

Marriage in Late Antique Mesopotamia', *Greek, Roman and Byzantine Studies* 29 (1988): 403–413.

30. See A. H. M. Jones, *The Later Roman Empire*, vol. 2 (Oxford, 1964), 862.

31. *J.Nov.* 14; *J.Nov.* 142.

32. See *Codex Iustinianus* 1.5.12.17; G. Greatrex, 'Justin I and the Arians', *Studia Patristica* 34 (2001): 72–81; and T. C. Lounghis, B. Blysidu, and St. Lampakes, *Regesten der Kaiserurkunden des Oströmischen Reiches von 476 bis 565* (Nicosia, 2005), 288.

33. See D. Pingree, 'The Sabians of Harran and the Classical Tradition', *International Journal of the Classical Tradition* 9 (2002): 8–35.

34. Malalas, *Chronicle* 18.119.

35. P. Sarris, 'At the Origins of the "Persecuting Society"? Defining the "Orthodox Republic" in the Age of Justinian', *Travaux et mémoires* 26 (2022): 407–422. I am grateful to Mr. Agostino Minichiello for discussion of Justinian's attitude to his imperial predecessors.

36. See *J.Nov.* 6 pr.

37. *Collectio Avellana*, in *Epistolae Imperatorum Pontificum Aliorum*, vol. 2, ed. O. Güenther (reprint, Cambridge, 2019), letter 187 (644).

38. *The Acts of the Council of Constantinople of 553*, vol. 1, ed. and tr. R. Price (Liverpool, 2009), 9, including note 4 (remarking on hints of Theopaschite sentiment in the 'Tome' of Pope Leo I).

39. See the testimony of Pseudo-Zachariah, *Ecclesiastical History*, in *The Chronicle of Pseudo-Zachariah Rhetor*, tr. G. Greatrex, R. Phenix, and C. Horn (Liverpool, 2011), 308.

40. D. Potter, *Theodora: Actress, Empress, Saint* (Oxford, 2015), 169–177.

41. Evagrius, *Ecclesiastical History* 4.10. See *The Ecclesiastical History of Evagrius Scholasticus*, tr. M. Whitby (Liverpool, 2000), 209.

42. See Procopius, *Anecdota* 10.13–15, 27.12–13.

43. John of Ephesus, *Lives* 47, in *Patrologia Orientalia* 18, 676–684. See *The Ecclesiastical History*, tr. Whitby, 209 note 28.

44. The classic work remains P. Brown, 'The Rise and Function of the Holy Man', *Journal of Roman Studies* 61 (1971): 103–152.

45. See C. Rapp, *Holy Bishops in Late Antiquity* (Berkeley, Calif., 2005), esp 137–154.

46. Evagrius, *Ecclesiastical History* 4.11. See *The Ecclesiastical History*, tr. Whitby, 210.

47. Potter, *Theodora*, 169–173.

48. S. Brock, *Syriac Perspectives on Late Antiquity* (London, 1984), sec. 11, p. 224.

49. *Acts of the Council of Constantinople of 553*, ed. and tr. Price, 1:12. For

the *Libellus*, see V. Menze, *Justinian and the Making of the Syrian Orthodox Church* (Oxford, 2008), 58–105.

50. The text is preserved in *Chronicon Paschale*. See *Chronicon Paschale*, tr. M. Whitby and M. Whitby (Liverpool, 1989), 129–130.

51. Menze, *Justinian and the Making of the Syrian Orthodox Church*, 187–188.

52. *Acts of the Council of Constantinople of 553*, ed. and tr. Price, 1:12; Menze, *Justinian and the Making of the Syrian Orthodox Church*, 174. For a full translation, see F. Haarer, *Justinian: Empire and Society in the Sixth Century* (Edinburgh, 2022), 178.

53. *Acts of the Council of Constantinople of 553*, ed. and tr. Price, 1:12.

54. Menze, *Justinian and the Making of the Syrian Orthodox Church*, 174.

55. See the testimony of Pseudo-Zachariah, in *The Chronicle of Pseudo-Zachariah Rhetor*, tr. Greatrex et al., 367, and Potter, *Theodora*, 173–174.

56. *Acts of the Council of Constantinople of 553*, ed. and tr. Price, 1:13.

57. Ibid.

58. *The Book of Pontiffs (Liber Pontificalis)*, tr. R. Davis (Liverpool, 1989), 52–53.

59. Potter, *Theodora*, 177.

60. P. Booth, 'Towards the Coptic Church: The Making of the Severan Church in Egypt', *Millennium* 14 (2017): 151–190, 155.

61. *Acts of the Council of Constantinople of 553*, ed. and tr. Price, 1:14 note 23. See also F. Millar, 'Rome, Constantinople and the Near Eastern Church Under Justinian: Two Synods of 536', *Journal of Roman Studies* 98 (2008): 62–82. In *J.Nov.* 42 c. 1.1 the teachings of Severus and his followers are deemed 'forbidden doctrines . . . foreign to orthodoxy'.

62. *J.Nov.* 42 c. 1.2 (dating from 536).

63. *J.Nov.* 131 c. 1.

64. See Pseudo-Zachariah, in *The Chronicle of Pseudo-Zachariah Rhetor*, tr. Greatrex et al., 399.

65. Ibid., 399.

66. *Acts of the Council of Constantinople of 553*, ed. and tr. Price, 1:13 note 22.

67. Evagrius, *Ecclesiastical History*, 4.10. See *The Ecclesiastical History*, tr. Whitby, 209.

68. Menze, *Justinian and the Making of the Syrian Orthodox Church*, 224, 222.

69. See C. Pazdernik, 'Our Most Pious Consort Given Us by God', *Classical Antiquity* 13 (1994): 256–281.

70. Malalas, *Chronicle* 17.19; Pazdernik, 'Our Most Pious Consort', 265.

71. Potter, *Theodora*, 198. See also Menze, *Justinian and the Making of the Syrian Orthodox Church*, 254–265.

72. Booth, 'Towards the Coptic Church', 159.

73. *Acts of the Council of Constantinople of 553*, ed. and tr. Price, 1:16.

74. M. Meier, 'The Justinianic Plague: The Economic Consequences of the Pandemic in the Eastern Empire and Its Cultural and Religious Effects', *Early Medieval Europe* 24 (2016): 267–292, 285, 287.

75. See Procopius, *Buildings* 1.3.1–2.

76. Pseudo-Zachariah, in *The Chronicle of Pseudo-Zachariah Rhetor*, tr. Greatrex et al., 426–427.

77. Meier, 'The Justinianic Plague', 287.

78. A. Cameron, 'Images of Authority: Elites and Icons in Late Sixth-Century Byzantium', in *Byzantium and the Classical Tradition*, ed. M. Mullett and R. Scott (Birmingham, 1981), 210.

79. Constantine Porphyrogennetos, *The Book of Ceremonies*, ed. and tr. A. Moffatt and M. Tall (Leiden, 2017), 497; M. McCormick, *Eternal Victory: Triumphal Rulership in Late Antiquity, Byzantium and the Early Medieval West* (Cambridge, 1986), 67, 208–209.

80. K. P. Wesche, *On the Person of Christ: The Christology of Emperor Justinian* (New York, 1991), 48, 35, 81.

81. *Acts of the Council of Constantinople of 553*, ed. and tr. Price, 2:273–274.

82. Wesche, *On the Person of Christ*, 165.

83. Ibid., 163–164, 19–22. With respect to Chalcedon, see N. P. Tanner, ed., *The Decrees of the Ecumenical Councils*, 2 vols. (Washington, D.C., 1990), 1:86. One of the most useful studies of the religious challenges faced by Justinian remains J. Meyendorff, 'Justinian, the Empire, and the Church', *Dumbarton Oaks Papers* 22 (1968): 43–60.

84. Wesche, *On the Person of Christ*, 198.

85. *Acts of the Council of Constantinople of 553*, ed. and tr. Price, 1:10, 1:16–27, 2:79.

86. Ibid., 1:23.

87. Ibid., 1:23, 1:45.

88. Ibid., 1:43–45.

89. Ibid., 1:166, 1:46–47.

90. Ibid., 1:47–48.

91. Ibid., 1:48–49.

92. Ibid., 1:172–173, 1:49.

93. Ibid., 1:173.

94. Ibid., 1:50.

95. Ibid., 1:50–51.

NOTES FOR CHAPTER 12

96. Ibid., 1:280–281, 1:52, 1:198.

97. Ibid., 1:52–53.

98. Ibid., 1:53, 2:75–80, 2:96–97.

99. Ibid., 2:215–219, 1:58.

100. Ibid., 1:33–36. On Gregory, see M. Dal Santo, *Debating the Saints' Cult in the Age of Gregory the Great* (Oxford, 2013).

101. Booth, 'Towards the Coptic Church', shows this was even true in Egypt.

102. See ibid. These separate churches, however, would remain relatively marginalized and insignificant until the Persian and Arab conquests of the seventh century, after which they would emerge as a major force. For the religious landscape of the seventh century, see J. Tannous, *The Making of the Medieval Middle East: Religion, Society, and Simple Believers* (Princeton, N.J., 2019).

103. Pseudo-Zachariah of Tel-Mahre, *Chronicle: Part III*, tr. Witakowski, 121.

104. See A. D. Lee, 'Evagrius, Paul of Nisibis, and the Problem of Loyalties in the Mid-Sixth Century', *Journal of Ecclesiastical History* 44 (1993): 569–585.

105. See J. Zouberi, 'The Role of Religion in the Foreign Affairs of Sasanian Iran and the Later Roman Empire', *Historia i Świat* 6 (2017): 121–132.

106. G. Fowden, *Empire to Commonwealth: Consequences of Monotheism in Late Antiquity* (Princeton, N.J., 1993), 100–137, is fundamental here.

107. See Roggo, 'Church and Crown in the Capital', 29–80, arguing that Eutychius was dismissed for other reasons.

108. See Sarris, 'At the Origins of the "Persecuting Society"'.

109. Procopius, *Anecdota* 8.23.

CHAPTER 13. THE FOUR HORSEMEN OF THE APOCALYPSE

1. Pseudo-Zachariah of Tel-Mahre, *Chronicle: Part III*, tr. W. Witakowski (Liverpool, 1996), 64.

2. Procopius, *Wars* 2.14.1–7, 2.11.1, 2.11.31–32, 2.10.4–5.

3. Procopius, *Buildings*, 2.10.2–25. For discussion of the archaeological evidence, see A. U. De Giorgi and A. Asa Eger, *Antioch: A History* (London, 2021), 208–216.

4. Procopius, *Wars* 6.20.23–30.

5. Cassiodorus, *Variae* 12.25. See Cassiodorus, *The Variae: The Complete Translation*, tr. S. Bjornlie (Berkeley, Calif., 2019), 493–495.

6. Procopius, *Wars* 4.14.5–6.

7. John Lydus, *de Ostentis* 9. See also, for Syria, *The Chronicle of Pseudo-Zachariah Rhetor*, tr. G. Greatrex, R. Phenix, and C. Horn (Liverpool, 2011), 427, where the author describes ash falling from the sky. He may, however, be describing a separate incident.

478

8. See D. Keys, *Catastrophe: An Investigation into the Origins of the Modern World* (London, 1999), 251–253. For an excellent recent summary, see also J. Preiser-Kapeller, *Die Lange Sommer und die Kleine Eiszeit* (Vienna, 2021).

9. Keys, *Catastrophe*, 120, 181.

10. See Preiser-Kapeller, *Die Lange Sommer*, 38–46, and K. Harper, *The Fates of Rome* (Princeton, N.J., 2017), 219.

11. See H. Büntgen, V. S. Myglan, F. Charpentier Ljungqvist, M. McCormick, N. Di Cosmo, M. Sigl, J. Jungclaus, et al., 'Cooling and Societal Change', *Nature Geoscience* 9 (2016): 231–236; now superseded by U. Büntgen, A. Crivellaro, D. Arseneault, M. Baillie, D. Barclay, M. Bernabei, J. Bontadi, et al., 'Global Wood Anatomical Perspective on the Onset of the Late Antique Little Ice Age (LALIA) in the Mid-6th Century CE', *Science Bulletin* 22 (2022): 2236–2344; E. van Dijk, J. Jungclaus, S. Lorenz, C. Timmreck, and K. Krüger, 'Was There Volcanic-Induced Long-Lasting Cooling in the Northern Hemisphere in the Mid-6th–7th Century?', *Climate of the Past* 18 (2022): 1601–2022. Some societies and regions would naturally have been more affected than others, and the Mediterranean may have been affected less or for a shorter period of time than many of the regions beyond the Alps. See M. Jacobson, J. Picket, A. Gascoigne, D. Fleittmann, and H. Elton, 'Settlement, Environment, and Climate Change in SW Anatolia: Dynamics of Regional Variation and the End of Antiquity', *PLOS ONE* (27 June 2022); F. L. Cheyette, 'The Disappearance of the Ancient Landscape and the Climate Anomaly of the Early Middle Ages: A Question to Be Pursued', *Early Medieval Europe* 16 (2008): 127–165; and P. Sarris, 'Climate and Disease', in *A Companion to the Global Early Middle Ages*, ed. E. Hermans (Amsterdam, 2020), 511–538. (Note that since the publication of this item the Ilipongo volcanic eruption has been redated to the fifth century, but a number of other Central American and Icelandic eruptions have been dated to the 530s and 540s.)

12. R. J. Sinensky, G. Schachner, R. H. Wilshusen, and B. N. Damiata, 'Volcanic Climate Forcing, Extreme Cold and the Neolithic Transition in the Northern US Southwest', *Antiquity* 96 (2022): 123–141.

13. See F. C. Ljungqvist, 'The Mid-Sixth Century Crisis in Recent Nordic Research', paper delivered at a Symposium on 'The First Pandemic: Transformative Disaster or Footnote in History', Hannover, Germany, 22 September 2021. See also B. Gräslund, 'Fimbulvintern: Ragnarök och klimatkrisen år 536–7', *Saga och Sed* (2007): 93–123.

14. I am extremely grateful to Dr. Elena Xoplaki for discussion of this point. Justinian's legislation reports severe famine in the Balkans in 535 that seems to have been unrelated to the period of climate instability that would follow. See

J.Nov. 32–34. Alternatively, the period of disruption possibly began in that year rather than in 536.

15. Harper, *The Fates of Rome*, 219, 249–259.

16. D. Oppenheimer, *Eruptions That Shook the World* (Cambridge, 2011), 248.

17. Procopius, *Wars* 4.14.6.

18. T. Malim and J. Hines, *The Anglo-Saxon Cemetery at Edix Hill (Barrington A), Cambridgeshire* (York, 1998).

19. M. Keller, M. A. Spyrou, C. L. Scheib, and J. Krause, 'Ancient *Yersinia pestis* Genomes from Across Western Europe Reveal Early Diversification During the First Pandemic (541–750)', *PNAS* 116, no. 25 (2019): 12363–12372 (preprinted in *bioRxiv*, 4 December 2018). For full references and an overview of the historiography, see P. Sarris, 'Viewpoint: New Approaches to the Plague of Justinian', *Past and Present* 254 (2022): 315–346, and G. Greatrex, *Procopius of Caesarea: The Persian Wars. A Historical Commentary* (Cambridge, 2022), 565–588. For the importance of the new genetic discoveries, see M. H. Green, 'When Numbers Don't Count: Changing Perspectives on the Justinianic Plague', *Eidolon*, 18 November 2019, https://eidolon.pub/when -numbers-dont-count-56a2b3c3d07, and M. Keller, C. Paulus, and E. Xoplaki, 'Die Justinianische Pest: Grenzen und Chancen naturalwissenschaftlicher Ansätze für ein integratives Geschischtsverständnis', *Evangelische Theologie* 81(2021): 385–400. The Justinianic plague did not necessarily reach Edix Hill from the Mediterranean. Rather, the disease may well have made its way to the east of England via a different route, such as the Baltic. See Sarris, 'Viewpoint', 343. For the possibility that there may have been a connection between the Justinianic plague and the pestilence recorded by the early sixth-century historian Gildas, see ibid., note 99. It is inconceivable that further genetic evidence for the disease will not be found in England as well as elsewhere (at the time of writing it has been identified at early medieval archaeological sites in England, France, Spain, Bavaria, Lebanon, and the Black Sea coast of Russia).

20. Sarris, 'Viewpoint', note 14.

21. See C. Tsiamis, *Plague in Byzantine Times: A Medico-Historical Study* (Berlin, 2023), 9–38, esp. 18–20. The study is out of date with respect to the historical literature but provides useful medical and biological context.

22. For furs and clothing as markers of status in nomadic society, see T. Alston, *Commodity and Exchange in the Mongol Empire* (Cambridge, 1997), and (on the Huns) Ammianus Marcellinus, *Res Gestae*, 32.2.5. For the importance of this cultural and economic context with respect to the later Black Death, see M. H. Green, 'The Four Black Deaths', *American Historical Review* 125 (2020): 1601–1631.

23. For rats in Justiniana Prima, see H. Yu, A. Jamieson, A. Hulme-Beaman, C. J. Conroy, B. Knight, C. Speller, H. al-Jarah, et al., 'Palaeogenomic Analysis of Black Rat (*Rattus rattus*) Reveals Multiple European Introductions Associated with Human Economic History', *Nature Communications* 1, no. 2399 (2022), https://doi.org/10.1038/s41467-022-30009-z. I am grateful to Dr. David Orton for discussion of rat finds in sixth-century Italy and the problems of the rat bone evidence in general.

24. See Tsiamis, *Plague in Byzantine Times*, 47–52.

25. S. Helama, L. Arppe, J. Uusitalo, J. Holopainen, H. M. Mäkelë, H. Mäkinen, K. Mielikäinen, et al., 'Volcanic Dust Veils from Sixth-Century Tree-Ring Isotopes Linked to Reduced Irradiance, Primary Production and Human Health', *Scientific Reports* 8, no. 1339 (2018), https://doi.org/10.1038/s41598-018-19760-w.

26. Tsiamis, *Plague in Byzantine Times*, 20–40.

27. For medical literature, see J. Mulhall, 'The Medical Response to the Justinianic Plague', *Journal of Late Antiquity* 14 (2021): 498–528.

28. See Sarris, 'Viewpoint', and Sarris, 'Climate and Disease'. Africa remains one of the most likely 'proximate' origins of the sixth-century plague. In *The Fates of Rome*, Harper argues for Central Asia. As noted in Sarris, 'Viewpoint', there are significant genetic differences, however, between the ancient strains of bubonic plague that have currently been identified in Central Asia and the strain we have evidence for with respect to the Justinianic plague, suggesting some evolution over the course of the migration of the disease (which thus must have taken time). New genetic finds are likely to resolve this issue. For the struggle for power in Arabia, see G. Fisher, ed., *Arabs and Empires Before Islam* (Oxford, 2015). For the relationship between Africa and the bubonic plague, see also M. H. Green, 'Putting Africa on the Black Death Map: Narratives from Genetics and History', *Afriques: Débats, méthodes, et terrains d'histoire* 9 (2018), retrieved from http:/journals.openedition.org/afriques/2125. For an excellent overview of the possible evidence for the impact of the Justinianic plague on Axum and as far away as the Congo rainforest in West Africa, where a major demographic collapse is discernible at this time, see P. Frankopan, *The Earth Transformed: An Untold History* (London, 2023), 299–300, 303–304. This book also provides a masterly analysis of the general issues relating to climate and disease in this period (see 282–308).

29. As suggested by the editors of *The Chronicle of Theophanes Confessor*, tr. and ed. C. Mango and R. Scott (Oxford, 1997), 322 note 1.

30. The seminar paper would later be published as P. Sarris, 'The Justinianic Plague: Origins and Effects', *Continuity and Change* 17 (2002): 169–182.

31. A point I owe to Dr. Philip Slavin.

32. We tend to fixate on rats and fleas in the transmission of bubonic plague due to their role in the spread of a later variant of it in the nineteenth century (known as the 'Third Pandemic'), but it is possible that the Justinianic plague and the Black Death were associated with greater face-to-face transmission between humans than this later outbreak. I owe this point to Professor Guido Alfani. The strains of bubonic plague that we now know on the basis of the genetic evidence to have led to both the Justinianic plague and the Black Death were very closely related, and followed very similar paths of evolution (such as with respect to parallel losses in their 'virulence factor', for example, an insight I owe to Dr. Gunnar Neumann). There is no reason to postulate that either strain was any less deadly than the other. As Dr. David Orton has pointed out, there appear to have been very few rats in Britain when the plague devastated the community at Edix Hill, so a model that focuses entirely on rats is not sufficient to explain the geographical reach of the sixth-century pandemic.

33. For the arrival and spread of the disease, see D. Stathakopoulos, *Famine and Pestilence* (Aldershot, 2004), and the groundbreaking study by L. K. Little, ed., *Plague and the End of Antiquity* (Cambridge, 2007), 3–32.

34. Procopius, *Wars* 2.22.3.

35. Ibid., 2.22.11–12, 2.22.17, 2.22.29–30, 2.22.36, 2.22.38, 2.23.1 (stating it was at its peak for three months but ran for four). For medical reactions, see Mulhall, 'The Medical Response to the Justinianic Plague'. Interestingly, the chronology of the plague in terms of the months it struck the city as described by Procopius would appear to have been very similar to that discernible with respect to the Black Death in Ottoman Constantinople. See N. Varlik, *Plague and Empire in the Early Modern Mediterranean World: The Ottoman Experience, 1347–1600* (Cambridge, 2015), 18.

36. Constantinople is likely to have repopulated relatively quickly, but only at the expense of other cities in its near vicinity. See discussion in C. Zuckerman, *Du village à l'empire: Autour du registre fiscal d'Aphroditô (525/526)* (Paris, 2004).

37. Pseudo-Zachariah of Tel-Mahre, *Chronicle: Part III*, tr. Witakowski, 74, 75, 77.

38. Ibid., 80–81, 86–90, 92–93. He tells us that the same was true in the great Egyptian city of Alexandria.

39. Ibid., 98.

40. See Sarris, 'Viewpoint', 326 note 42. Attempts to dismiss our contemporary accounts of the plague and its likely impact are largely based on a fundamental misunderstanding of the sources, the historiography, and the disease.

41. Procopius, *Wars* 2.23.6.

42. See J. R. Martindale, *The Prosopography of the Later Roman Empire*, vol. 3, *A.D. 527–641* (Cambridge, 1990), *PLRE-III-B*, 1248 (Theodorus 10).

43. *J.Nov.* 59.

44. Pseudo-Zachariah of Tel-Mahre, *Chronicle: Part III*, tr. Witakowski, 91.

45. Ibid., 91–92, 88.

46. Procopius, *Wars* 2.23.8.

47. Pseudo-Zachariah of Tel-Mahre, *Chronicle: Part III*, tr. Witakowski, 92.

48. Procopius, *Wars* 2.23.20, 1.25.2. For the possible attribution of the emperor's recovery to Saints Cosmas and Damian, see Procopius, *Buildings* 1.6.5–6. Procopius does not explicitly say that the illness from which they saved Justinian was the plague, but he does report that the emperor's physicians had given him up for dead. I owe this suggestion to Dr Michael Stewart. For the cult of these two saints in Constantinople, see P. Booth, 'Orthodox and Heretic in the Early Byzantine Cult(s) of Saints Cosmas and Damian', in *An Age of Saints? Power, Conflict and Dissent in Early Medieval Christianity*, ed. P. Sarris, M. Dal Santo, and P. Booth (Leiden, 2011), 114–128.

49. *J.Edict.* 7.

50. *J.Nov.* 118; Pseudo-Zachariah of Tel-Mahre, *Chronicle: Part III*, tr. Witakowski, 93.

51. *J.Nov.* 158.

52. *J.Nov.* 122; *J.Nov.* 128 c. 7–8; *J.Nov.* 77. For price inflation, see also the account of John of Ephesus in Pseudo-Zachariah of Tel-Mahre, *Chronicle: Part III*, tr. Witakowski, 88.

53. Procopius, *Anecdota* 23.19–21.

54. See G. Bransbourg, 'Capital in the Sixth Century', *Journal of Late Antiquity* 9 (2016): 305–414, 342–346, 394. Bransbourg's analysis of tax levels is more reliable than some of his other claims. See discussion in P. Sarris, 'Egypt in the Age of Justinian: Connector or Disconnector?', in *Egypt in the Eastern Mediterranean World*, ed. J. Bruning, J. H. M. de Jong, and P. M. Sijpesteijn (Cambridge, 2022).

55. See Sarris, 'Viewpoint', 332 note 66.

56. H. Pottier, 'L'empereur Justinien survivant à la peste bubonique', *Travaux et mémoires* 16 (2010): 685–691.

57. Revelation 6.7–8.

58. Procopius, *Wars* 2.18.1–26, 2.19.30–49.

59. Procopius, *Anecdota* 4.1–6. This strikes me as the most likely interpretation of the story reported by Procopius that Belisarius was accused of saying he would not recognize a 'second Justinian' set up in Byzantium. See Martindale, *Prosopography*, *PLRE-III-A*, 21.

60. Procopius, *Anecdota* 4.13–31, 4.38–39. For an alternative analysis of this episode, see the fascinating study by M. E. Stewart, 'A Tangled Web: Marriage and Alliance in the Shadows of the Plague', *Classica Cracoviensia* (forthcoming).

61. Procopius, *Wars* 2.28.7–11.

62. G. Greatrex and S. Lieu, *The Roman Eastern Frontier and the Persian Wars: Part 2, 363–630 AD* (London, 2002), 115–123. Justinian tried to negotiate a truce here in 551, but in vain. See ibid., 123–124.

63. M. E. Williams, 'The African Policy of Justinian I' (DPhil, Oxford University, 2015), 197–198, 233.

64. Ibid., 198–200.

65. *J.Nov.* 37 c. 5.

66. *J.Nov.* 37 c. 8.

67. Procopius, *Anecdota* 18.10–11.

68. Procopius, *Wars* 4.16.1–3.

69. Ibid., 4.16.6–7; Williams, 'The African Policy of Justinian I', 207.

70. Procopius, *Wars* 4.16.10–11.

71. Ibid., 4.16.12–13.

72. Ibid., 4.17.20–23; Williams, 'The African Policy of Justinian I', 208.

73. M. Whitby, *The Wars of Justinian* (Barnsley, 2021), 192–193; Procopius, *Wars* 4.17.30–35.

74. Williams, 'The African Policy of Justinian I', 208.

75. Whitby, *The Wars of Justinian*, 194–195.

76. Ibid., 195–196.

77. See Martindale, *Prosopography, PLRE-III-A*, 107–109.

78. Whitby, *The Wars of Justinian*, 196–197.

79. Williams, 'The African Policy of Justinian I', 228–231.

80. Ibid., 231; Procopius, *Wars* 4.28.42–51.

81. Ibid., 4.28.52.

82. Corippus, *Iohannidos* 3.343–389; L. K. Little, ed., *Plague and the End of Antiquity* (Cambridge, 2007), 14.

83. Corippus, *Iohannidos* 3.343–345.

84. For the plague in the Sasanian Empire, see M. J. Bonner, *The Last Empire of Iran* (Piscataway, N.J., 2020), 194–199.

85. As argued in Sarris, 'Climate and Disease', 528.

86. Procopius, *Wars* 7.33.1, 7.33.4–5, 7.33.14.

CHAPTER 14. PROPAGANDA AND DISSENT

1. Procopius, *Anecdota* 6.22. See Procopius, *The Secret History*, tr. G. A. Williamson and P. Sarris (London, 2007), 27.

2. See J. K. Knight, 'Penmachno Revisited: The Consular Inscription and Its Context', *Cambrian Medieval Celtic Studies* 29 (1995): 1–10, and A. Harris, *Byzantium, Britain and the West* (Stroud, 2003).

3. For indications that they may have been trying for children down to about 530, see D. Potter, *Theodora: Actress, Empress, Saint* (Oxford, 2015), 140. For machinations at court in the aftermath of Justinian's brush with death associated with the plague, see the excellent study by M. E. Stewart, 'A Tangled Web: Marriage and Alliance in the Shadows of the Plague', *Classica Cracoviensia* (forthcoming).

4. Procopius, *Anecdota* 5.8, 4.24–28, 16.6–17, 15.21–23, 22.3–12; P. Sarris, 'Viewpoint: New Approaches to the Plague of Justinian', *Past and Present* 254 (2022): 333–334.

5. Procopius, *Anecdota* 17.38.

6. Procopius, *Wars* 1.25.12, 1.25.15, 1.25.17–18.

7. Ibid., 1.25.19–30, 1.25.37–43.

8. Procopius, *Anecdota* 17.40.

9. Sarris, 'Viewpoint', 330. That this decline in output is not simply due to legislation getting lost or not being preserved (as proposed to me by Mr. David Rockwell) is strongly suggested by the fact that it is also reflected in a study by T. C. Lounghis, B. Blysidu, and St. Lampakes, *Regesten der Kaiserurkunden des Oströmischen Reiches von 476 bis 565* (Nicosia, 2005), in which the authors scour the literary and other non-legal sources to find evidence for lawmaking and other legislative activity. For the period from 527 to 546 they identified over 800 laws or enactments issued by the emperor during his period of sole rule, but from 547 to 565, only 131. See ibid., 151–347.

10. Procopius, *Wars* 7.32.

11. See *J.Nov.* 60 pr.

12. See B. Croke, 'Procopius, From Manuscripts to Books: 1400–1850', *Histos*, supplement 9 (2019): 1–173, esp. 74–89.

13. Procopius, *Wars* 8.1.1.

14. *The History of Menander the Guardsman*, ed. and tr. R. C. Blockley (Cambridge, 1985), 147 (fragment 14.2). On Menander and other late sixth-century responses to Procopius, see M. Jankowiak, 'Byzantine of Caesarea and His Byzantine Successors', and B. Croke, 'The Search for Harmony in Procopius' Literary Works', in *A Companion to Procopius of Caesarea*, ed. M. Meier and F. Montinaro (Leiden, 2021), 231–251, 28–58. Cyril Mango used to describe Procopius as one of the four greatest historians ever to have written in Greek.

15. Procopius, *Anecdota* 1.16–18, 12.31–32, 30.34 (the *archon* of the demons: this word is often used in medieval Greek for foreign rulers), 12.18–23, 18.1–45, 12.20–23, 11.1–19, 9.1–28, 17.16.

16. Potter, *Theodora*, 26–27.

17. For Procopius' narrative technique with respect to both Justinian and especially Theodora, see L. Brubaker, 'The Age of Justinian: Gender and Society', in *The Cambridge Companion to the Age of Justinian*, ed. M. Maas (Cambridge, 2005), 427–447, esp. 433–436.

18. Procopius, *Anecdota* 12.14, 12.16–17.

19. See discussion in Croke, 'From Manuscripts to Books', 74–89.

20. The best, if necessarily speculative, account of Procopius the man is to be found in G. Greatrex, 'Procopius: Life and Works', in Meier and Montinaro, *A Companion to Procopius of Caesarea*, 61–69.

21. Ibid., 62.

22. Procopius, *Anecdota* 11.25.

23. Procopius, *Wars* 5.3.6–9.

24. See P. Sarris, 'Introduction', in Procopius, *The Secret History*, tr. Williamson and Sarris, vii–xx.

25. Greatrex, 'Procopius: Life and Works', 64–65, provides an excellent summary.

26. Procopius, *Wars* 7.13.15 ('and it seemed to me' suggests he was present).

27. Greatrex, 'Procopius: Life and Works', 65–66 (discussing the Old Ethiopic *Chronicle* of John of Nikiu and the prefect mentioned by John Malalas).

28. See discussion in W. Treadgold, *The Early Byzantine Historians* (Basingstoke, 2007). Note, in particular, the map on p. 380, showing the birthplaces and workplaces of the early Byzantine historians.

29. A suggestion I owe to Mr. Ian Colvin.

30. Procopius, *Wars* 8.1–2.

31. Croke, 'The Search for Harmony in Procopius' Literary Works'; Procopius, *Anecdota* 1.3.

32. Procopius, *Anecdota* 1.2–1.4.

33. Although note the comments of M. Whitby, 'Procopius' Buildings and Panegyrical Effect', in Meier and Montinaro, *A Companion to Procopius of Caesarea*, 137–151, 138.

34. B. Croke, 'Uncovering Byzantium's Historiographical Audiences', in *Byzantine History as Literature*, ed. R. Macrides (London, 2010), 25–53, esp. 29–33.

35. See A. Kaldellis, 'The Classicism of Procopius', in Meier and Montinaro, *A Companion to Procopius of Caesarea*, 339–354. See also G. Greatrex, *Procopius of Caesarea: The Persian Wars. A Historical Commentary* (Cambridge, 2022), 8–19.

36. C. Mango, *Byzantium: The Empire of New Rome* (London, 1983), 125–128.

37. *J.Nov.* 8 pr.

38. Procopius, *Anecdota* 12.27.

39. For the role of genre and rhetorical form in distinguishing among Procopius' three works, see the groundbreaking study by A. Cameron, *Procopius and the Sixth Century* (London, 1985), and, more recently, Croke, 'The Search for Harmony in Procopius' Literary Works'.

40. Procopius, *Wars* 7.35.11, 8.35.20.

41. Croke, 'The Search for Harmony in Procopius' Literary Works', 52.

42. Croke, 'Uncovering Byzantium's Historiographical Audiences', 30.

43. Procopius, *Wars* 2.2.4–6.

44. Ibid., 2.3.32–48 (esp. 42–43), 2.15.19.

45. As argued by A. Kaldellis, whose work has inspired a new wave of Procopian scholarship, in *Procopius of Caesarea: Tyranny, History, and Philosophy at the End of Antiquity* (Philadelphia, 2004).

46. Ibid., 17–61.

47. Procopius, *Wars* 1.24.37.

48. Kaldellis, 'The Classicism of Procopius', 346; Kaldellis, *Procopius of Caesarea*, 36–37.

49. For a counterargument, see G. Greatrex, 'Procopius, the Nika Riot, and the Composition of the *Persian Wars*', *Travaux et mémoires* 26 (2022): 45–58.

50. Procopius, *Buildings* 1.2.7–10; Homer, *Iliad* 22.26–31. See Kaldellis, 'The Classicism of Procopius', 346, and Kaldellis, *Procopius of Caesarea*, 53.

51. As argued by E. Boeck, *The Bronze Horseman of Justinian in Constantinople: The Cross-Cultural Biography of a Mediterranean Monument* (Cambridge, 2021), 72–97.

52. Ibid., 85.

53. Procopius, *Buildings* 1.1.71, 1.1.78.

54. As argued by Sarris, 'Introduction'. For a dating of the *Buildings* to post-558, see also Whitby, 'Procopius' Buildings and Panegyrical Effect'.

55. J. R. Martindale, *The Prosopography of the Later Roman Empire*, vol. 3, *A.D. 527–641* (Cambridge, 1990), *PLRE-III-A*, 527 (Germanus), 750–754 (Fl. Mar. Petrus Theodorus Valentinus Rusticius Boraides Germanus Iustinus 4), 754–756 (Iustinus 5).

56. See discussion in P. Bell, *Three Political Voices from the Age of Justinian* (Liverpool, 2009), esp. 146, 177, 172–173, 152–158.

57. Ibid., 155, 178–179.

58. Ibid., 160–162.

59. See discussion in R. Scott, 'Malalas, the Secret History, and Justinian's Propaganda', *Dumbarton Oaks Papers* 39 (1985): 99–109, 103.

60. *Chronicon Paschale*, misplaced sub anno 531. See *Chronicon Paschale*, tr. M. Whitby and M. Whitby (Liverpool, 1989), 126.

61. Bell, *Three Political Voices*, 162, 105, 101, 108. See discussion in M. Hassall, 'Political Debate in the Age of Justinian I' (PhD diss., Cambridge University, 2022), 143. Justinian may have responded to such policy proposals: the emperor's active policy of improving the lot of the poor is emphasized by Procopius, *Buildings* 1.1.10.

62. Bell, *Three Political Voices*, 199–201, 190, 207, 192, 203–204. For his description of the altar cloth in the Great Church, see also C. Mango, *The Art of the Byzantine Empire 312–1453* (Toronto, 1986), 89.

63. Agathias, *Histories* 2.29.

64. R. Scott, 'Justinian's New Age and the Second Coming', in *Byzantine Chronicles and the Sixth Century*, ed. R. Scott (London, 2012), sec. 19.

65. For further discussion, see Hassall, 'Political Debate', and M. Kruse, *The Politics of Roman Memory from the Fall of the Western Empire to the Age of Justinian* (Philadelphia, 2019). The late Cyril Mango used to point out that even in Stalinist Russia, authors could sometimes get away with more than one might have imagined, especially if their literary reputation was sufficiently high as to offer a measure of protection.

CHAPTER 15. OPPORTUNISTIC IMPERIALISM

1. *The History of Menander the Guardsman*, ed. and tr. R. C. Blockley (Cambridge, 1985), 48–49 (fragment 5.1).

2. Procopius, *Wars* 7.1.28–33.

3. J. R. Martindale, *The Prosopography of the Later Roman Empire*, vol. 3, *A.D. 527–641* (Cambridge, 1990), *PLRE-III-A*, 614–615, 447–448.

4. Ibid., *PLRE-III-B*, 1328–1332; Procopius, *Wars* 7.2.7.

5. Procopius, *Wars* 7.4.10–32, 7.5.13–19, 7.6.1–6, 7.8.1–11, 7.9.7–18, 7.10.19–22, 7.9.21.

6. Ibid., 7.1.24, 7.9.5–6, 7.10.1, 7.13.15 (strongly suggesting he was present in person).

7. *J.Nov.* 116; Procopius, *Wars* 7.10.1.

8. Procopius, *Wars* 7.10.1–3, 7.11.13–16, 7.12.4–8, 7.12.10, 7.12.11–20, 7.13.1.

9. Ibid., 7.13.5–7, 7.13.20–22.

10. Ibid., 7.17.9–14, 7.17.19–20, 7.17.23–25.

11. M. Whitby, *The Wars of Justinian* (Barnsley, 2021), 237–240.

12. *The Chronicle of Marcellinus*, tr. B. Croke (Sydney, 1995), 50 (sub anno 543, written by the chronicle's continuator). For the plague in Italy, see,

especially, the highly important study by K. Harper, 'The First Plague Pandemic in Italy: The Written Evidence', *Speculum* 98 (2023): 369–420.

13. Procopius, *Wars* 7.24.2–4, 7.24.8–27.

14. Whitby, *The Wars of Justinian*, 241; Procopius, *Wars* 7.27–28, 7.30.1–2, 7.30.7–8. For Antonina, see D. Parnell, *Belisarius and Antonina: Love and War in the Age of Justinian* (Oxford, 2023).

15. Whitby, *The Wars of Justinian*, 241–242.

16. See discussion in A. Momigliano, 'Cassiodorus and the Italian Culture of His Time', *Proceedings of the British Academy* 41 (1955).

17. Whitby, *The Wars of Justinian*, 243.

18. Ibid., 244. See also A. Sarantis, *Justinian's Balkan Wars: Campaigning, Diplomacy, and Development in Illyricum, Thrace, and the Northern World, AD 527–565* (Prenton, 2016), 317 ('mainly Herul, Gepid and Lombard troops recruited from the Middle Danube area').

19. Procopius, *Wars* 8.26.7.

20. Ibid., 8.31.17–21.

21. For a detailed account of troop deployment and tactics at this battle, see Whitby, *The Wars of Justinian*, 245–249.

22. Procopius, *Wars* 8.35.20.

23. See discussion in M. R. Salzman, *The Falls of Rome: Crises, Resilience, and Resurgence in Late Antiquity* (Cambridge, 2021), 259–264. Localised Gothic resistance would continue to flare up until the year 561, but none of it posed a realistic threat to imperial control of the Italian Peninsula.

24. Procopius, *Wars* 8.34.1–4, 8.34.6–8.

25. See S. Lin, 'Justinian's Frankish War', *Studies in Late Antiquity* 5 (2021): 403–431, and *J.Nov. Appendix* 8.

26. See Salzman, *The Falls of Rome*, 36–196, 243–299.

27. *J.Nov. Appendix* 7.

28. See discussion in H. Börm, *Westrom: Von Honorius bis Justinian* (Stuttgart, 2018), 150–155, and Salzman, *The Falls of Rome*, 243–299.

29. See Salzman, *The Falls of Rome*, 335–336.

30. *J.Nov. Appendix* 7 c. 1.

31. See P. Sarris, *Empires of Faith: The Fall of Rome to the Rise of Islam* (Oxford, 2011), 171–177, and W. Pohl, 'Justinian and the Barbarian Kingdoms', in *The Cambridge Companion to the Age of Justinian*, ed. M. Maas (Cambridge, 2005), 448–477, emphasising how the stiffening of Roman defences often led to an intensification of barbarian attacks.

32. Sarantis, *Justinian's Balkan Wars*, 278–300, 306–323.

33. Ibid., 336–339.

34. Ibid., 339–340; Agathias, *Histories* 5.14.6–7, 5.15–20. See also John Malalas, *Chronicle* 18.129.

35. See P. Sarris, 'Climate and Disease', in *A Companion to the Global Early Middle Ages*, ed. E. Hermans (Amsterdam, 2020), 511–538, 518, and E. Cook, 'Megadroughts, ENSO, and the Invasion of Late-Roman Europe by the Huns and Avars', in *The Ancient Mediterranean Environment Between Science and History*, ed. W. V. Harris (Leiden, 2013), 89–102.

36. C. Baumer, *The History of Central Asia*, vol. 2, *The Age of the Silk Roads* (London, 2014), 88, 90–94. The group known to the Romans as the Avars was otherwise known as the Rouran. See W. Pohl, 'Ethnicity and Empire in the Western Eurasian Steppe', in *Empires and Exchange in Eurasian Late Antiquity*, ed. N. Di Cosmo and M. Maas (Cambridge, 2018), 21–49. The Turks with whom they were locked in conflict were led by the Ashina clan. For possible genetic evidence for Avar migration from Central Asia, see G. A. Gnecchi-Ruscone, A. Szécsényi-Nagy, I. Koncz, G. Csiky, Z. Rácz, A. B. Rohrlach, G. Brandt, et al., 'Ancient Genomes Reveal Origin and Rapid Trans-Eurasian Migration of 7th-Century Avar Elites', *Cell* 185, no. 8 (14 April 2022): 1402–1413.e21, https://doi.org/10.1016/j.cell2022.03.007. For the sometimes problematic nature of such genetic evidence, however, see M. Meier and S. Patzold, *Gene und Geschichte: Was die Archäogenetik zur Geschichtsforschung beitragen kann* (Stuttgart, 2021).

37. See R. Payne, 'The Reinvention of Iran: The Sasanian Empire and the Huns', in *The Cambridge Companion to the Age of Attila*, ed. M. Maas (Cambridge, 2014), 282–300.

38. Baumer, *The History of Central Asia*, 94; K. Rezkhani, *Reorienting the Sasanians* (Edinburgh, 2017), 140–143.

39. Baumer, *The History of Central Asia*, 173–206.

40. See discussion in the magisterial P. B. Golden, *An Introduction to the History of the Turkic Peoples* (Wiesbaden, 1984), 115–154.

41. Menander Protector, *History of Menander the Guardsman*, ed. and tr. Blockley, 49 (fragment 5.1).

42. Ibid., 48–53 (fragment 5.1–5.4), 253.

43. See G. Greatrex and S. Lieu, *The Roman Eastern Frontier and the Persian Wars: Part 2, 363–630 AD* (London, 2002), 122–129, 130–133.

44. Isidore of Seville, *Historia Gothorum* 47. See J. Wood, 'Defending Byzantine Spain', *Early Medieval Europe* 18 (2010): 292–319.

45. Jordanes, *Getica* 303. See Jordanes, *Romana and Getica*, tr. P. Van Nuffelen and L. Van Hoof (Liverpool, 2020), 364 (and note 937), and 12–13 (for the date of the expedition); J. R. Martindale, *The Prosopography of the Later Roman Empire*, vol. 2, *A.D. 395–527* (Cambridge, 1980), 677–681 (Liberius 3).

46. See discussion in P. Reynolds, *Hispania and the Roman Mediterranean* (London, 2010), and D. Donaldson, 'Byzantine Presence in Visigothic Spain' (PhD diss., Cambridge University, 2013).

47. Donaldson, 'Byzantine Presence', 20–21.

48. Ibid., 9, 25, 30, 102–103.

49. Wood, 'Defending Byzantine Spain'.

50. Donaldson, 'Byzantine Presence', 104–105, 99 (for imperial military investment in the Balearics).

51. See P. Sarris, 'Constantinople and the Eurasian Trading System at the End of Antiquity', in *Global Byzantium*, ed. L. Brubaker, R. Darley, and D. Reynolds (London, 2023), 316–331, and R. Payne, 'The Silk Road and Iranian Political Economy in Late Antiquity: Iran, the Silk Road, and the Problem of Aristocratic Empire', *Bulletin of the School of Oriental and African Studies* 81 (2018): 227–250.

52. Procopius, *Anecdota* 25.24.

53. Discussed in Sarris, 'Constantinople and the Eurasian Trading System'.

54. Procopius, *Wars* 1.20.12. See discussion in G. Greatrex, *Procopius of Caesarea: The Persian Wars. A Historical Commentary* (Cambridge, 2022), 262–270, and the much-neglected study of Byzantine trade with the East by N. Pigylevskaya, *Vizantya na Putyach v Indiou* (Leningrad, 1951), esp. 129–156 (on Cosmas Indicopleustes), 184–211 (on silk), and 260–335 (on trade via Himyar and Ethiopia).

55. Cosmas Indicopleustes, *Christian Topography* 11.17–19. See W. Wolska-Conus, *Cosmas Indicopleustès: Topographie Chrétienne*, 3 vols. (Paris, 1968–1973), 3:348–350. See discussion in F. Carlà, 'The End of Roman Gold Coinage and the Disintegration of a Monetary Area', *Annali dell'Istituto Italianiano di Numismatica* 56 (2010): 103–172, 54.

56. See discussion in Payne, 'The Silk Road and Iranian Political Economy'.

57. Cosmas Indicopleustes, *Christian Topography*. See C. Coedès, *Texts of Greek and Latin Authors on the Far East* (Turnhout, 2010), 130–131.

58. *J.Nov.* Appendix 5. See discussion in *The Novels of Justinian: A Complete Annotated English Translation*, ed. P. Sarris, tr. D. J. D. Miller (Cambridge, 2018), 1113–1114.

59. See P. Sarris, 'Banking, Credit and Loans in the Novels of the Emperor Justinian', in *Law and Economic Performance in the Roman Empire*, ed. P. Erdkamp and K. Verboeven (Leiden, 2022), 235–247, 246; Sarris, 'Constantinople and the Eurasian Trading System', 323–327; and Procopius, *Anecdota* 25.13.

60. Miller and Sarris, *Novels of Justinian*, 1113 note 1.

61. Procopius suggests it was late 551, while Justinian's envoys were

trying to persuade Khusro to negotiate with respect to Lazica. See Procopius, *Wars* 8.17.1–8, 8.16.1. See also Greatrex and Lieu, *The Roman Eastern Frontier*, 129.

62. Procopius, *Wars* 8.17.7.

63. Coedès, *Texts of Greek and Latin Authors*, 151.

64. R. S. Lopez, 'The Silk Industry in the Byzantine Empire', *Speculum* 20 (1945): 1–42; A. Muthesius, *Studies in Byzantine Silk* (London, 2004); C. Zuckerman, 'Silk "Made in Byzantium"', *Travaux et mémoires* 17 (2013): 323–350.

65. P. Bell, *Three Political Voices from the Age of Justinian* (Liverpool, 2009), 189–190.

CHAPTER 16. DEATH AND DECLINE

1. Procopius, *Wars* 2.30.49, 7.30.4 (after reigning twenty-one years and three months).

2. John of Ephesus in Pseudo-Zachariah of Tel-Mahre, *Chronicle: Part III*, tr. W. Witakowski (Liverpool, 1996), 124.

3. *The Chronicle of Theophanes Confessor*, tr. and ed. C. Mango and R. Scott (Oxford, 1997), 329.

4. J. A. S. Evans, *Justinian: The Circumstances of Imperial Power* (London, 1996), 256.

5. Procopius, *Wars* 7.30.3–25, 2.30.49–54, 7.35.1–3.

6. B. Croke, 'Justinian's Constantinople', in *The Cambridge Companion to the Age of Justinian*, ed. M. Maas (Cambridge, 2005), 60–86, 60. Croke says sixty years, but I work on the assumption that the young Petrus Sabbatius was sent to his uncle in about 490.

7. Ibid. See *The Chronicle of Theophanes Confessor*, tr. and ed. Mango and Scott, 342.

8. *The Chronicle of Theophanes Confessor*, tr. and ed. Mango and Scott, 345 and 346 note 2.

9. *J.Nov.* 127 c. 3.

10. *The Chronicle of Theophanes Confessor*, tr. and ed. Mango and Scott, 353. *The Chronicle of Theophanes* gives the year as 563–564. The remains of the church visited by Justinian are still visible.

11. See P. Niewöhner, G. Dikilitaş, E. Erkul, S. Giese, J. Gorecki, W. Prochaska, D. Sarı, et al., 'Bronze Age Höyüks, Iron Age Hilltop Forts, Roman Poleis and Byzantine Pilgrimage in Germia and Its Vicinity: "Connectivity" and a Lack of "Definite Places" on the Central Anatolian High Plateau', *Anatolian*

Studies 63 (2013): 97–136. For discussion of epigraphic evidence for Justinian's pilgrimage, see C. Begass, 'Justinian in Galatien', *Istanbuler Mitteilungen* 71 (2021): 239–248.

12. *The Chronicle of Theophanes Confessor*, tr. Mango and Scott, 344; *Anthologia Graeca* 9.641, translated in F. Haarer, *Justinian: Empire and Society in the Sixth Century* (Edinburgh, 2022), 198.

13. Agathias, *Histories*, tr. J. D. Frendo (Berlin, 1975), 5.14.1 (148), 5.14.2 (149).

14. D. Parnell, *Justinian's Men* (Basingstoke, 2017), 82–83.

15. *The Chronicle of Theophanes Confessor*, tr. Mango and Scott, 339. The growing 'sacralization' and 'liturgification' of the person of the emperor from the 540s onwards is a major theme in the work of Mischa Meier. See, for example, M. Meier, *Geschichte der Völkerwanderung: Europa, Asien, und Afrika vom 3 bis zum 8 Jahrhundert n. Chr.* (Munich, 2020), 964–973.

16. Parnell, *Justinian's Men*, 82, 134–135.

17. *The Chronicle of Theophanes Confessor*, tr. Mango and Scott, 345, 346 note 2, 347.

18. G. Bransbourg, 'Capital in the Sixth Century', *Journal of Late Antiquity* 9 (2016): 342–346, 394.

19. John Malalas, *Chronicle* 18.137. See *The Chronicle of John Malalas*, tr. E. Jeffreys, M. Jeffreys, and R. Scott (Canberra, 1986), 300–301 ('Jeffreys et al.' hereafter). The forced loans are alluded to in Corippus, *In Laudem Iustini Augusti Minoris Libri Quattor* Book 2 line 401. See Corippus, *In Laudem Iustini Augusti Minoris Libri Quattor*, ed. and tr. A. Cameron (Oxford, 1978), 59 ('Cameron' hereafter), and discussion in P. Sarris, 'Banking, Credit and Loans in the Novels of the Emperor Justinian', in *Law and Economic Performance in the Roman Empire*, ed. P. Erdkamp and K. Verboeven (Leiden, 2022), 235–247, 246.

20. Malalas, *Chronicle* 18.141 (Jeffreys et al., 301–303); *The Chronicle of Theophanes Confessor*, tr. Mango and Scott, 349–350. For Ablabius, see ibid., 351 note 7. For Aitherius' relationship to Justin, see S. Roggo, 'Church and Crown in the Capital: The Patriarchate of Constantinople Under Eutychios and John Scholastikos (552–582)' (PhD diss., Cambridge University, 2022), 67–70.

21. Malalas, *Chronicle* 18.141.

22. *The Chronicle of Theophanes Confessor*, tr. Mango and Scott, 350; Malalas, *Chronicle* 18.141 (Jeffreys et al., 303).

23. For Eutychius' relationship to Belisarius, see Roggo, 'Church and Crown in the Capital', 72.

24. Malalas, *Chronicle* 18.141; *The Chronicle of Theophanes Confessor*, tr. Mango and Scott, 350.

25. *The Chronicle of Theophanes Confessor*, tr. Mango and Scott, 350–351; Malalas, *Chronicle* 18.146 (Jeffreys et al., 304). Alternatively, the mob may have been attacking Procopius himself.

26. See *The Chronicle of Theophanes Confessor*, tr. Mango and Scott, 353, and Malalas, *Chronicle* 18.147, 149 (Jeffreys et al., 304–305).

27. Malalas, *Chronicle* 18.141.

28. See Roggo, 'Church and Crown in the Capital', 70 (citing the *Chronicle* of John of Nikiu).

29. See Roggo, 'Church and Crown in the Capital', 67–72.

30. Translation taken from Haarer, *Justinian*, 195.

31. John of Ephesus, *Historia Ecclesiastica* 2.10; Roggo, 'Church and Crown in the Capital', 73.

32. As carefully argued by Roggo, 'Church and Crown in the Capital', 29–80.

33. Ibid., 72–80; Evans, *Justinian*, 263.

34. Evans, *Justinian*, 263–264.

35. Ibid., 264. On the future emperor Tiberius II, see J. R. Martindale, *The Prosopography of the Later Roman Empire*, vol. 3, *A.D. 527–641* (Cambridge, 1990), *PLRE-III-B*, 1323–1326.

36. Corippus, *In Laudem* Book 1 lines 175–210 (Cameron, 90–91).

37. Evagrius, *Ecclesiastical History* 5.2–3. See *The Ecclesiastical History of Evagrius Scholasticus*, tr. M. Whitby (Liverpool, 2000), 256–257; *The Chronicle of Theophanes Confessor*, tr. Mango and Scott, 360–361 and 360 note 3.

38. Corippus, *In Laudem* Book 1 line 120 ('*pater inclitus orbis*') (Cameron, 89).

39. I owe some of my phraseology here to comments made by BBC journalist Gabriel Gatehouse with respect to Vladimir Putin in March 2022.

40. Corippus, *In Laudem* Book 1 lines 240–241 (Cameron, 92), Book 3 lines 40–61 (Cameron, 103).

41. See discussion in A. Cameron, 'Images of Authority: Elites and Icons in Late Sixth-Century Byzantium', in *Byzantium and the Classical Tradition*, ed. M. Mullett and R. Scott (Birmingham, 1981), 205–234.

42. Corippus, *In Laudem* Book 1 lines 236–238 (Cameron, 91), Book 1 line 365 (Cameron, 94), Book 3 lines 32–33 (Cameron, 103), Book 1 lines 225–235 (Cameron, 91).

43. Ibid., Book 1 lines 279–293 (Cameron, 92–93).

44. M. Maas, 'Roman Questions, Byzantine Answers: Contours of the Age of Justinian', in Maas, *Cambridge Companion*, 3–27, 8–9.

45. Evagrius, *Ecclesiastical History* 5.1. See *The Ecclesiastical History*, tr. Whitby, 254.

46. Haarer, *Justinian*, 140–141.

47. P. Sarris, *Empires of Faith: The Fall of Rome to the Rise of Islam* (Oxford, 2011), 179–180, 310–322; Isidore of Seville, *History* 70.

48. Sarris, *Empires of Faith*, 177–182.

49. For Roman-Avar relations at this time, see, especially, W. Pohl, *The Avars* (London, 2018), 21–100.

50. Sarris, *Empires of Faith*, 177–180. For discussion of recent possible genetic evidence of Slav settlement in the Balkans, see I. Olalde, P. Carrión, I. Mikić, N. Rohland, S. Mallick, I. Laziridis, M. Korać, et al., 'Cosmopolitanism at the Roman Danubian Frontier: Slavic Migrations and the Genomic Formation of Modern Balkan Peoples', *bioRxiv*, 31 August 2021, https://doi.org/10.1101/2021.08.30.458211. I am grateful to Mr. Zac Mee for bringing this to my attention.

51. See V. Ivanišević, 'Carčin Grad (Justiniana Prima): A New-Discovered City for a "New" Society', in *Proceedings of the 23rd International Congress of Byzantine Studies, Belgrade, 2016*, ed. S. Marjanović-Dušanić (Belgrade, 2016). I am grateful to Vujadin Ivanišević and Ivan Bugarski for having pointed out these 'burn layers' to me when I visited the site with them in September 2019.

52. Sarris, *Empires of Faith*, 226–306; J. D. Howard-Johnston, *The Last Great War of Antiquity* (Oxford, 2021).

53. Corippus, *In Laudem* Book 2 line 261 (Cameron, 99).

54. *J.Nov.* 148 pr.

55. See discussion in P. Sarris, *Economy and Society in the Age of Justinian* (Cambridge, 2006), 200–227.

56. *J.Nov.* 140; *J.Nov.* 145 pr.

57. Sarris, *Empires of Faith*, 236–242.

58. See Bransbourg, 'Capital in the Sixth Century', 342–346, 394.

59. See discussion in P. Sarris, 'Viewpoint: New Approaches to the Plague of Justinian', *Past and Present* 254 (2022), and P. Sarris, 'How a Lethal Pandemic Brought Catastrophe and Class Conflict to the Byzantine Empire', *Jacobin*, 28 September 2022, https://jacobin.com/2022/09/pandemic-plague-justinian-bubonic-black-death.

60. Sarris, *Economy and Society*, 222–227; Bransbourg, 'Capital in the Sixth Century', 394.

61. Procopius, *Buildings* 1.2.12.

62. See Sarris, *Empires of Faith*, 279–292.

63. See Agathias, *Histories*, tr. Frendo, 5.13.7 (148). For discussion of the complexities of this issue (and Agathias' coverage of it), however, see M. Whitby, 'Recruitment in Roman Armies from Justinian to Heraclius', in *The Early Byzantine and Islamic Near East*, vol. 3, *States, Resources and Armies*, ed.

A. Cameron (Princeton, N.J., 1995), 61–124, 92–110; C. Whately, *Procopius on Soldiers and Military Institutions in the Sixth-Century Roman Empire* (Leiden, 2021), 208–221; and W. Treadgold, *Byzantium and Its Army* (Stanford, Calif., 1997), 61–64.

64. See, for example, G. E. M. de Ste. Croix, *The Class Struggle in the Ancient Greek World* (London, 1981), 483–484.

65. For problems with the argument for widespread alienation, see J. Moorhead, 'The Monophysite Response to the Arab Invasions', *Byzantion* 51 (1981): 579–591.

66. See J. Horowitz, 'The Vengeance of the Jews', *Jewish Social Studies* 4 (1998): 1–39, and N. de Lange, 'Jews in the Age of Justinian', in Maas, *Cambridge Companion*, 401–426, 418–420.

67. See G. Bowersock, *The Crucible of Islam* (Cambridge, Mass., 2016); M. Donner, 'The Background to Islam', in Maas, *Cambridge Companion*, 510–524; Sarris, *Empires of Faith*, 258–268.

68. For the limitations of late Roman bureaucracy, see C. Kelly, *Ruling the Later Roman Empire* (Cambridge, Mass., 2004).

69. Cassiodorus, *Variae* 2.27.2.

70. See Sarris, *Empires of Faith*, 177–182.

71. *J.Nov.* 69 c. 4.1.

CHAPTER 17. IMPERIAL LEGACIES

1. Translation from A. Gerostergios, *Justinian the Great: The Emperor and Saint* (Belmont, 1982), 185.

2. Novel 1 in *Les novelles de Léon VI le Sage*, ed. and tr. P. Noailles and A. Dain (Paris, 1941), 10–13.

3. As noted by J. A. S. Evans, *Justinian: The Circumstances of Imperial Power* (London, 1996), 9.

4. For the deep-rooted continuities between the reigns of Anastasius, Justin I, and Justinian, see P. Sarris, *Empires of Faith: The Fall of Rome to the Rise of Islam* (Oxford, 2011), 134–145.

5. For the complexities of this term, see P. Maraval, *Justinien: Le rêve d'un empire chrétien universel* (Paris, 2016), 347.

6. As argued by M. Hassall, 'Political Debate in the Age of Justinian I' (PhD diss., Cambridge University, 2022), 81–93.

7. For the vibrancy of intellectual culture in the 'Age of Justinian', see C. Humfress, 'Law and Legal Practice in the Age of Justinian', in *The Cambridge Companion to the Age of Justinian*, ed. M. Maas (Cambridge, 2005), 161–184, and C. Wildberg, 'Philosophy in the Age of Justinian', in the same work, 316–342.

8. For the reception of Justinian in Byzantium, see the extensive survey by G. Prinzing, 'Das Bild Justinians I', *Fontes Minores* 7 (1986): 1–99, and R. Scott, 'Narrating Justinian from Malalas to Manasses', in his *Byzantine Chronicles and the Sixth Century* (Abingdon, 2012), sec. 17.

9. See K. Kovalchuk, 'The Founder as a Saint: The Image of Justinian I in the Great Church of St Sophia', *Byzantion* 77 (2007): 205–237, and Gerostergios, *Justinian the Great*, 182–202.

10. See discussion in E. Boeck, *The Bronze Horseman of Justinian in Constantinople: The Cross-Cultural Biography of a Mediterranean Monument* (Cambridge, 2021).

11. See Kovalchuk, 'The Founder as a Saint', and Boeck, *The Bronze Horseman of Justinian in Constantinople*, 144–145.

12. See P. Sarris, 'Introduction', in *The Novels of Justinian: A Complete Annotated English Translation*, ed. P. Sarris, tr. D. J. D. Miller (Cambridge, 2018), 14–20.

13. See, for example, the relationship between Justinianic law and that of the emperors of the eighth to tenth centuries as discussed in M. Humphreys, *Law, Power, and Imperial Ideology in the Iconoclast Era* (Oxford, 2015). For the post-Justinianic history of Byzantine law, see, most recently, D. Penna and R. Meijering, *A Sourcebook on Byzantine Law: Illustrating Byzantine Law Through the Sources* (Leiden, 2022), 91–205.

14. See sec. 17 in Scott, *Byzantine Chronicles*.

15. B. Croke, 'Procopius, From Manuscripts to Books: 1400–1850', *Histos*, supplement 9 (2019): 1–173, 12.

16. C. Mango, *Byzantium: The Empire of New Rome* (London, 1983), 4–5.

17. See Kovalchuk, 'The Founder as a Saint', 228–229 (and notes 63 and 64), discussing a source known as the *Parastasis Syntomoi Chroninkai*. For an English translation of this work, see *Constantinople in the Early Eighth Century: The Parastasis Syntomoi Chronikai*, ed. and tr. A. Cameron and J. Herrin (Leiden, 1984). See also Boeck, *The Bronze Horseman of Justinian in Constantinople*, 212 note 105, 184–191, 260–262. The identification with Heraclius was favoured by Crusaders from the West, for whom Heraclius was a hero. The identification with Constantine emerged in the fifteenth century, when the Byzantine government was on the verge of collapse.

18. See Kovalchuk, 'The Founder as a Saint', 227–228.

19. John Malalas, *Chronicle* 18.51. See *The Chronicle of John Malalas*, tr. E. Jeffreys, M. Jeffreys, and R. Scott (Canberra, 1986), 266. See also sec. 17 in Scott, *Byzantine Chronicles*, 45–46.

20. Boeck, *The Bronze Horseman of Justinian in Constantinople*, 233–262, 383–408.

21. See S. Runciman, *The Fall of Constantinople 1453* (Cambridge, 1965), 147, 149.

22. See, for example, J. Cole, 'Muhammad and Justinian: Roman Legal Traditions and the Qur'an', *Journal of Near Eastern Studies* 79 (2018): 183–196, and H. Zellentin, *Law Beyond Israel: From the Bible to the Qu'ran* (Oxford, 2022).

23. For a good overview of his reign, see A. Bridge, *Suleiman the Magnificent: Scourge of Heaven* (London, 2015).

24. See Boeck, *The Bronze Horseman of Justinian in Constantinople*, 324–325, and R. Ousterhout, 'The East, the West, and the Appropriation of the Past in Early Ottoman Architecture', *Gesta* 43 (2004): 165–176.

25. Boeck, *The Bronze Horseman of Justinian in Constantinople*, 332–333.

26. The plague had arrived in 542, and the column and statue were erected in 543. See Malalas, *Chronicle* 18.94. For the bubonic plague in early Ottoman Constantinople, see N. Varlik, *Plague and Empire in the Early Modern Mediterranean World: The Ottoman Experience, 1347–1600* (Cambridge, 2015), 131–159.

27. For an overview of Justinian in the early medieval western sources, see H. Gračanin, 'The Perception of Justinian in the Early Medieval Latin West', in M. B. Panov, ed., *Byzantium and the Heritage of Europe* (Skopje, 2016), 11–21.

28. See S. Lin, 'Justinian's Frankish War', *Studies in Late Antiquity* 5 (2021): 403–431. Isidore accuses Justinian of heresy. See Gračanin, 'The Perception of Justinian', 21.

29. On Bede, see Gračanin, 'The Perception of Justinian', 12, with note 14.

30. Paul the Deacon, *History of the Lombards*, tr. W. D. Foulke (London, 1907), 1.25 (44–45).

31. Ibid., 47.

32. Otto, Bishop of Freising, *"The Two Cities": A Chronicle of Universal History to the Year 1146 AD*, tr. C. C. Mierow (New York, 1893), 328–329.

33. Gračanin, 'The Perception of Justinian', 19, 15. See also C. Foss, 'The Empress Theodora', *Byzantion* 72 (2002): 141–176, 160.

34. See discussion in R. McKitterick, *Charlemagne: The Formation of a European Identity* (London, 2008), 339.

35. From Boeck, *The Bronze Horseman of Justinian in Constantinople*, 250.

36. See M. R. Salzman, *The Falls of Rome: Crises, Resilience, and Resurgence in Late Antiquity* (Cambridge, 2021), 300–336. For the construction of papal identity, see R. McKitterick, *Rome and the Invention of the Papacy* (Cambridge, 2020).

37. *J.Nov. Appendix* 7 c. 1.

38. For the 'Byzantine' context to Gregory's theology, see M. Dal Santo,

Debating the Saints' Cult in the Age of Gregory the Great (Oxford, 2013). For his pontificate as a whole, the best study remains R. Markus, *Gregory the Great and His World* (Cambridge, 1997).

39. See H. J. Scheltema, *L'enseignement de droit des antécesseurs* (Leiden, 1970).

40. See D. Liebs, *Die Jurisprudenz im spätantiken Italien* (Berlin, 1987).

41. See the groundbreaking work by L. Loschiavo, 'Was Rome Still a Centre of Legal Culture Between the Sixth and Eighth Centuries?', *Rechtsgeschichte* 23 (2015): 83–103, and *J.Nov. Appendix* 7 c. 22.

42. See C. M. Radding and A. Ciaralli, *The Corpus Iuris Civilis in the Middle Ages* (Leiden, 2007), 35–66.

43. The manuscript (which would end up in Pisa in the twelfth century, before being captured by the Florentines) is known as the *Littera Florentina*. See Radding and Ciarilli, *The Corpus Iuris Civilis in the Middle Ages*, 169–210.

44. Ibid., 35–65, 67, 133–168, and with respect to the rediscovery of the *Institutes*, 111–131. For the reception of the *Codex Iustinianus*, see also S. Corcoran, 'The *Codex* of Justinian: The Life of a Text Through 1,500 Years', in *The Codex of Justinian*, vol. 1, ed. B. W. Frier, based on a translation by F. H. Blume (Cambridge, 2016), xcvii–clxiv.

45. See S. Reynolds, *Fiefs and Vassals* (London, 1994); P. Stein, *Roman Law in European History* (Cambridge, 1999), 38–70; and B. Nicholas, *An Introduction to Roman Law* (Oxford, 1972), 44.

46. For a succinct overview, see L. Atzeri, 'Roman Law and Reception', European History Online (EGO), Leibniz Institute of European History (IEG), 20 November 2017, http://ieg-ego.eu/en/threads/models-and-stereotypes/model -classical-antiquity/lorena-atzeri-roman-law-and-reception. For the comparison between Justinian and Napoleon, see T. Weir, 'Two Great Legislators', *Tulane European and Civil Law Forum* 21 (2006): 35–51.

47. For the Justinianic influence on English common law, see P. Birks and G. McLeod, 'Introduction', in *Justinian's Institutes*, tr. Birks and McLeod (London, 1987).

48. Dante, *Paradiso* 6.10–12. See also D. Hernández San José, 'The Perception of Justinian in the Latin West: Considerations from Dante's Works', available at European Society of Modern Greek Studies, www.eens.org/EENS _congresses/2014/hernandez-san-jose_daniel.pdf, accessed 2 April 2022.

49. See T. Rüfner, 'Substance of Medieval Roman Law: The Development of Private Law', in *The Oxford Handbook of European Legal History*, ed. H. Pihlajamäki, M. K. Dubber, and M. Godfrey (Oxford, 2018), 309–331, 311–315, and A. Watson, *Slave Law in the Americas* (Athens, Ga., 1989). For the similarities

between forms of exploitation of labour in the sixth century and later periods, see J. Banaji, 'Agrarian History and the Labour Organisation of Byzantine Large Estates', in *Agriculture in Egypt from Pharaonic to Modern Times*, ed. A. Bowman and E. Rogan (Oxford, 1999), 193–216, and J. Banaji, 'Modernizing the Historiography of Rural Labour: An Unwritten Agenda', in *Companion to Historiography*, ed. M. Bentley (London, 1997), 88–102.

50. R. I. Moore, *The Formation of a Persecuting Society* (Oxford, 1987), 5, 146. See also J. Arnold, 'Persecution and Power in Medieval Europe', *American Historical Review* 123 (2018): 165–174.

51. For a collection of sources, see J. Arnold and P. Biller, *Heresy and Inquisition in France, 1200–1300* (Manchester, 2016).

52. For limited discussion of the papal reception of Justinianic law on heretics, see, for example, P. Riedlberger, *Prolegomena zu den spätantiken Konstitutionen: Nebst einer Analyse der erbrechtlichten und verwandten Sanktionen gegen Heterodoxe* (Stuttgart, 2020), 809–810. I am grateful to Professor Moore for feedback on this idea. The massive dislocation of the Byzantine state associated with the empire's seventh-century crisis probably served to disrupt the course of ideological development with respect to persecutions on which Justinian had set it, but see A. Cameron, 'Enforcing Orthodoxy in Byzantium', *Studies in Church History* 43 (2007): 1–24.

53. Nicetas Choniatis, *O City of Byzantium*, tr. H. J. Margoulias (Detroit, 1984), 357 (revised).

EPILOGUE

1. See the magisterial survey in B. Croke, 'Procopius, From Manuscripts to Books: 1400–1850', *Histos*, supplement 9 (2019): 1–173. For Ryves, see ibid., 80–82. For indications that some scholars had access to copies of the *Secret History* somewhat earlier, see ibid., 67. See also Procopius, *Secret History* 8.3.

2. G. Ostrogorsky, *History of the Byzantine State* (Oxford, 1957), 5. See also D. Potter, *Theodora: Actress, Empress, Saint* (Oxford, 2015), 208–209.

3. D. Womersley, 'Gibbon and Classical Example: The Age of Justinian in the *Decline and Fall*', *Journal of Eighteenth Century Studies* 19 (1996): 17–31, 21.

4. See Croke, 'Procopius, From Manuscripts to Books', 113–123, 120 (for Gibbon's focus on the *Secret History*); Womersley, 'Gibbon and Classical Example'; and A. Cameron, 'Gibbon and Justinian', in *Gibbon and Empire*, ed. R. D. McKitterick (Cambridge, 1996), 34–52.

5. Croke, 'Procopius, From Manuscripts to Books', 120.

6. Womersley, 'Gibbon and Classical Example', 27.

7. See Cameron, 'Gibbon and Justinian', and Womersley, 'Gibbon and Classical Example', 23.

8. As finely elucidated by Womersley in 'Gibbon and Classical Example', 28.

9. See, especially, the essays collected in R. Scott, *Byzantine Chronicles and the Sixth Century* (Abingdon, 2012), *passim.*

10. J. Bew, *Citizen Clem* (London, 2016), 630.

ILLUSTRATION CREDITS

INDEX

© John Deed

Peter Sarris is Professor of Late Antique, Medieval, and Byzantine Studies at the University of Cambridge. He is author or editor of eight books on the history of late antiquity, the early Middle Ages, and Byzantium, including *Byzantium: A Very Short Introduction*. He lives in Shepreth, United Kingdom.